HERLANDS

Herlands

. . . .

Exploring the Women's Land Movement
in the United States

Keridwen N. Luis

University of Minnesota Press
Minneapolis
London

Portions of chapter 3 were previously published in *Journal of Homosexuality* as "The Gender of 'Energy': Language, Social Theory, and Cultural Change in Women's Lands in the United States," 62, no. 9 (2015); reprinted by permission of Taylor & Francis. Portions of chapter 6 were previously published in *Journal of Lesbian Studies* as "Karma Eaters: The Politics of Food and Fat in Women's Land Communities in the United States" 16, no. 1 (2012); reprinted by permission of Taylor & Francis.

"THOSE TEARS" is reprinted with permission of the author, Chrystos; copyright 1991.

Copyright 2018 by the Regents of the University of Minnesota

All rights reserved. No part of this publication may be reproduced, stored in a retrieval system, or transmitted, in any form or by any means, electronic, mechanical, photocopying, recording, or otherwise, without the prior written permission of the publisher.

Published by the University of Minnesota Press
111 Third Avenue South, Suite 290
Minneapolis, MN 55401-2520
http://www.upress.umn.edu

The University of Minnesota is an equal-opportunity educator and employer.

Library of Congress Cataloging-in-Publication Data
Names: Luis, Keridwen N., author.
Title: Herlands : exploring the women's land movement in the United States / Keridwen N. Luis.
Description: Minneapolis : University of Minnesota Press, [2018] | Includes bibliographical references and index. |
Identifiers: LCCN 2018001928 (print) | ISBN 978-0-8166-9823-3 (hc) |
ISBN 978-0-8166-9825-7 (pb)
Subjects: LCSH: Women in agriculture—United States. | Land use—United States. | United States—Race relations. | Communities—United States.
Classification: LCC HD6077.2.U6 L85 2018 (print) | DDC 306.3/490820973—dc23
LC record available at https://lccn.loc.gov/2018001928

UMP LSI

"Just tell me," he says to Lady Blue, who is looking at the bullet gashes, "what do you call yourselves? Women's World? Liberation? Amazonia?"

"Why, we call ourselves human beings." Her eyes twinkle absently at him, go back to the bullet marks. "Humanity, mankind." She shrugs. "The human race."

—JAMES TIPTREE JR. (ALICE B. SHELDON),
"HOUSTON, HOUSTON, DO YOU READ?"

Contents

Introduction: Welcome to Women's Land, Here Is Your Umbrella	1
1. The Political Is Personal: From the Peace Camp and Women's Music Festivals to Women's Land	17
2. Are the Amazons White? Race and Space on Women's Land	45
3. "Now My Neighbors and Friends Are the Same People": Community, Language, and Identity	73
4. The Giving Tree: Gift Economies Planted in Capitalist Soil	105
5. The Mountain Is She: Gender as Landscape, Landscape as Gender	129
6. Primally Female: Agency and the Meaning of the Body on Women's Land	153
7. We Have Met the Enemy and She Is Us: Scapegoating Trans Bodies	187
8. The Hermit and the Family: Aging and Dis/Ability in Community	217
Afterword: Women's Lands, Women's Lives	243
Acknowledgments	251
Notes	253
Bibliography	267
Index	289

· INTRODUCTION ·

Welcome to Women's Land, Here Is Your Umbrella

After all, the real question, of course, is not whether women will practice separatism against men, but rather whether men will continue to practice separatism against women.
—Joanna Russ, "For Women Only, Or, What Is That Man Doing Under My Seat?"

Let's stop pretending that we have all the answers, because when it comes to gender, none of us is fucking omniscient.
— Kate Bornstein, *Gender Outlaw: On Men, Women, and the Rest of Us*

IT WAS OUR LAST NIGHT of the Landdyke Gathering at Turtle Mesa,[1] where the air was thin and the views went on forever. Although women usually sat around the campfire near the lovely cob house we were using as a shared kitchen, after dinner the oncoming rainstorm dispersed residents to their houses and visitors to their tents. My wife and I were staying in a dome tent just large enough for an air mattress and our luggage, placed among some pines near the edge of the mesa. As we said our good-nights, Marta, one of the residents, glanced at the sky and said, "If you have any trouble with your tent tonight, feel free to come to my place." We thanked her, sure that our tent would be okay, and set off.

Our tent was not okay.

It was raining hard by the time we navigated the twisty trails to the tent. Wary of the ways of nylon tents, I zipped our duffel bag shut and put it inside a large garbage bag I had brought for waterproofing purposes. I was pretty sure that the floor of the tent would leak; we had not been careful about positioning for water running downhill when we put the tent up in the blistering desert sun. As I worked, I felt something hit the top of my head. Shining my flashlight upwards, I watched as a spot on the top of the tent darkened and started to drip, right over the air mattress. My wife and I regarded the drip in silence for a moment. Then I noticed a second one.

Our decision was swiftly made. I started rolling up our bedding and Jude agreed to walk back in the dark and fetch the rental car so we could put our luggage in the (hopefully watertight) trunk and then drive to Marta's house, a mile away along the rutted red-dirt roads of the community. Jude set off into the dark with a small flashlight trained on her sandaled feet in order to avoid kicking any flying cholla cactus, insignificant plants that filled your skin with painful hair-fine needles at the slightest touch (I refused to wear sandals after kicking one on my first day there). I rolled up all the bedding, sealed it into more trash bags, and then lay on the air mattress, counting the leaks as they appeared. There were seventeen of them and I was getting a little damp by the time Jude got back, driving carefully because the fine red dust had turned into frictionless mud.

We threw our stuff into the car, left the tent and air mattress there for the night, and drove across the land to Marta's house. On the way there, a great horned owl launched itself from a short tree and drifted majestically across our headlight beams.

Marta's hand-built one-room hay bale house was full of women sitting around enjoying a slideshow about women's lands and dykelands across the United States. We had a grab-bag of dry clothing in the car (a lesson learned from previous years of camping), and I brought this inside, where Jude, soaked to the skin and shivering in the chill high desert night, changed into dry clothes. As the discussion wound down, I could feel Jude shivering, although she was sitting next to the woodstove.

Marta, who was about ten years older than us, had observed this as well. She announced that she was going to drive in her truck over to the sauna, did anyone want to come? With quick efficiency, she bundled me, Jude, and a couple of other women into her truck, and we were off for the wood-fired sauna. She and another resident stoked up the stove, and then we were all sitting naked and sweaty in the most delicious heat. The scent of woodsmoke combined with steam and fresh sweat, and Jude stopped shivering.

After that, Marta drove us back to her house, where she insisted that we sleep in her bed while she took the couch. We woke to sunlight and hummingbirds darting around the feeders on her porch. She waved off our thanks, saying that anyone would have done the same, as we set off to the collective breakfast around the campfire.

When we went to retrieve it, our tent had collapsed entirely under the onslaught of the desert rainstorm.

What are women's lands? The answer is at once both simple and complex: women's lands are independent living communities composed entirely of women. These communities form all over the world, although for the purposes of this book I have limited my analysis to those in the United States. They form as urban households, rural communities, and suburban communities, ranging from a cluster of houses at the Florida seaside to handbuilt one-room shacks with woodstoves and organic gardens deep in rural areas. Although some of my readers who know about such communities might assume that this style of living passed from existence sometime in the 1980s, there is a flourishing networked organization of such lands, the Association of Lesbians in Community, which last registered over one hundred such communities in the United States.

Women's lands have historically varied. They have included urban households, perhaps most famously exemplified by the Furies Collective, a lesbian group living at 219 11th Street Southeast in Washington D.C. from 1971 to 1973, who published *The Furies* lesbian newspaper (Sheir 2015). They have included rural lands, such as OWL Farm, founded in 1975 in Oregon, which operated as "open" women's land for a while (open to any women who wanted to live there), using a completely consensus-based and collective decision-making model (Lee 1985), and which is still extant, although no longer open. Many such communities and collectives were temporary, such as the 1971 takeover of 888 Memorial Drive, a Harvard-owned building, by women who wanted more equal division of the University's and city's resources; this event resulted in the founding of the Cambridge Women's Center, which still exists today.[2] They sprang from the passionate experimentalism of feminism, lesbian feminism, and women of color(s) feminism sometimes known as second-wave feminism, and are often thought to have quietly vanished along with the philosophy of lesbian separatism—often considered embarrassing by modern feminists.[3]

However, these places have not vanished. Many women's lands still remain, and new ones are even now being founded (including one I have only heard rumors of and was unable to obtain an invitation to—an alpaca farm run by trans women of color). "Lesbian separatism" is only one of the philosophies behind women's land—many of my informants did not identify as separatists—and their activism and ideas are still in active dialogue with the rest of the world. In fact, as I prepared this manuscript for press several friends excitedly emailed me about an essay in *Vogue* called "Country Women" (Bengal 2017). Written by Rebecca Bengal and illustrated with lovely photos and short gifs by Amanda Jasnowski Pascual, the article states, "Their stories are part of the evolving narrative of the feminist, lesbian, back-to-the-land movement, first told through their seminal '70s zine and more recently through a series of strikingly personal films."

What do women's lands and lesbian lands have to tell us? This book is an attempt to answer this question.

Who, What, When, Where: Methodology

In the course of my research, I have visited four women's lands (one in Massachusetts, referred to here as Oaktrust, one in Tennessee, referred to here as Mountainview, one in New Mexico, referred to here as Turtle Mesa, and one in Ohio, referred to here as Wild Uprising) as well as the Michigan Womyn's Music Festival, formally interviewed thirty-two women, and attended two Landdyke Gatherings. My informants include women who have participated in women's lands in New Zealand, Japan, England, and Eastern Europe as well as North America, although I have chosen to only excerpt portions of the interviews relevant to the United States and Canada. I also interviewed informants who had lived in women's lands in the past but who currently did not; "traveling dykes" who did not live at any one land but made a practice of traveling from one women's land to another; one woman who was living at a mixed-gender community as an out lesbian; and women who were involved in a women's-land community and who planned to move to women's land, but who had not yet done so.

Among my formal interviewees, only two of the thirty-two identified themselves to me as other than white (one woman identified as Chicana/Hispanic, the other as Native); the large majority of my interviewees either identified or passed as white. Two informants identified themselves as Jewish white women. About a dozen of my interviewees identified themselves as "older" women or crones, although few women specifically discussed their age with me. One woman identified as a Witch. Although a large majority (over twenty-five) of my interviewees specifically identified as lesbian, there was an overlap between this cohort and those who had children and/or had been previously married to men. I transcribed all my recorded, formal interviews myself and most of the quotations used throughout this book are word-for-word from recorded material.[4]

I also participated in typical women's-land activities, which ranged from weeding the garden to being part of consciousness-raising groups to playing Rummikub. I attended a funeral gathering and potluck suppers, cooked meals, discussed publishing lesbian land periodicals, sat in a sauna, showered using solar-heated water, and washed a lot of dishes. I kept a written field journal during my visits, and I remember one of the women laughing, and saying that she had been impressed with my dedication to journaling before I told her that I was doing research.

Although I do not have the kind of insight that would result from a year or more of living at a women's land (a project I contemplated but was prevented from by an issue that stops many women—lack of funds or means to support myself in a highly rural area), this project unites many different points of view.[5] By examining many different microcultures, this book provides an overall view of the interlocking network of women's-land cultures as they exist in the United States at this time. For indeed, these lands are not isolated at all—they participate in a larger network of culture maintained through individual friendships, paper publications such as *Lesbian Connection* and *Maize: The Country Lesbian Magazine*, email lists, and web presence. Thus, in addition to my visits and interviews I keep in touch with the community in general through the internet, email lists, and paper publications. This illustrates the larger network of "women's-land culture" along which ideas, news, goods, and people all flow.

Lastly, I supplemented my research in current women's lands with archival research at the Schlesinger Library at Radcliffe and Harvard University, for this is where the papers from the Seneca Women's Encampment for the Future of Peace and Justice are held. Two of my informants talked extensively about Seneca, and several had been there and spoke enthusiastically about the life-changing aspects of the women's camp and the protests against the nuclear missile facility there. After the women-only political protests ended, the land was turned into a women's land that outlasted the missile factory. This historical research enriched my understanding of the history of women's lands, and connected me to the extensive and active network of "Seneca graduates," activist women spread all over the United States.

Women's lands have a long and interesting history, but they are not only history. They are current, active places engaging with the culture around them.

How to Be a Lesbian Separatist without Even Trying

Outside scholarship on women's lands has been scant, although landwomen themselves have been prolific publishers of material about their experiences, much of it in periodical form. Mother Tongue Ink and We'Moon Company publishes calendars, art, music, books, and ephemera from a women's-land site.[6] Other important publications by land-women include (but are not limited to) Joyce Cheney's collection of essays, *Lesbian Land* (1985); Shewolf's *Lesbian Land Directory* (published periodically); Sue, Nelly, Dian, Carol, and Billie's *Country Lesbians* (1976); Juana Maria Paz's *The La Luz Journal* (1980); and Pelican Lee's *Owl Farm Stories* (2002). *Maize: The Country Lesbian Magazine* is currently published by self-identified landdykes, while historical publications such as *The Furies* were published by an urban lesbian collective. References to women's lands are also frequent in lesbian history and autobiography between 1978 and 1990; Lee Lynch's *The Amazon Trail* (1988) is an excellent example of this, as the very title is a reference to a highway in Oregon that passes by several women's lands.

Current scholarship includes La Verne Gagehabib and Barbara Summerhawk's *Circles of Power* (2000), which focuses on culture in women's communities in Oregon, and Dana Shugar's *Sep-a-ra-tism and Women's Community* (1995), which focuses on connections between utopian fiction and women's communities. Bonnie Zimmerman's *The Safe Sea of Women* (1990) also includes an overview of lesbian separatist fiction and how this has affected lesbian fiction as a whole. Catriona Sandilands connected lesbian separatist communities to queer ecology in her 2002 article based on her fieldwork in women's lands, "Lesbian Separatist Communities and the Experience of Nature: Toward a Queer Ecology," and in 1997, Gill Valentine published "Making Space: Lesbian Separatist Communities in the United States" in *Contested Countryside Cultures*. The *Journal of Les-*

bian Studies publishes both personal essays and scholarship on lesbian and women's lands.

Scholarly overviews, however, are scant. Why is this? Some of it must be due to the association of women's and lesbian lands with lesbian separatism, a philosophy that is highly embarrassing to many modern feminists. Yet the relationship between separatism and women's-land practice and culture is complex. In fact, very few of my interviewees identified as separatist, just as very few of them said transphobic things, at least to me. Yet the ways in which we imagine these communities associates them with a two-dimensional, simplified view of "separatism" which reduces both these communities and the philosophy and politics of separatism to a caricature. Both for the sake of the history of feminism in the United States, and for the sake of the three-dimensional women of these communities, I seek to flesh out this portrait.

In her essay "Will the Real Lesbian Community Please Stand Up," Esther Newton opens with an anecdote about a white anthropology student who was doing a project on "the lesbian community," which turned out to be entirely white (2000, 155). In this brief analysis of current social-science work on lesbians, she notes, with disapproval, the tendency to focus on white, middle-class women, and suggests that "even anthropologists and sociologists were victims of lesbian-feminist ideological hegemony" (156), which she defined as white, transphobic, middle-class, and as socializing primarily with other lesbians. Newton concludes that "sexuality is not inherently linked to *communitas*, . . . it can also be manipulated to express the structural elements of sociality" (164). Friendship groups established through couples, lovers, and ex-lovers reinforce class distinctions, "because lesbians overwhelmingly choose partners of like class, race, age, and so on" (164). Newton's essay both indicts and illustrates my own work, which was overwhelmingly with white participants. Indeed, while my informants largely rejected the idea of lesbian separatism, and sons, gay male friends, ex-husbands, and other men sometimes visited or participated in their communities, a form of unspoken separatism is still operating here: race separatism.

At the same time, work on particular queer groups remains obscure. "Within the last two decades the analysis of homosexualities and transgendering has become a *'supra rosa'* activity. To the extent that secrecy in the Foucauldian sense is productive rather than simply prohibitive, however, the legacy of silencing continues to shape the field" (Weston 1998, 148). Thinking about silencing as productive is useful and suggests that the ways in which these *particular* groups, these *particular* communities have been relegated to footnotes and assumed to have "vanished" is important and connected to larger issues in queer history, as I will explore in chapter 1.

I doubt even the most uninformed reader can imagine that the community of women on women's land can stand for the lesbian community as a whole, or even for lesbian separatism—not all land-women are lesbians, and very few of my informants identified as separatists. And although there are a surprising lot of women's lands extant for a movement that is largely imagined to be extinct, there are a great many more women who identify as lesbian or queer living in other communities: urban, suburban, small towns, on reservations, in colleges and universities, on houseboats, homeless. When land-women speak of their "communities," it is specifically about women's-land communities and the larger network of such communities that they speak. "Women's culture" refers to a similarly bounded phenomenon, which is neither global nor universal: the production of values associated with these particular microcultures.

Why, then, are we interested in women's lands and their cultures and communities? In part because all local cultures are particularized and individual; in part because they are an important part of feminist history here in North America; and in part because although these cultures are particularized, they are not isolated bubbles. They are embedded in the larger network of cultures in the United States, and ideas flow back and forth across the boundaries. As smaller nested cultures embedded in the larger matrix cultures of the United States, they demonstrate how individuals and groups of individuals agentially and actively process and change ideas and react to structural pressures.

Lastly, the amount of social and cultural change that has been achieved by these communities/nested cultures is impressive. As Gayle Rubin notes, "People often assume that if something is social it is also somehow fragile and can be changed quickly.... But the kind of social change we are talking about [relations of gender, sexuality, and kinship] takes a long time, and the time frame in which we have been undertaking such change is incredibly tiny" (Rubin and Butler 1997, 75–76). Therefore, the profound changes in gender, identity, and family relations that land-women have achieved are notable.

Living in the Matrix: Doxa, Nested Cultures, and Cultural Resistance

Why do I use the term *matrix cultures* rather than the more intuitive *mainstream*? For several reasons. First are the many problems with the term mainstream, including the major one of reifying the concept that there is a mainstream at all in the complex and plural society we live in. While I agree that the concept of mainstream is useful, I believe that we mostly use it as an imaginary goalpost rather than an actual, tangible set of cultural attainments and goals. Thus the mainstream is dependent on who is looking, when, where, and at what: it constantly changes with perspective and from moment to moment.

The term matrix cultures therefore, while not referencing a singular mainstream, does refer to a set of practices, values, and tangible artifacts that exert a considerable cultural pressure on smaller "nested" cultures (such as the women's communities I examine here) that reside within it. The term matrix refers both to the way that smaller cultural enclaves are "held" in larger cultural settings like stones in a geological matrix, and also to the fact that the matrix itself is not a uniform feature, but is made up of many cultural bits or strands. Like geologists, we can choose to focus our lenses on a macroscopic or microscopic scale. Unlike geologists, our matrix changes in human, rather than geologic time. I use the plural "cultures" to acknowledge both the plurality of cultures that have fed United States social norms and the wide variety of cultural and social settings across the geography of North America. Also, this term references Judith Butler's "heterosexual matrix" within which gender is constructed (1999). Just as queerness must emerge from and contend with an encompassing heterosexual matrix that "sets the terms" for cultural symbology, so too do nested cultures within the larger cultural matrix of the United States contend with the larger power of white middle-class normative capitalist cultural values.

Within the matrix cultures of the United States are many smaller cultural enclaves that I have chosen to call *nested cultures*. This term refers to cultural groups that are semidetached from the larger cultural matrix and exhibit a degree of cultural difference, such as immigrant enclaves, school campuses, and women's lands. These nested cultures engage in various forms of exchange with the matrix culture (economic, political, and cultural) and individuals pass through the boundaries that mark the nested culture from the matrix culture. Judith Okely, in her classic work on Travellers in Great Britain, noted that "the group's beliefs and rituals are not an abstract totality floating separately from the material circumstances and relations of production with non-Gypsies." She notes that although their culture is not, therefore, autonomous, "this absence of autonomy should not preclude the understanding that the group's beliefs and practices have a coherence and form a meaningful whole" (1998, 33–34).[7] Women's-land cultures exist in a similar relationship to the larger matrix culture of the United States, and have similar coherent, meaningful cultural structures. However, the matrix culture has a tendency to have a greater "weight" or pressure on the nested culture than vice versa in terms of adopting cultural ideals (a situation we also see in colonization) because of its greater economic and social importance. This often results in the adoption of what I have chosen to call, after Bourdieu, doxa.

Pierre Bourdieu used the term *doxa* and the adjective *doxic* to indicate when "the natural and social world appears as self-evident. This experience we shall call doxa, so as to distinguish it from orthodox or heterodox belief implying awareness and recognition of the possibility of different or antagonistic beliefs." Doxa is the unspoken social order, that which lies too deep to be spoken of, and which is taken for granted as the natural order of the universe. This is "the naturalization [of culture's] own arbitrariness" (1995, 164). In opposition to orthodoxy (which is set down or articulated and can be discussed) and heterodoxy (which is created in opposition to orthodoxy), what is doxic *appears* to be natural and inherent to human beings. Yet it is created by human beings and is, as Bourdieu observed, arbitrary.

Because doxa seems natural—so natural as to be self-evident and undiscussed—it is easy to adopt. Doxic ideas (particularly about gender and race) are often adopted within nested cultures from the matrix culture, even when those same nested cultures are deliberately trying to differentiate from the matrix. This seeming paradox results in situations such as the transphobia of the Michigan Womyn's Music Festival (discussed in more detail in chapter 7) and how whiteness becomes both an unspoken norm and a way of knowing (discussed in chapter 2) on women's land.

It would seem to be a given that before cultural resistance can occur, doxa must be raised to orthodoxy—that is, unspoken doxic ideas must be articulated so that a heterodoxy (the resistance) can also be articulated. However, this is not always the case. In actual practice, heterodoxy often causes doxa to be raised to the point of orthodoxy; that is, we are often not aware of doxa until heterodox practices challenge it. One excellent example of this comes from the history of sexuality: the term *heterosexual* did not enter the common vocabulary as a synonym for "normal" (or even "interested solely in male-female sexual relations") until after the term *homosexual* had been coined, and well after political and medical arguments about the normalcy of such sexuality had been enjoined (Blank 2012, 15–21). Similarly, we are often unaware of our doxa until someone directly challenges what we think of as the "natural" way of doing things by doing it differently.

In This Book

This book is arranged somewhat nontraditionally for an ethnography. In the first chapter, instead of introducing you to my informants and describing the history of the far-off and exotic place they live, I instead explore what preconceived notions we may already have about women's lands and lesbian separatists and how we got these ideas through literature and media. I also trace a brief history of, not women's lands per se, but music festivals and the Seneca Peace Camp, as events that helped shape and led to the establishment of women's lands.

The second chapter, "Are the Amazons White?" explores the issue of race and racism, both in the history of separatist philosophy and in women's lands today. Drawing on Carolyn Finney's idea of "whiteness as a way of knowing," I explore how aspects of women's-land culture rely on and reinforce assumed whiteness while rejecting racism. The third chapter explores community, language, and identity through stories of how women came to women's land, explorations of how women self-identify, and processes I call "feminist aesthetics of practice." As an example of the latter, I explore culture through language in the use of the gendered "energy" term.

Chapter 4, "The Giving Tree," explores the economics of women's land, commensality and gifting, and how this ties into cultural assumptions. The next chapter, "The Mountain Is She," delves deeper into the significance of land itself and the ways in which the gender of landscape and the landscape of gender both operate to create particular forms of culture. Chapter 6, "Primally Female," explores the multiple ways in which everyday body practice both replicates matrix ideas about gender and challenges it on women's lands. I use the examples of clothing and self-presentation, nudity and toilet practices, and finally the challenging ways in which food and the fat body are treated on women's land.

Chapter 7 deals with the issue of transphobia that always seems to be the first question that comes to mind when other scholars hear that I worked on women's lands, and explores both expressions of transphobia among my informants and events pertaining to the Michigan Womyn's Music Festival. Lastly, in "The Hermit and the Family," I address the ways in which women's lands deal with an aging population and attempt to open accessibility to disabled women, and how this illustrates important themes in women's-land culture and methods by which we might more actively address ageism and ableism in society as a whole.

What Do Lesbians Do?

What are land-women and what are women's lands? In this text I use several interlocking definitions, as I amplify in chapter 3: "women's lands" refer to autonomous residential communities composed entirely of women, while "lesbian lands" refer to such communities that restrict membership to self-identified lesbians or landdykes. Although many of these communities are rural, as the term "land" implies, there are communal shared households that are suburban or urban as well. "Land-women" refers to all women who participate in these communities, and is my own neologism; "landdyke" is a term created by landdykes themselves, and refers to lesbians who live in these communities.

The women's and lesbian land communities I have visited and most of my informants are "local" in that they live in the United States, as I do. This presents an interesting dilemma from an anthropological point of view—that is, is this anthropology at all? Anthropology as a discipline has long been based on the search for the exotic and the Other. Judith Okely notes dryly that "social anthropologists have usually selected as their object of study people geographically distant from their home country or institute of learning. The more apparently isolated from Western industrialisation, the more apparently appropriate" (1998, 38). The "field" is thus "supposed" to help define difference and otherness through geography. This difference at once defines both what/who is studied and the anthropologist herself, who becomes a "real anthropologist" through the rite of passage that is contact with the Other. When the anthropologist gathers data via the internet or invites informants home, as I have done, where does "the field" end? And, perhaps most importantly, how can we tell who is the anthropologist, and who are the people being studied?

Ellen Lewin and William Leap, in discussing the ongoing debate about how fieldworkers position themselves in regard to their work, write that "fieldwork is seen as different from daily life at home, precisely because this sort of identity management is required; it is assumed that people don't have to do this in their own communities, at least not with the same urgency. But the ordinary life course of lesbians and gay men depends precisely on this sort of management on a regular basis" (1996, 12). This type of identity management is not unique to queer people; however, the intensity and importance with which it is performed, and the ways in which it becomes part of one's daily habitus, are enhanced. The field, for those of us who already must manage our own identities so closely, can be seen as an extension of our daily round.

Akhil Gupta and James Ferguson continue the idea of the connection between "the field" and "home" when they raise the thorny question of the ethnographer's own cultural location, and point out that "for ethnographers as for other natives, the postcolonial world is an interconnected social space; for many anthropologists . . . the identity of 'one's own society' is an open question" (2001, 43). The interconnectedness of that social space reflects in my status and my identity, which are equally interconnected. There are strong advantages to this form of interstitial fieldwork. For one, I am less tempted to theorize my informants as living in separate "cultures"; that is, to commit the theoretical error of representing their multifarious and interlaced cultural settings as monolithic and bounded. My own experience of the field as interlaced with the matrix cultures of the United States has (hopefully) helped me overcome the temptation to portray women's lands as bounded, eternal, and unchanging.

At the same time, this work itself and the status of this work in the field are both impacted by my status as a native, or as Kath Weston would put it, a "virtual" anthropologist (1998, 189). The ways the work itself is impacted are myriad and intertwined with this book; the impact on its status is, as Weston points out, the ways in which the work will be criticized, set aside, minimized, and evaluated as marginal. "To the degree that queerness is read not only through your research but also through your body, hybridity becomes impossible to ignore" (90–93). I must establish myself as an authority in order to have this work taken seriously; however, I cannot do that in the time-honored ways of anthropology, because my sexuality places me in a suspect, even object position. This is precisely because sexuality is not limited to the study of what people do in bed: "Sexuality is inscribed in your history, your concepts, your most disciplinary desires" (27). Although Weston sees it as necessary to "bring research on sexuality into dialogue with writing on labor, race, colonialism, and the like, as a way of confronting the social forms that would confine eroticism to its own sphere" (26), sexuality is already intertwined with these things. And sexuality is most intimately intertwined with issues of identity, both for individuals and larger collectives.

What is an anthropologist to do? Ellen Lewin, in the debate over the ways in which anthropologists have been called upon to exercise less control over the expressions of those they purport to write about (cf. Lila Abu-Lughod's "writing against culture" [1993, 9]), suggests that although there is interpretation and filtering going on, such interpretation may be valuable.

> Personal narratives, life stories, and other products of inquiry that seek to avoid the dangers of "ethnography" by going to the "source" also depend upon theory and analysis in order to produce their documents. Individual accounts are as mediated as ethnographies to begin with; they are further shaped by the processes of questioning, recording, and editing. Cultural construction is a creative process which we need not repudiate. It is a process which imposes limits on the "native" perspective as stringent as those negotiated by the anthropologist. (Lewin 1991, 791)

Culture itself suggests interpretations to those who provide their stories to us. Our discourse, our answers to the question of what we are doing, are constantly shaped by our own ideas of what is important about this question, and what it means to "do" something. My interpretation and responsibility as the anthropologist is not only to respect the ways in which I hold the narrative reins, but also to frame this through my eyes and acknowledge it as my own.

Everyone, whether they have been trained in anthropology or not, brings their own interpretation to the table. Here is an example from Pelican Lee's "Kids Story," from her collection *Owl Farm Stories* (2002), about her time on a communal women's land in Oregon. This tells us about when the police, hostile to the women of OWL Farm, came and took their children away. Conflict between OWL Farm and the matrix culture, tensions and problem-solving on women's land, and varying ideas of what it means to be "a lesbian" are all neatly packed into Lee's retelling of this incident.

The women and men of the communities—OWL Farm had a neighboring gay male community at the time whom they consulted with over this incident—suspected that one of the neighbors had tipped off the police, but had no proof. After the police returned the children, because "they didn't have a case against us, it was all rumor" (Lee 2002, 21–22), the women all asked the children what their experience with the police and Child Services was like. One of the children responded:

> "The policeman asked me, 'What do lesbians do?'" She giggled behind her hands and shyly looked up at the circle of women gathered around her.
> "I said," and she beamed knowing she'd had the right answer, 'They go to meetings!'"

· CHAPTER 1 ·

The Political Is Personal

From the Peace Camp and Women's Music Festivals
to Women's Land

"Goddess! All this womon-energy is so . . . so healing!"
—Alison Bechdel, *Dykes to Watch Out For,*
"The Seven Ages of Lesbians"

RELATIVELY FEW WOMEN, even within the larger sphere of "lesbian cultures,"[1] have actual experience of women's or lesbian lands. Nevertheless, *we know* what these spaces and the women inhabiting them are like. *How* do we know? For we do: we find them reflected in media as diverse as Alison Bechdel's *Dykes to Watch Out For* series and the "many mothers" of Imperator Furiosa from the film *Mad Max: Fury Road*. Where does this knowledge come from? What is the relationship between these imaginary women's spaces and real women's spaces? How do ideas reach from actual women's and lesbian spaces to a wider queer space, and even into larger feminist and mainstream discourse?

The image of the "lesbian commune" or women's land is connected to the lesbian separatist, a figure very much associated with utopian ideals and the negative consequences of enacting them. The space is unwelcoming, cold, and hard work; the woman is stern and uncompromising, eats dreadful food, and knows how to run a consensus meeting but not how to make a joke. This dystopia-utopia meld is a form of what I call "reverse camp:" the separatist lesbian occupies the same symbolic space as the "old queen in a piano bar watering [his] drink every time they played Some Enchanted Evening" (Miller in Halperin 2012, 96). Both are part of a past we need to move away from (but the separatist lesbian also inhabits the dystopian future we must avoid); both are seen as comical; and both encode important queer cultural knowledge. But while the "old queen" encodes the knowledge of camp, I argue that the "old separatist" encodes "reverse camp": earnestness, utopian ideals, and a grim determination to go down fighting.

This chapter explores the ways in which knowledge production and community create each other. "Lesbian cultures" are constructed both by the knowledge and herstory of the women inhabiting them, and by the knowledge that transcends their boundaries. Women's land as a concept exists in a much larger discourse: about these spaces, about "women" and gender, and about identity, particularly lesbian identity. Women's land has become a cultural knot or center point in this web of knowledge. Knowledge moves both from the matrix culture to women's land, and from women's land outwards, into the larger web of matrix cultures.

My interviewees trace the history of women's lands and their own narrative histories of coming to live on women's land not to the utopian movements of the nineteenth century but to women's music festivals starting in the 1970s and to women's political activism, such as the Seneca Women's Peace Camp of the 1980s. Utopian movements and communes, along with the second wave of the feminist movement, combined at the same time to create the impetus for the creation of women's lands. Lesbianism became politicized and associated with particular forms of feminism at this time.

In this chapter, I will discuss three main examples to illustrate knowledge production about women's community. This knowledge about women's community, those who live in it, and larger ideas about gender, feminism, and sexuality are mutually constituted between women's lands themselves and people in the "matrix" community of the United States. The first example I have chosen is the Michigan Womyn's Music Festival, which is included as the most famous example of women's music festivals. It is connected with both the history of the creation of women's land and, perhaps more importantly, with the current dissemination of ideas about it. Music festivals serve as a "temporary testing ground" for utopian living ideas, and also demonstrate how such ideas can reenact larger structures of power rather than dismantling them.

The second main example is the Women's Encampment for a Future of Peace and Justice at Seneca Falls. The history of Seneca demonstrates political and cultural change from the micro to the macro level, and how ideas about gender, lesbian identity, and culture become points for conscious debate and action. Several of my informants were participants in Seneca, giving me a particularly good overview with several different viewpoints. Seneca, unlike music festivals, had stated political goals and is thus an excellent example of political embeddedness and action by women in women's space. Lastly, Seneca, as both open women's land and land on which decisions were made by full consensus, went "further" along the political spectrum than most music festivals. Seneca thus serves as both a good example of political and social change and flow in the United States and of how such spaces reverberate in the larger cultural network of women's community.

My last example is various portrayals of lesbian lands and land-women in literature published outside the circle of the land-women community. While most such portrayals originate in queer literature, they nevertheless serve to help create knowledge about such spaces. Here I argue that the over-serious "lesbian separatist" figure is an important figure of queer knowledge, standing opposite Halperin's "old queen" and representing what I call "reverse camp."

Throughout this complex history, a larger network of diverse cultures (lesbian and otherwise) has been widely influenced by women's and lesbian land. In this chapter I pull on the threads of women's music festivals, the Seneca Women's Peace Camp, and lesbian humor and literature to demonstrate first the historical roots of women's space (threads going into that knot) and then the influences of women's space on a larger cultural matrix (threads radiating outward). My evidence reveals that the saying about the personal being political holds particularly true when looking at knowledge production about gender, gendered identity, and gendered space. And the figure of the lesbian separatist is far from being simply a herstorical artifact. She, like the old queen, is an epistemological teacher, directing us to important queer ways of knowing.

We Are Everywhere and Nowhere: A Cultural History of Women's Utopia Traced from the Communitarian Movement to Women's Music Festivals

Although the women's-land movement and the intentional community movement are not deeply enmeshed, there are women involved with both, and similar cultural ideas can be traced. The concept of utopian living reaches back to the very roots of the United States, which was founded in part as a utopian religious community. Early communities can be loosely grouped as the "first wave" of utopian or communitarian living, including such famous experiments as Oneida and the formation of the Mormon state in Utah. A "second wave" of interest in communitarian living occurred during the social unrest and experimentation of the early 1970s, resulting in the "hippie commune," of which The Farm, still extant, is the most famous example. Today, the "third wave" of interest in communitarian living is represented by intentional communities such as cohousing, communal eco-villages, and the urban shared household. Intentional communities, communitarian societies, and communes: all of these have been seen as utopias.

My use of the first through the third wave terminology here, usually associated with the United States feminist movement, is hardly accidental. I have borrowed the terminology to point to the fact that these movements are also *social movements,* and have a larger social, cultural, and sometimes political impact. Although the women's-land movement looks largely to the second feminist "wave" of the early 1970s, women's music festivals, and post-Stonewall lesbian identity and political consciousness, there are also connections to the hippie commune "second wave." The back-to-the-land movement of the 1970s and its utopian ideals has also been an influence on women's land.[2] The second waves of both movements occurred at nearly the same time in the 1970s, a time many of my interviewees point to as the inception of the women's-land movement. This period of time established the Amazon Trail, a section of highway in Oregon along which several women's communities were established, as well as OWL Farm and other famous women's lands. This time also saw the rise of women's consciousness-raising groups, women's political groups, and women's music and women's music festivals.

Women's music festivals are transient, and women's lands are permanent communities; at the same time festivals are formed for a singular purpose, while "women's culture" and women's lands are much more all-encompassing. Yet the two phenomena are intimately linked despite these differences, and the women I interviewed made me aware of this at once.

"I wanted to live there all the time," said one woman, about her experience at a women's music festival. Another informant, Lillian, described her first experience of women's space, during an all-women's solstice festival in the Southwest: "I was just blown away. I just loved it, I just didn't wanna leave, I didn't want to go home, and I just like, the whole time, I kept thinking like, why would we ever go back? Why would we ever live any other way, you know? Why aren't we doing this all the time?" Thus the experience of women's "space" at the music festival was connected to the idea of "women's land." Several informants told me that the sense of empowerment that they first felt at all-women music festivals was the inspiration for either creating or seeking out women's land.

Women's music festivals and other women-only gatherings occupy a kind of utopian (but also dystopian, see below) discursive space. They are a space that is at once unstable and stable: that is, although such festivals often recur yearly in the same space, they do not exist constantly. As experimental spaces, such festivals are valuable for their periodicity; this enables them to bring together large groups of diverse women from a wide geographic range to exchange ideas, goods, and other cultural commodities. For example, the crafts sold at festivals become a means of networking outside of festival time: "Festiegoers grin when, 'off land,' they spot women about town wearing tie-dyed T-shirts from Snake and Snake or Willow Moon Designs. Products—art or clothing or music—become part of the lesbian code" (Morris 1999, 75). Note also that the festival itself is seen as being a "land." Bonnie Morris's overview book *Eden Built by Eves,* which includes many interviews with festival-involved women, provides a comprehensive history of women's music festivals. The women I interviewed testify as well to the importance such festivals possess in their lives.

Beyond its networking and celebratory capabilities, the music festival also offers the experience of women-only space and the utopian ideal of a female community. Morris writes that the Michigan Womyn's Music Festival in particular was "itself a political action. It is proof that women can perform every job required in the construction and maintenance of a city" (59). This serves as a projective space for women, in which they could "be themselves" and construct communal ways of living, such as the volunteer childcare and communal meals at Michigan. Such feminist projects are found alongside others such as antiracist work, eco-friendly policies, and antiviolence workshops. Thus the "thinking space" of the music festival is a rich ground for utopian ideals. This space provides inspiration, goals, and starting points for women who are interested in starting their own communities based on these or similar utopian designs. Yet Morris says, "For every festiegoer who sighs, 'If only the real world were like this!' there is usually a critic who replies, 'God *forbid!*'" (60).

At the same time music festivals, especially the primary example of the Michigan Womyn's Music Festival, illustrate how ideals that are utopian for some are dystopian for others. Incidents of classism, violence, racism, and transphobia show that such festivals are not free of larger structural forces. Indeed, transphobia has become a byword for the Michigan Womyn's Music Festival (Califia 2003, 227–29), so much so that it has tainted the very concept of women-only space. While I was doing this research, the transphobia of my informants was the first question asked by editors, other scholars, and casual discussants. However, while I did encounter some personally shocking incidences of transphobia, transphobia was not uniform across all women's lands or among all land-women, made up a relatively minor aspect of my research, and must be considered in the light of women's lands that explicitly welcome—or are created for the use of—trans women.[3] Yet, like racism, it cannot be lightly dismissed, for it is illustrative not only of problems within the community itself, but also of how unspoken ideas are adopted from United States matrix cultures.

The Crossroads of Politics and Gender: The Women's Encampment for a Future of Peace and Justice

The Women's Encampment for a Future of Peace and Justice in Seneca Falls, New York, opened in 1983 for the purpose of protesting the nearby nuclear depot. The land was purchased by a committee, but it was incorporated as a nonprofit and the Peace Camp was open to all women. The money for the purchase was raised through grassroots subscription because none of the local farmers were willing to rent land for women to camp on during the planned nonviolent political protests.[4]

The Peace Camp grew out of a disparate set of roots: the women's peace movement of the 1960s, which was largely white, middle-class, and did not identify as feminist (Swerdlow 1993, 2–3); the feminist movement, which had begun to incorporate consciousness-raising groups and other women-only spaces; the Women's Pentagon Action, which organized from 1979 through 1981 and included women of color and activism around reproductive freedom, gay rights, and eco-consciousness, as well as antiwar action[5] (King 1983); and the contemporary women's peace camp at Greenham Common in 1981 (Jones 1983).[6] Many of the women involved in the Women's Pentagon Action were also involved in planning the protests at the Women's Encampment for a Future of Peace and Justice.[7]

Louise Krasniewicz's ethnography of the event, *Nuclear Summer* (1992), focuses on misunderstandings, "the clash of communities," and violence. Two of my interviewees who attended the protests at Seneca heartily dislike the book, which characterizes the relationship between the town and the women as inevitably at odds, and the encampment itself as rife with conflict. While there was doubtless conflict with the surrounding community—a protest, even a nonviolent one, rather *presupposes* conflict—the Seneca archives and the women I interviewed present a much more nuanced and complex view of the event.

Despite the fact that everything was decided based on consensus,[8] the camp conducted several large and famous protests, had "Respected Policies" (their form of rules), and managed a large number of women who came in to participate in the protests at the depot. These protests included singing, art, theater, die-ins, marches, civil disobedience, and other peaceful types of creative demonstration. All of the demonstrations remained nonviolent, even in the face of verbal violence, harassment, and physical violence from local counterprotesters.

The Peace Camp was the site of a production of radical cultural difference, as previous journalists and historians have largely focused on. However, the camp also existed peacefully with the town of Romulus, purchasing supplies there, making friends, and socializing. One of my interviewees told me that many of the contemporary newspaper articles seemed to exaggerate the conflict between the citizens and the protesters. Yet there was violence, such as the Waterloo Bridge counterdemonstration, where local citizens barred the Peace Camp women from marching, shouted verbal abuse, and physically assaulted some of the women. Despite the behavior of the counterprotesters, the police chose to arrest the protesting women instead (Krasniewicz 1992, 180–83). One of the local women was also arrested in solidarity with the women of the camp.[9] Krasniewicz states that the women of the camp saw this incident "as the point at which many of the local people turned in their favor" (189). However, the women whom I interviewed about Seneca remember a much more complex narrative, in which relationships with local residents were begun well before the Waterloo Bridge incident and extended after.

The Peace Camp suffered many of the problems of consensual, anarchic government. Local organizations did not like the fact that they had no leaders. They had to make the same decisions over and over again; for example, where it was appropriate for women to smoke, and whether they would cut the fence into the depot that adjoined their property.[10] Essential work often went undone: the house on the property often had mold problems and always had rats from women being careless with food. One of the more charming examples was a sign Tamara told me about—it used to hang in the kitchen, reading "It is opressive [sic] to make others clean up your mess!" Tamara said that she and others used to joke about things that were "oppressive but not VERY oppressive—oppressive with only one p!"

Tamara said that one of the main problems with the openness of the Peace Camp, other than needing to make the same decisions over and over again, was that they were not equipped to deal with the kinds of problems some women had. She noted that some women there "had nowhere else to go in the world, no resources." Although she felt that the camp knew what had brought women to that pass—sexism and racism and similar forces—and were fighting those things, "there were women we didn't help and didn't know how to help because they—we—didn't have the resources." Tamara added, thoughtfully, that there had been a woman who had a "mental health breakdown," who had gone around the camp in a white sheet, disturbing people. "She left her ID behind and vanished. What happened to her?" The Peace Camp simply did not have a safety net to catch women who needed this kind of help.

Yet enormous amounts of work did get done. Privies were dug, hundreds of yards of wooden walkways constructed for handicapped access, plumbing put in and taken down for the camp, the barn winterized, windows repaired, fifty apple trees planted, and so on. Eventually, when the Peace Camp evolved into something else, long meetings (called Transform or Die meetings) were held, and the open women's land was changed into a land trust with a semi closed board membership.[11]

While journalist Margaret Doris concluded dismissively that "the encampment of women outside waits for evolution to teach it how to live in a world with warheads" (1983, 30), the women's land established at Seneca outlasted the missile factory. Krasniewicz suggests that the camp "did not seem to provide any particular benefits" (1992, 236). She thinks that it served as a symbol of the "dangerous woman" who "ruins" things such as "patriarchal modes of representation" (240). Yet the women I have spoken to about the Peace Camp and the subsequent women's land do not see their experience as symbolic but as literal, practical, and transformative. They were not there to "ruin" but to build. Journalists and scholars seem to want to box the Seneca Women's Peace Camp into a safe and simple category, assuring us that it was not very effective, did not create anything lasting, and was "only symbolic." But what if it was effective?

In either case, the women of the Peace Camp did not base the value of the camp solely on its political goals. When I interviewed women about the Peace Camp, they spoke of the radical sense of accomplishment that came from being part of an organization of women: "It was exhilarating," one woman told me. "Imagine learning to use a tool one day and teaching another woman how to use it the next." Another woman said, "We were stretching ourselves to our limits." All of my informants who had participated in the Peace Camp agreed that they had participated in the creation of a different culture that had affected their subsequent lives powerfully.

The Seneca Women's Peace Camp was a point of transformation. Doris, looking only for change on the massive and immediate level, was unable to see the ways in which Seneca was transformative on an immediate personal scale, and *also* on the slower, greater political scale. The nuclear installation did not close instantly. But the peace camps of Seneca and Greenham and other demonstrations helped shift the weight of political thinking. Transformation happens individually, and at the same time, there is a larger cultural thread that becomes visible in society as antiwar and antinuclear sentiment becomes more acceptable and common.

While academics find it tempting to view communities like Seneca as unique, uncommon, fragile, and ineffective—indeed, Doris compares them to the white deer, supposedly a product of nuclear-waste exposure mutation, that lived near the missile factory (1983, 30)—this stems from larger cultural imperatives to view women's work as trivial and ineffective and anything women build as fragile or temporary. By focusing on the conflicts between the Peace Camp and the local community, Krasniewicz positions the women of Seneca as disruptive and their political work as temporary and fleeting. Most problematically, she characterizes them as "symbolic" rather than as human agents of change.[12] Academics need to abandon this tendency to dismiss the work of women because of their gender, and instead consider the ways in which such communities of change operate on many levels at once.

My informants who attended Seneca did not see the Peace Camp as ineffective, or effective only symbolically. Indeed, they viewed Seneca as effective personally, empowering them and other women politically and socially. The Peace Camp was a political awakening for many women who went on to continue political work elsewhere; but this is not its only impact. For two of my informants, the Peace Camp also served as an introduction to living on women's lands. Tamara, who went on to live at the women's land founded at Seneca after the main political protests were over, watched women's land grow directly out of political protest. Bea, who attended the Peace Camp and lived at other women's lands, connected her experiences at Seneca to women's lands through the sense of community and empowerment that the Peace Camp fostered.

Political action and impact are intimately tied to women's lands. Many of my informants reported intense political engagement with local LGBT organizations, labor organizations, and ecological activists. Another one of my informants, when asked about political engagement, referred to the hundredth monkey principle, which she described as the notion that even if one monkey out of a hundred does something differently, it provides the opportunity for the others to watch and learn. That is, by living alternatively, she said, women's communities generate ideas that would not otherwise have occurred to the people around them. Women's lands, therefore, are in and of themselves a form of activism.

As Seneca shows, women's community and space can be an important point of transformation both for individual lives and for larger political movements. The history of Seneca demonstrates the connective points between political organization and women's land, and the cultural changes these make in the lives of individual women and in the larger matrix culture of the United States.[13] If we are to look for Seneca's *symbolic* importance, it is not in the political activism that occurred there, but in the ways it now appears in literature (see the next section, "Dangerous Places") to represent both women's space and political activism. Yet this symbolic importance is not static or past-tense: it is still currently used to create identity.

Lastly, the academic tendency to downplay the importance of Seneca raises the question of scale—on what scale do we look for change? If women report that Seneca made significant impacts in their lives, why do some academics contrast this with an *assumed* lack of impact on a political scale? What does this mean in relationship to the fact that the Peace Camp was run entirely by women—how is this tendency to assume or argue that Seneca was ineffective gendered? And what does this mean for the relationship between any form of activism—a protest, the creation of a community, the writing of a book—and the larger context in which it is meant to be effective?

Dangerous Places: The Women's Commune in Literature and Visual Media

In addition to affecting the larger matrix of cultures through political action, women's communities affect the production of *meaning* itself. The "nested cultures" of the intentional community or utopian movement and women's lands are caught in cultural webworks connecting them intimately to the larger matrix of culture in the United States. Cultural meaning flows both ways along these networks as women's and lesbian lands influence our conceptions of lesbian identity, what women's lands are, and ideas about feminism itself. One excellent example of the creation of cultural meaning is in the fictional portrayal of the "women's commune" in literature.

The connections between literary and lesbian or feminist utopias are many. Dana Shugar explores, for example, the influence Sally Miller Gearhart's *The Wanderground* and Suzy McKee Charnas's *Motherlines* have had on women's lands in part three of her ethnography *Sep-a-ra-tism and Women's Community* (1995). In *Eden Built by Eves,* Morris notes that "the birth of festival culture in the 1970s dovetailed with an emerging literature of lesbian-feminist science fiction classics that particularly emphasized the idea of utopias for women" (1999, 60). In addition to the works already mentioned, she notes *The Mists of Avalon* by Marion Zimmer Bradley, Katherine V. Forrest's *Daughters of a Coral Dawn,* Marge Piercy's *Woman on the Edge of Time, The Left Hand of Darkness* by Ursula K. Le Guin, and *The Female Man* by Joanna Russ as important influences. I would add Marion Zimmer Bradley's Free Amazons books (*The Shattered Chain, Thendara House,* and *City of Sorcery*) and Joanna Russ's famous short story "When It Changed," along with James Tiptree Jr.'s (pen name of Alice Bradley Sheldon) "The Women Men Don't See" and "Houston, Houston, Do You Read?"

Bonnie Zimmerman, in *The Safe Sea of Women,* calls women's community "the third formative myth in lesbian literature, and the keystone of lesbian feminist culture" (1990, 120). She calls this myth "Lesbian Nation," after the term coined by Jill Johnston in a 1971 *Village Voice* article and which later became the title of her well-known book (1973). Zimmerman notes that "novels about lesbian community (whether they belong to the genre of speculative fiction or not) tend to be intensely idealistic and utopian. They may establish myths of origin explaining or justifying all-female collectivity" (1990, 121). Zimmerman sees the development of such literature as arising from political sources such as the gay liberation movement, 1960s counterculture, and radical feminism, as well as the adoption of particular literary symbols such as the Amazon and the island of women (121–26). Although we may attempt to trace the development of feminist, lesbian, and separatist communities to the influence of such literature, the truth of the matter is that there is no simple, directional, cause-and-effect vector. The influences, causes, and motivations are complex, networked, and interpenetrate each other: literature makes community makes literature (or perhaps community makes literature makes community).

Zimmerman traces the impact of several lesbian novels about community/separatism, starting with a chronicle of literary or "realistic" literature focusing on community in a broader sense, through lesbian bars, community work, or political activism. Throughout, she concentrates on the issue of culture:

> Lesbian feminists... have used two tactics to rehabilitate lesbian culture and community. One has been deliberate separation: rather than waiting to be thrust into a gay ghetto, many lesbian feminists take the initiative and withdraw both actually and symbolically from the dominant society into Lesbian Nation. We refuse to continue the debilitating struggle against oppression. Inside Lesbian Nation we pursue the second tactic, creating our own history, tradition, and culture. In a profound way, this culture defines and sustains the community. A woman becomes a citizen of Lesbian Nation, a lesbian feminist, through the books she reads, the music she listens to, the heroes she identifies with, the language she speaks, the clothes she wears—even if at times she resents the required codes. (159)

Prominent and important questions of feminist, lesbian, and separatist philosophy are raised both in "fantastic" depictions of all-women's space, and in more "realistic" depictions of women's collectives, communes, and love lives. Furthermore, as Zimmerman aptly notes, knowledge of and consumption of these texts is an important part of membership in a larger, dimly-defined lesbian culture.

Lest we should doubt the influence of the fantasy and science fiction feminist utopias on the lives of real women, in the introduction to *Free Amazons of Darkover* (an anthology of short stories dealing with women-only communes in her patriarchal society of Darkover), Marion Zimmer Bradley writes,

> I had no notion, when I created (out of a dream) the Free Amazons of Darkover, that they were to become the most attractive and controversial of my creations, drawing more fan mail than all other subjects put together. Not only are there now several Amazon Newsletters among female fans, there are at least a dozen women that I know of (not counting those I don't) who have legally changed their names to the Free Amazon style; as well as a number of Guild Houses in various cities where women try to live by some version of the Amazon, or Renunciates Oath. (1985, 7)

If the Free Amazons were inspiring women to change their names and to create women-only communities in the 1980s, well after the first surge of women's-land creation in the early 1970s, then clearly these books had a considerable real-world impact. Later in this introduction, Bradley notes that "it is a rare sf convention where some would-be Amazon fails to ask me to accept her Amazon Oath. I usually question the women seriously to see if they are aware of the number of restrictions and renunciations involved in this and if they seem to be serious, I accept their oath" (12). This is further evidence that women found inspiration in this fictional depiction of women's community. Bradley did not take her influence, or the women who were inspired by her, very seriously, ending this paragraph by saying, "It is a fantasy, I expect, at least no more harmful than the 'adoption' of Cabbage Patch Dolls," thus infantilizing these women and lowering their life commitments to "play."[14] Despite this there is evidence that her books had real impact.

Not all women involved in women's land, of course, think that fiction of any sort can or should have an impact on the political and social lives of land-women. I vividly remember an incident from my first Landdyke Gathering, when one woman asked me how I came to be interested in women's land. I mentioned that I had first heard of it through reading fantasy and science fiction novels written by women that included all-women societies, whereupon she declared that such fiction was "wish fulfillment" and proceeded to go out of her way to treat me rudely for the rest of the Gathering (including insulting my cooking to my face—a serious breach of manners among land-women). At the same time, women who live in women's-land communities still produce such fiction. Diana Rivers, whom I met at the Michigan Womyn's Music Festival and who lives on women's land, writes a series of fantasy novels[15] that contrast a utopian women's society called the Hadra with surrounding warring societies. Thus the utopian image of the all-female society both produces and is produced by women who live in women's communities.

The image of the women's community is not limited to the utopian, but ranges from the comic/dystopic to the realistic. Zimmerman suggests that the "myth of community," while most often appearing as utopic, is also criticized and even satirized, including novels that refer to it as a "fairy tale," depict communities of those who compete for a "most victimized" label, spell "women" eleven different ways in four pages, have protagonists who feel alienated from their communities, and depict racism, classism, and homophobia both within the community and serving to keep the community itself in check (Zimmerman 1990, 157–58). Depictions of lesbian communes, women's lands, women's music festivals, and lesbian farms abound, particularly in lesbian literature. These depictions help construct the image of the women's community itself, and also form a type of social keyword, an important image of what it means to be lesbian.

I do not mean that all lesbians must have some connection to, or even be aware of, women's lands. But women's lands or lesbian communes are potent symbols in the construction of lesbian identity. Through depictions of them in literature and jokes, ideas of what it means to be a lesbian (or, perhaps, a particular kind of lesbian?) and to know about lesbian culture are formed. David Halperin, in his work *How to Be Gay*, proposes that gay male queerness is a cultural rather than a sexual performative and that it entails particular forms of cultural, especially aesthetic, knowledge. Similarly, ideas of what it means to be a lesbian, to be a queer woman, to rebel against "stereotypes" of lesbianism, and to construct queer female identity are to a certain extent constructed with regard to women's land and images of women's land, even for those of us who have never heard of it.

Halperin argues that gay male culture uses camp, "which involves not taking seriously, literally, or unironically the very things that matter most and that cause the most pain" in order to "suspend the pain of losses that it does not cease to grieve" (2012, 218). Camp, therefore, along with the appreciation of aesthetics that produce camp, such as emotion-laden musical theater, opera, or early Hollywood film, serves as a means of both acknowledging and relieving pain, of making it bearable by turning it into something else. Halperin further argues that rejection of camp and association of it with earlier generations of gay culture then becomes "necessary":

> Perhaps that is another reason why gay male culture produces so much aversion in gay men, why it elicits so much denial, and why contemporary gay men tend to project it onto earlier generations of archaic, pathetic queens—onto anyone but themselves. Traditional gay male culture is a way of coping with powerlessness, of neutralizing pain, of transcending grief. And who nowadays wants to feel powerless, who wants to think of himself as a victim? (218–19)

Therefore this aspect of gay culture is rejected, precisely because it is necessary to gay pride. That is, the pursuit of acceptance within mainstream society necessitates the rejection of this aspect of the social experience of gayness, the erasure of erasure. Halperin suggests,

> It is understandable that a set of cultural practices designed to cope with the reality of suffering, to defy powerlessness, and to carve

out a space of freedom within a social world acknowledged to be hostile and oppressive would not only fail to appeal to many subordinated people nowadays, but would constitute precisely what most of us—including women, gay men, and other minorities—must reject in order to accede to a sense of ourselves as dignified, proud, independent, self-respecting, powerful, and happy in spite of everything. (219)

He goes on to note that the solution of gay pride to this problem is essentially an appeal to utopianism—"aspiring to a better future—better, that is, than the world as we know it."

Yet in the case of lesbian culture, the relationship of queerness and utopianism is more complex. The "continuing appeal of utopianism" (219) is heavily tainted with the shadow of lesbian separatism, and the scapegoating that separatism has endured. Joanna Russ observes perceptively that "it's pretty clear that feminist attacks on separatists and feminist horror stories about separatists are a form of scapegoating, just like the scapegoating of the 'undesirables' of one's own sex or ethnic group" (1998, 85). How is it that lesbian utopianism has become, instead of a shining futuristic appeal, a point to scapegoat? Apparently, a utopianism without men is, even for lesbians, *unacceptably radical*. Russ's characterization of this is particularly pointed: "We haven't gone too far; *she* has. We aren't crazy; *she* is. *We* aren't angry or bad or out of control; *she* is. *We* don't hate men (the sin of sins); *she* does. Don't punish us; punish *her*" (85). Separatists are frequently scapegoated, misrepresented, made mock of, and generally not taken seriously either in scholarship or in "mainstream" feminist work.

Thus the "utopianism" of gay pride merges with a different, inverted kind of camp in the image of the lesbian separatist utopia: instead of camp itself, which mocks and makes light of, these images are seen as *too* earnest, *too* extreme, and *too* radical, and thus *reverse camp*.[16] The old lesbian separatist is the opposite side of the coin from the old queen; where one is antipolitical,[17] mocking, and camp, the other is entirely political, antifun, and earnest. Yet the same flavor of embarrassment tinges both; both are associated with "previous generations" of gay culture; and both are rejected in favor of looking to a more heteronormative future, where our marriages are "just like yours, only gayer."[18]

Michael Warner, in *The Trouble with Normal*, uses the terms "stigmaphobe" and "stigmaphile" (borrowed from Erving Goffman) to discuss how queer culture deals with ambivalence about sex and stigma (1999, 43).

In his conception, those looking towards the more heteronormative future, the ones who "express the greatest desire for conformity" are "stigmaphobes," while "stigmaphiles" are those who "find a commonality with those who suffer from stigma, and in this alternative realm learn to value the very things the rest of the world despises." However, only considering two groups oversimplifies this issue: the lesbian separatist is not a "stigmaphile," although she is highly stigmatized and rejected by those who adhere to mainstream queer respectability politics: the "stigmaphobes." Indeed, lesbian separatism has produced its own set of respectability politics and sexual shame, and as Warner notes, power tends to accrue unevenly in such situations: "power lies almost exclusively on the normal side" (44). Esther Newton notes that

> in different ways, both "political lesbians" and traditional middle-class women are still, in Erving Goffman's phrase, "normalizers." Lesbian-feminists insist that they are the healthy ones, and everyone else is "sick" or "unreal." Their political rhetoric about "egalitarian sexuality" emphasizes a traditionally female ideal (tenderness, affection, communication) and proscribes "male" genital sexuality (promiscuity, power relations, sexual excitement for its own sake). (2000, 161)

Thus the image of the "proper" lesbian separatist is complex and shifts as she crosses boundaries: stigmatized and embarrassing to mainstream queer politics; the arbiter of the "normal" within women's community and one who maintains standards of strict, almost puritan, sexual shame. (This in spite of the fact that there are widely varying standards of sexual practice on actual women's lands, as well as individuals who practice BDSM.)[19]

Images of the lesbian separatist in the United States are almost always white.[20] Or, perhaps it would be more accurate to say that the key symbolic character—the one who is depicted as being unpleasant, prudish, humorless, political, the heart of reverse camp—is depicted as being white, although supporting characters and more sympathetic characters may be depicted as women of color. This is despite the fact that black and Latina women have been involved with women's community since its inception, and women of all races (and cultures) worldwide have participated in various forms of women's separatism. The association of separatism with whiteness is pervasive enough that black separatists, writing in the 1970s and

1980s, felt the need to address it. However, as we will see below, *women's community* is not always depicted as a racially uniform space, and characters of color are depicted as participating in various forms of women's community.

In larger spheres of lesbian culture, the image of the lesbian separatist is both culturally important yet denigrated as being too "radical." The utopianism of the women's community or lesbian commune itself is contrasted with a cynical overlay of doubt; the communities are presented as extreme, unworkable, and often unpleasant. Yet at the same time, knowledge of these communities, ideas about and from these communities, and experiences of these communities are interwoven into the lesbian cultural overlay, the same way that cultural knowledge of camp and how to do it is woven into gay male culture. Furthermore, that knowledge is important: we must *recognize* the lesbian separatist and her place in culture, even if we are ignorant of part (or all) of her history.

One excellent example of this is the use of women's space in Alison Bechdel's *Dykes to Watch Out For.* These collections, which have appeared in countless gay publications around the globe and have been translated into many languages, are a touchstone for a large portion of the queer and especially lesbian community. The comics are set in a lesbian community in a small fictional town and reflect daily life; over the years, Bechdel has chosen to address a wide range of issues facing the queer community, ranging from current politics to motherhood, gender transition, the women's bookstore as community center, vegetarianism, online dating, and academia.

Her mentions of women's land (ranging from music festivals to lesbian communes) are few but significant. The first few mentions occur in the first volume and tend to be indirect. "Summer Grooming Tips" (47) makes reference to both "at the music festivals" (the tip is "Do braid your armpit hair!") and "at the peace camps" ("Don't bring your blow-dryer!"). Both music festivals and peace camps are references to women's space. In "Summer Sublet" (51), one of the jokes depends on "the bed's not big enough for the whole collective," referring to a nonmonogamous lesbian group living together (pictured as five women of various races and a baby). But the most relevant early cartoon is "The Seven Ages of Lesbians" (68–69) in which the Baby Dyke (first panel), exclaims, "Goddess! All this womon-energy is so, so healing!" in front of a fence labeled "Army Depot, Keep Out," further decorated with a "Zukes, Not Nukes" sign. Here the reference to women's energy and the illustration of the army depot are clear references to the Seneca Women's Peace Camp. The last panel in this

Originally published in *Dykes to Watch Out For* by Alison Bechdel. Copyright 1986 by Alison Bechdel.

comic shows an old lesbian scaling the fence, labeled the Tireless Activist. Involvement in women's land and activism, within this comic, is part of the "lesbian life cycle," and frames the entirety of it. Activism is symbolized by the Seneca Women's Peace Camp *itself*, which is the space in which activists feel "women's energy" for the first time, and the group the old lesbian joins to continue her political work.

Bechdel tackles the lesbian communal lifestyle head-on in many cartoons. For many years, prominent characters Sparrow, Lois, and Ginger lived together in a communal house. It is notable that two of the characters—Sparrow and Ginger—are women of color (Sparrow is Asian and Ginger is black). Sparrow is perhaps the character closest in tone to a "stereotypical" lesbian communard: she is a vegetarian, works in a women's center as an abuse counselor, and follows new age beliefs of meditation and herbal healing. However, Sparrow departs from the "typical" depiction in many ways. In addition to being Asian instead of white, she is very open-minded and exhibits a firm practicality underneath her warm outward demeanor. For example, in one early strip, she uses her role in picking up the house and the mail to convince her roommates to do their share of the cleaning: "Maybe I should just never reveal the whereabouts of a particular black leather jacket and a certain overstuffed mauve envelope that arrived in the mail this morning addressed to Ginger 'Angel Lips' Jordan" (implied: unless she gets some help) (Bechdel 1993, 15). In later years, she takes a male lover and has a child with him. In this depiction of the communal lesbian household, not only do we see women of various races and backgrounds, but as Sparrow demonstrates, they are rounded, full characters rather than stereotypes or bywords.

Lesbian lands remain more in the background, but in a series of consecutive strips titled "Hell House," "The Visitation," "You Are What You Eat," and "Sermon on the Couch," Bechdel chronicles a visit to this communal household by Milkweed Moongarden, a woman who lives on a "lesbian farm" (Bechdel 1990, 79). In this series of strips, Milkweed, a white woman, is an abrasive and unlikeable character who apparently cannot answer the phone or take messages properly, throws away lightbulbs because they are "products of the military-industrial complex" (81), and is highly judgmental of other people's eating habits, herself eating only a vegan organic diet (83).

This stereotype of land-women or "lesbian separatists" derives its humor largely from an assumed audience familiarity with the stereotype,

Originally published in *New, Improved! Dykes to Watch Out For* by Alison Bechdel. Copyright 1990 by Alison Bechdel.

as well as from exaggerations of typical feminist concerns, such as "the military-industrial complex." Milkweed's earnest and humorless aspect also plays on the reverse camp image of the lesbian separatist, although the strip itself—lesbian humor!—slyly undercuts this.

A later mention of lesbian lands occurs during a discussion between Toni and her midwife while she is pregnant, in a strip called "The Fairies' Midwife." When Toni complains about her partner Clarice being distant, her midwife (a white woman) remarks that she had the same problem with her husband, and the solution was that she "left him and moved into a lesbian commune." Toni's response here is particularly important—she states that not only does she not want to leave Clarice, but that she thinks "they don't have lesbian communes anymore" (Bechdel 1993, 89). Here, lesbian communes are no longer presented as an essential part of the "lesbian life cycle," but as a part of lesbian *herstory*. We as readers are still expected to have an idea of what a lesbian commune is, though.

The humor in these panels both depends on our knowledge of music festivals, women's political peace activism, and lesbian communes, and re-

Originally published in *The Essential Dykes to Watch Out For* by Alison Bechdel. Copyright 2008 by Alison Bechdel. Reprinted by permission of Houghton Mifflin Harcourt Publishing Company. All rights reserved.

inforces or *provides* that knowledge. In addition to providing the reader with a sense of "belonging" when she—or he—reads these jokes, they also *construct* that knowledge, telling us both that lesbian communes exist and what kind of people (in the case of Milkweed) we can expect to live there. These spaces are at once constructed by Bechdel as utopic, as in moving to a lesbian commune when leaving a husband, and as full of undesirable extremists, like Milkweed. The contrast is played for humor, and depends on cultural ideas about these spaces already extant: including the idea that these distant cultural spaces are inhabited by white women.

Comic artist Roberta Gregory, in her *Bitchy Butch: World's Angriest Dyke* (a play on her earlier title *Bitchy Bitch*), has Bitchy Butch fondly remembering her days "living in the country with wimyn" (Gregory 1999, 54). In back-to-back panels on a single page, Bitchy Butch remembers building her own house in two weeks, homegrown apples, and a women's spirituality circle contrasted with rain, an outhouse, sick goats coughing, and "Let's hold a healing circle for hepatitis." With admirable economy and a sense of ironic humor that depends on these extreme contrasts, Gregory not only tells a complicated herstory of women's lands, including positive and negative depictions, but also connects them to the life of her main character.

Later in this volume, Bitchy Butch narrates a history of the gay movement that includes much more idyllic—even utopic—representations of women's land and other collectives, including representations of women's farms, bookstores, alternative families, processing circles, and finally an "ideal society" (85–86). However, these are presented as part of the past and an idealized, utopic future; a fantasy rather than a present influence on lesbian culture. This contrasts with Milkweed from *Dykes to Watch Out For*, who may be characterized as unpleasant, but who was presented as existing in the present day of the original publication and who interacts with the main characters.

Moving to text from comics, Laura Antoniou's *The Killer Wore Leather* (2013) is an excellent example for illustrating conceptions of women's space for several reasons: First, mysteries with lesbian detectives are a popular genre; second, the setting, which is a BDSM convention, is about as far as one can get from lesbian lands in terms of queer culture; and third, the reference to women's lands is particularly clever.

The Killer Wore Leather presents mysteries on a number of levels (a murder mystery; who is going to win the Global Leather title; who is leaking information to the protester sending threatening emails; why do people run conventions anyway?), but the most relevant to this discussion

Originally published in *Bitchy Butch* by Roberta Gregory. Copyright 1999 by Roberta Gregory. Reprinted by permission of Roberta Gregory. All rights reserved.

is the mystery of who wrote a set of novels called the Zod books, a thinly disguised parody of the Gor novels.[21] The Zod books have a significant role-play/lifestyle following in which people pretending to be Zodians consider themselves part of the kinky community because of how the books portray master/slave relationships between men and women.

Late in the book (chapter 30, 275), it is revealed that a lesbian anthropologist who both writes about and is involved in the BDSM community (Dr. Abraham) is the actual author of the Zod series. This creates drama, because the books are supposedly for the titillation of conservatively heterosexual men who want "slave women" and women who don't mind playing such roles. Soon, however, phyl'ta, a role-playing Zodian, reveals that she doesn't care who wrote the books, because they enabled her to meet men who thought she was attractive and "didn't even have to say things like, I was sexy *despite* being fat, like some guys do"—and then, "Because last night, I came six times! Six! Because he thinks it's his duty as a Zodian master to make me 'weak in the love furs,' and so he figures that means getting me off so much I have to beg him to stop" (293–94). Despite their patriarchal trappings, these books seem to be beneficial to women, or at least, this woman.

Later, when she is questioned about her motives for writing the books, Dr. Abraham, after saying she could "retire on those royalty checks" (325) and that originally it was a joke, explains:

> If you read the men as stone butches, it works. But . . . just read the damn things! If you can bear to. Look at all the cultural signifiers I put in there! The girls wear rainbow silks, and lavender veils. The sigil of the greatest of the clans is a fucking labrys crossed with a crescent moon! They eat tons of goddamned . . ."
>
> "Tofu," Nancy said, wonderingly.
>
> "Yes! Grilled tofu! And in one book, they even get food poisoning from it, an actual historic event well known in the why-mins community." (328)

The books serve as a complex double joke both on the role-playing "Zodians" and on the women's community itself, in which their culture becomes not just welcoming of kink *but a kink itself.* In the end, though, this may be one of the most positive depictions of women's land; Dr. Abraham receives a suggestion that she should "Make them admit you're the real dom of doms!"[22] And then, in simple language they'll understand, write their rulebook for them . . . tell them how to treat their ladies right and they'd have to listen!" (330). That is, force the male-dominant role-players to accept that their "play" should be for the benefit of women. This suggestion (which she seems to accept), makes the utopianism of women's land into a *rulebook* and a way to influence even the lives of (supposedly male-dominant) straight people. In this story, women's land has the last laugh: not only is it erotic, not only does it work as long as you don't *know* it's women's separatism, it's also everywhere you never thought to look for it. Reverse camp, indeed.

It is perhaps unsurprising to find references to women's lands and lesbian separatists in lesbian humor comics and mysteries. Yet nonqueer media also presents us with images of "women's lands" and "separatists," and these images show not only the ways in which information disperses through the matrix cultures of the United States, but also how various discourses reflect and refract these images. For example, in Amanda Cross's 1981 mystery novel *Death in a Tenured Position* (set at Harvard University), a major player in the mystery is Luellen, a woman involved in a women's commune in Cambridge and fighting to keep custody of her children because of her possible lesbianism and involvement in the commune.[23] The women of the commune use the term "sisters," explained by Joan Theresa, another commune member:

> Women who are sisters have no part in the male establishment, no part in patriarchal institutions at all. Furthermore, they despise them. They feel that patriarchal institutions have suppressed and used women, and the sisters want nothing to do with them; they would, in fact, like to destroy them, but at least they know they're rotten. Women who are not sisters play along with the rottenness, either liking it or thinking it changeable. (11)

The women of the commune, who run a coffee shop called Maybe Next Time Coffee House, refer to proper fem dress as "drag," and who have been in marches "where people were arrested" (64–73), yet are depicted surprisingly sympathetically given the framing of the novel. The main character, academic Kate Fansler, admits, "I think I like Joan Theresa [a sister/communard] better than Janet Mandelbaum [the Harvard professor she's been asked to help]" (25). The sisters are portrayed as part of the present and necessarily entangled with the plot of the novel, which has to do not only with murder but with the age-old "woman question."[24] They are depicted as over-serious, involved with politics, and deeply concerned in particular with the purity of one's sexual politics (reverse camp). One character notes, "There was no way those women, outside the institutions and living in a commune, were going to come to the aid of straight women" (25). Yet here are separatist women ("sisters") operating a coffee shop in the heart of Cambridge in 1981, entangled in Harvard's murder mystery as well as in their own custody troubles, politically involved, running their own business, and, rather to my surprise, much more likable than any of the Harvard professors, despite their deliberate prickliness.

That was 1981. Surely female separatists and women's lands have faded away from our cultural zeitgeist by now? Yet they have not, as the recent film *Mad Max: Fury Road* (2015) makes clear. Not only is the main character (Imperator Furiosa) given an implied past on women's land (she calls herself the daughter of "many mothers" and remembers being kidnapped from "a green place" to which she hopes to return), but a number of characters, including older women and women of color, comprise a women-only community who are given a heroic and key part of the film's plot.

These characters, who are rooted in their women's separatist background, are symbolically connected not only to the "better past" that makes up the background of apocalyptic/dystopian narratives like the *Mad Max* films, but also to a more hopeful future. The women of the separatist clan (including Miss Giddy, Valkyrie, Keeper of the Seeds, and the motorcycle-riding Vuvalini),[25] are associated with Imperator Furiosa's "green place" of the past, in a film whose desert setting is both symbolic and a visual synecdoche for the series itself. This "green space" (vanished/ruined though it is in the present of the film) and the bag of seeds kept by the Keeper of the Seeds connect these women with powerful nurturing and Earth-harmonious images that might have come directly from the culture of land-women. These images stand in opposition to the desert and the many references to "destroyed" or "poisoned" earth or land that are made throughout the film. For example, the wives of the warlord who are rescued by Furiosa write "Who killed the world?" on the walls of their empty harem, and scream it back at the army of the warlord Immortan Joe pursuing them, a question that implicates both Immortan Joe and the entire system of war and corporate greed. It is through the action of the separatist women, who are both violent and heroic in the film, that Imperator Furiosa is able to release the water in the Citadel, overturning a warlord/corporate-run culture. At one point, one of the wives tells the separatist women that Immortan Joe keeps control by keeping the water, which he pumps up from underneath the earth but only gives out in small shares; she adds, "He calls it Aqua-Cola," a reference to today's bottled water market.

Lesbian subtext in the film is present but remains "in the shadow kingdom of connotation" (Miller 1990, 119). The subtext includes how Furiosa introduces herself, the lost daughter of the community, as the daughter of "many mothers" and the fact that not only does the community have no men, but Furiosa's immediate reaction to seeing the motorcycle grannies is to say that she will "vouch for" the two men she brings with her (saying nothing of the other women, who presumably can vouch for themselves). Within the harem, the wives refer to each other as "sisters," but their appearance does not support genetic sisterhood; their extremely close family bonds can be read several ways depending on the preference of the viewer. Lastly, there is no overt inevitable heterosexual love plot for any of these women (most notably, Furiosa herself). While our culture tends to see all people as "straight until proven otherwise," women holding military status or being in close emotional proximity to other women endanger this automatic straight privilege. Thus, as with other women's communities, the shadow and "abiding deniability" (118) of lesbianism hovers over these women.

The film not only references separatist women's/lesbian community, but also makes it central to the plot of the film. A corporate warlord who trains young men to gladly die for him and hoards resources such as water, women, even women's breastmilk (an early scene in the film shows a "secondary harem" of women hooked up like cows to milking machines) is the villain. By creating a plot that begins with a female soldier (Imperator Furiosa) helping women escape from a harem and enlisting the aid of a women's separatist community to bring down the Immortan and create a new "green place" (literally healing an apocalyptic landscape), the film casts women's community in the central heroic role. As in *The Killer Wore Leather,* women's community is suddenly everywhere—it is in the harem, it is in the history of the female soldier, and it is surviving in the apocalyptic desert with the bag of seeds that will save humanity and heal the earth. Thus *Mad Max: Fury Road*—a film that one could argue is itself camp, with its over-the-top aesthetic and postapocalyptic plot—embraces the reverse camp of the separatist lesbian, and acknowledges her role in leading us closer to utopia.

· CHAPTER 2 ·

Are the Amazons White?

Race and Space on Women's Land

No matter how sensitive you are
if you are white
you are
No matter how sensitive you are
if you are a man
you are
We who are not allowed to speak have the right
to define our terms our turf
These facts are not debatable
Give us our inch
& we'll hand you a hanky

—Chrystos, "THOSE TEARS," 1991

AS I WRITE THIS CHAPTER, it is October and November in the year 2014, and the events in Ferguson, Missouri, and the aftermath fill my newsfeed. I cannot escape the ways in which racism is encoded into the very fabric of American society, either via tweets that attempt to excuse the murder of minors by those minors' petty misdeeds, or a student's comments attempting to justify stop-and-frisk as "crime-stopping." As a white woman in the United States, I live in a very different world than that of my black colleagues and friends: my embodiment is predicated on my ontological right to exist. I garner no curious looks at the faculty meeting, I am not expected to "speak for" my people when writing about race, and no one questions characters of my race appearing in works of fiction.

This ontological "right to exist" is part of the racial privilege of whiteness. While establishing whiteness's right to exist, this frame of thinking assumes the "otherness" of other racial embodiments, producing the white/nonwhite dichotomy. In turn, the dichotomy helps construct the unmarked (white) and marked (nonwhite) in American space. This works in concert with the invisibility of racial privilege to make the policing of other races in "white space" seem natural while remaining brutally effective.

Despite efforts made on the part of many land-women to resist, subvert, and change aspects of American culture, race and racism remain stubbornly present. The women's-land movement is largely though not wholly white, thus the embodiment of white women has shaped its culture. Those who do not personally know what it means to be black, Latina, Native, Asian, or any race that falls into the "marked" category are those who have articulated the "body" of the women's-land movement. The blind spots of this culture are numerous.

One of the most persistent blind spots of women's land is how land is referred to, interacted with, and imagined. Carolyn Finney notes that "we have collectively come to understand/see/envision the environmental debate as shaped and inhabited primarily by white people. And our ability to imagine others is *colored* by the narratives, images, and meanings we've come to hold as truths in relation to the environment" (2014, xii). If our culture has a tendency to imagine the outdoors as "belonging" to white people,[1] then women's land is imagined as a space for white women. Finney suggests that "whiteness as a way of knowing becomes *the* way for understanding our environment, and through representation and rhetoric, becomes part of our educational systems, our institutions, and our personal beliefs" (Sundberg 2002; DeLuca and Demo 2001; and Smedley 1993; cited in Finney, 3). These beliefs shape women's land and how landwomen and those in the matrix culture react to it.

This chapter will examine the construction of race on women's land as I experienced it. I will focus on three aspects of race: First, the construction of whiteness as absence of race or racial marking. Second, how this assumed absence of race/presence of whiteness serves as a hidden cultural marker within the community, producing what Finney calls "whiteness as a way of knowing." Third, how racism is constructed as "other," portrayed as something which is done both *by* and *to* other people. Racism is also often depicted as being parallel to, rather than intersecting with or constituent of, other forms of injustice or oppression such as sexism and homophobia. At the same time, the writings of lesbians of color early in the women's-land movement describe what would later become known by the term "intersectionality" in talking about these forms of oppression (Crenshaw 1991).

This is not to imply that the women I worked with were terrible racists (they were not) or that being white somehow, in and of *itself*, produces racism. It is also important to note that "whiteness is not now, nor has it ever been, a static, uniform category of social identification" (Saxton 1990; Jacobson 1998; Roediger 2005; cited in Twine and Gallagher 2008, 6), as I hope to show with regard to my informants later in this chapter. Whiteness does, however, interact with our culture in such a way as to generate a "protective shield" that is not available to people of other races, and this shield can produce some curious results, which I seek to document here.

Before I speak about my own observations and the experiences of my informants with regard to race, it is necessary to put the women's-land movement and lesbian separatism into context. There is a long history of writing about race with regard to lesbian community, lesbian separatism, and "women's culture."

"Not Necessarily Contradictory": Writing about Separatism and Race

Women of color within women's communities have long written about racism and racial issues. However, different perspectives between women of color and white women often clash, and while some women of color assert that separatism is not inherently racist, others point to ways in which racism has remained from the dominant matrix cultures and has gone unexamined. Others suggest that "separatism"—not the same thing as living in women's community, but the philosophical and political position—is in fact racist. Separatism as a philosophy and the culture of women's lands are two different things: most of my informants did not identify as separatists. However, separatism has historically been associated with women's land and lesbian land and is often credited with its creation.

The ways in which racism operates in women's lands through pressure from the matrix culture are often linked to how women are permitted, by themselves and others, to assert power and agency. Although women's lands maintain strong cultural boundaries with the U.S. matrix culture, there are certain aspects of this matrix culture that "pass" those boundaries, either through unspoken, doxic beliefs and understandings, or through larger cultural pressures such as economics. At the same time, women's lands also engage in active resistance, and racism is a point at which unconscious adoption and active resistance both occur.

The proto-articulation of the "separatist" position, which is regarded by feminists as framing the general philosophy of women's land, is often traced back to articles in 1970s feminist newspapers. These include the Radicalesbians' "The Woman-Identified Woman" (1970), "How to Stop Choking to Death, Or: Separatism" by the Revolutionary Lesbians (1971), and "Lesbians in Revolt" by the Furies, in the newspaper of the same name (1972). "The Woman-Identified Woman" includes the statement, "Our energies must flow towards our sisters, not backwards towards our oppressors" (Radicalesbians 1991, 21). "How to Stop Choking to Death" bluntly states "as long as men are getting the attention and energy of women they will not face their sexism" (Revolutionary Lesbians 1991, 24). "Lesbians in Revolt" notes that "women in women's liberation have understood the importance of having meetings and other events for women only. It has been clear that dealing with men divides us and saps our energies and that it is not the job of the oppressed to explain their oppression to their oppressor" (Bunch for the Furies Collective 1972, 9).[2] Similarly, the Combahee River Collective Statement is often framed as the concomitant opposition of women of color to lesbian separatism: "As we have already stated, we reject the stance of Lesbian separatism because it is not a viable political analysis or strategy for us. It leaves out far too much and far too many people, particularly Black men, women, and children" (Combahee River Collective 1986, 14).

Barbara Smith, in her forward to the Kitchen Table Press edition of the Statement, suggests that "what made the Combahee River Collective most unique was the fact that it was a *progressive, multi-issue, activist* Black feminist organization" (1986, 5). Although, as I argue later, many women on land also see themselves as activists, the philosophy of separatism itself was often seen as isolationist in ways that were only tenable for white women: "Our situation as Black people necessitates that we have solidarity around the fact of race, which white women of course do not need to have with white men, unless it is their negative solidarity as racial oppressors" (12). Yet women's land in practice is not exactly isolationist, far from it. In fact, one of the main problems that women of color face in such communities is that it is impossible to isolate such communities from larger oppressive systems of racism, classism, and capitalism.

"Separatism, we feel, is based on the erroneous assumption that the patriarchy is the only system that we must overthrow and seems to suggest that the needs and interests of all lesbians are somehow identical" (Gibbs and Bennett 1980, 2). This criticism is one that is echoed over and over within feminist work; it is certainly not limited to criticism of separatism alone. However, the problem of the "common lesbian experience," is particularly prickly in the case of community. If entrance to and acceptance into community is based on assumed shared experience, women of different racial, class, ethnic, cultural, and ability backgrounds will be excluded. Audre Lorde noted the same dynamic when she wrote, "to imply, however, that all women suffer the same oppression simply because we are women, is to lose sight of the many varied tools of patriarchy. It is to ignore how those tools are used by women without awareness against each other" (1983, 95).

Yet the case is not how white lesbians supported separatism (not all did in the 1970s, and certainly it is unpopular today), while black lesbians did not. There were white lesbians opposed to separatism (McCandless 1980) and lesbians of color—black, Latina, and Asian—who identified as separatist, who were involved in women's land, or both. For example, Anna Lee, in her essay "A Black Separatist," writes about how important separatism is to her: "Becoming a separatist encouraged me to realize that the world can be interpreted through my lesbian eyes" (1991, 87–88). She also addresses the problems of racism in the community: "While I believe that white separatists are no more racist than other white feminists, I also know that being a separatist does not automatically exclude the possibility of being a racist." She also noted the other side of this struggle, the way that separatism was labeled racist and therefore not part of black feminism: "Finally to all my sisters who perceive separatism as a white ideology, I reject that notion. . . . Separatism and blackness are not necessarily contradictory" (90–91).

Naomi Littlebear Morena, in "Coming Out Queer and Brown," notes a similar problem in the narrow path between being the token woman of color in the lesbian community and the problems of being a lesbian in her Chicana community. She writes, "for a brown woman to denounce her brother/oppressor, it's a political crime" (Morena 1991, 347). She notes that there are power imbalances: "It's a hell of a lot easier to call someone racist than for a chicana to call her 'brother' a sexist jerk. . . . i agree, me and my 'brother' both been screwed by the system, but when he started screwin' me he is the system and when white liberals start telling me to 'take it but don't shake it' they're the system too." In her analysis, she notes that the racism of white lesbians is as problematic as the sexism and homophobia of her own race; she does not erase the problems she has encountered with either group.

The "system" identified by Morena and the divisions between feminism and antiracist work identified by Lee are pointed out by Kimberlé Crenshaw as the focus of what she calls intersectional analysis. Crenshaw, in her groundbreaking work "Mapping the Margins: Intersectionality, Identity Politics, and Violence against Women of Color," points out that certain identities are often subordinated or made invisible by more dominant definitions of identity: being male and black as the dominant identity of the antiracist movement, and being white and female as the dominant identity of the feminist movement (1991, 1240–41). She writes, "My focus on the intersections of race and gender only highlights the need to account for multiple grounds of identity when considering how the social world is constructed" (1245). As illustrated by Morena and Lee, ten years before Crenshaw identified intersectionality as a key concept for feminist analysis, women writing about lesbian separatism were approaching that concept, identifying racial marginalization in the lesbian-feminist milieu and sexuality/gender marginalization in antiracism work as key interlocking problems faced by lesbians of color.

Critics of separatism often point to problems of racism and classism inherent in separatist policy (see "Capitalism Has You Surrounded" in chapter 4 for more discussion of class critique). Joan Gibbs writes:

> I was never a separatist because it doesn't speak to the reality of the world I live in or my needs as Black woman. . . . So, when separatists talk about the problem being men or straight people, I know they are not talking about my problems. When separatists talk about moving to the country and buying land, I know that I can't and don't want to do that—isolate myself from Black women, men and children. Why would I, a Black woman, even be interested in buying land in the first place, when Third World people, Black, Native, and Hispanic peoples—within the current borders of the U.S. are fighting for liberation, for land? (Gibbs and Bennett 1980, 2–3)

This analysis connects the separatist stance with social withdrawal (a connection also made by Cathy McCandless) and suggests that the act of buying land in a capitalist, colonized state contributes to violence against marginalized and colonized peoples. This is complicated by the question of land for women of color and Native women. However, the rejection of "withdrawal" from alliances with men of color is one of the foremost criticisms of separatism, one that is echoed by the famous statement made by the Combahee River Collective in 1977: "We feel solidarity with progressive Black men and do not advocate the fractionalization that white women who are separatists demand" (1986, 12).

That solidarity, however, is not always reciprocated. Vickie Mays points out that although there is a long history of woman-woman marriages in Africa, there is a continued resistance to acknowledging the validity of black lesbian experience; not only is it "labelled as something white, middle-class and bourgeois," black lesbians face an increased risk of violence from black men (1980, 97–98). Mays suggests that black lesbians, despite coming from a culture that values woman-woman bonding, are often isolated: "The Afro-American woman who chooses to be open and visible about her lesbianism may often lose the support of her friends and society at large, as does the Euro-American lesbian, but she also loses the support of her family and the Black community" (100). While such sweeping judgments about the black community's homophobia can be problematic (and seem dated), there is considerable evidence that black LGBT Americans still face particular problems from the intersections of racism and homophobia, and may feel more pressure to be closeted (Woody 2014). Mays points out that because of this enforced invisibility, black lesbians are in greater need of community support and the "Euro-American lesbian community fails to provide this supportive function by the sharing of resources or by facilitating the gathering of resources so that the Afro-American lesbian may build a community and be visible" (102). Thus not only the separatist philosophy is problematic, but the dynamics of the larger lesbian community as well.

Before turning to discuss such dynamics, I would like to introduce the three women of color communities that I have experience with: Arco Iris, which I know from several articles and from interviewing women from its sister community, Sassafras; Maat Dompim, which some of my informants had visited or helped fundraise for; and La Luz de la Lucha, which I know from Juana Maria Paz's account in her autobiography. Arco Iris is about 400 acres located in the Ozark Mountains near Fayetteville, Arkansas, and still exists as a sanctuary "not only for women and children of color, but for all who come in peace and in search of sanctuary" (Águila 2015, 51). Maat Dompim, 109 acres (with another twenty-four under a quitclaim deed) in Buckingham County, Virginia, was founded as a place that would "accommodate a *flow of women* rather than a static community." Although "women were enthusiastic" and the land is paid for, no one is currently living there, and Blanche Jackson and Amoja Three Rivers, the founders, do not live on the land due to personal concerns (Mushroom 2015, 154–5). La Luz de la Lucha (The Light of the Struggle), started out as Limesaddle, a heterosexual commune that converted to women's land as men left and women stayed, and consisted of twenty-four acres, a farmhouse, and smaller cabins built by residents (Paz 1980). It is no longer listed in Shewolf's *Directory of Wimmin's Lands and Lesbian Communities*. Women of color land is rarer than women's land, and faces more extreme problems of funding and support.

Violence against women of color within the lesbian land community illustrates larger race politics in the lesbian community and the matrix culture(s). The *La Luz Journal*, Juana Maria Paz's account of living on women's land for two years, records several incidents of violence. In one such incident, there were white women at La Luz, land originally intended for women of color. Paz was having a fight with Peru and Cypress.

> They came back. I was afraid. They came to kill me, I thought. I felt it as they came in one by one and surrounded us. There's something wrong here, I thought, it's the wrong way 'round. It's supposed to be the wild natives who come and surround the civilized whites and scalp them. We're supposed to be wild and savage when we do it, make loud war cries and dress in wild colours. It's not supposed to happen like this, with two native womyn and sleeping child quietly listening to music and civilized white people enter and invade, calmly, methodically, with efficiency and purpose. It was insidious. (1980, 64)

This "efficiency and purpose" is emotional violence and implied threat. Paz left and the women in the house "discussed" her; she did not want to discuss her relationship with Flying Thunder, one of the women on the land, in front of an "angry mob" (65) of white women and thus she was disempowered and silenced by the situation. That power is inherent to skin color in this situation—an ability to silence and take over because of the authority inherent in whiteness. Paz herself is aware of this, as she inverts and ironically makes use of racial stereotypes to demonstrate such uses of power, simultaneously showing them to be false and ridiculous while also using them to critique the very concept of who is "civilized."

This situation demonstrates why women of color might want their own land, connecting the problem of violence to the central issue of *agency*. Yet Paz writes, "Did it begin at that moment or was it an illusion from the beginning? Did the white people always hold La Luz?" (58). She questions whether white privilege might always have trumped the agency of women of color. Even learning about La Luz demonstrates this—Paz learned about La Luz while she was staying at another women's land: "The rest of the womyn couldn't go there because they were white. They let me know that they felt real bad about that, excluded and hurt and oppressed by the unsisterly behavior. From a group of womyn who hadn't said a civil word to me in weeks, I thought they had a hell of a nerve" (2). The women who told Paz that they felt "excluded and hurt and oppressed" were evading the question of whether they, as white women, were part of a larger problem of racism by framing themselves as victims of oppression. This connects to Ellen Scott's analysis of feminist organizations on the West Coast and their antiracist efforts within their own organizations; she found "a silence" about everyday racism that was supported by political discourses in which individuals are shuffled into one of two binary positions: victim or perpetrator (2000, 126). Paz illustrates this when she writes about vulnerability and antiprejudice work:

> It seemed that I lost power by affirming out loud that I must be anti-Semitic since I've grown up in America and it's part of the cultural baggage that I carry, like racism and classism and a personal feeling of powerlessness. After I admitted that it seemed like anything the white womyn did to me was all right, to them, since they had been somewhat restrained by the racism consciousness in the tribe but now they had something on me, too. And what came out was all the white womyn's anger at having to deal with racism in the first place. (Paz 1980, 60)

This reversal of racism—this willingness to "forget" one's own privilege in asserting one's rights as a victim—is framed on simplistic notions of a victim as innocent and a perpetrator as guilty, without acknowledging that one may both suffer racism and perpetuate it. Assigning victim/ perpetrator thus does not actually address any underlying problem. And finding out that one has one type of "oppressed" status does not liberate one from examining one's own privilege, any more than accusations of racism are worse than actual acts of racism.

Scott notes dryly that such a "discourse of agency in racial politics paralyzes action. Activists tend to vie for membership in the victim category and attach a great deal of shame to belonging to the perpetrator category" (2000, 126). This process is doubtless familiar to my readers and I have observed it myself many times. Scott suggests that "new subject positions must be created" in order to escape this problematic binary and facilitate coalitions, alliances, and new forms of antiracist activism.

In the case of the women who claimed they were "oppressed" by being excluded from La Luz, however, the binary framing of victim/perpetrator was being used in order to define who should have *agency*, and in this specific instance, access to women's land. Agency thus becomes linked to space/land: it is not only a valuable resource, but also provides the opportunity for women to develop agency. These issues are intertwined. As women's land is space for women to develop agency, land for women of color is space for women of color to develop agency in ways they cannot in communities dominated by white women.

Arco Iris, a land for women of color, is located in Arkansas in a rugged mountainous location. A conversation about Arco Iris's history appears in *Lesbian Land,* a collective volume about various lesbian lands edited by Joyce Cheney (1985).[3] The women of Arco Iris clearly articulate an ethos of agency (Mujeres de Arco Iris 1985, 36–37). When Lucia asks, "Why is there a need to have a womyn of colors community?" Maria responds with a long reply that concentrates on agency. She states first that there is a "need" for the community, and goes on to say "we feel that we must have this freedom to be self-determined because throughout our lives we have lived in a white European society. . . . Everywhere outside Arco Iris that's the way it is; not just on other womyn's lands, but everywhere, surrounding us." Thus land or space is connected to agency and autonomy. Maria states that this space is needed because of racism:

> The few cases that I have heard of, of womyn of color living together with white womyn have all been very difficult situations. The racism is always the problem. Even though white womyn are working on their racism, there are generations of problems that they have to go through in order to overcome them. Regardless of

whether or not they are sincere in their efforts, this does not make the problem any easier on womyn of color.

Claiming this autonomy does not remove white women's responsibility to deal with their own racism, but it places it squarely where it belongs—on their own shoulders, instead of on the shoulders of the women of color. As Audre Lorde points out, "now we hear that it is the task of women of color to educate white women—in the face of tremendous resistance—as to our existence, our differences, our relative roles in our joint survival. This is a division of energies and a tragic repetition of racist patriarchal thought" (2001, 24). By removing themselves from that context, the women of Arco Iris created a space where racism could be openly questioned and unlearned.

The invisibility of whiteness among white informants is not universal; while it is still partly an unmarked category, as it is in the matrix culture, some of the women involved in women's-land communities and lesbian separatism are aware of the issues of white privilege and are working to educate themselves and others about them. Women of color also have a long history of involvement with lesbian separatism and women's lands, and thus their perspectives and voices are a significant thread in how race and racism are approached. From the analysis of intersectionality to the consideration of violence, agency, and autonomy, the voices of women of color have been part of the history of women's lands for many years.

"The Common Lesbian Experience": Whiteness as Absence of Race

The Women's Encampment for a Future of Peace and Justice in Seneca Falls, New York, opened in 1983 for the purpose of protesting the nuclear depot in the area, and wound up operating as open women's land. This meant that any woman was permitted to come and participate—although whether she *felt* welcome was another matter.[4]

One of my informants, Tamara, remembering her time at the camp, related an incident in which a woman arrived with a gun, contrary to the nonviolent sensibilities of the other women. My informant said that this woman would clean her gun openly and the other women felt threatened by it. "What were we going to do?" she asked rhetorically. "We didn't want to bring the police into it, since we thought the police were part of the problem. Also, it was a very rural and racist region, and the woman was black. We *really* weren't going to bring the police into it, and she knew that."

What does it mean that a black woman who was surrounded mostly by white women felt that she needed a gun? Was it to protect herself in "a very rural and racist region"? Was it an assertion of social power? Tamara was clearly aware of the larger race and political implications when she stated that she and the other women were opposed to calling the police, against whose power the single black woman with a gun would have been very badly matched. Yet there were clearly other issues. Were the other women afraid of the gun itself or of our culturally entrenched beliefs about black women's potential for violence?

This enigmatic incident is only one story told from a single perspective. What stands out to me is that alone of the stories told, this is the only one marked in my notes with any indication of a woman's race. Blackness is *inherent* to this story in ways in which whiteness is *not* in other tales of camp violence. These other stories included behavior classified as mental illness, violent threats, and rumors of rape: none were told with racial identifiers for either victims or perpetrators. Whiteness is seemingly not important with regard to mental health, violent threats, or rape. It is a non-marker, a non-race.

One of my informants has repeatedly said to me, "We brought our problems with us," and these problems included racism. Racism is one of the major investigations in Gagehabib and Summerhawk's ethnography of women's lands in Oregon (2000). "White lesbians spoke of a universal movement and expressed belief in a common lesbian experience that women of color could not relate to" (168). That universalization erases the experiences of women of color where they differ from those of white women. The common discussion of class in women's lands can acknowledge where class and race interact in complex ways, yet can also serve to obscure discourse about racism that moves beyond a simple race-and-class linkage. Speaking about race is difficult when race itself tends to be obscured in a false universalization of experience that is itself a form of white supremacy.

Women's lands have dealt with racism in a variety of ways. Mixed-race lands have instituted various means for educating members about racism, and lands have been created that were solely for women of color. Of the women I interviewed, only two identified themselves to me as women of color. I could not fail to be aware of the overwhelming uniformity of racial identity among the women I worked with.

Yet not all the women who count as "my informants" are white, although certainly it appears that the majority are. It is important not to erase the presence of women of color at Landdyke Gatherings, on women's lands, and at women's festivals. Race is cultural, not biological, and can never be wholly read by appearance. Therefore, I cannot with surety assign "all the rest" of my informants as white, for it is possible that they may have identified with any one of a number of racial identities. However, the racial hegemony needs to be openly addressed; whiteness is something that should not be invisible or taken for granted. "Women" as a category are *not* only white.

The concept of race itself is cultural and historically situated. In 1997, the American Anthropological Association published a "Statement on 'Race'" that stated flatly, "biophysical diversity has no inherent social meaning except what we humans confer upon it" (2003, 124). Yet the *social* reality of race continues to inform our lives; the fact that race does not "exist" as a biophysiological object discoverable by genetics does not obviate the ways in which it operates on a cultural level. Race's status as "cultural" does not make it any less *real*; simply because it is a human invention does not mean that it is not complex, important, and sometimes highly rigid in how it operates. Sarah Daynes and Orville Lee suggest that this persistent cultural form is "desire for race" that stems from "thought, fantasy, and the body, as well as the sense of danger that pervades negative feelings towards racial Otherness" (2008, 20). Racial identity is thus constructed, and that construction fulfills needs and desires that perpetuate inequality. These discourses "*of* race," come in forms shaped by the invisibility—the non-race—of whiteness as opposed to the visible presence of the otherness of race.

Lorraine Delia Kenny, in her ethnography of white, middle-class suburban schools, notes that color blindness is part of a "culture of avoidance" (2000, 112). The white culture she studies, like my informants, "had moved to this quiet, effectively homogenous community, to get away from the culture of conflict they imagined a more diverse metropolitan setting to harbor." Although the source of the conflict(s) for my informants often came from different sources (such as sexism and homophobia), the creation of a relatively homogenous community which through its very homogeneity excludes others is strikingly similar. Indeed, Bonnie Zimmerman suggests, tongue-in-cheek, that, "the 'true path,' or central myth of lesbian feminism is that we are all one, all sisters; our lesbian nationality or culture overrides, even obliterates, 'minor' differences among us" (1990, 174). This is similar (but not identical) to *communitas* as used by Victor Turner, who defines it as "a spontaneously generated relationship between leveled and equal total and individuated human beings" (1974, 202). This mutual feeling, which Turner specifies is related to Tönnies' *Gemeinschaft* "insofar as it refers to a directly personal relationship" (201) depends on similarity or assumed similarity between the participants, as Zimmerman aptly points out. Thus, the "culture of avoidance" is avoiding the other, and "communitas" depends on emotional connections with those *like ourselves*.

Bell and Newby (1972) note that the term "community" itself has *nostalgic* overtones and also connect this back to Tönnies' *Gemeinschaft* and *Gesellschaft* of 1887. Thus I use "communitas" not to refer solely to a brief moment of liminal ritual-space connection (the Turner definition), but to the nostalgia and longing for community that is present in the very term community itself. Edith Turner, in *Communitas: The Anthropology of Collective Joy*, states that "communitas is togetherness itself" (2012, 4). However, as I use it, communitas is not only the transcendent moments of feeling that mark moments of "togetherness" but the *concept* of togetherness as well. While Edith Turner states that "it does not take sides; it does not rush to 'in-group/out-group' competitiveness" (5), the *concept* of togetherness/community does indeed always imply those who are included versus those who are not. Iris Young writes that "the ideal of community expresses a desire for social wholeness, symmetry, a secure and solid identity which is objectified because confirmed by others unambiguously. This is an understandable dream, but a dream nonetheless, and, as I shall now argue, one with serious political consequences" (1990, 232). These political consequences include the literal exclusion of others, as well as ways in which a particular model of the self (whiteness, for example) is accepted as the unspoken norm.

Moreover, Kenny and other scholars of race have suggested that "whiteness in the United States—especially in its middle-class, heterosexual configuration—occupies a hegemonic position precisely because it cannot and will not speak its own name" (2000, 114). This refusal to self-name, this invisibility or non-raced-ness of whiteness, persists despite the fact that many of my informants self-identified as poor or working class, and none of them identified as heterosexual. When asked about their backgrounds and self-identity, my white (or white-passing) informants mentioned gender, sexuality, and class, but only one of them explicitly mentioned whiteness.

In fact, whiteness positions itself not as a "race" per se but as an absence of one, as the generic and neutral position. Frances Winddance Twine, in her work examining the racial self-identification of young women of mixed ancestry brought up in suburban spaces, found that her informants identified as "white" despite African features such as brown skin or curly hair (1996). Twine notes that due to immersion in family and cultural networks where whiteness was the social norm, these women (in childhood) came to see themselves as racially and culturally neutral, like their peers. Two important concepts emerge from Twine's work that are relevant to my own: the first is the reaffirmation of the ways in which white identity is seen as a position of "race neutrality" (211), and the second is how whiteness as a category is not defined strictly by biological characteristics, but is instead a cultural category. This latter issue is very clear in how Twine's informants move from the white category to the black category over time (as they become politicized at the University of California, Berkeley) but also in terms of the language they use: "I didn't try to fit into white culture. I was white culture. Both my parents were white" (Natasha, informant with a black father, and a white mother and stepfather, 209).

White culture includes particular modes of interaction. Twine notes that "the multiracial women, who acquired a white cultural identity, did not position themselves, and were not positioned by those around them, as culturally distinct from their peers of exclusively European descent in behavior, dress codes, speech, practices, or interests" (208). Similarly, among my informants, nonwhite women in primarily white settings were not seen as culturally distinct (although I think these women were unlikely to self-identify as white): the larger arc of "women's culture" or "landdyke culture" was positioned as a unifying, homogenous force, as exemplified in the Gagehabib and Summerhawk quotation about the "universal lesbian experience" (2000, 168). Thus, although the Peace Camp, lesbian land, and women's land are positioned as *oppositional* to middle-class whiteness, they nevertheless operated as "white culture." The cultural distinctiveness of these spaces is steeped in practices that assume the normativity of white skin. Zimmerman suggests this when she writes "white women shaped Lesbian Nation as a room of our own with a door that appears transparent and open from the inside, but opaque and firmly closed from outside" (1990, 175). Evelyn Hammonds criticizes the very terms of queer theory when she points out that theorizing about sexuality, including lesbian sexuality, focuses on the assumed white body and excludes the experiences and theory of women of color (1997, 138). She suggests that theorists must explore the notions of "the politics of silence" as well as the way certain aspects of black women's lives, such as sexuality, have been made "invisible" (143, 145). This invisibility of the experiences of black women (and of other women of color) dovetails with the invisibility/normality of whiteness to create an assumed lesbian whiteness.

Twine identifies particular practices which tend to *produce* whiteness, including "color blindness" and emphasis on the individual rather than on connection to a larger racial or cultural group; immersion in a primarily white setting; and the ability to participate in middle-class material consumption. The whiteness produced in women's lands, however, must be distinct from the whiteness of middle-class suburbia, as connection to a larger cultural group (lesbians, women, or landdykes), and *rejection* of middle-class consumption are very prominent cultural markers among my informants.[5] Emphasis on the individual and "color blindness" are aspects of white culture that do appear in women's-land culture. Whiteness is thus multiple and specific in its incarnations: Twine and Gallagher note that "whiteness [is] a multiplicity of identities that are historically grounded, class specific, politically manipulated and gendered social locations that inhabit local custom and national sentiments" (2008, 6).

Whiteness, however, was not fully available to most of the women in Twine's study, who became racially marked through heterosexual dating rituals in high school in which they were often seen as unacceptable mates for white men (1996, 216). Similarly, although nonwhite women participating in women's-land culture are not marked by heterosexual mating rituals, they occupy a similar marked/unmarked position, in which they are invisible/"assimilated" with regard to some aspects of culture, but also, at times, occupy a marked, excessively "visible" position as racial outsiders. For example, Maya Sundance-Woman (interviewed by Gagehabib and Summerhawk) stated that she felt inaudible because of her nonwhite status: "I feel that, as a woman, I not only do not get listened to at the dominant culture level, I also do not get recognized as having a valuable point of view in the counter culture" (2000, 28). Similarly, Shaba Barnes, writing as a member of the only African American couple in a lesbian retirement community in New Mexico, stated, "I shared that I felt like an outsider, that people turn their heads rather than speak, that some look into my face and still don't speak. I told them how much it means to me to be addressed by my name and not that of another African American sister who is visiting for a week or month" (2005, 52). On the other hand, Canyon Sam experienced a curious form of assimilation/invisibility: while at an outdoor festival she happened to see her reflection in the mirror of a parked car and "was so startled that I looked so different from them... when you are the only person of color and you are looking at everyone else... you think you look like them" (Gagehabib and Summerhawk 2000, 29).

This "racial gaze" is difficult to escape. The relevance of a black woman's race to her presence at the Peace Camp with a gun is multileveled—relevant to the reaction of the other women, her situation (and sense of safety or lack of it) among a largely white population, and to how my white informant told the story. Race *cannot* be left out of this story. Yet the double linking of race occurs not in the story itself but in the absence of race in *other* stories about the Peace Camp, or even about violence at the Peace Camp or directed at members of the demonstrations. Race is only relevant when it becomes the object of the "racial gaze" and this gaze is only turned towards others, never towards a white-identified gazer. There is a dual presence and absence of race. Race is absent in the very way in which whiteness is constructed: whiteness as the *absence* of racial characteristics. Race, however, becomes very present when someone of a racial cline too different to pass as white is present; in the absence of an understanding of whiteness as a race, they become doubly invested with race, the "marked category," the "person of race."

Assimilation/invisibility signals a disciplinary adherence to white cultural standards. Despite being marked as "people of race," many of Twine's informants noted that they still "felt comfortable" in groups of mostly white people, which also demonstrates comfort with and adherence to those cultural minutiae. "At one point during the interview Angela [one of the biracial informants] described black students as 'extreme' and implied that blacks are deviant, which is in opposition to her identity as a 'normal' person" (1996, 218–19). Whiteness does not only provide a comfortable sense of racial "invisibility" and "normalcy": it also guides particular ways of thinking about visible race and otherness. Whiteness is thus not solely a matter of culture but also a *way of knowing* (Finney 2014, 3).

What does it mean when women who do not identify themselves as belonging to a "race" are the primary constructors of culture? What is included and what is left out? How does this create a "white way of knowing" within the larger structure of a "feminist" way of knowing within "women's culture?"

The Un-hearable Whiteness of Being: Doxa, Race, and White Ways of Knowing

If doxa serves as a set of unarticulated cultural "rules" as well as culture's "naturalization of its own arbitrariness" (Bourdieu 1995, 164) then whiteness as a cultural form is doxa: like whiteness as a race, it hides itself in its own seeming normality or neutrality. But doxa, like race, is not neutral or natural: it is a particular set of rules and ways of doing things. Thus, "white ways of knowing" are particular forms of culture, even as they hide themselves by presenting as the natural order.

This "natural order" is encoded in the people who participate in women's land, and also in the land itself. In representations of who cares about, who uses, and who enjoys wilderness or wild land, U.S. matrix culture depends largely on images of white people, affecting who has access to this resource (Finney 2014). Thus "narratives about our 'natural environment' [inform] our environmental interactions and shap[e] the institutions concerned with environmental issues (thereby shaping how we represent, perceive, and construct the identities of racial 'others' within our society). The dominant environmental narrative in the United States is primarily constructed and informed by white, Western European, or Euro-American voices" (DeLuca and Demo 2001; Jacoby 1997; Taylor 1997; cited in Finney, 3). This environmental narrative is twined around the culture of women's lands, in which wilderness and the land itself figure prominently as important concepts.[6] This land is conceptualized as devoid of current inhabitants of color, as Native peoples are erased through the image of them as ghosts, existing only in the past (Bergland 2000). The "whitewashing" of wilderness affects the culture of women's lands. As women's lands conceptualize themselves as including or adjacent to wild spaces, a lack of women of color can be naturalized and erased through ideas about wilderness that have implicitly taught that such spaces are primarily for white people.

Such implicit ideas adopted from the matrix culture shape many aspects of various women's lands. However, "white ways of knowing" are difficult to point out in academia due to the fact that academia itself is shaped by white ways of knowing. Such cultural forms, ideas, and habits of thinking align neatly with those of the academy, and afford no contrast. Noting, for example, that most women's lands tend to have an individualistic ethos (following Twine 1996) leaves open the question of whether this is a form of "whiteness" adopted from middle-class American values or some other cultural ideal. However, contrasts between the experiences of white women and women of color who participate in women's land illustrate some important differences.

White women and women of color tend to see racism very differently. One of La Verne Gagehabib and Barbara Summerhawk's informants articulated this dilemma very well: "These women said there was no racism because there were no women of color there. The women of color saw the opposite and connected racism with their not being there" (2000, 78). This clearly articulates how in the absence of people of color, a "white way of being" does not obviate racism. The burden of antiracist work raises another question: the white women suggest that this has already been done, or else is the responsibility of women of color. The women of color, on the other hand, place the responsibility squarely back in the court of the white women. Another example of this sort of thinking comes from an article on the Dragonwagon community in which the author, a resident of the land, states, "Similarly, why have no wimmin of color chosen to live at Dragon? But better the wimmin of color give the answer to that one" (Brown 1985, 48). Such a statement ducks responsibility for exploring both racism and a culture of whiteness. Zimmerman also notes that "many white and middle-class women are socialized to dislike and avoid confrontation" which she points to as one of the reasons for defensive and avoidant reactions to discussions of racism (1990, 176).

So, what happens when women of color participate in women's land? In a section titled "A Woman of Color Perspective—La Verne," Gagehabib writes:

> One major concern that arose from our research is the fact that only three land groups composed of women of color exist today anywhere in the United States despite many other existing communal and private women's lands. None of the lands of the women of color are in Oregon.[7] In the beginning of the women's land movement, there were several land groups of women of color that formed, but disagreements, changes in collective members, theft, and violence among the women caused these lands to be foreclosed. They were not replaced or saved. With other women's land that has been saved under land trusts, most, if not all, of the women who live there are white. (2000, 18–19)

Gagehabib points out that many women of color communities have been lost. Communities are transient, but how long communities last is a question linked to issues such as economic power, social stability, the number of women who can contribute, and the status of those women. Also, as Gagehabib points out, the problem is not only transiency but the fact that the communities have not been replaced with new ones. There are economic stresses: women of color are among the least advantaged in the capitalist system of the United States. However, other issues such as support or lack of support from the larger network of women's-land communities, overt or covert racism in the matrix culture where the community is planned/located, and intersectional difficulties (such as sexism from a local antiracist or people of color community, or racism from a local feminist or lesbian community) also contribute barriers.

Residual cultural material from the matrix cultures plays a large part in how women deal with race and racism in women's land. Summerhawk and Gagehabib write:

> Although women of color have visited and related to this community [Southern Oregon Women's Community] since the beginning, very few long-term resident white women can name these women. Recently, one woman tried unsuccessfully to recall the names of two Japanese women who stayed at WomanShare for several months and who shared Kionna, the visitor's cabin located near WomanShare's main house. While foreign names are especially hard to remember, it seems these women have faded into an anonymity not uncommon to women of color. (2000, 27–28)

This anonymity is particularly problematic in a culture where news is often via word of mouth, and where one's welcome and reputation in various communities may depend on being "known." Introductions are important in a culture where traveling among various communities is common, but communities are open or not depending on word of mouth. In my own experiences, my access to and welcome in different women's communities has depended on introductions from land-women, communications about me from friends to friends, and my ability to demonstrate connections to other land-women. This affects how "open" women's communities are to women of color, perhaps without the white women involved being aware of any "selection" on their part at all: the operation is invisible/forgotten, like the names of the women who lived in Kionna cabin.

Gagehabib and Summerhawk note that women of color tended to have a much less idealistic view of the values of lesbian land cultures, often viewing them "as simply a repeat of patriarchal values transferred to a matriarchal setting" (168). On the other hand, it was not solely these problems that prevented more women of color from settling in this particular community: "Each also expressed that it was not so much the attitudes of the women in the Southern Oregon Women's Community as the oppressive atmosphere of rural white Oregon that placed limits on their desire to remain in the community." The rural location of many women's lands can also present a cultural and social barrier.

Race illustrates both influences from the matrix cultures and ways in which women's-land communities deal with power, agency, and conflict in culture and community creation. Agency in particular is an important issue in terms of women of color space, and yet that space is still marginal due to pressures from both the matrix society and from women's-land culture. Invisibility is also important as women of color often feel that they are not heard within women's-land culture. Many of these issues are also seen in larger matrix cultures of the United States, but seem to loom larger within the context of women's-land cultures because of their egalitarian and feminist ethos.

Racism as "Wrong-Feeling": The Otherness of Racism and the Otherness of Race

Several of my informants spontaneously spoke about racism and their experiences with it as white women. These narratives were often intimately tied to their sense of themselves as also excluded from "the norm." This sense of exclusion was often framed as providing an almost instinctual or emotional understanding of racism as wrong; at the same time, the narratives were rooted in an unspoken framing of their own experiences as invisibly race-neutral.

This connects again to Scott's analysis and her contention that in feminist organizations there tends to be "a silence" about everyday racism due to the binary discourse of victim or perpetrator (2000, 126). While my informants were not immune to this problematic binary through the connection of racism to other forms of prejudice, they framed themselves as allies, or at least as neither victims nor perpetrators. However, their narratives fall prey to another problem with how we understand racism in the United States: what Scott calls "the prejudice model." In this model "racism is seen as the product of negative attitudes derived from wrong beliefs, falsely generalized and expressed about individuals and groups" (130). However, such a view of racism fails to see the ways in which our culture, beliefs, economy, educational systems, justice systems, and the very cities we live in have been shaped by a profoundly racist history. Scott notes that the prejudice model is common in the United States, and "has historically dominated other perspectives and understandings of racism" (131). Thus it is not strange that my informants, like hers, primarily use it in their articulation of how racism works.

Fascinatingly, both the land-women I worked with and Scott's informants were able to articulate and speak about a larger, structural model of racism as well. Scott suggests that "racism as a system, a set of institutions and social meanings and practices, is obscured and can be misconstrued as simply individual attitudes and behaviors. Thus it was easy for the activists in West Coast Women and El Refugio [Scott's locations of investigation] to construe racism in the daily life of the organization as a problem of individual beliefs, although in other aspects of their organizational discourse and action they clearly articulated a structural analysis of racism" (131). Similarly, my informants discussed racism as structure when discussing *outside* issues, such as universities or politics. However, they tended to switch to the prejudice model when discussing their own experiences.

Below I will analyze two narratives about racism from my informants, and show how these articulate a new subject position that is neither victim nor perpetrator through the construction of racism as "wrong-feeling." At the same time, these still tend to uphold a "race-neutral" position for the narrator. Both racism and race itself are, therefore, presented as "other." Narratives about my informants' own experiences thus employ the prejudice model, while at the same time connecting this model to other forms of prejudice.

One informant, Marie, told me about her experience of moving to the South with her husband of the time, who had just been assigned to Fort Bragg. This was in the 1950s, when segregation was still enforced by law, and it was uncommon for married women to work outside the home. Marie, however, worked as a nurse in the local hospital.

I went to work at University Hospital. Well, why wouldn't I have wanted to work? I was just out of training, why wouldn't I have wanted to work?

I was in the preemie [unit], where the preemies were, and you couldn't feed them all,[8] they were all black. 'Cause the black women had to come in and go out in twenty-four hours. The "stork club." How about that for a euphemism? They called it the stork club.

ME: Wow.

MARIE: They allowed them to come in and have their babies and go out in twenty-four hours. And anywhere you went there were signs. Black—you know, colored, colored—they didn't call them black, they called them colored, fountains. You didn't see them in the movie theater, so I said to somebody, where are they? And they said, oh, they're up in the balcony, that's where they like to go.

Now, this is interesting. When I was kid, our movie theater, if you went up to the balcony area, they called it "nigger heaven." Well, I had no concept. I don't think I even knew what "nigger" meant. You know. Somebody had been South in our town—probably the guys in the service—and come back and called that "nigger heaven." And I didn't get this together until . . .

ME: So they knew that, in the South, they had to go and sit in the balcony.

MARIE: Right, right.

ME: Wow.

MARIE: And they [the signs] were everywhere. I was appalled. I said to Don, this was '57, "What if we just went where it said 'Colored Only,'" like lunch counters you know, "What if we went and sat there? Isn't that horrible?" We were both pretty horrified. And he said, "I think you'd get arrested."

I wasn't quite gutsy enough. Now I would do it, but I wasn't quite gutsy enough to do it at that time! [Laughter]

Marie discusses segregation in both the northern and the southern United States. In fact, she relates earlier that when she was a child living in a northern state, her town was all white: "When you went to the city, you would see black people." Her reaction to racial segregation in the South—which she encounters for the first time because her childhood town entirely lacked black people—is emotional. Her imagined approach to this is to suggest she could be "like them"; a strategy that was employed by white sympathizers during the civil rights movement a few years later. In other words, she does not see herself as participating in a larger system of racism, but as an *outsider* who, if she were "gutsy enough," could try to undermine it: neither victim nor perpetrator. The lack of black people in her own home town is not portrayed as segregation and does not elicit the horror that "Colored Only" signs in the South do. Thus the significance of her story seems to be in the ways in which she is telling me—another white woman—about how she *emotionally* experienced racism: her feelings of wrongness about the oppression of *others*.

In Marie's narrative we can find traces of how whiteness is an unquestioned norm *that does not need explaining* in many ways. In her narrative, she does not speak to any single person of color. In the story of theater balcony seating, her informant is another white person who simply "knows" that "that's where *they* like to go." This is partly an artifact of segregation; but it is also a narrative highly constructed around white perspectives. I do not believe this is a narrative that would have been elicited if I had not presented as white.

This invisible normativity is one that many of my white-identifying interviewees still struggle with. Since my white informants are very aware of the ways in which they are not normative in the matrix cultures of the United States, race normativity can become invisible. Yet at the same time, some of my informants use their own experiences of being othered in order to approach racial othering.

Another antiracist story was told to me by Glorious Dyke, who spoke about how racism impacted her upbringing as a white child in a poor family in the southern United States:

> GD: It was just like the racism—when I was 4—in a boxcar, where a couple lived and we were having dinner with them. And the reason we were was because my mother's male partner was involved in the unions. And there was this black couple, so we were having dinner with them, and this woman made this great dinner. And I ate and I was sitting there.

And of course I'd been taught racism, I mean, unbelievably by this time. And she walked around and was offering me another biscuit. And she touched my arm, and I stared at my arm like—oh my God! It's going to rub off on me!

And she looked at me in the kindest way and she said, right in front of everybody, "Honey, it's not going to rub off on you."

ME: Wow.

GD: It was so precious to me. And then before I left there she gave me this beautiful little black baby doll.

ME: Um hmm.

GD: I don't remember ever having a baby doll in my life. But I had this one, and I loved it! And I had it for—[choking up] I'm talking, and feelings can come up, you know, it's really interesting.

ME: Um hmm.

GD: Okay, so, I had this little baby doll for not all that long. And then, I woke up one morning and it was gone! And my mother's male partner said to me, "Oh, you left her—you left her out on the porch and she got all wet, and fell apart and she was thrown away."

ME: Mmmmm.

GD: So it was my fault.

ME: Um hmm.

GD: And well. And from then on, I had some clarity that they were wrong. Really, really wrong.

Glorious Dyke presents a conversion narrative, in which a black woman speaks to her as a racist and terrified small child about how "it's not going to rub off." This is a complex moment—the black woman is dispelling contagion myths, and at the same time, by reassuring the child, she is addressing that fear. She deals with the contagion fear of a small child with dignity and grace. This becomes an antiracist teaching moment that the child remembers many years later as an important part of her life narrative.

The second part of Glorious Dyke's story centers on "a beautiful little black baby doll." Here we completely subvert the idea of "contagion," with Glorious Dyke, as a child, willingly taking "blackness" into her "imaginary family" in the form of a doll. She has adopted it. The significance of doll play and doll narratives is striking here, since only a few years later the immensely famous Clark doll tests, also using black dolls as well as white dolls, would begin.[9] In this narrative we see a kind of reversal of the Clark test, in which a black doll teaches a white child about acceptance of others. However, the adults around her make the doll disappear because of that boundary-crossing, and then blame her for the disappearance. Yet Glorious Dyke, even as a child, sees through this narrative and the untruth of it helps her construct her own sense of "wrong-feeling."

My white informants approached whiteness from the perspective of the unmarked category. When racial awareness is brought up in the context of life histories, women often provide narratives about breaking through barriers in the context of approaching the Other. Whiteness remained largely an unquestioned neutral category by white women. However, their narratives were not simply those of presenting themselves as normative and other racial categories as Other. Through their own experience of being othered as women, lesbians, ethnic, or class others, they draw parallels that compromise and break down a strict binary of self/other and provide ways for them to approach race that do not *completely* adhere to the racial binary that the norm of whiteness suggests.

Such narratives by white women cannot approach the experience of racism "from the inside": the tacit comparisons made by my informants are vulnerable to the criticism of false equivalency. However, these two stories do not openly compare their *own* experiences with being nonnormative to *experiencing* racism. Instead, they provide complex narratives about the "wrong-feelings" of racism and how they came to reject the dominant narrative of white supremacy. These are emotional stories about the relationship to racial Others, rather than examination of one's own privilege. However, these are not *negative* aspects of these stories—these stories are firmly rooted in their own experience as white women, and do not attempt to appropriate the experience of women of color.

The narratives are focused outwards—the experience of racism is of racism directed at other people; this helps whiteness itself remain invisible. Yet remember that speaking from their own experience is the only intimate subject position and contact my interviewees *could have* with racism, and many of them told similar accounts as integral parts of their life histories. Experiences that broke down early prejudices were seen as very important. Such prejudice was also overtly or implicitly connected to homophobia. For example, Glorious Dyke's story sprang directly from the tale of how her family separated her from a girl she had a crush on at eight years old (four years after the doll incident). "It was just like the racism" at the beginning of her tale refers to how her family refused to tell her where her friend was or speak about her again. To Glorious Dyke, the two events were connected, even though she had to jump backwards in time to tell me the doll story, and so the two types of prejudice are connected. Thus she approaches the Other in race through the lens of her own experience of othering. It is implied that her family did both those things—separate her from her friend and steal her doll—for the *same reasons*.

Another white informant, Sealion, is deeply involved in antiracist activism and regularly attends workshops and conferences on this theme. After attending the 2007 White Privilege Conference, she wrote:

> I learned why we have to go beyond diversity. It's because diversity education has become reduced to tacos and tofu, without talking about systems of oppression and privilege and social justice. The talk about racism is no longer just about discrimination that people of color face, but also about systems of invisible advantages for white people. Feminism and gays and lesbians were visibly present. (email to landdykes listserv, April 22, 2007)

This awareness of the systems of invisible advantages for white people goes beyond the "emotional moment" of the other stories; this recognizes the invisible and doxic systems of privilege. So it is not simply on the emotional level that white land-women approach race issues: a larger awareness of racism as a system is present. However, as in Scott's analysis, *experiences* of racism tended to use the prejudice model, rather than a larger systems model, perhaps because this model explains individual incidents or experiences better.

The invisibility of whiteness as a race continues to make many of the race issues in women's-land culture difficult. White lesbians, so well aware of the ways in which they lack privilege due to their gender, sexuality, and social politics, can be unaware of the ways in which they wield racial privilege. Yet this is certainly not universally true, as Sealion's participation in the White Privilege Conference and similar antiracist activities attests. Some of my white informants are able to use their own experiences of othering to approach racial othering, although the invisibility of whiteness remains unquestioned.

While women's-land culture largely constructs itself as "race-neutral" (or "color-blind"), this depends on the categorization of whiteness as the absence of race, and the absorption of the experiences of other-raced women into a larger (false) universalization. However, the writings of women of color who identify as separatist lesbians help form alternate cultural threads, pointing out the problems of this universalization, emphasizing the differences in cultural background, and hinting at the conflicts that Crenshaw calls intersectionality. Even the different cultural backgrounds of lesbians who identify as white can help undermine a strict binary between "white" and "Other" when white lesbians are seen as ethnically or culturally Other.

However, it is undeniable that women's lands continue to be mostly white, and this assumed "absence of race"/presence of whiteness serves as a hidden racial marker within the community itself. This produces "whiteness as a way of knowing," which marks not only whiteness as normal, but particular forms of white culture as normal. Within this way of knowing, both race and racism are constructed as "other." That is, as race marks certain people as other, racism is something that happens to other people, and *both* are marked as nonnormative through the prejudice model (Scott 2000, 130). This is inevitable, as even the most intimate experiences of racism from a white perspective provide a "spectator" point of view.

This would be a very different culture if more of its culture-creators understood racism from the inside, or as a larger system in which all people, including its members, were complicit. But while the ontological "right to exist" of lesbians and even women has been under fire, the right to exist of whiteness passes without question.

· CHAPTER 3 ·

"Now My Neighbors and Friends Are the Same People"

Community, Language, and Identity

And that doesn't mean that we know that the minute that we come out that we're free. We don't. Most lesbians today are still trying to be good girls and behave and trying to say, you know, "it's only what you do in bed." Well, that's bullshit! It's not just what you do in bed. It's absolutely everything to do with freedom and love!

—Glorious Dyke

Now my neighbors and my friends are the same people.

—Freddie, resident of Mountainview

A GROUP OF TINY CABINS in a remote mountainous region in New Zealand built out of mahogany shipping crates; cob and straw structures on a high desert butte in New Mexico, colored warm adobe and molded with snakes along the walls; metal-roofed cabins and trailers hidden in the woods in Virginia; a farmhouse and barn and wide grassy fields in Oregon; beach houses with flat roofs clustered together on a Florida shore. Houses of mud, houses of straw, houses made from recycled wood and windows. In some cases, the houses are produced entirely by the labor of women. In most cases, the houses reflect different aesthetics and priorities than those you would find in a typical commercially-built home in the United States. These structures vividly illustrate how women's-land cultures produce difference. Yet despite the difference in these living spaces, all are part of the wider community of women's lands.

Women's communities do not present the same sort of forms—architectural or cultural—that the largely imaginary mainstream of the

United States does. They do not present the same cultural ideas that the many and varied matrix cultures of the United States do. Women's communities were created in order to foster deliberate and profound cultural difference. As Sirocco, a landdyke from the Pacific Northwest, says:

> The lesbian community is an entirely different culture and I use the word culture because it is. Some people have a real hard time accepting that the gay and lesbian lifestyle is a culture but it is. We have our own language. We have our own spiritual beliefs. We have our own ways of doing things which are acceptable and aren't acceptable amongst ourselves. Everything from how we dress to the language we use.

Those differences spring from different ways of doing, creating, and thinking about culture.

One main way women's communities create difference is through what can be called a feminist consciousness. This feminist consciousness influences cultural items as diverse as decision-making by consensus, communal living, ecological consciousness, and nonmonogamy. These seemingly diverse threads of culture are in reality closely interwoven through the cultural perception that consensus, communal living, ecoconsciousness, and the land itself are all feminist or feminine. Thus these aspects of what landwomen often call "women's culture" serve as threads that both tie together diverse and physically distant women's lands, and serve to differentiate these cultures from the larger matrix cultures around them.

I divide the feminist consciousness that runs through women's lands arbitrarily into three parts: community, commensality, and what I will call here a feminist aesthetics of practice. Ideas about community, who belongs to it, and the network of community are important aspects of women's culture and also a foundational principle in that women's lands were born out of women's community. Commensality—which as I use it covers shared resources and communal decision-making—is seen as so integral that many of my informants take it for granted that consensus is feminist. Lastly, there is the category of what I call "feminist aesthetics," a group of beliefs and practices that vary a little more widely from group to group, but that all partake of what the women practicing them assert are specifically *feminist* ideals. These range from a feminist basis for nonmonogamy to feminist connections to ecoconsciousness. All of these cultural items—community, commensality, and feminist cultural gestures—are *gendered* by the participating women. Thus *women's* culture in particular is created, and gender is the key point of the difference between these communities and the matrix culture.

My use of the term "feminist aesthetics" is somewhat different from the way it is commonly used in feminist discourse, where it most often refers to literary or media production. Rita Felski, in *Beyond Feminist Aesthetics,* notes "the impossibility of a feminist aesthetic, defined as a normative theory of literary or artistic form that can be derived from feminist politics" (1989, 2) and it is not my intention to go over that old argument here. Felski, indeed, makes an excellent case that "it is impossible to speak of 'masculine' and 'feminine' in any meaningful sense in the formal analysis of texts" (2).[1] However, gender in the context of this ethnography is not limited to single, simple concepts of "masculine" or "feminine"; gender is interrelational and dependent on the actions, decisions, and statements of my informants. Thus, the crux of the matter is not whether I, or you the reader, find "masculine" and "feminine" meaningful in relation to these items but whether and in what contexts my *informants* do so.

Furthermore, I am not applying the concept of "feminist aesthetics" to literary texts (or, at least, not to literary texts alone). I am using it to refer to a wide range of practices that land-women consider to reflect feminist ideals. However, this is similar to aspects of the more narrow literary usage that Felski carefully deconstructs, especially in "the assignment of an innate value to women's bodies and the claim that women possess a privileged affinity to nature and to peace" (75), ideas that recur many times in my informants' statements.

> Aspects of feminism tie in here with . . . current reactions against industrialism and technology and in the increased prevalence of ecological and back to nature movements. Mary Daly, Susan Griffin, and other "cultural feminists" espouse a dualistic vision which counterposes a conception of a holistic, harmonious, and organic "femininity" against an alienated, rationalist, and aggressive masculinity. These dichotomies constitute a significant dimension within feminist ideology, which in turn finds its expression in numerous fictional texts. (76)

Such ideas certainly inform a large proportion of what I am calling here "feminist aesthetics" (what I might more strictly call "feminist aesthetics of practice") among my informants, and such dichotomies are still active today.[2] Felski's arguments about the problems of such dichotomous thinking are solid, but are irrelevant in the face of the fact that these narratives are still widely used by my informants, and are still recognized by them as both feminist and female-gendered.[3]

My use of the term "women's culture" follows the same principles. Just as "feminist aesthetics" as a term is intended to reflect practices and ideas that land-women espouse, "women's culture" is not an anthropological term. I am not claiming that there is a cross-cultural group of people called women that I can usefully analyze;[4] I am not claiming that there are essential differences between "women's culture" and "men's culture"; and I am not claiming that women "naturally" produce a particular form of culture. Instead, I am using a term that my informants do to refer to a particular phenomenon: how these cultural products, gestures, and ideals are seen as *gendered* and how that gendering is then used in order to link different cultural practices and communities together. That is, I examine the way the women *of these communities* deliberately create local cultural difference and see this difference as gendered.

This gendering is rooted in particular local cultural practices, historical ideas, and bodies. If community is a foundational principle of women's land, then the fact that so many lands are inhabited by mostly white women reflects something fundamental about the overarching ideas about community. Communitas looks for those who are like us, those who match without ambiguity, and as Kath Weston notes, in her analysis of gender systems, "ambiguities are as raced and classed as they are gendered" (2002, 27–28). Thus the "feminist consciousness" and "women's culture" that I explore here is not only located in time and culture, but born from a specific history and connected to particular ideas about race and raced behavior. The community is predicated on what Finney calls "whiteness as a way of knowing," although the cultural items integrated into "feminist consciousness" (in the limited way I use the term here) make copious use of nonwhite thinkers and concepts. It is important not to erase either the participation of women of color or the integration of cultural items that do not originate from white thinkers. Yet whiteness is seen as normative and invisible, and this serves to marginalize and "other" nonwhite participants in important ways. This is particularly noticeable in terms of how women join these communities.

In this chapter, I explore how ideas about self-identity are woven into ideas about the identity of women's lands. What does it mean that such spaces are largely considered and labeled "separatist," for example? What is the relationship between lesbian identity and women's lands? Self-identity, however, is more complex than simply labels, whether they are applied to the self or to the community. Through the life histories of a few of my interviewees, I hope to demonstrate some of the great variety of land-women's lives, including how they came to become involved with women's space. Most land-women have not lived their entire lives on women's land.

Identity, however, is only half the picture. We must also consider the process of women's lands, the ways in which women actively build structures, processes, language, and different ways of thinking—a culture that is different from the one they came from. A sense of benefiting women is worked into processes as varied as models of community governance, forms of artwork, forms of architecture, forms of language, and forms of social interaction. That is, decisions as varied as fundraising and food practices can be seen as *related* as long as they are both chosen for their benefit to women as a larger political group.

Language serves as an especially good case study for how what I am calling "feminist aesthetics of practice" both shapes and is shaped by ideas about gender in women's space. The use of terms such as "women's energy" serve both as community signposts indicating group affiliation but also as practical terms that these women use in order to comment on, analyze, and perhaps change gendered social interactions.

Who Lives Here? Identity, Sexuality, and Separatism

About one-third of the thirty-one women I interviewed (I interacted with many more) had once been married to men, and several of them had children.[5] I interviewed one woman who was raising a young child while living in community part-time with her partner, who was the birth mother. Most of my interviewees identified as lesbians.[6]

While about two-thirds of my informants were living on women's land at the time of the interviews, some of them lived on the land only part-time, some women had lived on land in the past, and some women were seeking to live on land. I also interviewed two "traveling dykes" who traveled from place to place staying at various women's lands and women's festivals. One woman was living in a mixed community but attended the Landdyke Gatherings in order to stay in touch with the larger landdyke community. Three of the women I interviewed were in the process of moving to their land and retiring from their current jobs. One woman I interviewed had been considering moving to a particular women's land and had recently decided against it because of interpersonal issues, but was still interested in women's land.

While a good number of my interviewees (about 60 percent) were women old enough to "retire" in terms of the U.S. matrix culture, most of them were still active in economic pursuits. For example, one woman drove a taxi in the winter for money, and grew her own vegetables and kept ducks in the summer. Other women worked as nurses, kept a local artists' co-op, worked as university professors, were jewelry artists, or worked office jobs. Hobbies and leisure activities included keeping a therapeutic riding stable for local disabled children, participating in the local volunteer firefighters, political and organizing work (including in the local LGBT community, among the Native community, and labor organizing), art in many forms, cabinetry, and attending women's gatherings such as music festivals.

Only two of my informants identified as nonwhite: one as Native and one as Chicana/Latina. Although both these women mentioned their racial identity at some point during my interactions with them, neither of them spoke to me about *identifying* as such explicitly. This is parallel to the white and white-passing women I interviewed, almost none of whom thought it necessary to mention their race when we discussed identity. The only exceptions to this rule were the Jewish women I interviewed (two), both of whom noted their Jewish identity explicitly and in response to questions about identity.

The terminology involved with these identities is complex. The term "land-women" is my own creation, an umbrella term used to refer to all women who live, have lived, or who plan to try living on women's land. Land-women themselves use a multitude of overlapping terms. "Landdyke" is a very common one, used for the Landdyke Gathering, a yearly conference of land-women identifying as dykes held at a hosting women's land. *Maize*, an important publication serving a large part of the land-women community, is subtitled *The Lesbian Country Magazine,* and provides another term, "lesbian country," that embraces a larger lesbian community and the space that itself houses that community. This term is possibly also a play on *Country Lesbians,* the title of the 1976 book (Sue et al.) about the WomanShare community. Both of these terms presuppose a particular sexual identity as well as a gendered one; however, not all women's lands are limited to lesbian or queer women.

Several women's lands, including some of the oldest and longest-running, were explicitly founded for the use of women, full stop. This came up in discussion at one of the Landdyke Gatherings, when Sirocco, who was living with her partner and their child at one of the oldest women's lands in Oregon, discussed the openness of this space to straight women with a number of other landdykes, some of whom disapproved. I arrived at the end of the discussion, and Sirocco walked away with me and talked about how the charter of Firefly Farm explicitly stated that the land was for the "use of all women," thus the objections of landdykes "who didn't even live there!" were irrelevant. She was committed to making the space available on a permanent (residential) or temporary (festival or camping) basis for all women who needed women's space. It came out in conversation that all the current residents of Firefly Farm identified as lesbian, but, Sirocco stated, that did not mean that it was "*lesbian* land." While Gagehabib and Summerhawk (2000, 38–39) define women's/lesbian lands following Bethroot Gwynn, as a division between lands allowed for public events and deeded to women (women's lands) and land simply owned/lived on by lesbians (lesbian land), this definition did not obtain among my informants. For Sirocco and the women arguing with her, the difference between women's land and lesbian land is not a matter of inheritance or community use, but a matter of who is invited to the land. Thus the rubric "women's land" *includes* "lesbian land."

Gender itself and terms of gender are also contested within women's-land culture. One of my informants, Glorious Dyke, objected to my using the terminology "woman," because, she said, "woman means slave." When I asked whether this meant that she thought of all heterosexual women as slaves, she responded, via email,

> YES, all weMEN are slaves. Lesbians are runaway slaves who are in process of learning Freedom and Love. tha word ALL throws me a little, haven sakes Lesbians (out Lesbians) suffer from tha slavery within y rule, so very likely y serving x's would even more so. One of tha benefits of Lesbians in community/ LandDykes is to distance ourselves enough to explor FREEDOM. I say to even learn

bits and pieces of FREEDOM we need to release doMANence/ patriarchy/ use and abuse. (Glorious Dyke, email communication, 2/8/2009)[7]

She identified solely and simply as a "lesbian," and said that she was working for the freedom of "all X people."

Another informant, Joanne, said "I identify as a radical feminist, I don't identify as a lesbian. I am a lesbian. But I didn't identify as heterosexual when I married either. That to me is not who I am. You know, who I sleep with is not who I am. I am a radical feminist, and understanding what that means and how that impacts my life is pretty much focus for me." Thus the importance of sexual identity varies from person to person.

Sexuality remains an important source of identity for the women I interviewed because of the historical association of women's lands with lesbian separatism and the use of women's land and lesbian land as a safe space for queer women. The relationship of nonlesbian women to the association of lesbian identity with women's lands is complex. Bisexuality was not a topic of conversation that I explored with my informants; however, the fact that sexual behavior changes over the lifespan is very clear from the life histories that my informants provided me. Only some of my informants identified as lesbian from young ages—and many of those who did still married. One stated that she married a gay man in a marriage of convenience, and they had children. While my informants largely identified as lesbian, those who did not expressed no anxiety or tension over living in largely lesbian communities. An interesting example was Jan and Sara, who were founding their own community, that they explicitly stated was to be "queer-friendly" and "trans-friendly" but "for women." They did not give a sexual identity for themselves.

Many of the women I interviewed used alternate spellings of "women" in order to symbolize freedom from defining women as the marked category to the male unmarked category. "Wombyn," "wimmin" and "womyn" (the latter can be singular or plural) are all spellings I ran into frequently. Glorious Dyke connected the issue of spelling and aesthetics with deeper cultural issues of naming and expectations:

And I use the word Dyke Haven, instead of Dyke Heaven, the lie h-e, "He" in "Heaven" would not work for dykes, because so many dykes speak in terms of the patriarchy, as in "Heaven," they hold onto the patriarchy, thinking that it is important to identify that pie in the sky, but actually if you drop it then you permit it to be Dyke Haven, which can be Dyke Haven here in earth and Dyke Haven hereafter.

Glorious Dyke connects the "he" (male) in the word "heaven" with patriarchal views of "pie in the sky" used to keep women in line. By rejecting that, she creates a unified vision of a good life for dykes, now and in the future.

The women I interviewed had many reactions to the term "separatist." Glorious Dyke identified as a separatist, and stated that her community was a worldwide net of lesbian separatists, including ones she had met in Japan, Wales, and Scotland. However, Arcadia, who identified as a lesbian currently living on women's land, said,

> I'm not a separatist per se, but I am for any minority group having the right to draw back and separate to find out who they are and what they are and what they can do uninfluenced by the mainstream, the dominant culture. And that you know includes if African-Americans wanted to set up a place to be by themselves . . . it has to do with figuring out who you are when you're not being told anymore who you are.

This is a very separatist philosophy, but she declined to be called a "separatist per se." Sirocco gave the following description:

> I am not a separatist, I at times have a real hard time considering myself a radical feminist, because I don't consider myself a feminist, I consider myself a humanist. I, however, have extreme respect for women who chose separatism and feminism as a way of life, and I kind of take what I need from that for my own daily life.

In 2015, a woman who subscribed to the *Maize* email list but who did not self-identify as a lesbian was asked to leave by the other subscribers of the list. She did so, but not without some verbal conflict. This policing of the boundary of lesbian identification is a form of separatism, whether or not the actual term is used. In virtual space, where one would think separatism would be more difficult to police and enforce, separatism is more likely to appear, although in my experience less likely to be named as such.

Separatism as a philosophy is highly varied, and usually dated to the Furies' 1972 statement about rejecting male dominance. Bev Jo notes: "Separatism is a dirty word in the 'women's' and lesbian communities. In my experience, of all the groups of lesbians who exist, separatists are the safest to attack" (1991, 74). This hostility is acknowledged within the women's-land community: separatism as a philosophy is sometimes regarded with suspicion. It is considered extreme, it is considered "leaving men to their own resources"—as Russ pointed out, "Haven't they got any?" (1998, 92). Yet, in 1978, the Gorgons wrote, "we are Lesbian Separatists because we love women and want women to be happy" (1991, 394). This is at the core of most separatist statements—the valuing of women's happiness, development, abilities, and freedom. Zimmerman, in her overview of separatism, notes both that it was "never one monolithic theory," and also that it originated in feminist, not lesbian, theory, which in turn drew from the black separatist philosophy of *autonomy* (1990, 127). Such autonomy was often conceived of as a nonviolent way of withdrawing from a patriarchal, capitalist, racist, hierarchical, and violent society.

Charlotte Bunch, one of the founding members of the Furies, recalls how straight feminists shut lesbians out in the second wave of the women's movement, and concludes that "separatism was the only way we saw to create lesbian-feminist politics and build a community of our own in the hostile environment of the early seventies" (1994, 435). She suggests that "thanks in part to this time of separation by lesbian groups in many cities, lesbian communities can now exist openly and proudly throughout the nation as the backbone of many feminist, political, cultural, and economic activities. Most women's groups now recognize the 'legitimacy' of lesbians' civil rights in society, as well as our right to exist openly in their midst" (436). She therefore suggests that separatism is not simply a philosophy of autonomy, but also one that allows lesbian and queer women's presence to become more visible and their civil rights to be more acknowledged.

Bunch also notes that "while I am as glad as any woman that the most painful days of separatism seem to be behind us, we must not lose sight of why they happened in the first place. Separatism happened for a reason. It happened because straight feminists were unable to allow lesbians space to grow" (442). Separatism is thus not solely because of heterosexism, but because of the ways in which straight feminism was unwilling to make room for lesbians. Moreover, she credits separatism with both political analysis and "structural innovations" (442), the latter of which recall collectives and women's lands.

The rich background of the "separatist" term that is one of the identity threads of my informants—sometimes chosen, sometimes forcibly applied—demonstrates the wide range of how separatism, lesbianism, even the term "woman" are defined. Each of my informants had a different definition of herself, her sexuality, and her choice to live in a women's community. Identity is at one and the same time both an intensely individual and a publicly debated and contested ground.

Women's Lives on Women's Lands

Women come to women's lands by various and varying routes. Some set out to create women's communities, while others find women's land via friends, other forms of women's community, or by chance. Here are some examples of how my informants have come to women's land. Although these stories are not comprehensive or "representative," they do illustrate some of the varied backgrounds women bring with them to the project of women's land.

Sophia, an older white woman, began her story with how she struggled to come out as a lesbian in her mid-twenties, living in Florida. She remained celibate for a number of years, then became part of a strong lesbian-feminist community and became "radicalized" in the 1980s, in her fifties. She said that around this point, she started talking with a group of women who were concerned "about retaining our lesbian culture when we age, when we're old." This group developed the concept of the Star[8] community, of women supporting each other as they aged. They met until 1987.

Sophia was working as a physical therapist and a bookseller at the time, selling radical feminist literature out of her van. She visited women's communities and mixed communities all over the United States. In 1997, she retired from both of these businesses, and went to live with a woman in the southern United States who had invited her to stay in an apartment in her house, in order to begin a community based around the Star ideals. However, that community did not "get off the ground."

Then Sophia heard about Mountainview and the land owned by Mountain's Daughters nearby. Although she wasn't interested in trying to start Star as a part of Mountainview, the idea of being near other women's land was appealing. So Sophia gathered together a group of women, negotiated with Mountain's Daughters, and began a year and a half of labor, working together and building houses. However, as I relate in more detail in chapter 4, there was a disagreement over the use and ownership of the land, and the Star women ended up leaving. When I interviewed her, Sophia was committed to Star, although still in the process of mourning its failure at Mountain's Daughters. She said "I have not lost the vision of [Star], though, it's a very important vision, I think." She said she planned to try again, with a new community, as the women she had been working with had all moved on with their lives.

Jan and Sara were also building a community, planning an artist's colony in the Southwest. Jan said of her childhood, "My parents were hippies in the '70s when I was born, and we lived in a van for a while, and kinda traveled around, and lived in a commune for like a year and a half, two years, while I was five. Four, five, six. So I guess maybe two and a half years. And so that was my early exposure to it. But that was over when I was six or seven. And then I had a more traditional and very fundamentalist Christian upbringing."

Jan and her partner Sara visited a number of women's communities in various states, and decided to build their own community where they own the land and the members of the community "rent" space. Their physical space was an old hippie commune with some residents still living there. Jan said that "for about twenty-five to thirty years it was a Gurudeep artist community, which is a Sufi-based teaching. There were twenty-one hippies who were living out there and they built all the structures and there's even an underground bunker and when we bought the place we didn't even know about it."

The transition from the old community to the new one was difficult, Sara noted. They inherited three people from the old community, who "had very set ideas about how things should go. And they weren't people who had lived there for twenty years, they were people who had lived there for six months," Jan said. They didn't want to kick anyone out, but it was clear that Jan and Sara had a very different community in mind, and eventually the previous residents left.

They were in the process of making the space friendly to artists. Jan said, "we have a painting studio, a pottery studio, a welding and woodworking studio, and then I have my own jewelry studio." There are shared gardens and shared space, but also private retreat space and sleeping quarters. They planned to have the land open to all visitors, but as a living space for queer women only.

Sirocco's story is best told in her own words, as she told it to me:

> First of all I'm [Sirocco], and I came from a family of four siblings, there were four kids in the family, so I have one brother and two sisters, and my mother raised us as a single mom. We came from a poverty-stricken background, and I was raised primarily in [rural Oregon]. All of my life—I was born and raised there.
>
> And I think at about age twelve was when I finally recognized what I was. And how that came to be was that there was an article in a magazine or a paper or something that a couple of people were discussing about some pedophile who had molested some boy children and they referred to the pedophile as a queer and how "those queers are child molesters." And I remember asking somebody "What is a queer?" and "A queer is somebody who sleeps with or is attracted to somebody of the same sex." And I knew immediately that they were talking about me. And I knew that I would have to keep my mouth shut because I didn't want to be perceived as a pedophile.
>
> And then I went through (also at that same age)—my mother became a Christian and started attending church and taking us to church and stuff, and the faith that my mother belongs to does not accept homosexuality whatsoever, so I knew I could never speak out about what I was and what I was feeling. So I tried to hide it. I tried really hard at times to even be straight. And, of course, I never really was attracted to men, so that didn't work for whatever reason.
>
> I had my daughter when I was seventeen years old. And proceeded on the road of motherhood to the best of my ability. I was also fairly heavy into drugs in my early teens. And so that had—my drug addiction had a big impact on my life. At age nineteen, I finally recognized that I was a lesbian and proceeded to look at lesbian information and tried to find ways to come in contact with other lesbians. However, I had never had a physical experience with a woman until I was twenty-one.
>
> And that lasted like six months. Like many of us, you know, we were fairly promiscuous in our early twenties and I did a lot of sexual exploration around my sexuality.

And I think I was twenty-one years old when I finally discovered [Firefly Farm]. And I think that was in 1984. And for me it was a major life-changing experience because I never even knew that land like that could exist. Somebody had taken me out there for a work day or something, and I immediately fell in love with the place. It was like a real spiritual connection for me.

There were eight women, eight of us that were living out there at the time. We lived communally. We each had our own separate sleeping spaces, but we ate together, we cooked together, we worked together, we shopped together, we did laundry together, it was definitely a 100 percent communal effort. And I lived out there mostly during the fall and winter months. It was about a six-month period, the first time.

And through that experience, I came in contact with the women's community in southern Oregon, and met a lot of wonderful older lesbians who took me under their wing and taught me about women's spirituality, taught me about the women's community, taught me about separatism, taught me about feminism, women's history, all those things that I don't believe I would have had the opportunity to know about if it hadn't been for my experience at [Firefly Farm]. My experiences out at [Firefly Farm] were fabulous. I would not trade one single day of it. So that's my prelude.

These three life stories illustrate how different women come to community in varying ways. Very few women are born into women's community, although Jan had the experience of being partly raised in a hippie commune; most land-women are deliberately seeking out the different culture of women's lands. That different experience is self-built, continually in process, and focused on the idea of female space.

Building Community, Building Culture: The Process of Women's Lands

Women's communities did not spring fully formed upon the land like Aphrodite from the waves. First there was the idea of creating such communities, and then there were women who built them. Thus community and the perception of community are extremely important. The women I interviewed included urban living arrangements in their history of women's community, as well as referencing women's centers, help lines, political protests, and especially music festivals. Several informants told me that the sense of empowerment and women's space that they first felt at all-women music festivals were the inspiration for either creating or seeking out women's living communities. "I wanted to live there all the time," said one woman. It is clear that feminist *community*—the sense of being with other feminist women—is an important origin for women's lands.

One informant, Joanne, told me that her first woman's community was a suburban household she described as "collective":

> But anyway, so, you know, the, doing, having decisions made by consensus was important, and establishing collective. . . . In 1975, we formed an intentional living-together collective in [large Midwestern city], and there were five of us. We lasted ten years, and I would say that what came out of the women in that group was amazing.

She stated that they had a system by which women would track the use of foodstuffs from the pantry on a list on the refrigerator, and women took it in turns to go to the market with the list, using a communal fund. She said the system worked well. There was a general feeling that most of the residents contributed fairly equally to the rent, the fund for groceries and utilities, and the housework.

> And the main thing for me was economic efficiency. Um, I don't think we need a washer or dryer for every two people. I don't think we need a refrigerator for every two people. I don't think we, we even did this thing, now this is city stuff, we even did this thing for a while where we really tried to share vehicles, so that we didn't have a car for each person. And it, you know, it took some work, but we did it. . . . And that was our main thing, you know, let's put our assets together, so that we can have this, knowing that, if it was just me, I would never have that. I would never have this land, I would never have this house, I would never have all these resources. So, economic efficiency was certainly a piece of it. The other thing is, the mechanics of living. If all we do is exist as individuals or as couples, the mechanics of living take up your energy. Making your meals,

doing your shopping, doing your laundry, you know. All of that stuff, there's no time left. So, but if you only have to make a dinner once a week, then you've got time to do something else.

Joanne's description foregrounds sharing as both an economic principle and as a timesaving one—by sharing resources, more women get to use those resources, and also have more time for leisure, work, or other activities. This description is particularly important because of its connection to class—by sharing domestic work and space communally, the women of the household were able to have both more resources and more access to time/leisure.

Joanne's situation illustrates how particular women's lands often arise from experiences at *other* women's communities. That is, women move from community to community. They use their experience to refine their ideas of what community should be like, and then build new groups. She said, "Well, in the community that I did live in for, the one that stayed together longest was ten years, and then there was another one. It shifted some of the people for another, I would say, another seven years." This shift from community to community produces an important cultural flow, a commonality of terms, ideas, and people, although different groups preserve important cultural differences. Indeed, some communities often go to great lengths to create differences not only from the matrix culture but from other women's lands.

Arcadia told me that she left one community saying, "I will never live on land again that doesn't have a conflict resolution procedure." She felt that there were intense conflicts—that land was famous because it had started as a mixed community in the 1970s. Arcadia characterized it as "the men—essentially well-meaning nice hippie guys—got pushed off the land." She didn't want to stay after that due to the conflicts that the remaining women continued to have with each other, so she left with her lover and wound up creating another community, Lilith's Land. Lilith's Land operates on consensus minus one, which Arcadia said was "sort of a craziness clause because you can always have a person who decides that the position of power is the oppositional position." She added that they have been studying nonviolent communication, but when I asked about the conflict resolution procedure, she said, "And we *still* don't have one!"

However, despite this lack, Arcadia felt she had helped build a community more free from the conflicts she found problematic. In contrast to "pushing men off the land," Lilith's Land, though all women, is more relaxed about such things:

> And for me, I'm living in a quasi-separatist community, I have two sons who I am trying to include in my life, we're all doing sort of a dance about men in the main house (it used to be no men in the main house). This last spring, my son [Al], who is teaching nonviolent communication for couples, came and gave a workshop for five lesbian couples—or four lesbian couples and two singles, whatever—on nonviolent communication, he and his girlfriend. So I thought there was some humor in this. And we loved it. The workshop was a big success, [Al] really enjoyed it, and so did [his girlfriend Elaine]....
> We do have the power to determine our own lives, so we don't have to be so uptight about it as we used to be.

This shift to "having the power to determine our own lives" is linked, in Arcadia's narrative, to their ability to build a women's community. A strong community leads to confidence that means that the boundary of sex segregation does not need to be policed as stringently.

The confidence that Arcadia demonstrates stems from the successful creation of difference. This process of creating cultural difference is painstaking and often difficult. I would like to focus now on two particular ways that women on women's lands create cultural difference: commensality, including both communal decision-making and the sharing of resources, and feminist aesthetics.

Although commensality is also seen as feminist by my informants, I have chosen to discuss it separately from other feminist practices because of its primary importance. How a community makes decisions is fundamental, and a focus of much thought and experimentation by land-women. When asked about their communities, my informants never failed to tell me how decisions were made and why that procedure was chosen. Consensus in particular was often cited as being a particularly feminist way of organizing decision-making, although many women were also quick to point out the problems of trying to reach consensus with a large group of women or a group which was strongly divided on a topic.

Arcadia's group, and its consensus-minus-one model, was one example of working around some of the problems of consensus. Other groups, committed to the process of consensus, are willing to invest a great deal of time and effort into their meetings. Marie of Mountainview described how their group's commitment to consensus served as a barrier to some women:

> So they do try—[the parent group] does try to—you know, they try to get women who have sort of the same values I guess you would say. Now when the last group of cottages was developed, [two women] came from [town], California, and they came to our meetings—this was part of the breakup of [another community]. And they said, "You rule by consensus? You do things by consensus? Ooh, that takes too long!" We would run the Center, you know, they were eight-hour meetings, so that the supporters would be happy. Vegans, non-vegans. "Oh! That takes too long. You don't do things. You're just middle-class people, you're just middle—that's not, that's not—just raise your hand, that's how you do it!" They would leave a meeting if we didn't raise our hands. They would not sit through consensus.

Note how the process of consensus was defined by these two women as "middle-class," and how they withdrew their participation in protest over the effort. Here we see a conflict between consensus and class: if consensus is feminist, but also "middle-class," what does that say about this particular feminist aesthetic?

Consensus is often seen as an essential part of creating what landwomen call "women's culture." It is the primary decision-making process of all of the lands I visited, and the Landdyke Gatherings as well. In fact, it is so essentially integrated into "women's culture" that most women took the connection for granted, as in Marie's example above. Discussions about consensus were not about whether it was feminist, but rather about how to make it work better, the history of consensus, and problems with the process.[9] Robin, from Mountainview, sees consensus as "standard feminism." "The first night is a business meeting where we go through all the issues. No one is required to come to meetings, but most of the women do. And we have a standard feminist program with a little grounding and a facilitator, and a time limit, and all those good things to run a meeting, and we have very experienced meeting people."

Communal living was also often cited as inherently female or feminist.

Joanne stated, "But just women create spaces that are generally, and you know, I know all the objections, but are generally, more shared." Although the women are aware that there are communal living societies with mixed genders, commensality was still seen as a component of specifically *women's* culture.

It is important to note that while many of my informants provide essentialist arguments for particular aspects of culture being female/feminist/feminine, particularly in the case of consensus, these arguments are not solely grounded in an essentialist view. Many of these aspects of culture, such as communal sharing, are also presented as feminist for purely *practical* reasons: they *benefit women*. Thus, consensus is often presented not simply as something innate to women, but instead as something that is simply *fair to all the participants*, who are all women, and therefore feminist. Thus essential views of the feminine/female are interwoven with more empirical or functionalist reasons for choosing these particular processes.

A feminist aesthetic runs through all of these discussions of women's community. What I mean by a feminist aesthetic is the use of feminism to inform space and practice as well as ideas—a feminist will-to-creation as well as will-to-action. This can be seen in many aspects of women's land, including in religious practice, interaction with the natural environment, and even love relationships.

One feminist aesthetic that often springs from the idea of commonality is a rejection of monogamy. Several of my informants reported that they had participated in open and consensual nonmonogamy. Pelican Lee writes,

> At Owl Farm we believed in non-monogamy. We believed that couples were like capitalism—possession and ownership and hoarding love. Couples were a tool of the patriarchy to isolate us from all but one another. To be single meant sharing love in a circle, being independent and communal with our energy. We believed in the power of the circle. (2002, 6)

Another of my informants, Glorious Dyke, stated that she would "never want to own another beautiful dyke," presumably referring to marriage. In *Country Lesbians,* Billie writes about nonmonogamy in "Opening Up" (Sue et al. 1976, 75–76). She notes that "we approve of couple energy and the intensities that accompany it, but we also feel the need to change our culturally conditioned attitudes about jealousy, possessiveness, and exclusiveness." Billie analyzes nonmonogamy, noting that "I had learned from the male culture that 'letting go' means *losing* and 'losers' are powerless to control our own lives.... But women are creating new rules! Letting go does not have to mean losing!" In this analysis, Billie suggests that patriarchal ideals of ownership and objectification are tied up in monogamist ideals, and instead presents nonmonogamy as a feminist reframing of love, power, and freedom.

Several of my informants who stated that they had practiced nonmonogamy in the past were currently in traditional two-person relationships. Gagehabib and Summerhawk noted a similar shift away from nonmonogamy in the Southern Oregon Women's Community: "Women wanted some balance between those two forces during a time of community-building and began to reaffirm their needs for privacy, space, and personal style. By the early nineties, serial monogamy was the dominant relationship pattern in the Southern Oregon Women's Community" (2000, 151). While I definitely met many women who were in long-term stable relationships with one other woman, my experience was not as uniform as Gagehabib and Summerhawk's.[10] In fact, the "general availability" they speak of during the days of nonmonogamy was also not as simple as it sounds; it is hedged around with courtship rituals, taboos, and complex relationships.

Religion and religious practice are an important feminist aesthetic in many women's lands. *Mountainview* has many practitioners of feminist Goddess spirituality, including Robin, who identifies as a Witch.[11] One member's backyard had a permanent circle in it, marked with large stones,[12] and I was taken on a long hike to two other sacred locations, one formed by enormous glacial boulders resembling recumbent women, and the other a clearing on top of the mountain with a very impressive view. These spaces, the hiking trails that connected them, the improvements, decorations, offerings, and sacred objects in the ritual spaces, and the relationship of the women to the land all reflected a feminist aesthetic. On the other hand, not all religious influence in women's communities is Goddess worship. My first interviews were with members of a community formed around a group of women who had met while studying in a Methodist theological seminary. Thus their group, while highly influenced by feminist and religious concerns, worshiped in a different manner.

Another important ethic is feminist ecoconsciousness, or ecofeminism. While ecological consciousness is a theme common to many intentional communities, many women's lands specifically connect this to feminist ethics. Lily from *Mountainview*, for example, in response to a question about how the community tried to make itself different from society as a whole, noted first that, "For one thing, we're all women, which is a big thing. I think we try to live more cooperatively rather than hierarchically. Although, we do have that issue, too. We try to—we really try to take care of the environment, to tread lightly on the earth." Note the flow of thoughts—gender to cooperation to taking care of the environment—all of these are connected into the production of a culturally different and feminist place to live. She adds, "But as much as we can, we're trying to be environmentally sound and conscious. And I think that doesn't hold in the outside community a whole lot."[13]

Community, commensality, and certain cultural forms are seen by land-women as being *gendered* as well as being feminist. The community is gendered by being composed of women, but also because community itself has positive and feminine connotations. Commensality is perhaps the most strongly gendered of these items, as many women stated that consensual decision-making and communal living were both inherent to women and benefited women. Lastly, feminist ideals shape such aspects of culture as religion, love and family ties, and the relationship of the individual and the community with the earth. Thus, gender influences these aspects of culture, and is constantly invoked when land-women think about and construct their cultures. Gender is a constant concern in the deliberate creation of cultural difference.

Essential Difference: Community and the Importance of Boundaries

The boundaries of women's lands can be physical—resident households, land-based communities' geographic edges—or intangible, like the edges of social networks. In the case of women's land, gender, sexuality, and identity are all bases on which boundaries are constructed. Additionally, a sense of nostalgic communitas leads to the adoption of particular unspoken ideas about class, race, culture, and gender that also serve as boundaries.

The members of any intentional community are engaged in cultural exchange with the surrounding matrix culture(s). Boundaries serve as walls, but they are also where cultural exchange occurs, as Sally Ward notes, they are "between the local and the global, dwelling and movement, home and away, past and present, physical geographies and cognitive maps. Many ground such an abstract realm of in-betweenness in those people who make or have made crossings between those realms, those who live in the borderlands" (2003, 87). Border crossings, as Gloria E. Anzaldúa reminds us, are always significant. Furthermore, "Borders are set up to define the places that are safe and unsafe, to distinguish *us* from *them*. A border is a dividing line, a narrow strip along a steep edge. A borderland is a vague and undetermined place created by the emotional residue of an unnatural boundary" (2007, 25). To a certain extent, my informants live in the borderlands. Their communities, nested within the matrix culture, are engaged in a continuous "bordering" with it, a negotiation of cultural differentiation. Thus this creation of boundaries in order to create community, even by those who are displaced/minoritized by a larger culture, is also an act of power.

Community itself can be a difficult term. Colin Bell and Howard Newby (1972) emphasize the nostalgic connotations of the term *community*. This is relevant in dealing with women's-land communities that depend on a sense of *nostalgia* to define those boundaries. A *sense of belonging* is thus an important part of such community. Jack Halberstam notes this in particular: "The reminder that quests for community are always nostalgic attempts to return to some fantasized moment of union and unity reveals the conservative stakes in community for all kinds of political projects, and makes the reconsideration of subcultures all the more urgent." Halberstam gestures to Sarah Thornton's assertion that community is linked to residence, neighborhood, kinship, and family. He then contrasts this to the notion of subcultures, arguing that they "suggest transient, extrafamilial, and oppositional modes of affiliation" (Thornton 1997, in Halberstam 2005, 154n2). Yet while lesbian and women's-land space is subcultural in some senses, it is also based on the ideals of nostalgia/sense of belonging—indeed, on that "fantasized moment of union and unity." It is part subculture and part communitas.

This nostalgic sense of community is very important. However, it may *depend* on drawing boundaries. For many lands, biological sex is a boundary. Sexuality or sexual identity is also sometimes used as a boundary. Not all of the women's-land women are lesbians, and thus not all of them are land*dykes*. The Landdyke Gathering is for "self-defined landdykes at heart,"[14] thus, any woman who wishes to self-define that way. The term itself, because of the use of the word "dyke," calls for self-identification with a lesbian identity.

Such boundary-drawing sometimes leads to the expression of surprisingly mainstream gender ideals. For example, one of my informants told me casually one day that she felt uncomfortable around butch women, as opposed to "dykes," whom she seemed to define as more androgynous women. She said that she found butch women too "masculine" and lacking in the female energy she sought at women's lands. In this case, we see the significant "energy" term (discussed below) used to convey ideas about social gender performance. She was clearly looking for a socially *feminized* space rather than a space with a diversity of female gender expression.

Other informants expressed the idea that women's space was "safer": land-women talk about violence perpetrated by men, but tend to elide violence perpetrated by women. "It's a safe space to go home to. Where I can really be who I am. We can be a couple there like anyone else, holding hands," said Meg. Other common ideas included that women's society was about "discussion rather than about hierarchy" and that "women love to talk!" Such ideas are then woven into a nostalgic idea of specifically female-gendered community, and become part of a "gender boundary."

However, despite this "gender boundary," ideas about gender are challenged in these spaces. I believe that the challenge that women's space represents to ideas about femaleness/ femininity paradoxically creates a need for an essentialist, often bodily (see chapter 6) definition of gender. Because women in these spaces *must* take on all kinds of roles and *can* behave in ways that are not seen as a polar opposite to the male, conventional social definitions of gender are unmade. For example: women on women's lands build their own houses, operate chainsaws, do their own electrical wiring, and repair their own cars. They also fight with one another and are engaged in politics. But these circumstances also set up paradoxical questions: if women can do and be anything, then who are women? What makes them different?

Boundaries are essential to maintaining a community in all of its nostalgic as well as its literal sense. Iris Young writes, "I have criticized a predominant tendency in participatory democratic theory to deny or think away social differences by appeal to an ideal of community" (1990, 256). What she criticizes in her work is the notion of community based on *sameness*, leading to exclusion and oppression. For example, Marsha Ritzdorf notes that the legal definition of what she calls the "mythical nuclear family," by excluding many American households not comprising a married heterosexual couple and their children, functions as a racist, classist, and sexist discrimination tool (1997, 83, 87). Communities can be a way of holding on to classist and especially racist privilege—a stark reminder that communitas is not always based on equality. In this community model, there is no way to work with the Other, for strangers are automatically excluded from the community.

Some of the same forces are at work within women's communities. The women creating these communities are shut out in many ways from the communities of the matrix cultures. This lack of access operates not only from direct homophobia but also through more subtle means, as these women do not have access to heterosexual privilege.[15] Women's communities, therefore, often actively attempt to give access to goods and privileges to a generally nonprivileged group.

Because of this awareness, land-women are eager to create space benefiting "their people." However, the definition of that group is influenced by a nostalgic sense of communitas, in which many of these women wish for a space where there are others *like them*. Many of these women were raised in environments where there were no out lesbians. Meg, who was seeking a women's-land community, said, "I feel like an outsider in the general community." However, a sense of community as sameness also excludes. The greater proportion of the inhabitants in the women's communities are white. One of my white informants told me that her community was "open" to women of color, but in the absence of any women of color in that community, what does that openness mean? If communitas is based on unspoken similarity, the answer is clearly no, it is not open. Racism remains a powerful "silent partner" in terms of how communitas operates to exclude women of color.

Boundaries are therefore both explicit and implicit. These communities are often composed of women who seek an experience of communitas. Underlying this is a thread of the similarity spoken of by Young: in order to find this community, some people must be excluded. In particular, gender is most often called upon to serve as part of the communitas, and some of the gender ideas or ideals that women use to create that sense of "like us" are gender essentials drawn from the matrix culture but more importantly, from particularly raced bodies performing a particularly historic and cultural form of gender. Thus at the same time, the sense of communitas implies exclusion, both open exclusion of "masculinity" and hidden exclusion of those whose femininity does not perform the proper raced, cultural gestures. Community has an uncomfortable underside.

Land-women are often aware of that underside. Meg, for example, spoke eloquently of the experience of feeling excluded from a women's land she was hoping to join because of ideas about the unfitness of her body (see chapter 6), and many women openly worried about the lack of younger members, discussing what could be alienating younger women from women's-land community.[16] A less discussed topic—but one that did come up—was why women of color lands were dwindling and women of color were rare in women's lands and gatherings.

Gender and Language: Women's Energy as Social Theory

The concept of "energy" emerged early on during my interviews with women's-land participants. In particular, the idea of *gendered* energy, the idea that a person "projects" energy that is either male or female, often appeared in answer to questions about gender. Although at first glance the "energy" term appears to deal with something metaphysical, what it refers to is "meta-physical" in the literal sense: it is a way of talking about social theory, how physical people interact. "Energy" refers to the spoken and unspoken ways in which an individual interacts with others in society, and women's-land women have correctly identified that gender is a major factor in how those social interactions pan out.[17]

The energy term has a long and interesting history. Bonnie Zimmerman traces it back to the development of separatist politics:

> A kind of separatist physics developed, positing that every woman has a quantifiable and limited amount of "energy" constantly in danger of being ripped off and given to men. If a woman loses some of her energy, her power is diminished; should a man receive some of it, his is enhanced. Straight women, or even another lesbian who "gave energy" to men, were the medium by which energy was exchanged and hence were to be avoided. (1990, 128)

This illustrates a complex political embeddedness to the energy term, including an implied sexual dichotomy as well as a zero-sum game in which every person has not only energy, but a limited amount which can be "taken."[18] Most interestingly, while men take energy from women, the reverse does not seem to be true.

My informants did not use "energy" in the same way as is reported by Zimmerman about the early days of the separatist movement; while there is an implied resistance to "giving attention" to men, the energy term was mostly used to discuss gendered *styles* of interaction, not intangible near-economic transactions as above. In other words, no one "gave" or "took" energy in my informants' discussions. However, the implied gender difference was much more important to my informants. In fact, I believe that the term "energy," because of how it is used in women's space and because of its roots in the separatist movement, signals a certain alignment to particular gender ideals that are often interpreted as hostile to the inclusion of trans women. While this does not necessarily follow for all of my informants, the way the term is used outside of women's lands often indicates an adherence to gender beliefs that exclude trans women as having flawed (or no) "female energy." (For more on this, see chapter 7.)

What is "female energy?" One woman said: "Well, things are just different when the community is all women. It's a kind of female energy." Sirocco said, bluntly, "Women's energy is so different from men's energy." "Energy" is thus an expression that has an implicitly binary gendered component and refers to that difference, and it is usually used about social interactions. There are a wide variety of coded gender beliefs in this term, and my informants use it as shorthand to refer to many gendered linguistic and social behaviors.

Indeed, throughout my work with my informants, I *never once* heard anyone use the energy term without an actual or implied gender adjective added to it. The term seemed to be a way of expressing the performance of gender itself. In her overview of studies of the "linguistic performance of gender diversity," Cameron notes, "gender is not just performed differently in different communities or subcultures; some range of gendered performances can be found in the repertoire of every group, and indeed every individual subject" (2005, 493). The energy term, with its wide range of applications and meanings, illustrates that range of gendered performances while still pointing to some very specific ideas about gender: what Cameron calls "local practices" of gender (489).

The energy term tended to be used in certain almost mythologized ways. "Female energy" or "women's energy" occurred in all-women settings. "Men's energy" could occur even when only one man was present. And there was a particular story that several of my informants told, a kind of social theory parable: the story of the man who walks into the room full of women. One woman, Acorn, gave me this example: "Women listen better. When there's a man in the room, he's the center of attention—energy goes to him like he's a magnet. Even if they're all dykes!" This example of the single man in the room changing or claiming the "energy" of the room was referred to by several interviewees. Here are some more examples of "the man in the room":

> Women-only space frees up a great deal of energy in women to not be coping with fending off men. That's the way it is. When women are together and there are no men around, they're busy chattering and carrying on—a man walks into the room—everything stops. And he automatically ends up taking over. Even the nicest of men. Because they're different. Because you don't know what they're going to do, you have to look and see. So, it just stops what goes on. (Robin)

> Oh, the other thing I wanted to say is, and it never fails, the other thing, the other reason, that we need to keep men out of women-only space, is because women defer to them. Every single group I'm in which is, any more, rare if there's a man in it, but if a man comes in, the women right away defer to him. Let him speak first, listen to his opinions better, makes you crazy. But anyway. And until women stop deferring to men, we have got to have our own space, in my opinion. And that includes trans men. (Joanne)

These examples show an *observable social phenomenon* that is spoken of using the term "energy." Robin attributes it to "difference," to women not being able to predict what a man is going to do; Joanna attributes it to the way women have been taught to defer to men. She includes trans men in this definition, thus placing them in the category of "men." In other words, "energy" and "the man in the room" are being used to discuss actual gendered social interactions.

So, what *exactly* does energy refer to? Here I asked Lily a little more about how she understood the term "female energy":

LILY: Yeah. Um, I don't know, you sense it, it's just that it's there, I can feel it. I think women do tend to act differently when they're in an all-woman space than they do on the outside, especially straight women. When they—like in the festival that I'm going to in June—it's largely straight women who come, it's a spirituality festival, and they just relax when they get into woman-only space. For them, it's very, very different. And they love it. [Laughter]

There's just a whole different feel, and I, I can't explain how it's felt. I don't think there's a mechanism, you just feel it.

And we, uh—I react different in all-women's space than I do out, having to talk to men. Just, uh—my guard is up, for one thing. If they say anything unfeminine—unfeminist, you know, I . . . And just my guard is up generally with men I don't trust, I don't care very much for them.

Lily speaks here of female energy as something you "just feel," but as something that is at the same time very profound. Here, "female energy" refers to social interactions again ("women do tend to act differently") and those interactions are ones that do not need to be "guarded" in the same way that interactions with men need to be. Yet at the same time, she states that there is no "mechanism," nothing measurable or *deliberate*. It is observable—"felt"—but not controllable. In fact, the energy term is used as a way of describing social interactions.

What specific social interactions are being spoken of here? There are a number that could be included under this rubric, both verbal and nonverbal. My informants refer to "attention," which correlates closely to Fishman (1978) and Hirschman's (1973, in Maltz and Borker, 1982) early work on gendered communication, which observed that women tended to do more of the conversational work to keep an interaction going, including asking questions, making minimal responses, and doing what Fishman has famously referred to as the routine "shitwork" of social interaction (408).[19] Some informants are, in fact, referring to dominance or relative status—Joanne said, "if a man comes in, the women right away defer to him. Let him speak first, listen to his opinions better, makes you crazy." But Robin spoke only of "difference," and Lily of "trust." Neither "difference" nor "trust" implies that the interactions between women and men in "the man in the room" scenario are necessarily unequal in terms of status. So the "energy" term covers both difference in conversational style and the problems of male dominance in conversation.

While we usually think of social interactions as being composed of voluntary actions—things we say or do as agents—putting social interactions in the rubric of "energy" casts a new light on the subject. "People just interact differently" does not sound very voluntary. Acorn and Lily made it sound *entirely* involuntary. The very term "energy" creates an image of radiation, an almost Star Trek vision of a force field emanating from someone's body, and this does not necessarily imply something someone can control. The image of energy radiating outward, like light or warmth, two of our most common cultural synonyms for energy, is not one that we picture as necessarily even *being* controllable. It is plain from this language that *involuntary* aspects are important.

Thus, this image conveys the involuntary aspects of social interaction in a compact way. In fact, the idea of gendered energy is a way of talking about paradigm and hegemony in more accessible and concrete language. "Female energy" refers to a kind of female social paradigm that "male energy," implied in the presence of a man, being hegemonic in the matrix culture, has the power to disrupt. An excellent example of this is Lily's observation that even straight women relax in women-only space. Lily states that women *involuntarily* relax in a social setting composed only of women. There is something going on here that is both gendered and not entirely within conscious control. In fact, what we have here in the gendered energy term is a way of talking about deep structures that does not use the fancy language that social scientists do. It is workable folk social theory.

"Female energy" raises some fascinating questions about categories. What about this energy is particularly "female"? If energy *can* be changed, can it become more or less female? What creates female energy—the fact of its creator being a woman? If so, then how is a woman defined? Each woman uses this term a little differently, and thus the larger scope of the terminology itself is multivocal and encompasses a wide variety of meaning. Yet the term seems to be widely understood. However, underneath the way the term is used—its assumptions—is an invisible doxa of the primal, precultural and sexed or gendered body: the idea that women's energy *exists* and can be named because there is a natural class of *women,* and that this natural class is biological and precultural.

Joanne's explication relies on these unspoken binaries:

> You know, when I go into a space, and I don't mean this to sound airy-fairy, you know, I think that women's energy is different. It's not as aggressive, it's not as violent, and, I know there are aggressive women, I know there's violence, violent women, but as a group, as a class of people, I think that our objectives are always more toward sharing, toward trying to help.

Joanne does not want to sound "airy-fairy" and instead cites common, almost stereotypical adjectives that are used to describe women's interactions and social behavior. She suggests that women are essentially different from men—for example, she uses the word "always"—and that this difference obtains among women as a group.

However, this is not the *only* way in which the energy term is used. Remember that Joanne, when speaking of energy and women-only space, said, "And until women stop deferring to men, we have got to have our own space, in my opinion. And that includes trans men." That statement opens up an entire world in which gender can be changed, and when gender is changed, so is the gender or character of "energy." This change is rooted in both social behavior (an ability to stop deferring) and bodily changes (such as those trans people undergo). Thus, it is clear that energy is not always something rooted in an unchangeable body and gender identification.

It is difficult to escape doxa: doxa is not only culture's "naturalization of its own arbitrariness," but also masquerades as nature itself. Therefore, it is not surprising that land-women, most of whom have been raised in one strand or another of the United States matrix culture, retain certain aspects of its doxa, even its gender doxa. The idea that women comprise a "natural class,"—for biological or other reasons—is enmeshed in United States culture, and this springs from the assumption that gender is binary, on-off, female-male.

This therefore makes it all the more interesting that land-women have taken a simple term like "energy" and used it to critique, comment on, and make clear aspects of how gender works in a social setting. The "energy" term has fascinating implications, especially in its connections with spiritual terms, as those connections imply that certain aspects of gendered social interactions—*even if they are involuntary*—can still be changed. "Energy" at once captures the way we acquire a certain habitus without being consciously aware of it, and points to particular ways we might become aware of it, and thus change our cultural and social behavior. The term's use seems to have changed from examining gender as a social transaction to thinking about gender as *doxa*.

Gender as nostalgia is thus the "acted-upon identity" that forms the boundary around the network of community of women's lands. That is, nostalgic ideas about "women like us/me" form ideas about community that invisibly exclude others; these are "acted upon" in terms of who is welcomed into a community, and this helps form a particular community.

Gender thus becomes a significator for nostalgic definitions of community, yet that sense of nostalgia incorporates matrix/doxic ideas about women as nurturing or more communal. This nostalgia also serves to exclude those who do not fit that image: nonfeminine women or women of the "wrong" class or race. At the same time, however, the single-sex world of women's lands also actively unmakes mainstream ideas about gender because women can and indeed must take all roles, such as leadership and the use of previously "masculine" skills (like home repair). This leads women to both question those doxic matrix gender roles and to build new ideas about the female gender.

Within community, deliberate acts of what are seen as feminist or feminine ways of living, including commensality, ecoconsciousness, and the process of community-building itself, are used to create "women's culture." Within this network of cultures and this larger web of women's community, individual histories and identities are woven into a larger complex of identity and community. These individual histories and identities may even be at odds with the nostalgic ideas about communitas and gender that help form the community's borders; but the network at large still expresses a sense of community as "people like us."

· CHAPTER 4 ·

The Giving Tree

Gift Economies Planted in Capitalist Soil

And it's a way of stepping outside of that, having the whole pie instead of just half of it, or a third of it.

—Robin

A GIFT IS ALWAYS MORE THAN JUST A GIFT. Whether given anonymously, or in expectation of a return, whether it is of time, money, something handmade, something purchased, something you know the recipient desires or something you feel obligated to give, a gift implies a world of other connections, meanings, and knowledge. A gift is a transaction, a connection, a symbol, and sometimes an enormous fuck-you to the entire capitalist system. Other times, gifts are the product and backbone of that same system.

Knowing the right thing to give is important. When visiting one women's land in Tennessee, I agonized over the correct hostess gift to bring to the generous woman who was letting me stay in her house, and eventually decided on a box of local (Boston) chocolates. These were received with puzzlement, if not indifference, although my hostess thanked me politely. However, when staying at a women's land in New Mexico during a Landdyke Gathering, just before I left one of the local women took me aside and told me that she had noticed I had been "taking up the slack" in terms of dishwashing and kitchen cleanup. "Thank you," she said sincerely. "We really appreciate the gift of your time." Without agonizing over it, I had hit upon the correct gift on that occasion.

Gifts indicate and regulate not only relationships between individual women, but also the ethos of an entire economy: what I have chosen to call here generalized reciprocity, after the anthropological term. This ethos of giving deserves exploration because it is a very important part of the economic systems of many women's lands and intertwined with ideas about community. Generalized reciprocity—giving a gift without expecting a return—is also often seen, by land-women and by others, as being in direct contrast to capitalist modes of interaction. Yet capitalism also influences women's communities, not only because these communities are surrounded by and enmeshed in a capitalist system, but because capitalist ethics inform many ideas about class.

Ideally, women's lands are spaces that resist matrix cultures' concepts of class and class divisions, but in actual operation, capitalist ideas about class and wealth divisions play an important role. The ethos of generalized reciprocity serves as a way to resist ideas about class, but also sometimes incorporates these ideas, particularly with regard to monetary gifts.

The question of money leads to the discussion of land, the largest purchase these communities must make, and to the ways in which land is viewed in distinctly noncapitalist ways. Land is regarded as partly inalienable, a thing with which women have personal and intimate relationships that cannot be wholly ruled by deeds and monetary access. However, at the same time, access to land, especially to land to settle/live on, is still highly governed by access to purchasing power. Yet one of the major examples within this chapter is a literal gift of land, moving land itself into the gift economy.

Thus the economics of women's lands reveal a great deal about how these cultures operate, particularly in how they produce cultural difference while still enmeshed with the matrix culture. The arbitrariness of the capitalist system is laid bare and resisted, but also incorporated, sometimes invisibly. A gift is always more than just a gift. It is a symbol, a connection, sometimes an exercise of power and influence, and always a demonstration of how well you fit into a community.

What Counts? Feminist and Anthropological Approaches to Economics

This book takes an anthropological approach to what counts as "economic," rather than limiting our view to neoclassical or strictly Marxian definitions. I consider all survival and work activities, exchange, and gift transactions as being economic in nature. This includes housework and other nonrecompensed labor, as the use of money as a medium of exchange or value is irrelevant to whether or not an activity is "economic."

Although anthropological approaches to economics often focus largely on subsistence and nonmonetary transactions, economics as a discipline focuses solely on capitalist, monetized transactions among governments, large corporations, and individuals. Feminist economics, which brings gender, race, and other forms of social difference into the analysis, seeks to consider such topics as unpaid/lesser-paid labor such as household, domestic, and slave labor (Chang 2000); shadow economies, such as illegal trades like prostitution (Sterk 2000), untaxed cash economies (Kümbetoğlu, User, and Akpınar 2010), and informal/part-time labor that is contingent and unprotected by law (Elgeziri 2010); and the ways in which finance is dependent on the differential production of laboring bodies (Roberts 2015). Since this chapter focuses on gifts and reciprocal exchanges (often outside of a money system) a few concepts from feminist economics will be helpful as a framework. This is not a comprehensive overview but a cherry-picked set of concepts relevant to the matter at hand.

Gillian Hewitson (1999), critiques the central figure of neoclassical economic theory, "rational economic man," and notes that "feminist economists using the gender approach argue that rational economic man must be expanded to become 'rational economic human.' My analysis, on the other hand, shows that the masculinity of the economic actor is constitutive of neoclassical economics, and cannot be dislodged or generalized without threatening the coherence of this body of knowledge" (166). Hewitson argues that such a rational economic actor is premised on assumptions that deliberately exclude and otherize the body, the "feminine" (however it is defined), and marginalized classes of people. Indeed, the discipline and markets both incentivize and make invisible such inequality, as "there are material incentives for the construction of racial categories and boundaries" (Saunders and Darity Jr. 2003, 101). As early as 1988, Marilyn Waring discussed the ways in which women, indigenous people, and racial minorities were deliberately excluded from both economic calculation ("nonproducers" or "economically inactive") and participation in the upper regions of capitalism, while being used as fodder for exploitative activities. My informants, in their attempts to deliberately withdraw from such markets and create an alternative, may be counted as "nonproducers" although they are not literally so.

Feminist economic analysis also examines the larger neoliberal capitalist global economy, an economy in which smaller economies are embedded willy-nilly, despite attempts on the part of my informants and others to withdraw. As Valentine Moghadam observes, the ones who reap the greatest benefits are profiteering transnational corporations and bankers (a very small percentage of the population as a whole), while those who bear the highest social, economic, and ecological costs are the most vulnerable and poorest members of the community, often women and children (2011, 33). Moghadam connects this back to what she calls "hypermasculinity," which she states "is also a defining feature of the corporate domain—with its risk takers, rogue traders, reckless speculators, and manipulative financiers" (2011, 37). This is similar to Lourdes Benería's criticism of "Davos Man," the neoliberal financier (placed in philosophical and racial opposition to the Asian financier), who has brought on so many global financial crises through greed (1999).

In this vein of feminist critique, deliberately different means of economic subsistence, transaction, and networking can be seen as an embodied feminist resistance/critique of the larger hypermasculinity of the corporate capitalist economy. What forms of economy resist hypermasculinity? Is there such a thing as a "feminine" economy—as opposed to an economy that runs on the unpaid labor of women (Russ 1998)? How do land-women resist integration into this capitalist hypermasculine machine? Currently, capitalism is theorized as having "no outside," as a form of "systemic embodiment" (Gibson-Graham 2006, xxiii–xxiv). They write, "where we might stand to combat capitalism or to construct something 'noncapitalist' is not at all clear" in this context. However, forms of resistance are common.

In the introduction to *The Woman-Centered Economy*, Loraine Edwalds writes, "the woman-centered economy is rooted in an emotional investment in women that cannot readily be paid for with cash." Like the anthropological understanding of economy, this "woman-centered economy" takes into account "women creating and being part of organizations that give definition to our community and culture," and "women changing the way things are done in the mainstream in order to benefit other women" (1995, 2). Is lesbian-ness a challenge to a masculinist economy (as Marilyn Waring suggests) because we have removed ourselves from economic reproduction/reproduction economics (1988, 206), and if so, how is a woman-centered economy that includes women's land and lesbian land different? Karen Williams sarcastically points out that "part of the unspoken vow that we took when we became lesbians was the vow of poverty" and suggests that lesbians should be unashamed of having money but should support the women's community by spending their money at lesbian events and bookstores (1995, 179). In contrast, Genevieve Vaughn, writing about the community center Stonehaven, opines that "women's nurturing is free gift-giving and does not require an equivalent repayment" (1995, 293). Both of these approaches to "woman-centered" economy suggest inversions of the capitalist ethos.

Williams's humorous jab about the "lesbian vow of poverty" references both how women are disadvantaged economically and also how poverty/money issues are then internalized as a moral force. Karen Rudolph, writing about fund-raising, suggests that "people with money are seen as smart, hardworking, and successful. People without money are seen as dumb and lazy. As feminists we know that isn't correct, so some of us just turn that proposition on its head." In short, these writers acknowledge the emotional aspect of economic choices and constraint: "Underneath our politics we have layers of emotions about money." Yet, as she then goes on to point out, "our fundraising cannot be absolutely politically pure because we live in a capitalist society" (1995, 95, 97). Capitalism and money influence these non-monetary or anti-monetary systems by literally surrounding them. The doxa of money and class can be inverted, but it cannot be erased. This suspicion of capitalist "success" is a strong thread in land culture, and helps explain why gifting and alternative economies are so favored. Yet money is not entirely dispensed with.

The Spirit of the Gift: Generalized Reciprocity and the Ethos of Giving

Gifts are important and meaningful objects/acts. However, on women's land there are different types and forms of gifting, regulated not only by what is being given and to whom (as it is in U.S. matrix cultures), but also by a larger unspoken ethos of how gifting replaces other economic forms of exchange.

Among land-women, although varieties of gifting similar to the matrix culture appear (such as birthday gifts, which are formally "no strings attached"), there are other forms as well. Most obvious to the observer, because largely absent in matrix cultures, is the gift as replacement for other economic exchange. While donations of labor, money, and other goods are certainly common in the United States, such transactions are usually differentiated from "normal" transactions, either through the intervention of a charitable organization or through a sense that "donating" is not an *economic* exchange. My favorite example of the gift-as-economy on women's land is woman-built housing. "Woman-built housing" often signifies not only a type of "gender accomplishment," but an enormous defiance of capitalist forms, for these houses are usually built not only with women's labor, but with gift labor. These houses are common on women's lands: while materials must be scavenged or purchased and land itself must often also be purchased (as I will discuss later in this chapter), other land-women will often gift their labor to help build homes. For example, in *Country Lesbians,* "the hexagon" is described as "built in 3 months by 32 women," and was initially lived in by Nelly (Sue et al. 1976, 152). Such gifts of labor, moreover, are not transactional in a strict sense: the women who will live in the house may not be seen as "owing" the laboring women themselves a reciprocal gift. Instead, those who have received the gift of labor may owe the larger community.

Women's lands operate on a different economic ethos, where the very idea of community can also mean a certain open flow of goods and services that is different from the capitalist system. There is a great deal of visiting from one women's land to another, women may move from one land to another,[1] and various communities keep in touch, creating a constant flow between them. This flow consists not only of people and news, but also of goods and services. Within the women's community this flow is best described as "generalized reciprocity" (also sometimes called "communal sharing") in the classic anthropological sense. As will be explored below, however, the ways in which giving is structured and the expectations of individuals and different communities are complex and differ.

Generalized reciprocity also extends to money, which tends to be both a scarcer resource and one that is universally useful. Fundraisers and donations in order to sustain institutions, lands, or individual community members are common features of the larger community. Such fundraisers are particular features of the email listservs, often focusing on helping individual women with healthcare expenses.

Among anthropologists, "generalized reciprocity" is used to refer to situations where goods are distributed as equally as possible without expectation of either immediate or delayed return from the giftee to the gifter. Things are expected to "even out" over the long run, rather than everyone keeping track of what they have contributed and what they have received from everyone else. The classic example of such a society is the Dobe Ju/'hoansi in the foraging era. Richard Lee repeats Marshall Sahlins's claim that the same economic system has been observed in all known foraging societies (Lee 1979, 118). Although I have used the term to refer to the ethos of giving among women in women's-land societies, I am referring to the *ethos*, rather than to all individual practices. As among the Dobe Ju/'hoansi—not to mention every other case of generalized reciprocity that I am personally aware of—individual women are usually aware of what they have given and to whom, and of who tends to do more work in the community and who does not. Although no one is formally "keeping track" of who gives what, everyone is pretty much aware of who tends to be more on the giving end, and who on the receiving end. Furthermore, the ethos of generalized reciprocity does not preclude transactions of balanced reciprocity.

Balanced reciprocity—giving a good or a service in the expectation of an immediate or delayed return that may or may not be negotiated beforehand—is another important economic transaction. Examples of balanced reciprocity often include land transactions, in which women trade money or services (such as elder care) for access to or the right to stay on women's land. Land transactions, because of the importance of access to land, are usually (but not always) explicitly negotiated. However, there are more informal examples of balanced reciprocity, including "guesting": allowing women to stay at your home or land in the expectation that sometime in the future, if you need a place to say, those women will put you up.

"Guesting," however—a word I have coined to describe a phenomenon that is prevalent and recognizable, but not explicitly named—also partakes of the ethos of generalized reciprocity. Women are expected to provide houseroom or camping space to other women when possible even when there is little or no expectation that those *particular* women will be able to return the favor. Due to the ethos of guesting, any woman who is part of the larger network of community should be able to ask for houseroom. Women who do not have permanent space of their own cannot return this particular favor, and women who are helping to maintain large land-communities are far more likely to be called on to provide guesting than to ask the community for it. Nevertheless, the larger ethos holds that to turn down a request for a place to stay is rude.

This particular aspect of generalized reciprocity wound up having quite an impact on me and my wife after I was incorporated into the houseroom network of a few "traveling dykes" (a term used by women who like to travel from women's land to women's land). For several years, we would receive occasional phone calls from women who needed a local place to stay, and we agreed. Indeed, it would have been difficult not to agree, given how important such hospitality is considered to be.

This situation, however, caused me some personal difficulty around one particular visit, after which my wife informed me that this guest was no longer welcome at our house. We were already used to guests who were unsure of when they were arriving, who had particular dietary needs, or who were allergic to cats. However, my hospitality does have limits. One woman attempted to arrive a week early and was extremely persistent even after I pointed out that we were unable to cope with guests that weekend because my wife had just had a very traumatic dental surgery and was on heavy-duty pain medication. Later, during the actual visit, she saddled us with several boxes of books "because your house is so big, you'll have no trouble storing them!" and then kept asking us to attend long evening religious events and classes with her, even after we had politely declined several times because of our work schedule. She then phoned from the event, asking whether she could bring a friend she had met back with her because this friend did not have any other place to go; I had to decline this offer while the newfound friend listened to the conversation. The final incident happened during dinner when she made several racist remarks and then said that since she was going to be traveling abroad to India soon, would we look after her cats for her for a few months?

I then had to consider that while I wanted to give back to the community of land-women, perhaps I could do so through means other than providing houseroom. This illustrates one of the problems with generalized reciprocity: it is almost impossible to give "to a larger community." Your gifts or obligations are almost always claimed by particular people. This is also one of the ways in which race, class, and culture influence the gift economy: class affects ideas and ability to gift and receive gifts, and sometimes time and effort are "invisible" compared to more tangible gifts. It is also not difficult to imagine how race might affect the practice of "guesting." Would women of color be received as readily into the homes of white strangers? Would white strangers be as willing to ask for houseroom from them?

There is a strong ethos among land-women that one should "give back to the community," and this refers to generalized reciprocity. I call this an ethos rather than a belief because it remains largely a thing of action rather than discussion. In fact, while I observed many women behaving in a manner I would categorize as "generalized reciprocity," far more often women *discussed* balanced reciprocity—expecting a return, though sometimes far in the future, for certain gifts. The discussions I was a part of did not target specific women as owing these returns, although specific *categories* of women might be mentioned. For example, in several cases I witnessed discussions of aging on the land in which older women expressed the expectation that younger women "owed" them labor and time due to their own previous contributions to the community. Yet despite these discussions, women often gifted labor, time, knowledge, money, goods, space, and services without discussion of and apparently without expectation of return.

Materials that women gave away without expectation of return included goods such as tools and building supplies, food and items such as crafts for specific events, and especially services such as labor and skills. It is not unusual for women to travel from community to community, donating labor and teaching skills, and being supported—even though where the labor is donated and where they may stay may *not* be the same community. Thus the sense of generalized reciprocity is very strong indeed, and although individual women often complain of not receiving as much from the larger community network as they give, the *ethos* of giving continues. This ethos is one of the ways in which a larger community of women's lands is bound together.

This flow creates what I call the gift economy among women's communities. These gifts uphold the ideals of collectivism and egalitarianism, and at the same time represent ways in which individual women connect with one another. One particularly moving example was located at Mountainview. Two women were showing me the house they had built themselves, with help from the community and from traveling women, and were pointing out features when I happened to admire the lovely doors. One of the women smiled and told me that Falcon had given them the doors. "She used to go for long walks in the city when she was living there," she explained, "and then come back with her truck if she saw anything on the sidewalk that she thought anyone could use. They're from a Victorian house that was being torn down, and she got them just for us, since she knew we were building a house." The connection between the salvaged doors and the memory of their friend was tangible. Among land-women, gifts are important because of how they create a connection to the person who gave them.

Marcel Mauss, in his classic monograph, asks, "What rule of legality and self-interest ... compels the gift that has been received to be obligatorily reciprocated? What power resides in the object given that causes its recipient to pay it back?" (1990, 3). The form of this question has clearly been shaped by capitalism—the only form of economy in which power adheres to the person who acquires more rather than to the person who gives more. Objects do not possess power as such, not in women's-land cultures and not in their matrix cultures, either. Objects, however, are invested with *meaning*: whether it is the purely capitalist meaning of their purchase value or more cultural and personal meanings attached to the object due to the object's history or symbolic value. Among land-women, the *history* of objects— particularly the history of who has owned or given them—lends them significance and meaning far beyond their use value or purchase value.

In a certain sense, therefore, some of these objects are "inalienable possessions" as Annette Weiner explains; they remain identified with the giver (1992, 46). Yet, like the Ju/'hoansi, who "don't trade with things, we trade with people!" (Lee 2003, 119), it is the connection with the person that is important. Neither culture considers the items they are trading to be as important as the relationships created and maintained by the trade or gift network. Among land-women, the act of remembering the person in the gift is one of connection. Even gift labor is remembered as coming from particular women—at a land in Ohio, for example, I was informed by a small sign who had built an outhouse I was using, and in New Mexico, women were eager to inform me who had built the house we were using as a communal kitchen. Connections are clearly what is important: the object, building, or act is remembered as the gift of a particular woman and takes its value from that connection and the act of remembrance.

This is not to say that the ability to gift others might not extend a woman's power and influence, but that influence is restricted by the ethos of generalized reciprocity, which limits the obligations of other women in return. The ethos of generalized reciprocity is part of a collective of values, which may include such items as recognizing the value of a woman in the community as theoretically independent of her ability to contribute economically, and disvaluing paid/capitalist notions of "work" altogether. Lillian, a traveling dyke, stated flatly that she did not believe in the "job" system. She herself did not have a job in the capitalist sense.

Another prominent feature of the gift economy is the dignity of the woman or women who receive the gift. The right to dignity also limits the obligations of the receiver. Although the recipients of any gift have this right to dignity under the ethos of generalized reciprocity, there are still ways in which individual women may forget this, and from cultural training in the matrix culture, expect something back: gratitude, acknowledgment, cultural recognition as a "good" person, or even economic or social obligation on the part of the recipient. Yet the ethos of giving still operates, and women who are recipients of economic donations, whether in money, goods, a place to stay, consumables, labor, or other such items, thus have a space to assert their own dignity.

There is also a certain amount of creative play between what is given in generalized reciprocity and what is given in delayed reciprocity; among land-women, there is often no clear-cut divide between when a gift expects a return and when it does not. Although in some cases, fund-raising for example, it is clear that no return can possibly be expected, in others, such as house-raising or work donation, it is less clear. Perhaps women will be able to return the favor in the future. Perhaps not. But the general ethos of giving makes this a much less potent issue, and becomes a great equalizing force.

Beyond Equality: Or, How the Giving Tree Got Its Roots

Although the ethos of generalized reciprocity limits the power and status that can accrue to any particular woman through the act of giving, such acts do extend a woman's influence. The one who provides—whether it be money, goods, time, organizational force, or land (especially the latter)—is able to demonstrate her status in the community and acquire a certain form of social power. However, that social power is limited, both by the ways in which reciprocity is limited and by how land-women regard such social power.

Because acts of giving are by their very nature unequal, many land-women regard them with some distrust, while at the same time lauding those who unselfishly give of themselves for the greater good of the community. It is possible to have more than one narrative, ethos, and feeling about the act of giving, and one of these narratives suspects that giving is a road to power. As Jo Freeman writes in "The Tyranny of Structurelessness" (1970), "A 'laissez faire' group is about as realistic as a 'laissez faire' society; the idea becomes a smokescreen for the strong or the lucky to establish unquestioned hegemony over others." Gifting is one of the techniques that can be used to establish hegemony, especially when what is given (access to land, for instance) is vital and cannot be replicated. The status of the giver is a status of power: what is given can be taken away.

One excellent example of this is the now-defunct Michigan Womyn's Music Festival, in which the final word on access to the festival depended solely on the woman who owned the land where it was held, Lisa Vogel. The news that the festival was closing was posted on Facebook on April 21, 2015, a move that seemed to come as a surprise to most, although the post said, "We have known in our hearts for some years that the life cycle of the Festival was coming to a time of closure" (Vogel in Ring 2015). Discussion among my informants shifted quickly from the issue of the exclusion of trans women (and others, such as disabled women) to the fact that as the sole owner of the land, Vogel had the ability to shut down MichFest whenever she pleased, as well as to enforce other polices: her ownership prevailed. Her gift of the land for the previous festivals was appreciated, but my informants noted, perhaps with an eye to how this can apply to land-communities, that the money for the land had been raised communally, yet Vogel had wound up as the only owner on the deed. This provided her with enormous and largely unquestionable power over the festival—her gifts of time, land, and organization thus proved a form of power for her to shape the fate of the festival.

The power of the gifter, however, is limited by how those who receive the gift perceive and discuss the gift, reciprocity, and analysis of how gifting provides power within "structurelessness." It is also limited by a relationship that Joanna Russ (1985, 44) powerfully called the "Magic Momma/Trembling Sister" dyad, in which women are expected, due to doxic ideas about power and femininity, to never use their power or success for themselves. Russ writes:

> If you've been forbidden the use of your own power for your own self, you can give up your power or you can give up your self. If you're effective, you must be so for others but never for yourself (that would be 'selfish'). If you're allowed to feel and express needs, you must be powerless to do anything about them, and can only wait for someone else—a man, an institution, a strong woman—to do it for you.

This toxic situation causes rage and division between women who take on (or are forced into) the Magic Momma or Trembling Sister roles, and the disintegration of women's communities. Since these roles are dependent on hegemonic ideas about femininity, it is difficult to eliminate them entirely. Russ notes that "what makes the MM/TS scenario so stubborn is the hidden insistence that a woman cannot, must not, be allowed to use her power on her own behalf" (48–49).

That insistence is reinforced by cultural products ranging from the mainstream U.S. media to the very premise of gifting itself, since according to the tenets of capitalism—the system most of the residents of women's lands grew up in—gifting cannot accrue power (only receiving goods is associated with accruing power). Yet it clearly does; this is the heart of the conflict. The Trembling Sister can see the Magic Momma wielding power and influence, while the Magic Momma sees the labor and self-sacrifice involved, since her power and influence cannot be used for herself. As Russ points out, both these positions "are engaged in ritually sacrificing the possibility of a woman's being effective on her own behalf, not needy and ineffective, not effective and altruistic, but *effective for herself*" (54). This paradox is inherent to hegemonic Western/U.S. models of femininity, and can only be escaped when we are willing to give up the premise that women are supposed to exist for others alone. Although Russ does not explicitly reference race in this essay, these roles—particularly the Magic Momma, who can in certain lights look suspiciously like a Strong Black Woman—inflect variously raced notions of femininity.

Thus, adopted doxic ideas about femininity affect how effectively gifting can be used as a means to extend one's influence and power, as is commonly done in noncapitalist cultures. Issues of power remain around obligation, especially where land and money are concerned. Because of the nature of the gift, and particularly gifts of money and access to land, gifting is sometimes seen simultaneously as required (women should be effective for others/the community) and also a means to power (to help shape the hegemony of the community). Thus in Shel Silverstein's *The Giving Tree* (2002) the Magic Momma/Trembling Sister dyad reappears, with the Magic Momma (the Tree) depicted as willing to give up her entire life for another (the Boy), but also enabling and shaping the life of that dependent other. The figures in this dyad are linked by capillary power: if the Tree has the power to give, the Boy has the power to lean; the Tree suggests, the Boy executes; they are unable to escape one another. In the context of women's communities, the Boy becomes the Trembling Sister, while the Magic Mommas distribute those demands for giving into the network of the Tree. I have chosen to borrow the image of the Giving Tree precisely because of its disturbing and eventually unsustainable nature. In the book, the Tree's resources are eventually exhausted—this model of giving, while it does not fall upon a single person as heavily as the Magic Momma/Trembling Sister dyad, is in the end unsustainable.

Money is a potent force in a capitalist culture, and it is one of the ways by which the Giving Tree is distributed, so that no one woman need feel the vampiric pull of being a Magic Momma/Giving Tree too much. Indeed, the nature of the Giving Tree is the fact that it *is* distributed, in order to prevent the power/drain of the Giving Tree from accruing too much to any one woman. Over time, everyone within the community is expected to contribute something, to form one of the little rootlets of the Giving Tree. At the same time, individual interactions—specific times when one woman contributes time, labor, land access, or money, or another woman needs these—demonstrate the same uneven distribution of power, and can cause the same angry reactions that Joanna Russ called out as "trashing" in her essay (1985, 47), as well as the uncomfortable realization that money and class create inequalities. Unequal access to money and class are issues that women of color have noted especially, and form one of the ways in which unaddressed racism helps shape the current form of women's communities. In the end, capitalism, while it provides a method for distributing the responsibilities of the Giving Tree, is also the reason the Giving Tree is disturbing and unsustainable. Capitalist understandings of gift dynamics obscure emotional responsibilities, and encourages the drain which in the end reduces the Tree to a stump.

Capitalism Has You Surrounded: Issues of Money and Class

Yet money is not something that women and women's communities can do without. Tracy, one of Gagehabib and Summerhawk's interviewees, noted keenly, "But when we are in this society, we are in this society, even if you drop out. The preference for barter here is the dollar. You cannot pay your taxes with tomatoes or goodwill or anything else that has to be done" (2000, 77).

Tracy's analysis is particularly sharp. The necessarily close interaction between the larger money-based matrix culture and the smaller women's communities is the source of a great deal of friction. Money *cannot* become a disused or even a trivial medium of exchange—as Tracy points out, one still needs to pay taxes. All of the women come from not only a money-based society, but a capitalist one—a society where the value of things is measured in money, and which makes certain bone-deep assumptions about possession, value, labor, and class. In addition, women do not have equal access to those tangible and intangible resources. Although women's lands are structured to try to throw off these assumptions, it is exceedingly difficult to achieve even a semblance of equality in such a completely unequal matrix culture. Lastly, issues of access to land, attitudes towards women who are financially able and those who have less, and the use of public assistance all contribute to a complex understanding of class issues among women who often ambitiously wish to eradicate class from their own communities.

Joyce Cheney, in her collective book on lesbian lands, interviews some of the women of ARF, a women's land located in the American Southwest, about the class issues they dealt with. In this interview, Rose describes how the "gypsy women" (women traveling together from women's land to women's land), arrived at ARF and a number of conflicts ensued. "There were some women who felt that we were elitist, capitalist, racist, classist snobs, taking our privilege with our private land; they didn't respect private land. This was women's space, it was safe space to get off the road, and they were going to live here, period" (1985: 15). Pelican Lee, one of the traveling women, responds, "We expected ARF to be open to us, but the five women who lived there felt invaded by the fifteen or so of us who arrived over a two-month period" (163).

Women of different classes clashed over such points, but further issues arose from different approaches to the *problem* of class. Lee's group, the nomadic Nozama Tribe, approached the problem of class by rejecting materialism—they moved from place to place camping on land that technically belonged to others—while other women founded women's lands that provided wilderness and home space to all women (Lee 1985). Lee points out that the differences on this level not only obfuscated issues but also caused women to forget their "basic unity with each other against much larger forces" (162). Class can be a divisive force not only in and of itself but also politically and philosophically.

Despite the general uneasiness of U.S. matrix cultures in discussing class, issues of class and money are discussed openly and often among land-women. My informants have universally been willing to discuss their monetary arrangements and difficulties and their financial relationship with the various lands they live on.

Women's lands are organized in several basic ways. They can be owned by an individual woman or a couple of individual women, who then agree to make the land available to other women; they can be owned by many women in common under an incorporation; or the land can be held under a trust agreement. Land trusts seem to be currently gaining in popularity. Under a trust agreement, the land is "owned" by the trust itself and managed by a board and women sign agreements or "leases" to be allowed to live on the land. The problem with all situations in which land is held in common is that it is not possible for individual women to get mortgages on the land in order to raise funds to purchase building materials or labor. Because of the differing requirements of land trusts and capitalist banks, banks refuse to loan to women living on land trusts, meaning that the labor, building materials, and homes on women's lands must be funded by other means. If the land itself is not alienable, the bank will not allow a mortgage on it—it could not foreclose on the land should the loan be defaulted on.

Money is therefore an important issue. Even a one-room house without running water that utilizes a lot of scavenged materials will probably require some materials to be purchased. Women's-land housing is created under constraints that housing in the matrix United States is not, and this impacts not only the physical lives of women living on land, but also the way women think about living on land. For example, one woman referenced in the Dykelands slide show[2] insisted on having a house "with an indoor bathroom and a paved road," by which insistence we can infer that these things are not necessarily standard, and see that not everyone is willing or able to adapt to living without them.

Lillian, a traveling dyke, noted that problems arise due to money on women's lands she has visited:

> A lot of the conflict that women have seems to be around money, too. You know, who's contributing more, and who owns what. And so, a lot of the discussions are around money, and a lot of the women's land, like [land name] has the hammock [business] going on, and that's become like—you know it used to be a farm, but now the community has become about the hammock business, you know? Like if the land has a certain cottage industry or something going, the community tends to be about that, and it becomes more like a business, I think.

Other problems can arise from values associated with women's land itself. One of Gagehabib and Summerhawk's informants, Maria, noted that her class within the community was actually lower because of her lack of ownership of land, despite her degree[3] and the fact that she was working to support herself (not all women on the land were monetary contributors):

> Even though I have a Master's degree in social work, nobody took my word or my professional advice. I was contradicted often with totally off the wall [comments]. Somebody with more money and more land.... If you had land, whether you had a lot of money or not, if you have land you have more credibility. They would say incredibly off the wall things about social services and things that I know about. They would have credibility and I would not. It was like I was completely discounted as a human being and my knowledge was not only not heard but it was suspect.
>
> Q: You think it was about the money thing?
>
> A: Yeah, and it was because I didn't own land. Because I chose to live the lifestyle I was living in a rural community, I was caught. I couldn't earn what I could normally earn in that profession as a lesbian on land. There was prejudice in both camps. I wasn't totally accepted either way. (2000, 77)

In this case, even more important than access to money is access to land itself, which is only then mediated by one's standing in the mainstream matrix culture. Land is the primary status symbol, which is hardly surprising, since it is the very thing that makes these communities possible. Yet at the same time access to it is generally mediated through money.

Critics of separatism have often focused on racism and classism as important issues that are inadequately addressed by separatists. Cathy McCandless notes that "social separatism" is different from economic separatism, and devalues that first as "the political equivalent of sulking." However, she also notes that "3rd World and working class" separatists tend to be involved in anti-capitalist struggles, and that such struggles are vitally important. These struggles are important because without them, we remain unaware that "under this capitalist system we live in, *someone's* going to end up doing the shitwork for white high-class men, and if you merely withdraw and refuse to do it without doing anything to change the system itself, you just leave that much more shitwork for others, generally women who are poorer and more exploited than you" (1980, 108–9). McCandless analyzes the problem of separatism in monetary terms: the wealthier a woman was, the more "separatist" (i.e. without social contact with men or heterosexual women) she could afford to be. "The cost of that barrier was high, and they weren't the ones who had to foot the bill. The price was paid by the community as a whole, for the barrier these women had so systematically constructed serves as often as not to sever women from other women and even divided Lesbians up into castes, each more-separatist-than-thou (and therefore holier)" (111).

This analysis of separatism as a social achievement and way to divide the lesbian community into "castes" has, however, become outdated. Separatism is far too unpopular a creed in the present day; in fact this analysis may seem comical to some of my readers. However, historically the idea of having women-only and lesbian-only space was exciting for a great many women. The resulting stratification is problematic and disappointing, although perhaps not surprising. McCandless blames wealthy white women not only for divisions within the community, but also for the bad name of separatism itself:

> At the very least the women were hoarding wealth that wasn't theirs. Moreover, in their attempts to hold onto control of it, they were doing the work of the white supremacist capitalist patriarchy itself, and that's about as unseparatist as you can get. Nevertheless, many of these relatively wealthy white women claimed to be true practicing Lesbian separatists, the vanguard of the feminist revolution. It was they, I believe, who gave separatism a bad name throughout the progressive political community. (111)

McCandless suggests that the anti-capitalist side of separatism must be deliberately sought, rather than relying on social separatism. Thus, separatism must engage with larger struggles.

In *Country Lesbians,* Dian chronicles how difficult it was for her to put the deed for the land in the name of all the women who lived there: "I felt that if i put their names on the deed i would be letting go of a lot of money. How could i do such a thing? Such behavior was contrary to my whole life's upbringing. And, especially, how could I share land-money with women who did not (i believed) love me?" Dian provided the money to purchase the land for WomanShare, which meant that the initial deed was in her name; later, after hearing about collective land and women who shared large sums of money throughout the lesbian community, she slowly began to see the matter of "ownership" in a different light (Sue et al. 1976, 72–73). At the end of her essay, she writes, "i realize now that i couldn't live here and work on the land and believe the things i believed about cooperation and collectivity and continue to privately own the land. It was a living contradiction. i had to unite my beliefs and my actions" (73). This is an excellent illustration of the emotional conflicts that arise between how capitalism becomes doxa in one's upbringing and learning different ways of relating to money and land.

OWL Farm is described as "the first experiment of its kind," a nonprofit corporation run by open women's meetings where all the women had equal say. It was a place where, in principle, any woman could live and where all the women had equal control over how it was run. "But structurelessness doesn't work, as was noted in the early feminist classic, *The Tyranny of Structurelessness* [Freeman, 1970]. At OWL Farm, women came up the road with all the dysfunctions, pain, and neediness America's mainstream society helps create" (Gagehabib and Summerhawk 2000, 123–24). Although OWL Farm went through many changes before finally becoming a closed land trust in 1999, it provided open women's land for many years. Unfortunately, race and class issues still arise on open women's land; it is not a cure-all despite its radical form.

The question of how to deal with money equitably and/or collectively and how to create a culture that provides equal access out of a world that is based on inequality is profoundly difficult. These difficulties demonstrate that some of the most profoundly unexamined foundations of the United States matrix cultures are *predicated* on unequal access to goods and resources. This makes it extremely hard to create any community that attempts to provide equal access to goods and services, because it must compete with the outside society on two levels. First, on the level of the unconscious assumptions of everyone's doxa, those ideas that have been shaped by the cultures they have grown up in. Second, on the level of their interactions with the matrix society, which is larger and exerts not only obvious pressures in the form of such things as trade, taxes, media, etc., but less obvious pressures in the form of social expectations. Yet there are many ways in which women's land actively works against those expectations.

For example, there is Arco Iris, a land for womyn of colors where the land itself was donated by a larger, white-dominated women's land. Paz notes, "The rich white womyn, who originally bought the land, was struggled with and convinced after much bitterness and tension to deed the most remote part of the land to womyn of colour" (1980, 78). Although she recounts this as a difficult struggle, it is significant in that it *happened*. In many forms of U.S. culture, it would be unthinkable to ask a private person to deed their land to "people of color" simply because it is the right thing to do. In the network of women's community culture, this request was both understandable and granted. The *awareness* that this is a way to try to create a form of equity is there. Bitterness and misunderstanding might arise—from the women of color *having* to ask; from the woman who owned the land feeling that it belongs to her; from guilt feelings over having when other people do not; from seeing other people have when you do not; from seeing inequality when you are committed to a culture of equality. But the gift happened; changes happened.

It Owns Us: Economics, Land, and What One Cannot Possess

The process by which Arco Iris was deeded to womyn of colors by the Sassafras collective and the land's owner is recounted by Maria, an Apache-Aztec Native American woman. This tale intertwines differing ideas about land, capitalism, class, and right action.

> All of the womyn except one, the womyn who had bought the land originally, and is a million/heiress, agreed to sign the land over in the first councils that we had together as groups. She would always maintain that she did not want to give up the land; she did not want to divide the land. Finally, after several councils, several meetings broken, several agreements broken that they had made with me, I have a final council with them and I called on all the forces to be with me. All the spirits came and circled with us down at the river. At that time, the one womyn said that she would sign the deed, finally, but the whole time I could see in her eyes that she was resisting, but her will had been overcome by a greater spirit because the Great Spirit was able to do these things, and she was not able to resist any longer. (Mujeres de Arco Iris 1985, 35)

Maria's story credits spiritual forces—spiritual force that comes from *the land itself*—with winning her battle. She envisions it as a contest between spiritual and material, where "spiritual" encompasses and promotes social awareness, equality, and racial justice, while the "material" stems from capitalist ideals. Similarly, Águila (Maria Christina Morales, aka Sun Hawk; the same narrator under a later name) recounts that she had a vision that the "land was to be a sanctuary, a safe space, for women and children of color" (2015, 46). Here we see one woman swaying the group with her spiritual/social will and the other holding fast with ingrained beliefs about ownership of land, but then yielding. The deed was written up, but Maria says, "as I looked over the deed, I realized that it was very complicated and I felt uneasy about being rushed into signing it, so I asked her to leave the deed with me for a while so I could read it more thoroughly and understand it. She knew that I only had an eighth grade education" (Mujeres de Arco Iris 1985, 36). This again brings up the issue of class.

> To her, her heritage had taught her that land was money. To me, land is our survival, and our future. I knew that I had to be very careful with this womyn because she was a very shrewd businesswomyn. Finally, she agreed to leave the deed with me for a few hours. I then asked a couple of friends that were there at the house with me to help me read over the deed thoroughly. We all found, in the end, that the deed that she had drawn up was ultimately a fake deed because in the last statement in the deed it stated that if this land were ever to be sold it would revert to the original owner. We called up an attorney and asked what that meant, and she said that, in court, it wouldn't hold up as being our land. The womyn came back to the house to pick up the deed and when she came in I was very upset and angry. I gave the deed back to her and told her that I didn't want that deed; I didn't want another broken treaty; I didn't want her phony words and her phony tears and her phony apologies; we were tired of hearing all these lies and we would take care of drawing up the deed ourselves.

Maria gives a very good cultural analysis in the beginning of this passage—land-as-money versus land-as-survival, which echoes the conflict between the capitalist ownership/possession of land and the women's culture inalienability of land. Yet to both women and from both cultural perspectives, land is a primary, important resource. Maria's language casts "the phony deed" in the light of treachery to the Native peoples of this continent—"another broken treaty." The use of this term brings up the image of hundreds of years of oppression of Native peoples, giving Maria a greater moral weight. It also refers to how *all* these lands were Native once, thus invoking the powerful idea that what the other woman is doing is returning stolen land back to Maria and other women of color, returning something that is already rightfully theirs. Maria constructs her argument powerfully. "The original owner was the very last person to sign the deed. I felt the Great Spirit move her hand to sign her name. The Great Spirit has a way of having Her will be done, and Her will was done. Ho!" (36). In this case, the ethos of non-ownership of land (Arco Iris is a land trust), support of other women, and the moral justice of the arguments of the women of color prevailed over the capitalist construction of land as an ownable object of value.

At a later period (2007) I spoke to Arcadia, one of the white women who had been part of Sassafras. This interview was informal and not recorded; when I asked about this incident, Arcadia stressed, according to my memory, two things: the first was that she was willing to give them the *use* of the land, and the second was that while she felt supportive of women of color land, she did not feel that many women of color were interested. By stressing that she was willing to give them the *use* of the land, there was an echo here of wanting to retain capitalist possession and ownership of it. She stated that Arco Iris was closed, and that she had not had other requests from Native women of color to "give back the land." At the time she spoke to me, Arcadia was living at a completely different women's land (called here Lilith's Land). I remember that she said that she would support Native women's lands, if there were any; but she spoke as though such projects were the responsibility of women of color.

However, Arco Iris is not actually "closed." As reported by Águila, Arco Iris incorporated in 1984 into a nonprofit "survival camp" for women and children of color, gained 501(c)(3) status in 1994, and in 2000, they asked for and received the land that had housed Sassafras, which had been abandoned. Arco Iris, now divided into Arco Iris as a whole and a living area called Rancho Arco Iris, is still thriving (Águila 2015, 49–50). Águila writes, "I will never forget that this sacred land was returned to the hands of poor, indigenous, two-spirit women. It was placed in our trust, so that we could have sovereignty and autonomy, so that we could reclaim within ourselves our sacredness, our purpose, and our strength" (50). Currently, Águila and her son live on Arco Iris, running men's and women's lodges, living off the grid, and acting as land stewards (51–52).

This struggle illuminates the ways in which the doxa of the matrix society regarding class and race still continues to influence women's lands. However, within women's-land culture, that doxa is often orthodoxy—it can be spoken of, put into words, and thus struggled with and resisted. The significance of women of color challenging the capitalist and class dictates of who owns/has rights to the land of Arco Iris is great: this undermines the class, capitalist, and race conceptions of ownership, control of space, and power that surround us in the U.S. matrix society. The struggle brought those ideas out into the open and made them visible. In this case, the values of women's-land culture seem to have triumphed over those of the matrix United States. The gift economy, the ethos of egalitarianism, the struggle against white supremacy, right-doing, and the importance and inalienability of land to those who live on/care for it are all illustrated in this interaction. It also shows how difficult the struggle against doxa is, with capitalist white supremacist ideals undermining even the best-intentioned women.

As can be seen here, the gift economy is complex: it defies capitalism but is also shaped by it. It creates alternative structures and egalitarian modes of transaction but also provides a means for particular women to accrue power or enforce their own ideas. Lastly, it supports the struggle of minorities by undermining ideas about ownership yet also reinforces hegemonic hierarchies by reproducing class, gender, and racial power relations from matrix United States cultures. Thus, the gift economy both represents a powerful tool for undermining one of the primary movers of U.S. matrix culture—capitalism—but is also shaped by that mover. This is an excellent example of Foucault's notion of resistance: forms of resistance that are shaped by the very thing they are resisting against. "Where there is power, there is resistance, and yet, or rather consequently, this resistance to power is never in a position of exteriority in relation to power" (Foucault 1990, 95). Yet this does not mean that resistance itself is constrained within the larger system or subsumed by it—rather, that resistance is not singular, but instead happens at many points and is part of larger, more complex ways in which systems are changed. Foucault writes about the nature of "power relationships":

> Their existence depends on the multiplicity of points of resistance: these play the role of adversary, target, support, or handle in power relations. . . . Hence there is no single locus of great Refusal, no soul of revolt, source of all rebellions, or pure law of the revolutionary. Instead there is a plurality of resistances, each of them a special case: that are spontaneous, savage, solitary, concerned, rampant, or violent; still others that are quick to compromise, interested, or sacrificial; by definition, they can only resist within the field of power relations. (95–96)

Individual acts of noncapitalist economy—gifting, delayed reciprocity, generalized reciprocity—all act as various points of resistance or friction to the larger capitalist ethos of the United States. These points of resistance are necessary, but they are also not subsumed into the system—"this does not mean that they are only a reaction or rebound, forming with respect to the basic domination of an underside that is in the end always passive, always doomed to perpetual defeat" (96). These points of resistance in Foucault's "dense web" reverberate through the web itself. These "points of resistance" do not only apply to economic modes of thinking, but to many other aspects of culture that are resisted or challenged in women's-land spaces.

I do not think that we live inside a seamless system, and neither, I believe, do most land-women. Each way the gift economy resists capitalism helps weaken, challenge, or shift the overall system. But more than that, the gift economy is itself a webwork of relationships, memories, herstory, and *power*. As Russ reminds us, "'Successful' feminists aren't immune to the terror of power; all the women I know feel it. We take the risk anyway. That's the only secret" (1985, 54). By resisting that terror, women who participate in this subversive economy both resist the doxa of capitalism and the doxa that women are never allowed to be effective for themselves. The gift economy, when it operates to accrue power to the gifter—or to the giftee, as in the example from Arco Iris—is *also* subversive; subversive of hegemonic ideas about femininity and proper ways of behaving as a woman (even a feminist woman).

· CHAPTER 5 ·

The Mountain Is She

Gender as Landscape, Landscape as Gender

The tomatoes grow faster and the beans.
You are learning to live in circles
as well as straight lines.

—Marge Piercy, "Digging In"

ONE OF MY INTERVIEWEES TOLD ME a story about living on a remote mountaintop somewhere in the rural United States with a group of other women. They were camping on the land while looking for a place to settle more permanently. On the other side of the mountain was a spiritual retreat center run by a guru.

One day, a group of the women went on a long walk, and they encountered some of the people who were staying at the spiritual retreat. There were mutual greetings and conversation, and finally one of the retreat center attendees asked the women, "But who is your teacher?"

There was a momentary baffled silence, and then the woman said, "You're standing on Her."

What difference does it make if a mountain is She rather than It? On women's land, it makes a profound difference; these are not simply spaces *for* women, they are female-gendered spaces. This particular cultural gesture, making a connection from the body to the land through gender, is an important symbol for many of the inhabitants of women's lands. Through this gesture, the feminine becomes the default, the unmarked, and the world.

Women's lands, literal and embodied localities where the environment itself is gendered and shaped, form the physical backbone of the culture my informants create. They are also used in creating community, which operates as a more metaphysical or conceptual "space" in which individual women move. Throughout this process, ideas about gender help create cultural difference, and language is how ideas about gender are both conceptualized and applied.

Women's lands are unique in their production of a gendered difference that goes beyond the creation of space "for women" to the creation of literally female space. While there are other spaces within the United States that are gender divided—perhaps most obviously bathrooms, recalling Garber's analysis of Lacan's "urinary segregation" (1992, 13–15)—the space *itself* is not seen as masculine or feminine. There are also some spaces—fiber arts shops, for example—considered "feminine" in their atmosphere. Yet we do not tend, in the matrix culture, to declare that space has gender in and of itself. But women's land is not only land for women, but also gendered female in and of itself—the landscape itself, the features, flora, and even wildlife may all be considered female by its inhabitants. This creates a different conception of both gender and space.

This concept of the land as female is related to some early types of ecofeminism, to the land as spiritually important and a space for home, and to wilderness. This connects historically to images of land during the land-grab era of the United States, which persist to the colonized present. In this present, ideas of wilderness and the ecofriendly use of land continue to be connected with white bodies rather than with bodies of color (Finney 2014), which are either excluded or seen as past historical adjuncts or ghosts residing on the land itself (Bergland 2000). Thus there is also a racial component to the gendering of space.

In such spaces, land-women create a sense of intimacy through the shifting boundary of the public/private. This both blurs the domestic/public distinction—indeed, we might be hard put to it to decide whether women's lands were domestic or public spaces—and queers space as it is used in ways outside the heteronormative household. Women's land spaces make use of a "fractal" (Gal 2002) public/private divide, along which community members move over time as they shift from "strangers" to "chosen family." That is, privacy in women's lands is often determined solely by present intimacy between those who inhabit them, not, as one might imagine, by gatekeeping or preventing those who are less intimate from entering certain spaces.

Land-women also create a sense of emotional rooting and home through connections to the landscape, creating a "sense of home" and bringing us full circle to the inclusion of the land itself in the concept of gender. The gendering of landscape also personifies and humanizes the landscape, making it an emotional player in this complex dance of relationships among women.

Mountain, City, Stone, and Stream: The Gender of Place and the Place of Gender

Throughout my talks with land-women "the land" loomed large in the conversation. My informants told me that women needed space to "go back to the land" and that women needed "access to the land." "Nearly all of our respondents agreed that the core of the community is women's land" (Gagehabib and Summerhawk 2000, 37, writing about the southern Oregon women's community). What was so important about *land*?

Land is viewed as a deeply important resource. Land-women take this importance as given; some women may touch on its spiritual importance, but more often the importance of land is simply not explained. The spiritual importance of land is manifest in wilderness; for example, women who follow a feminist-Goddess tradition explicitly revere the earth and worship outdoors when possible. The land itself is often seen in these contexts as female or feminine, and also as divine (Starhawk 1989, 91). However, other important functions of land are often not articulated, and women who do not follow this religious tradition still regard land as extremely important. May, one of my informants, said, "I just like the peacefulness of being out here in the woods."

The ideas of wilderness, unspoiled or virgin land, and nature itself have largely been gendered as feminine in U.S. matrix cultures, and this cannot be ignored when examining the relationship of women to land. Wilderness or "virgin" land—not tamed, civilized, farmed, or homesteaded—codes for the woman who is "untamed," unmarried, nonchildbearing, or not working within the bounds of patriarchy (Kolodny 1975). The colonial land-grab was, in the United States and elsewhere, often coded in these half-hidden sexual terms.[1] Indeed, Henry Nash Smith's book on the literary tropes of the American West takes advantage of this in its very title, *Virgin Land: The American West in Symbol and Myth* (1970). Smith notes the sexualized terms in Walt Whitman's poetry: "America, the mistress" (from his "A Broadway Pageant," 46). James Fenimore Cooper's romanticization of "forest freedom" in the Leatherstocking Tales (62) and Charles W. Webber's "themes of primitivism—the decadent impulse to go back to nature" (73) illustrate similar "myths." These "myths" guide not only our concept of the West and how it was colonized but also ideas about wilderness and human relationships with nature. Bonnie Zimmerman takes this parallel further in her analysis of lesbian fiction, suggesting that "at least partly because of the antiurban bias of the 'Woodstock generation' and the revision of traditional gay urbanism by contemporary lesbian feminists, lesbian fiction displays an ironic similarity to the dominant American literature of the nineteenth century with its pairs of men escaping civilization for the frontier" (1990, 137). This similarity is actually neither ironic nor coincidental—it is the product of a particular colonial history enmeshed with the idea of feminine wilderness.

That history of colonial settlement cannot be ignored when considering the project of "going [back] to the land," especially in a queer context. Mark Rifkin (2011) notes that settler colonialism focused on Native kinship, sexuality, and governance as alien and other in order to legitimate the state, so that heteronormativity "naturaliz[es] not only the privatized domestic space of the (white) marital household but also the domestic space of settler nationalism" (38). Queer critiques help foreground the political project of heteronormativity, but as Andrea Smith (2010) points out, queer studies is not immune to reifying colonialism, especially in its construction of time. Smith suggests that "the subjectless critique of queer theory can assist Native studies in critically interrogating how it can unwittingly re-create colonial hierarchies even within projects of decolonization" (63). Scott Morgensen goes on to argue that settler colonialism is "a key condition of modern sexuality on stolen land" and that "queer politics produces a *settler* homonationalism that will persist unless settler colonialism is challenged directly" (2011, 2). Morgensen, in his analysis of how indigenous and aboriginal nonheteronormative sexualities are appropriated, referred to, incorporated, and otherwise entangled with white queer sensibilities and politics, also notes that in the settler state, these relations "blur easy distinctions of 'colonial' from 'anticolonial'" (28).

The history of such settler colonialism informs the sensibility of relationships between women and land. My informants may be literal homesteaders, in that they build houses and plant gardens, but their relationship with the land is seldom expressed as one of mastering, taming, or owning. Instead, they speak of relationships, harmony, and the *value* of wilderness. These values, however, are framed in a history of colonialism which, in being made invisible, also makes the appropriation (settling) of colonized land invisible. Morgensen notes that "Radical Faeries apply back-to-the-land principles to a mobile practice that made retreat to rural space a conduit for urban and itinerant people to realize portable truths ... [and] as a means for non-Native gay men to liberate an Indigenous gay culture and integrate it into their everyday lives" (2011, 127). Similarly, women's land makes seemingly-universal values available to "all" women—space, nature, healing—and while I did not observe the same systemized utilization of Native culture on the lands I visited, American Paganism, which was definitely present, is not innocent in this regard.

Smith warns that "in the move to 'postidentity,' queer theory often reinstantiates a white supremacist, settler colonialism by appropriating colonized indigenous peoples as foils for the emergence of postcolonial, postmodern, diasporic, and queer subjects" (2010, 63), and this trend can partially be seen—where are the indigenous people in this story of mutual healing between women and the land? However, indigenous and aboriginal women are actively involved with this movement, as we will explore below, complicating this notion of indigenous people only as "foils." For example, Arco Iris was founded on the very notion that it was ethical to give land *back* to indigenous women. Morgensen also noted that Radical Faerie work had been adopted by some Native queer and Two-Spirit people as a vehicle for decolonization (2011, 130).

The language my informants use to speak of land includes privacy, loneliness, community, connection with wilderness, and refreshment of the soul: all themes associated with the frontier in nineteenth century (and later) American fiction. These are not new themes, but they are deployed in particular and gendered ways by my informants, who seek neither to conquer the wilderness nor to prove their own civilized nature, but instead to escape or repair the damage of a patriarchal civilization and an already-colonized world. Catriona Sandilands, in her ethnography working with land-women in Oregon, found similar sentiments:

> Certainly, separatists began their experiments in community with the sense that nature was not yet fully incorporated into patriarchy and that lesbians could thus create a new and more innocent world in this relatively new and more innocent space. But that is only one thread. It is important, for example, that none of the lands was a "wilderness" before the women arrived; in all cases, they understood themselves as taking over an already "damaged" landscape. (2002, 145–46)

The notion of "healing" from damage was also very prominent and important to my informants, who apply it not only to their lands (for example, seeing organic gardening not only as an end-unto-itself but also a way to "heal" the land from previous use of pesticides) but also to themselves. Access to lonely, wild, or becoming-wild land is seen as healthful to the spirit and the body. One land, Oaktrust, was located in Massachusetts specifically as a retreat for women who identified as disabled. The main resident (Acorn) was sensitive to chemicals and saw living in the wilderness as a way not only to prevent her illness from becoming debilitating, but also to heal herself physically from its effects. This healing effect was also cited by other informants, who saw living on women's land as an antidote to social and physical ills imposed by the matrix culture.

Queerness is often associated with urban space rather than rural space or wilderness (Riordan 1996, xi). However, this does not mean that queer people do not live outside the city. Indeed, "queer identity work done in places thin on privacy, reliant on familiarity, and shy on public venues for sustained claims to queer difference produce differently—not less—mediated or declarative queer pronunciations than urban LGBT communities" (31). Women's lands also produce differently mediated queer pronunciations, although their engagement with rurality is different from the experiences Michael Riordan describes for Kentucky queer youth living in small towns and on farms.

Space to be in or near wilderness is regarded by most of my informants as a deeply important psychological or social resource. One informant, Lillian, described this benefit, talking specifically about the need for wilderness: "But, so my interest has been largely about just being, living with nature, in a wild, natural way, as opposed to in, you know, this structured society." The resource of wilderness is seen as essential to a particular means of "natural" living contrasted to "structured society."

Space is significant to the formation of culture, both in its physical sense, as it interacts with the body and as the body interacts with and changes physical spaces, and in the metaphorical sense. David Harvey notes that "the figure of the city as a fulcrum of social disorder, moral breakdown, and unmitigated evil—from Babylon and Sodom and Gomorrah to Gotham—also has its place in the freight of metaphorical meanings that the word 'city' carried across our cultural universe" (2000, 157). Likewise, the figure of the garden or the wilderness takes on an opposing utopic garment. Utopia, as Harvey describes it, is a cityscape, claiming that "the figures of 'the city' and of 'Utopia' have long been intertwined" (156), yet for land-women this is palpably untrue. The use of space reveals clearly that the city is not the model for women's-lands communities. Wilderness is valued, along with space and privacy and a sense of retreat; conversely, communal use of resources, including wilderness, kitchen spaces, workshops, and in some cases sleeping spaces, reinforces a sense of community opposing the anonymity and fragmentation of the city. Ultimately, wilderness or garden is seen as female/feminine. Many of my informants call the land or land features by feminine pronouns, gendering the landscape.

The coding of land and women's space as gendered is part of how land-women create women's culture. This is what Ina Rosing calls "the gender of space," and "is the product of symbolization (*genderization*); no real persons, no biologies are implied" (2003, 191). Yet among the Andeans that Rosing investigates, there are many genders (she identifies ten), and the landscape that people interact with is gendered in both masculine/male ways and feminine/female ways. According to my informants, *every* place on women's land is female/feminine, whether it is indoors or out, high or low, watery or dry, public or private. Rosing notes that "in Western culture all talk about 'Women's space' is talk about gendered space, not gender of space" (205), but the space on women's land is both gendered, in that it is reserved to the use of women, and possesses gender in that it is considered feminine/female.

Women who inhabit women's communities, lesbian lands, and women's lands seldom spend their entire lives on one land. They are a highly mobile population, and often move from one community to another. Such movement illustrates the webwork of culture among women's communities, and also points to "a new awareness of the global social fact that, now more than perhaps ever before, people are chronically mobile and routinely displaced, inventing homes and homelands in the absence of territorial, national bases—not in situ but through memories of and claims on places they can or will no longer corporeally inhabit" (Malkki 2001, 52). Land-based memories and claims are an important part of identity formation for land-women, who not only track their own identity and history through such connections and claims, but also weave the herstory of the entire larger community through them. Yet the members of this population are "moving targets" (Malkki 2001, 53), who pass through the boundaries they themselves help create, who shift identity in different contexts, and who deliberately draw on the ideas of rooting, nostalgia, territory, community, and nature in inventing or creating these homelands and identities.

Land-women engage in a reversal of how land can be defined as the "'people of a country,' as in 'the land rose in rebellion,'" (Malkki 2001, 55)—a type of metonymy where the land stands for the complex of territory, people, and culture as a whole. Malkki notes that "the territory itself is made more human." While the "territory is made more human" for land-women, it is done so in reverse—instead of "standing for" people, it is an individual in its own right. It is gendered female, and the relationship a woman has with a women's land as a space may be viewed as a separate thing from the relationship she has with the community inhabiting that space. Thus the land itself is seen as a key factor in emotional commitments to particular communities.

These relationships with land are very important. Photographs of land are often posted to the Landdykes email listserv. Pamela Stewart and Andrew Strathern note that "the sense of place and embeddedness within local, mythical, and ritual landscapes is important. These senses of place serve as pegs on which people hang memories, construct meanings from events, and establish ritual and religious areas of action" (2003, 3). Permanent religious circles have been built in Mountainview, along with long hiking trails intended to serve as ways for the women of that community to commune with the land. In addition to houses, women build outdoor fireplaces, gathering grounds, and altars on women's lands, supporting particular relationships with the community of that land, their own religious beliefs, and the mountain itself.

Lastly, the gender of that space is extended not only to land and to features of land, but to all the inhabitants of that space. If the land is gendered female, it seems to actively gender its inhabitants. For example, Hawk Madrone, in her autobiography about living on women's land, calls an unwelcome visitor to her henhouse "her": "I yelled at the skunk, got her attention, then grabbed the first tool at hand off the outer wall—a grass whip—opened the door and banged the handle on the floor, hoping the noise and my anger would at least frighten the skunk into letting go of the hen" (2000, 91). This genders the world female in varying gradations. Defining things as female can be a linguistic act of defiance against a language in which the male is still "default," and also a spiritual act in which women consciously invoke a feminine presence into the world around them.

Hawk Madrone also, in a more significant gendering, consistently refers to the mountain her land is located on as "her."

My informants did the same: animals and birds whose sex was unknown were always "her." However, this did not mean that everyone and everything was female; I vividly remember a conversation about hummingbirds in New Mexico (hummingbirds, unlike skunks, are sexually dimorphic) in which a woman commented about the aggression of the male birds in particular. We were watching a number of birds compete for five or six feeders hung from a trellis, and she remarked, "Look at him, attacking [for space at the feeder] like that. And there's plenty of space elsewhere, too." The bird in question was clearly marked male by his plumage, but the incident also led me to wonder how much human-gendered behavior tends to be projected onto the landscape and the wildlife that also inhabits it. Of course, such attribution of human characteristics is not a habit that is unique to the inhabitants of women's lands.

Earth/Body: Ecofeminism, Race, and Bodily Ways of Knowledge

Ecofeminist responses to relationships between the body and a larger (ecological, economic, and social) landscape may have helped shape the ethos of women's land. From an outsider's perspective, there is a clear connection. However, from an insider's perspective the relationship is more complex, as the connections between women and women's lands are more intimate and less theorized, than ecofeminism; and not all inhabitants of women's land subscribe to its theory. Ecofeminism tends to be more specific. Just as there are many "branches" of ecofeminism, there are complexities in the relationships of land-women to land, how they speak about landscape and gender, and how they construct bodily ways of knowledge. Perhaps it will be more useful to use Donna Haraway's concept of "naturecultures" (2003) to cover "livable politics and ontologies in current life worlds" (4).

Ecofeminism has been accused of reifying the male/female binary and thus the hegemonic identification of the masculine with culture/technology and feminine with nature (see for example Sherry Ortner's classic anthropological essay, "Is Female to Male as Nature Is to Culture?" [1972]). Cultural ecofeminism links the female body with "nature" through reproduction, while social ecofeminism emphasizes how social and economic hierarchies force women as a class into greater proximity with such "natural processes" (usually those associated with the human body). This latter form of ecofeminism also notes that women have more restricted access to natural resources and that capitalist development often curtails this further (Bauhardt 2013). Land-women discuss both of these strategies when talking about ecofeminist concerns, but often move directly to activism by *assuming* that there is a feminist concern with ecology rather than theorizing this link intensively. Indeed, the theoretical link between ecofeminism and land-women is one that resides mostly on the ecofeminist side (which is not to say that no land-women have read and/or practice ecofeminist theory).

While modern ecofeminists recognize the problematics of the equation of "female" and "nature," at times it is that very cultural association that powers land-women's economic, activist, and spiritual relationships with their land. As Catriona Sandilands notes, "At the height of lesbian feminism in the 1970s and 1980s, lesbian 'separatists' who moved to rural settings to live collectively away from urban heteropatriarchy had a clear idea about the importance of nature in their culture, and the importance of their culture to ecology" (2002, 132). At the same time, this cultural equation, which can be found in works as diverse as Mary Daly's classic *Gyn/Ecology* (1978) to Starhawk's *The Spiral Dance* (1979) is a reflection of social norms or doxa from the matrix cultures of the United States. The simple equation of the female and feminine with nature is also, as Mohanty reminds us, a reflection of the white middle-class Western "feminine" and tends to either erasure or simplification/commodification of the experiences of nonwhite women (1984; 2002).[2]

Greta Gaard notes that ecofeminist scholarship has been extraordinarily broad, yet the concept of ecofeminism, "tainted" (not unlike the concept of lesbian separatism) with the charge of essentialism, has consistently been dismissed or outright attacked in feminist publications. Gaard particularly notes a long-running series of articles in *Signs* (2011, 32–38), and Alaimo (2000, 8) suggests that this division stems from (or possibly helps result in) the division between feminist theorists and feminist activism. At the same time, Gaard writes,

> In conjunction with the charges of essentialism were the criticisms of ecofeminism's allegedly essentialist spirituality that both gendered the earth as female and led to elite, apolitical retreat and individual salvation rather than inspiring engaged struggles for

local, community-wide, and global ecojustice. Yet, ecofeminist theory, spirituality, and practice have consistently been rooted in activism that challenges any notions of essentialism" (38).

Some land-women see retreat as political: Gentian, one of my interviewees, once told me about the "hundredth monkey principle," which she described as "a sixties concept" in which simply serving as a visible alternative to a mainstream/hegemonic lifestyle is a form of cultural intervention. Land-women are also often involved in politics at a local and global level: for example, in 1992 the southern Oregon women's community fought Ballot Measure 9, a constitutional clause that would have forbidden all mention of "sexual deviance" in any public forum in the state, and went on to be very involved in creating the Human Rights Coalition, a broad-based political group that became nationwide (Gagehabib and Summerhawk 2000, 83).

Niamh Moore further problematizes the very concept of essentialism, noting that the debates between essentialism and anti-essentialism have resulted in problematic oppositions, exclusionary politics, and similar naming of "outsiders" to "proper" feminist theory (2008, 470). These issues of feminist epistemology are also issues that touch on the everyday life of my informants; I will never forget the day one of the land-women turned to me and said, in a tone of despair and disgust, "They call us *essentialist*," as if that were the worst insult possible. This illustrates the contingent and uncertain ways in which land-women as a group and my informants in particular were impacted by both ecofeminist theories and by the greater feminist response to those theories. While it is clear that some of my informants were aware of these debates, I do not know how many of them were well-read in ecofeminism, felt themselves to be influenced by ecofeminism, or were even aware of the larger debates in ecofeminism. None of my informants actually identified herself to me as an ecofeminist—although this does not, of course, preclude the possibility of any of my informants identifying that way. Sandilands, in her ethnography of lesbian separatists in Oregon, notes that the "essentialist rhetoric" of her informants "is only part of the story"; indeed, that "just as their ideas on gender and sexuality have changed, so too has their ecological wisdom, even if the desire for a counterhegemonic lesbian culture of nature has not" (2002, 133).

Land-women integrate everyday activism with notions about the importance of ecological consciousness and spiritual practice. Their statements can be read as essentialist at times; but keep the above critiques of anti-essentialist politics in mind, and consider how ideas about essence are strategically deployed. Acts of everyday activism include the use of ecologically friendly housing, including rainwater catchment, composting toilets, and gardening for vegetables; the setting aside of a percentage of certain lands as wilderness and/or wilderness recreation area (such as women's campgrounds); and personal choices about purchases, food intake, and the use of renewable resources (such as using glass jars to store water for meetings, rather than purchasing bottled water). These acts are not always placed in an explicit feminist frame, but when they are, their connections to ecofeminist theory are diverse.

For example, Sadie, in an interview, answered a question about why women would want to live on women's land: "A lot of women love to live in the country, and this is—you know, it's just not like having a whole lot of acres and you're farming, but it really is living in a remote area, and they're probably women similar to me, who just would love the idea of there being a women's community that they could function in." Here the connection between women and living on land is expressed purely through *desire*: women's lands function as a way to provide women with a desired way of life. This is neither essentialist nor anti-essentialist, but purely functionalist: it is a positive thing to organize to provide women with a good such as women's land, simply because there are "a lot of women" who want to access that good.

A different example of connection to theory can be seen in how land, features of landscape, and even the default gender of animals is shifted to the feminine. This is a deliberate, political act that identifies the interests of land-women and the land itself as in common because they share a common gender. However, gendering the landscape is not solely the "essentialist" act that it seems to be on the surface; indeed, it serves a number of deliberate social functions. These include assuring the femininity of all women on the land, even if they do not adhere to cultural standards of femininity; reminding all present of the humanity/sacredness of the space; and defying usual linguistic norms in which the gender of the unknown is either masculine or neuter. This last function connects in important ways to ecofeminist theory, since in referring to animals, birds, and plants as "she," my informants not only humanize them but suggest a connection. Jennifer McWeeny, in her essay reflecting on "topographies of flesh," suggests that "a feminist ontology should not ask us to choose one side of the dualism between connection and difference; it should instead give us tools to reframe the conversation nondualistically, enabling us to think connection and difference simultaneously" (2014, 270–71).

Race is a strong but often silent shaper of the public imagination when it comes to the relationship between humans and our environment. Carolyn Finney, in *Black Faces, White Spaces,* writes that "along with a lack of visible African American participation in mainstream environmental activities, visual representations of wildlands and other green spaces remain largely focused on a Euro-American experience of the environment" (2014, 27). Finney focuses on the ways in which national parks and forests in particular "become sites in which African Americans experience insecurity, exclusion, and fear born out of historical precedent, collective memory, and contemporary concerns" (28). However, her argument that the United States has a general association of wilderness and nature with a *white* body follows also for both ecofeminism and women's land itself, as such land is often seen as contiguous with (or partly) wild or "natural" landscapes. The exclusion she writes of twines around not only the Sierra Club and the Grand Canyon, but also more intimate relationships with nature.

This dovetails with what France Winddance Twine and Bradley Gardener call "the white spatial imaginary," after George Lipsitz (1998). This concept covers why "predominantly white residential neighborhoods appear to be 'natural' and how white supremacy" is thus inscribed invisibly on physical space (Twine and Gardener 2013, 5). Thus, it is not only that the white body is the "correct" body to inhabit wilderness, but also that communities composed largely of white people go unquestioned as "natural." Lipsitz notes that "this imaginary does not emerge simply or directly from the embodied identities of people who are white. It is inscribed in the physical contours or the places where we live, work, and play and it is bolstered by financial rewards for whiteness" (1998, 29). These spaces are the segregated neighborhoods, schools, and marketplaces of the United States. While land-women often seek to create spaces away from those of the matrix culture, the whiteness of a large portion of women's land helps shape its "imaginary" and contributes to similar segregation.

Twine and Gardener also note that while privilege is "not fixed and assumes various forms" (2013, 8) within these spatial relationships, it "describes a very specific kind of power, one that is often rendered invisible, at least to those who benefit from it" (9). Invisibility as a concept cuts both ways: the invisibility of privilege renders it more powerful. However, at the same time, a system of privilege can also render particular people invisible and thus *deprive* them of social power.

These interactions are dependent on particular relations between the body and the environment. Finney emphasizes this when she wishes to "challenge the universality that denies the differences in our collective experiences of Nature in the United States" (2014, 34). The cultural background, knowledge, experience, and *race* of a body changes its relationship to what we call nature: the assumed relationship between the feminine and nature is heavily inflected by how that body is raced. The presumed "neutrality" of the white body (which is a position of power, and not neutrality at all) provides that body with an unproblematic relationship to "nature" that is not available to bodies of other races.

Setha Low notes that "when critically examined, space and spatial relations yield insight into unacknowledged biases, prejudices, and inequalities that frequently go unexamined" (2011, 391). In her work on spatial anthropology and spatialized culture, Low connects notions of enclosure and security to the development of neoliberal policies. In her ethnography of gated communities and co-ops, she notes that these provide an enhanced notion of security, an enhanced fear of others, and furthermore that "desire for social and economic homogeneity also produces environments in which minority residents feel singled out and where racist and exclusionary behavior can be more easily exhibited" (2011, 402). Thinking back to Marie's statement about the "comfortableness" of living with women, we are led to wonder how gender masks ways in which this space is further exclusionary, and ways in which middle-class doxa from the United States about desirable "people like us" informs even communities of "outsiders" like land-women.[3]

Thus, the importance of wilderness or rural space as a concept and the importance of access to these spaces is not simply expressed through attachment to particular women's lands (although individual women may become very attached to individual spaces). This is a dialogue of concepts and access. By actively deploying doxic concepts about the feminine nature of Nature itself, as well as the female gender of women's-land space, land-women *use* ecofeminist arguments to further an agenda of making rural and wild space accessible to women. However, the "invisible" status of the white body as normative helps shape both these arguments and these spaces as part of the "white imaginary."

Alien Landings: Creating a Sense of Place and Rooting

The relationship of women to land is extremely complex. It is economic, as women sometimes depend on it for food as well as for shelter and community, and yet women also regard their relationship to the land in philosophical, social, and spiritual terms. Land is both alienable, according to the laws of the United States, and inalienable, according to some women's relationship with their land. Inalienability is a statement of love, homecoming, and spirituality, in which women make statements about the sacredness of the earth and their connections to it. Land is feminine and female, land is a source of authority, and land is a literal space.

The anthropology of space and place "has liberated and challenged anthropologists to examine cultural phenomena that are not fixed in a faraway, isolated location, but surround us in the cities and countries in which we live" (Low and Lawrence-Zúñiga 2003, 2). Most anthropological study of space and gender has concentrated on the domestic (see for example Michelle Rosaldo's 1974 work on the domestic and the public), taking as its model the famous analysis of the Kabyle house done by Pierre Bourdieu (1979). While women's lands can be seen as domestic, they are also more than that, and an analysis of communal space cannot rely on the usual dwelling-equals-domestic equation, as the dwellings of land-women may be communal, shared, public, or private depending on the particular land community and on the woman in question. Nor can there be a domestic:public::female:male analogy made in a situation where both the domestic and the public (or the inside and the outside) are populated entirely by women.

In fact, the division between public/private is contested, especially when it comes to queer space. Megan Sinott notes in her work on women's homosociality and same-sex sexuality in dormitories in Thailand that the very division of space into public/private, in which the public is linked to global processes, emancipation both sexual and social, and higher status, is a Western divide (2013, 334). She states that the dormitory space she studied both encourages proper gender behavior (modesty and unmarried women living apart from men) *and* queerness (open same-sex sexuality), as well as serving as a domestic space that is intimately connected to the global. Similarly, women's lands challenge the domestic/public divide, and while providing a space that encourages same-sex sexuality, also encourages certain mainstream ideas about feminine behavior, such as the equation of femininity with "nature."

Doreen Massey (2005) suggests that space is the product of social relationships and "imagining," and thus that while the concepts of public and private are relevant, we cannot assume that these concepts map perfectly with other oppositions such as global/local. Massey in fact notes that much "public" space excludes, while oftentimes "private" space includes more than first appears (152–53); as she says, "all spaces are socially regulated in some way." Women's lands are highly private at times, but very open at others, hosting events and setting aside land for women's open camping. These spaces are both "privatized" (privately owned by particular women, or by collectives of women) but also "public" in that larger communities are invited. The social regulation is done via both explicit rules (public?) and nonexplicit standards of behavior in the community. Indeed, while these spaces are clearly socially bounded and imagined, they are difficult to define as either private or public.

This space itself challenges the North American concept of the domestic, with "domestic" activities, such as bathing or excretion, often moved outside or otherwise in the open. This claiming of "public" or "semipublic" space for "private" activities is reminiscent of John Hollister's argument about queer sex, in which he states that privacy and sex help define each other, thus marking particular spaces such as gay cruising suites as "collective private spheres" not unlike chat rooms online, where privacy is defined by different terms than bedroom walls or legal definitions (1999, 63). The idea that sex creates its own privacy is probably traceable to Richard Mohr (1996), but the important notion here is not sex itself, but the movement of "the private" into the outdoors, which helps to erode a clear public/private divide. This divide, similar to the public/domestic, is based on assumptions about interiority/exteriority, use of space, identity, and gender (recalling Rosaldo's 1974 work again). These assumptions are social and do not entirely pertain to queer uses of space, including women's land. Similarly, Nancy Duncan (1996) argues that marginalized groups tend to undermine the coherence and application of the public/private binary, especially in reference to how spatial areas are held to have particular sexualities.

Susan Gal (2002) writes:

> Contrary to customary scholarly parlance and commonsense usage, "public" and "private" are not particular places, domains,

spheres of activity, or even types of interaction. Even less are they distinctive institutions or practices. Public and private are co-constitutive cultural categories, as many have pointed out. But they are also, and equally importantly, indexical signs that are always relative: dependent for part of their referential meaning on the interactional context in which they are used. (80)

In her analysis of "public" and "private" as a primarily semiotic phenomenon, Gal further notes that this division is what she calls "fractal": that is, it "can be reproduced repeatedly by projecting it onto narrower contexts or broader ones" (81). These reproductions can grow infinitely smaller and larger; her examples include the private inside of a house contrasted with the public outside; but within the house, the living room is public while the bedrooms are private (82). Thus, the outdoor space of women's land becomes "public" to the group inhabiting it, while home space (or tent space) might represent the private. If we apply this again with Mohr and Hollister in mind, space is only as "private" as the activities occurring there, or the relationship between the women inhabiting that space; the privacy of space is not contingent on location or walls, but on relationships and activities.

This complex restructuring of the public/private is only one way in which space is queered in women's lands. Sandilands (2002), in her analysis of queer ecological politics, focuses on two important issues: the ways in which sexualities are organized via geography (such as within urban natural spaces, such as parks and strolls) and the ways in which ecofeminism has criticized compulsory heterosexuality. Both of these combine in how the landdykes interviewed by Sandilands contribute to a queer ecology, an understanding of a landscape which is itself queered by its use by women and lesbians.

Lesbianism and the "natural" have a complex relationship. "As women, lesbians can be encoded or can identify themselves as 'close' to nature, but, as queers, they have been denigrated as 'unnatural'" (Alaimo 2000, 165). Sandilands also notes this, contrasting how homosexuality is seen as "unnatural" with the way it is also called "uncivilized," thus positioning queers in a liminal zone with regard to the classic nature/culture dichotomy (1994, 21). Although efforts have been made to recast nature as a "tough bitch" (Margulis quoted in Alaimo, 179), a "butch" (Sandilands 1994, 20) or a "wild and rowdy woman, a bad and unruly broad with no concern for her children" (Vance quoted in Alaimo, 179), the connection of nature with the "reprosexual" (Alaimo, 165) is still profound in the Northern imagination. Sandilands, in her work on the inclusion of queerness into green politics, writes, "Position drag 'in' nature both to suggest that 'nature' may be partially performative and to challenge the boundaries between 'truth' and 'artifice.' Speak of nature and artifice as non-mutually-exclusive to suggest that the truth may be stranger than we could ever imagine" (1994, 23). By challenging both the inherent essence of male/female (reprosexuality?) and nature's "lack of artifice," Sandilands creates space for queerness in nature. Similarly, the creation of "queer space" is connected to the positive connotations of "natural" that must reach beyond more conventional ideas of what "nature" implies or how it functions.

While Halberstam writes that "queer uses of time and space develop, at least in part, in opposition to the institutions of heterosexuality, the family, and reproduction," (2005, 1) women's land is also a space in which the family and reproduction thrive. OWL Farm, as Pelican Lee notes in her gently humorous "Kids Story," is a place where many children were raised—much to the chagrin of the heteronormative matrix culture (2002). The complex layers of meaning in "chosen family" (Weston 1991) become even more complex on women's land. This occurs as women share space that shifts between "public" and "private" with a group of people who might also shift between "acquaintance/community member" to "chosen family." In fact, emotional intimacy between members may be one of the ways in which space itself is temporarily designated as "private" or "public," similar to Mohr's suggestion about physical intimacy (1996).

Sense of place in women's land is not only local. John Gray notes that placemaking involves both places "viewed or imagined *at a distance*" and in how people interact with and in particular, name places (2003, 227–28). Both of these types of placemaking are involved in women's lands. First, there is the act of creating mental maps, of imagining lands as places where meaning can be inscribed, as in Lee's *Owl Farm Stories* (2002). Second, there is the act of living on, walking on, and interacting with the land itself, creating a discourse with other women in which the land is physically present, as in the case of Mountainview, where hiking trails, named places and roads, and religious circles inscribed on the land bear witness to the ways women interact with the mountains they live on. Lastly, there are the ways in which women name and refer to women's lands and landscapes that are distant, using the names of places to "root" themselves in a larger network of land-women.

Territory and rooting are both significant in the relationship between women and land. Liisa H. Malkki writes:

> "To be rooted is perhaps the most important and the least recognized need of the human soul," wrote Simone Weil ... in wartime England in 1942. In our day, new conjunctures of theoretical inquiry in anthropology and other fields are making it possible and necessary to rethink the question of roots in relation—if not to the soul—to identity and to the forms of its territorialization. The metaphorized concept of having roots involves intimate linkages between people and place—linkages that are increasingly recognized in anthropology as areas to be denatured and explored afresh. (2001, 51)

Those "intimate linkages" also impact the economic and emotional relationships of women to land, and help shape relationships women have with each other in such spaces. The underlying idea that people are connected/rooted to land whether by birth or by choice is the metaphor through which these relationships are elaborated. Land-women *choose* their lands, but that does not mean that the attachments are viewed by them as any less legitimate or profound than those which happen via an accident of birth. There is a similar agency of choice in the language used by many queer folk in the concept of the "chosen family" (Weston 1991).

The relationship of women to land is thus extremely complex and intertwined with the most basic aspects of economy and identity, community and right living. Relationships between humans and land encompass ideas about wilderness, nature, connection with the earth, ecological niches, life-systems, and spirituality. Thus the inalienability of land goes beyond the inalienability of one community location from its community; it is considered extremely important for women *as a group* to have access to land *as an entity*. Ni Aodagain, a former resident of OWL Farm, suggests this when she states that "women without resources *have to be able to go back to the earth*" (Gagehabib and Summerhawk 2000, 127, emphasis mine). This is a statement about women's access to a way of *correct living*.

This is not to say that land-women are inextricably entwined with their various locations, although some may perceive themselves this way. Many women are transient; communities also undergo change with the addition and departure of members. However, even for limited periods of time, profound relationships may develop with the land. Land provides not only space for community and shelter but also identity and the intangible but valued good that comes from contact with wilderness. Land-women who had been living in urban spaces have told me about the importance of getting out to wilderness—not a particular land, but wilderness or women's land in general. As one informant simply described it to me, "it's space to *be* in."

"To plot only 'places of birth' and degrees of nativeness is to blind oneself to the multiplicity of attachments that people form to places through living in, remembering, and imagining them" (Malkki 2001, 72). She aptly points out here that the attachment of people to place goes beyond the imaginings of "native land": the creation of "home" is something constructed and can happen outside of a birth relationship with a country or location. Certainly the relationships that women have with women's lands are carefully cultivated and not usually created by birth; yet they are complex, seen as fully legitimate, and moreover invested with important emotional and spiritual burdens of meaning. These relationships are inalienable; at the same time, paradoxically, the same women are often mobile and live at multiple women's-lands over a lifetime.

A Land of One's Own and the Imaginary of Home

Land is the site of important struggles. At Mountainview, the main division between the founders of the community and the current group of women living on the land had to do with deeds to individual plots of land. Several of my informants from Mountainview related this story to me: Because of how the parent group purchased the original large land lot, they could not release deeds to the women purchasing smaller lots within it before a particular year. Some women purchased these lots, and then, in the process of building, discovered that they needed a deed in order to get a mortgage. Two women hired a lawyer and forced the parent group to release their deed, whereupon some of the other women of the community began to ask about their deeds. One of my informants, May, explains:

> There's the three developers [the parent group] that have their ideas that basically it feels like a matriarchal type thing. And then

there's the rest of us. . . . For a while the developers told us they didn't want to come to anything because we might ask 'em a question that they didn't want to answer. Or couldn't answer. Or were uncomfortable answering. And . . . there's been some struggles between the two groups.

However, Marie said,

> And, uh, you know when I come they approach me about it [the deed issue] and I say, "Well, I don't know what to tell you cause I'm not here full time and I can't be until I get a job and I don't really care about my mortgage. I'm honoring what they said we would have, you know, I'll take my deed when I take my deed."

Not all the women have issues with the process. However, the lack of a deed, which inhibits the ability of some women to build houses, demonstrates a basic conflict between the needs of capitalist society and the community. The pressures of the capitalist society continue to influence the economies of land.

The complexities of the relationships among women, land, and money are further illustrated in a painful story related to me by Sophia. Sophia is an older woman who has lived at a number of women's lands. She and a number of other older land-women were putting together a community that she hoped would be a permanent community for older lesbians (called "Star" here), and they elected to purchase land from another women's community, Mountain's Daughters. Star, after many community meetings discussing their ideals, met with Mountain's Daughters and arranged a land-transaction for some of the land that Mountain's Daughters (a community with a board of directors) administrated. Star members began building houses on the land allotted to them and then Mountain's Daughters decided that the land would not be allocated to Star. There was a legal wrangle over land rights, and Star left the land, and in many of the cases, homes they built themselves.

Land rights, trust, and economic concerns all weave a very tangled web indeed. The Star members believed that Mountain's Daughters had given them a right to the land they were building on, while Mountain's Daughters clearly believed no such thing; in Sophia's narrative, betrayal of trust was one of the most important themes. It formed perhaps the most painful part of the story, along with losing a home. Sophia acknowledged that she felt she had been wronged—as the users of that land, it was clear that Star members felt they had (an inalienable?) right to it. It was a particularly difficult episode because Sophia in particular, and perhaps other Star members, were looking for a permanent home. Thus the story is not only about ownership and right usage of land, but also about home and home-seeking.

Land rights are inevitably also influenced by the beliefs of the matrix culture regarding property ownership, alienability, and proper use. Mountain's Daughters had greater rights to the land in terms of legal ownership, yet Star believed that they would abide by the precepts of women's-land beliefs and acknowledge that the work Star had put into their land and their emotional attachment to it was also important. In the end, however, the ideology of capitalism prevailed—the land was claimed by the women who owned it via deed. Yet it was clear from the reactions at the Landdyke Gathering that Mountain's Daughters would have to frame their claim in terms of women's-land rights in order to make their actions morally right in the eyes of other land-women.

These struggles over land illustrate the complex dance between alienability and inalienability, ownership of land and use of land, attachment to land, and the importance of home in the landscape of women's-land cultures. Concepts of home and homecoming are important and pervasive in the language that land-women use to refer to women's land. Many of my informants referred to being on women's land as "coming home," both in the context of personal histories and as an imagined, future homecoming. Sally Ward, in examining how "home" has been studied in anthropology, notes that "home can be severed from particularities in time and space; it need not be somewhere in particular, grounded and static" (2003, 89). For my informants, "home" can be where they live, a place they visit, a women's music festival that only exists for a few days out of the year, a friendship network, or a virtual network of like-minded women. "Whereas place can imply mere point or location, home implies belonging and conjures up images of the greatest intimacy, security, and familiarity." (2003, 89). The nostalgia brought up by the concept of home is intimately involved with inclusion and exclusion, and thus with issues of identity: who is included within the homesite. This again calls up *communitas*: community and nostalgia/desire for community shaping each other.

These complex relationships with female land and the gendered space women have created form an important branch of identity among land-women. "As people fashion places, so too do they fashion themselves" (Feld and Basso in Ward 2003, 86).

Land, the physical place/space of "women's lands" is a complex and potent aspect of how these communities define themselves. The land itself looms large as a shaper of such cultures, but it is also shaped by them. This is true both in a literal physical sense (homes built, roads created, gardens planted, and trails marked) but also in the sense of how the women of these cultures shape their means of interacting with, symbolizing, and using the landscape. A gendered landscape holds a different meaning than a landscape that simply happens to house women. The mountain being "she" signifies political action, emotional commitment, and marking the landscape as an emotional player in and of itself: the tenor of one's relationship to the land can thus be marked as legitimate and significant.

The relationship of women's-land culture(s) with the land is various and profound. As Moore (2008) reminds us, the act of gendering need not refer to some essentialist assumption about gender, and we can trouble the binary assumptions we have around essentialist and nonessentialist uses of gender (which can too often code for nonacceptable and acceptable). How can a landscape essentially be one thing or the other? Gendering a landscape is a choice, a political act, a strategy, a poem.

This ties into the ways in which this landscape has been gendered *before*. No longer seen as a virgin eagerly awaiting colonization, this landscape is a teacher, a mentor, a wise crone, who provides both a space for queering our expectations of what the public and the private are, but also operates with the nostalgia of home. That nostalgia can be dangerous, tying into ideas of a "safe community" and the white imaginary. Yet the land, and the attachment of land-women to the land, remains primary.

· CHAPTER 6 ·

Primally Female

Agency and the Meaning of the Body on Women's Land

The repossession by women of our bodies will bring far more essential change to human society than the seizing of the means of production by workers.

—Adrienne Rich, *Blood, Bread, and Poetry*

To some degree I walk around in denial. To me, I'm a normal person walking around living a normal life. . . . It's something we don't talk about.

—Meg, about food and fat politics in the women's-land community

THE AIRPORT CAR-RENTAL PLACE offered me and my wife a cheap upgrade from the compact we'd reserved when they heard where we were headed. As we powered that six-cylinder sedan over seven arroyos carved in the steep dirt road to the mesa top, 6,000 feet above sea level, we were grateful.

Halfway up, we came to a gate. I got out, worked the combination lock—we'd gotten the combination in an email—and opened the gate for the car. I made sure to refasten it securely and snap the lock in place. And then it was about another mile before we got our first glimpse of the Gathering.

There was a round mud-brick house with turtle and snake shapes molded on the outside, with a few canopies set up for shelter. A claw-foot bathtub stood next to it, hooked up to a rain-catching water tank, atop a wood-burning stove for heat. Women of all shapes, sizes, and ages were parking vehicles, walking around, hugging, chatting, unpacking their camping gear. I got out of the car, eager for a bathroom—we'd been driving two or three hours since our lunch in Santa Fe.

We greeted women we'd met at the first Landdyke Gathering we attended two years earlier in Ohio. We were introduced to some of the women from this land, and after the initial wave of conversation, I politely asked where the shitters (common landdyke terminology) were. One of the land-women took me on a brief tour.

The red sandy soil was peppered here and there with flying cholla, a small, low-lying cactus that was prone to being kicked by unwary feet. I had changed from sandals to heavy boots immediately upon getting out of the car, after an inadvertent introduction to one. There were stands of scrubby pines and tall cacti. Practically everywhere we had a spectacular view off the edge of the mesa: angular mountains covered in twisted trees and cut by raw red canyons, their layered colors slightly subdued under a pearly sky promising the long-awaited rain. There were few houses or other signs of human habitation.

We rounded a stand of pines to an especially amazing view. My guide gestured almost triumphantly to the five-gallon bucket topped with a toilet seat.

"The toilet paper's in the coffee can—be sure to put the lid back on it so the dew doesn't get in—and the sawdust is in the blue bucket," she said. I looked at these arrangements, then back at the main trail between houses, which was not quite obscured by the short trees: one of the women I knew waved cheerfully at me. I looked back at my guide, who wasn't going anywhere. She was standing right next to me, naming the distant mountains for my edification, and I realized, to the distress of my bladder, that she didn't feel privacy was required.

Welcome to women's land.

Women's land is not simply composed of ideas, discourse, or language; women's lands enfold the body as well as the mind. There are different ways of eating, different ways of building and living in buildings, different ways of bathing, and even different ways of excreting. All of these practices lend themselves to different ways of being in the body. Bodily practice inflects bodily experience. Women's bodies shape women's lands, and vice versa.

Some anthropologists have suggested that the very act of sharing space and experiences with our informants changes how we anthropologists look at the world and helps us approach, if not necessarily share, how informants perceive their worlds (Desjarlais 1992; Sklar 2001). Culture is not something located only in the mind. In examining how intimate bodily practice helps shape the culture of women's land, or how women experience women's-land spaces, it is useful to refer back to Nancy Scheper-Hughes and Margaret Lock's famous concept of the "three bodies." These are defined as the individual body, the social body, and the body politic (1987, 7). These three bodies illuminate the ways in which the body as a concept, as an experience, and as an object is differently treated, experienced, and made use of. Individuals each have their own personal experiences living within and reacting to the body cultures of women's lands. Socially, bodies are seen and understood in different ways in women's lands; the meaning of the female body itself and how women's bodies interact change profoundly in this context. Lastly, the ways in which bodies are controlled, viewed, and categorized—the body politic—changes according to the cultural frameworks of women's land and the physical ways women live in them. How women view their own bodies, other women's bodies, and social bodies are influenced not only by different discourses but also by their day-to-day interactions.

Using the division between the individual body-self, the social body, and the body politic offered by Scheper-Hughes and Lock, this chapter traces some of the connections among bodily experience on women's land. However, these divisions are not "pure": the body-self affects the social body, which affects the body politic. Day-to-day experiences of being in the body affect, and are affected by, the ways in which women's-land political culture expresses itself through the body. Simultaneously, the body remains a potent symbol in definitions of self and culture. The body is a cultural artifact—both creating culture and experiencing itself through culture—despite a tendency in both United States matrix culture and women's-land culture to look to the body as a precultural, "raw," biological truth. But we do not experience the body *before* culture, and the doxa of the United States is both threaded through and undone via bodily action and experience in women's lands. Thus embodiment and the meaning of embodiment is, as always, both personal and political.

Body-Self: What Do I Wear to Women's Land?

One of the ways my cultural non-knowledge was particularly evident at the beginning of my research was in my clothing. Although from my point of view I was dressed in a very similar manner to my informants (jeans, T-shirts, sneakers or sandals), there were important subtle markers I missed. The color, logo, and origin of the T-shirt mattered. Other markers included varieties of jewelry (particular items indicating class, feminism, religion, and varying degrees of femininity), buttons with logos, and tattoos. All of these items bore important meaning, and similar items have been significant in the history of women's activism and queer liberation (Penney 2013).

Anthropologists have long been interested in the ways in which the body is adorned.[1] The complex meanings of clothing are embedded within other disciplines and investigations in anthropology; clothing has been investigated as a discourse, a semiotic play, and an element of consumption, "conceived not only as markets and economic actors but as cultural processes that construct identity" (Hansen 2004, 370). As I am focusing on the body, clothing and other bodily adornment are both experiential and social, helping to construct the identity of the individual and the individual's integration into the community, following Terence Turner's concept of the "social skin" (1993). Although we are agentic in selecting particular clothing styles, haircuts, and other body forms, the meanings of these forms are communally created and cannot be individually controlled, creating a "self" that is both exposed to the outside world and also at least partially constructed by it (Woodward 2005, 22). Within these constructions, gender, race, sexuality, and class are made visible. Clothing at once "allows us to assert ourselves as individuals [and] it also allows us to identify ourselves as part of a social collective" (Polhemus and Procter 1978, 11). The values of the group are largely communicated via the "fashion/anti-fashion" that is identified with that group.

Queer readings of the body and gender must be understood in a larger matrix-culture context that privileges male bodies, masculine genders, and heterosexualities over others. However, the performance of the body is always contingent, and queer performances help to elide and change the "reproduction" of gender systems (Butler 1993a). Research suggests that the "butch" or androgynous woman is a primary image of lesbianism/queer women in the matrix culture of the United States (Hammidi and Kaiser 1999; Hillman 2013; Levitt and Horne 2002; Maltry and Tucker 2002). Identities, such as butch identity, are expressed through the body and clothing, although it is important to keep in mind that body shape, cultural background, and race have a significant impact on how such performances are viewed or "pressed onto" particular bodies. For example, women of color are often interpreted as "butch" by white women despite other aspects of their presentation (Hammidi and Kaiser 1999, 60; Hillman 2013, 165). Butchness is sometimes reported as "favored" in queer contexts, with more fem women reporting that they have their queerness questioned, or feel that they don't fit in (Clarke and Turner 2007; Levitt and Horne 2002; Maltry and Tucker 2002).

On the women's lands I have visited, there was a preference for "dyke" presentation, which is more androgynous than fem presentation and less masculine than butch presentation. (This does not go for all individuals—some residents are more feminine-presenting and some of my informants identified as butch.) The "dyke" aesthetic connects to the criticism of the butch/fem dynamic that was contemporary with the advent of lesbian feminism (Maltry and Tucker 2002, 93) and which centered on the "heteronormativity" of the butch/fem dynamic. The "androgynous" presentation I encountered is similar to that discussed by Betty Luther Hillman (2013) in her article on 1970s feminist gender politics, in which clothing, hairstyle, makeup (or lack thereof), and body hair were all used as political statements by both feminists and lesbians:

> By adopting what would come to be known as an "androgynous uniform" (or, for lesbians, a "dyke uniform")—often consisting of jeans, button-down work shirts, and work boots, often without makeup and bras, and sometimes with short hair—these women's liberationists and lesbian feminists visually displayed their political goal of creating a society free of gender distinctions, defying expectations that men and women ought to "look different" from each other. (162)

However, in the context of women's land, the goal of the more androgynous look is not to state that men and women are not so different after all, but to express other cultural and political sentiments. These are similar to those of the lesbian feminists cited by Hillman, such as freedom of movement, comfort, and practicality. "The clothes I wear help me to know my own power" (Liza Cowan, "What the Well-Dressed Dyke Will Wear," in Hillman 2013, 162). By dressing this way, my informants also *visually* reference the ideals of the feminist movement and align themselves with a particular branch of lesbianism. This rejection of mainstream/matrix culture's demands on the female body comes to be signified by its own aesthetic. However, some of my informants still connect "dykeness" to rejection of the butch/fem aesthetic. One of my informants told me casually one day that she felt uncomfortable around butch women, as opposed to "dykes." She said that she found butch women too "masculine."

As this analysis suggests, queer coding is seldom as simple as research on "butch/fem" aesthetics might imply. Although a number of researchers report that butch/"masculine" presentations have not only received the most attention in the literature but also in queer culture (Hammidi and Kaiser 1999; Levitt and Horne 2002; Maltry and Tucker 2002), there are actually a wide number of presentations that can be read as queer depending on the context, time, cultural inflection, and personal performance. Clarke and Spence, in their recent investigation of queer women's appearance practices in the United Kingdom, report that "there is no longer a lesbian 'uniform' or 'dress code'" (2013, 27). Clarke and Spence also note that gender presentation changes over time, is connected to a sense of inner authenticity, and can be actively manipulated "to express a mobile sense of self" (29). However, as with all clothing and bodily presentation, there is always slippage between presentation and how that presentation is received by others.

Shaving the body is a political statement as well as an aesthetic one, connected to the idea of a "natural body." Hillman notes that refusal to shave one's legs and armpits was seen as a political stance by feminists of the 1970s; such refusals could also connote masculinity or lesbianism (2013, 162). Later, debates on whether or not feminism "required" not shaving armpits or legs, as well as similar "beauty sacrifices," turned into a politics of choice argument (164). Similar arguments still rage today, mainly online, where debates over cultural pressures to maintain mainstream beauty standards versus choice still appear (Cliffe 2013). It is important to note that removal of any body hair (as opposed to head hair) is conceptualized as artificial by many of my informants, and also as producing a proper, "docile" feminine body (Bartky 1997 notes that body hair removal is central to this).

As I did not ask direct questions about body grooming, I am relying on two things for my conclusions here: my observations of other women's nude bodies (as women often go nude, especially for swimming and bathing, on women's land), and other women's reactions to my own body. While negative reactions to another woman's body were generally frowned on in women's-land space (see next section), I believe my body practice made me more acceptable and comfortable in the space. However, there was another aspect of my presentation I am fairly sure marked me as an outsider: my hair. Most of my informants chose to wear their hair short, in ways that made care and styling extremely simple (Hillman 2013 notes that this was also a characteristic of 1970s feminism and lesbian feminism). I wear my hair very long and usually twisted up into a bun to get it out of the way—a style marked in American mainstream culture as feminine, despite also being unfashionable. Maltry and Tucker actually begin their work on the multiplicity of fem performance in queer culture with an (admittedly tongue-in-cheek) story about a young lesbian who feels constrained to cut off her long hair in order to be accepted as queer (2002, 89–90).

Although none of the women I encountered during my fieldwork remarked upon my choice of hairstyle, it was noticeable to me that my way of wearing my hair was different. I was more feminine-presenting and easily picked out as an outsider. In this case, the idea of the "natural"—for my hair was arguably just as "natural" as a short haircut—was overridden by its gender significance. Hillman writes of the 1970s feminists, "Perhaps the most controversial decision that some feminists made was to cut their hair, ridding themselves of the long locks that defined both traditional femininity (at least for white women) and membership in the 1960s counterculture" (2013, 161). Yet now perhaps it is as controversial—at least among lesbians—to *not* cut one's hair. Hammidi and Kaiser suggest this, noting that long hair intersects with racial and class markers as well (1999, 60). In fact, the conflict between short and long hair is arguably another instance of white ways of knowing (Finney 2014, 3), as hair has such different expressions on differently raced bodies.[2]

The significance of wearing the "correct" type of T-shirt also has to do with politics. The T-shirt is a complex and important form in North America, and, indeed, globally: Minh-Ha Pham suggests that "the financially attainable T-shirt symbolizes the essential American style of democracy" (2010, 401). Joel Penney writes that the gay and lesbian T-shirt in particular serves as a form of body project for public visibility "by circulating images of gay and lesbian identity and advocacy in public space via the chests of wearers, this practice draws attention to ... expressive, visual, and embodied modes of political participation" (2013, 289). The readability of these shirts (whether directed at a previously-informed audience through subfusc symbols or outwardly-directed through easily readable terminology) serves multiple functions: community-building, raising awareness, and creating collective identity (292). In this instance, in order to be part of the larger collective identity, it was important for me to show both knowledge of the larger identity and solidarity through wearing the forms on my body. One of my informants kindly provided me with appropriate markers after I visited her land by gifting me with a women's-land T-shirt.

Since women's land is a relatively small part of the larger QUILTBAG[3] political spectrum, the signs and symbols referencing it directly (like T-shirts printed by particular women's lands) are mainly of importance to those within the community, rather than for communication to the larger matrix culture. (This does not mean that such T-shirts are never worn off women's lands or used for such purposes, however.) Other important T-shirt logos include women's bookshops, women's music festivals, feminist artists, and feminist sentiments in general; these are all part of a larger aesthetic that helps establish identity, community, and belonging.

The "natural body" was an important signifier for many of my informants, who judged personal adornments and style according to this aesthetic. Interestingly, such adornments and body style must be consciously created, as Woodward notes about one of her (presumably heterosexual) informants: "She has consciously to create such a 'natural' unthought look" (2005, 27). The "naturalness" of this style of personal adornment connects to the concept of the land itself as "natural." However, gender as a marker overrides naturalness in the matter of hair, where short hair (which must be clipped) tends to be preferred over long. The significance of the (largely gender-neutral, see Pham 2010) T-shirt in this aesthetic has to do with both the looseness and neutrality of the shirt as well as its easy adaptation to homebrew political messages (Penney 2013). Personal body practices interact with larger aesthetic and cultural ideas in the formation of both identity and community; the meanings of particular embodiments are always social.

The Social Body: From the Shitters to the Spirit

One of the oft-repeated sayings about women's land is, "It is just different." When I took my first field trip to a women's land in the Midwest, I thought I was prepared for things to be "different." I wasn't. I suppose, since my field location was in the United States, of which I am a native, and my informants were lesbians, a population to which I belong, I was unconsciously expecting a culture that was not *too* different. Instead, I experienced severe culture shock.

To a great extent this was due to the different physical way these women had of being in the world on women's land. The physical acts that made up women's relations to the land, women's relations to each other, and women's relations to their own bodies were different. These differences were attributed by my informants to the literal absence of the male gaze. This was explicitly noted by land-women as one of the main reasons for the creation of women's land: to have a space where women are free of the perceptions of men.

In this cultural context, male gaze is both Foucauldian, in that it implies self-policing, as well as literal, in that it is dependent on the presence of actual men. This definition is thus a paradox. As Sandra Bartky (1997) points out, Foucault's analysis of the production of "docile bodies" is extremely useful for examining the particularly gendered "docile bodies" of women. I am using his analysis of the panoptic gaze as it applies to how women internalize the heterosexual norms of the female body and apply those norms to themselves. I call this the "male gaze" (Mulvey 1999) for although the lookers may be of any gender, the standards applied are those that are considered to be attractive to heterosexual men—the patriarchal definition of "the feminine." This is also a "male gaze" in that although the gazers are not always male, the ways in which the gaze disciplines female bodies are seen by my informants as ways that specifically *benefit men*. Men benefit twice from this application of the assumed-male gaze: the first is the application of presumed heterosexual, dominant, mainstream tastes to the female body, producing the outward shapes of the "docile body" (Foucault 1995); the second is how such docile bodies are secondary and subservient even when they are coded as white, upper-class, or otherwise dominant (Bartky 1997, 142). While it may benefit an individual woman to discipline her body into attractiveness—for example, it may help her gain a professional job—the customs that state that attractive women are more likely to gain jobs benefit men, who do not have to invest the same amount of time and energy into appearance in order to compete for the same jobs (Bartky 1997, 139).

My informants state that outside of women's land, they sometimes participate in self-policing, thus becoming part of the panopticon of the male gaze—that "design of subtle coercion" in which "(s)he who is subjected to a field of visibility, and who knows it, assumes responsibility for the constraints of power; (s)he makes them play spontaneously upon [her]self" (Foucault 1995, 209, 202–3). Yet the male gaze is also perceived as being physically located within men: in the absence of male human beings, women's lands are conceived of as being freed or partially freed from the male gaze. Victoria Brownsworth (2015) writes about the Michigan Womyn's Music Festival: "But in the week during which it is all women, all the time—women of different races, ethnicities, ages, sizes, abilities—the world feels like a very different place. A place where there is no male gaze and no threat of catcalling or body shaming or sexual assault." The absence of the literal male body becomes a synecdoche for the absence of the larger phenomenon of the male gaze. In this section, I will explore three results of this perception: the expectation that everyone is female, public excretion, and nudity.

On women's land, one of the most important assumptions is that only women are present. This leads to the assumed absence of the embodied male gaze. One incident that neatly illustrates this assumed absence happened on Turtle Mesa in New Mexico. A meeting about the history of consensus in one of the homes located on the land was interrupted by the arrival of a male telephone technician. We were all sitting in the house, a single-room hay bale adobe structure with wide-open glass doors and large windows, when one of the women interrupted the current speaker, saying: "That's a man's voice." After a moment's silence, during which we all listened—indeed, there was a masculine voice speaking outside—three of us immediately pulled our shirts on or closed and the woman to whom the house belonged left the circle of chairs and hurried outside. She spoke with the technicians while the rest of us sat tensely, our previous discussion silenced by this unexpected and unwelcome arrival. This was all the more surprising because Turtle Mesa is located on a remote desert plateau beyond five gates and up a long and unpaved road. The woman to whom the house belonged returned and explained that the man was a telephone technician who had to "trace the line," and that being associated with a utility, he had the combination to the gates.

One woman left to escort the technicians off the land when they were done, and afterward, the meeting continued. Another participant stated dryly that the technicians would have had to drive past the outdoor shower structure to get to the house we were meeting in, and another commented that she had heard the voice earlier but "could not believe it was what it sounded like." This reflected my experience as well, for I had heard the voices outside and noticed that one of them sounded male, but dismissed the evidence of my ears because men were not *supposed* to be in that space.

This illustrates both the assumption of female space ("of course that's not a male voice") and how a literal male presence stands in for the metaphorical male gaze. Note how we immediately covered up our bodies, shielding them from the gaze of the male stranger, and note also how the discussion ceased until he left. Within these practices are encoded both unwillingness to be nude or partially nude in front of that "gazer," and unwillingness to allow him to participate in the culture of women's land, even superficially. Note also the *assumed absence* of male presence—to such an extent that some of us were slow on the uptake.

Another theme that often comes up is safety. Women often place great emphasis on the fact that women are "safe" or "safer" on rural women's lands, that women can travel on foot around the lands alone, and that women do not fear being outside in the dark. Rose, one of my informants, told me:

> Well, it's safer and more free to be whoever you are at any moment. And that's not to say that I think all my neighbors agree with everything, but they're not going to harass me if—you know, if something is important to me and I'm being that way, or doing that, or putting that in my yard, if they find it offensive they would explain why. . . .
> And being safe, I know we talked some the other night. I've never lived anyplace where at night I felt I could just go out by myself and walk around. And feel—I know I've done it, but there's that edge of really paying attention to are there other footsteps or whatever, and that feels very safe in that way.

Rose connects social safety, the ability to "be who she is" and free from harassment, with physical safety, feeling safe walking around by herself at night. These different types of safety are connected to the absence of men. Brownsworth quotes playwright Carolyn Gage: "At MichFest, she can experience a degree of safety that is not available to any woman any time anywhere except at the Festival. And what does that mean? It means she achieves a level of relaxation, physical, psychic, cellular, that she had never experienced before. She is free, sisters. She is free. Often for the first time in her life" (2015). A lack of need to police the self both socially and for physical safety is connected to the lack of male presence.

Marie implied some of this when she touched on the problems of living in her old neighborhood—saying that "a man might be looking in your window" in a suburban area. This lack of privacy and autonomy is mediated by the *gaze*: a male someone looking in a window. Women's land provides "safe space" for women, and part of this safety comes in the form of privacy and aloneness. Sirocco also spoke of safety as an important aspect of women's land, and connects it with other social goods:

> I find that there's a sense of safety. Having women's land I think is extremely crucial that other people even know that it's there because I do believe that there may be a time in women's lives when they need someplace to go, even if it's for a week, to try to get their thoughts together or whatever, and to know that that's accessible, that that is a reality. Throughout my lifetime, no matter what has gone on in my life, there's always been a little index card filed away that says, "I always have a place to go. I always have a place to belong."

Here Sirocco speaks of a sense of refuge, and then went on to connect it to safety in an uncertain world.

However, land-women do not always feel safe. One informant told me about a women's land in Mississippi where she felt that the male neighbors hated them and the women living on the land were in constant danger. She reported that she often saw trespassers on their land, whom she thought were their neighbors proving to them that they weren't safe in order to "put them in their place" and police them. The feeling of being unsafe was one of the reasons she and her lover both chose to leave that land. More famously, a women's land that often served as a lesbian gathering place in the southern United States, Camp Sister Spirit, was harassed for several years in the 1990s by neighbors leaving threatening letters and dead animals in their mailbox.[4]

The male gaze serves as a disciplinary mechanism in the larger schema of rape culture. While rape itself is highly feared by American women (Bart and O'Brien 1985; Miller and Biele 1993; Starling 2009), it is also connected to larger issues in rape culture, including colonialism and the genocide of indigenous peoples in the Americas (Smith 2005), gendered violence and rape in prisons (Critical Resistance and INCITE! Women of Color Against Violence 2006), institutionalized violence against immigrant women (Falcon 2006) and law enforcement violence against women of color and queer people of all genders and races (Ritchie 2006).

However, despite the ways in which rape is universalized by many feminist theorists (and my land-women interviewees), rape is not a global human phenomenon (Helliwell 2000; Sanday 2007, 6).

Christine Helliwell exemplifies this in her fieldwork story from the Gerai, in which a man crawls into a woman's mosquito net at night, to her vocal indignation; after she raises the alarm, the household chases him out, disheveled and ashamed (2000, 789–90). When Helliwell asked the woman if she was frightened, she replied, puzzled, "Tin [Christine], it's only a penis. How can a penis hurt anyone?" (2000, 790). Lacking models of genital difference and having a concept of sex as fully mutual rather than male-aggressive, female-passive, the Gerai appear to have no concept of rape, which Helliwell uses to argue that rape is one of the mechanisms by which gender is created and performed in rape cultures. It is hopeful that there are cultures that do not have a concept of rape and in which rape does not appear to happen; if rape is neither biological nor a human universal, then rape culture can be changed.[5]

Yet rape is perceived by my informants as permeating North American matrix cultures—and, indeed, there is evidence that many discourses promoting rape culture persist, both among political conservatives and liberals (Filipovic 2008; Jervis 2008). As the women's lands I worked with were embedded in this space, rape culture was an important factor in women seeing all-female space as safer than mixed-gender space.

Many of my informants stated that the physical safety of women's lands was one of its positive benefits. Due to the gendered nature of violence in North American matrix cultures (Campbell 1993), my informants perceived women as less likely to commit acts of violence, including rape. Some separatist literature identifies rape as a male domain (Lee 1991, 88–89), but this erases rape and violence between women, which is reported on women's lands. For example, Juana Maria Paz reports extensively on violence against herself on women's land (1980, 19) and her own impulses to violence (48–49). Similarly, my informants reported violence on women's lands, as well: Bird (who is white, unlike Paz) mentioned that she and her lover had to leave a community because one of the women there felt threatened by them. This community had an anarchic system in which anyone was allowed to come and stay on the land, as long as they introduced themselves to all the other residents, which Bird and her lover did. The couple was living on the land when one of the permanent residents came and told Bird that if she didn't move off the land, the resident would kill her. Bird was deeply disturbed and frightened, not only by the threat but also by the lack of response among the other community residents; she and her lover ended up leaving.

Rape culture is not only expressed in physical violence. The disciplinary male gaze is also objectifying, and is seen by my informants as expressing itself in many ways, from street harassment (New York City Hollaback!, 2015) to images in the media (Conley and Ramsey 2011; Kilbourne 2010). The pressure of the male gaze is considered to be fraught with danger, especially in terms of nudity and the body. Therefore, it is significant that nudity and public excretion and bathing are important aspects of women's-land culture, and these activities are connected to the assumed absence of the male gaze, and the rape culture it enforces.

One woman told me, for example, that she thought that a lot of women's anxiety and repressions in the United States came from bathroom anxiety and restrictions—from having to "hold it" until reaching a place of suitable privacy. She said that she felt that one of the best things about women's land was that women were permitted to pee anywhere outside, whenever and wherever the need struck, and that this permitted a more natural and healthy relationship with the body. In fact, she was squatting and urinating while speaking to me.

Excretion is neither a matter for intense privacy nor a taboo subject in many women's lands. Land-women are not unique in their disdain for bodily privacy: Sarah Lamb notes that both defecation and urination in the Bangladeshi village where she did her fieldwork typically happened out in the open; in this context, the lack of privacy implied social surveillance as to whether one was properly bathing following defecation (2000, 184, 195). And Isabel Fonesca notes that not only did the Mechkari Gypsies she lived with excrete outdoors, but that they were such firm believers in the non-necessity of privacy that someone would accompany her to the outdoor toilet site every time, resulting in her becoming "intransigently constipated" (1995, 25). This parallels my first experience with the non-necessity of privacy rather uncomfortably.

There are a wide variety of cultural practices and taboos about excretion. Horace Miner, in his satirical but none the less accurate study of American body habits, emphasized the premier importance of privacy for the "rituals" of both excretion and bathing (1956). Mike Dimpfl and Sharon Moran note that "pulling open the bathroom door reveals a tangle of experiences tied up in the construction of the body as fundamentally *other-than* its waste-making proclivities" (2014, 423). Taboos about excretion are tied not only into unspoken doxa about the proper body but also into gender, the state, and the proper domestic household. The expectation that such privacy is not necessary on women's land follows cultural lines about pollution, modernity, nature/urban location, and the body's role in these.

The flush toilet is a common icon of modernity, associated with cleanliness, urban life, and proper sanitation, yet also hidden from view architecturally and socially and engendering privacy (Dutton, Seth, and Gandhi 2002). Margaret del Carmen Morales, Leila Harris, and Gunilla Öberg discovered in their work investigating sustainable and dry toilet systems in Buenos Aires that the flush toilet and the concept of "flushing" (or making vanish) sewage are central to how urban dwellers think about citizenship and modernity. "For many in the Global North, urban life means that your shit is not your problem.... Distance from shit, facilitated by a connection to a centralized, waterborne, linear end-of-pipe sanitation system, may nonetheless be essential to imaginaries of urbanity and modernity" (Morales, Harris, and Öberg 2014, 2817). It is therefore clear that a lack of the flush toilet and an embrace of more sustainable options is a cultural *choice* that rejects this urban model. A rejection of the flush toilet is a rejection of the city and modernity, and an affirmation of "nature" and rural life through bodily practices: "Low-tech options are often considered to be more ecologically sound." Such ecologically sound toilets are embraced by a wide variety of cultures, ranging from communards, to eco-friendly city-dwellers, to those who are concerned about sanitation for underserved urban populations (2817).

Judith Okely reports that Travellers in the British Islands separate excretion from the indoors because it is polluting: "Gorgios [non-Travellers] design lavatories for their caravans: proof of their dirty habits.... Whereas Gorgio hygiene consists to some extent in containing, covering, or hiding dirt, for the Gypsies [sic] polluting dirt can be visible, but it must be a clear distance from the clean" (1998, 86). In this case, the rejection of the flush toilet is because of ideas about pollution; Pickering further suggests that it is also a rejection of state control (2010, 45). For land-women, rejection of the city/modernity, rejection of state control, aesthetics, and concepts of *anti*-pollution are woven together into the adoption of alternatives to the flush toilet. That is, they recast the products of the body as not polluting, and therefore not needing to be "flushed."

On women's land, bucket toilets come in many varieties, from the elaborate outdoor "Poogoda" of Fly Away Home (Madrone 2000) to the lovely indoor toilets of two of my informants at Mountainview. They maintained two bathrooms—one for solid waste, and one for urine—and said that they generally only emptied the buckets into an outdoor composter every three days. Their bathrooms were clean and odor free. The separation of shit and urine was a fairly common practice; due to the perception that urine was less contaminating or impure, and that it was good for plants, many women's lands permitted urination anywhere outdoors. At one land, the outhouses had separate buckets for shit and urine, but most women used them only for defecation, preferring to urinate just off the trails, which is where the urine buckets would be emptied in any case, the shit buckets being destined for a more elaborate composter.

Not all women's lands have or use open-air public toilets. In addition to the indoor bucket toilets, I have also encountered traditional indoor flush toilets that made use of running water and individual septic systems, flush composting toilets, and at festivals, portable toilets serviced by a septic truck. However, many women view composting as a political or even spiritual choice as well as a personal one. Composting toilets of whatever variety use little to no water and return nutrients to the soil, and are also extremely easy and cheap to build. Comfortable ones can be created in little time with few materials. The politics of composting go beyond "ecological consciousness" or monetary necessity to the idea of women's bodies as acceptable, non-disgusting objects that connect themselves with a larger landscape through *valued* products: shit and urine.

Women's lands are not the only spaces where outdoor urination and the rejection of the flush toilet are culturally and politically embraced. Lucy Pickering notes that the very idea of the toilet as connection to a larger state is rejected, as is the notion of the "purified private self" by hippies in Hawai'i (Hawkins 2006 in Pickering 2010, 40). Pickering argues that toilets and plumbing are *relational*, connecting the private self to a hidden public system and regulating private cleanliness and public sanitation (45). Therefore, her hippie informants "can be read as having rejected not only a particular type of toilet but also the connection to the state it entails," in favor of a connection with "natural" cycles of recycling, composting, and fertilization through the use of drop toilets, composting toilets, and outdoor urination (40). She suggests that "this group creatively reframes faeces and urine—those substances which transgress body boundaries—not as potentially polluting substances but as generative, life-giving matter" (34). This is very similar to how women's-land inhabitants conceive of bucket toilets, composting toilets, and urination: shit is not considered something that needs to be hidden and separated from daily life, and urine was considered beneficial for plants, similar to the views of Pickering's informants (46). These substances are no longer "dirt" but are now "earth," connecting human bodies with the landscape.

This engenders a *bodily* relationship with the land, in which human bodily products are seen not as "waste" to be disposed of in secret but as a product that is part of a larger natural cycle and beneficial to the land. In contrast to how human waste is often seen as a "dirty" or even "polluting" substance (Chun 2002; Morales, Harris, and Öberg 2014; Okely 1998; Pickering 2010) in urbanized settings, on women's land it is valued or at least, not something that must be instantly hidden. Pickering's hippie informants valued it for its ability to grow plants such as cannabis (2010, 49); my informants did not use it on crops intended for human use, but valued the *act* of composting human waste as a connection to the land in particular and the concept of natural cycles in general.

This is greatly at odds with how we view excretion and our bodies in the matrix culture of the United States. In this model, bodily functions become practical matters rather than shameful ones. The creation and usage of open shitters emphasizes the right of women to perform these bodily functions in the outdoors, relying upon the absence of a male gaze.

Why must the male gaze be absent? In the matrix culture, it is not only women who are not supposed to pee in public, although men generally have more freedom in this area. It is notable, for example, that Pickering only speaks of male public urination in her work on hippies in Hawai'i (2010). However, the fact that bathrooms still tend to be gender-segregated in the U.S. matrix society suggests that a gendered gaze is still implicated. This connects back to Garber's discussion of Lacan's concept of "urinary segregation" and how this reinforces and helps create the gender binary (1992, 13–15). This "bathroom problem," as Halberstam (1998, 20) puts it, polices gender within the restroom, making those who do not adhere to gender binaries, such as butch women, vulnerable to a curiously public gaze. Thus it is not merely the lack of the "male gaze" but also the lack of a gender binary that allows women on women's lands to claim not only "the women's room," but everywhere on women's lands. The interpretation of bodily functions as both natural and valued allows women to assert that their bodies are also natural and valued. Thus, women's land is claimed as space where a variety of bodies can exist without constraints of shame.

Nudity is an immediately "obvious" result of the assumed absence of a male gaze. Nudity and partial nudity are common in women's lands, and I often saw women on women's lands and in women-only space such as music festivals going topless, or going to and from the showers wearing only towels or nothing at all. Swimming areas are suit-optional, and I have never seen a woman wearing a bathing suit in a women's-land setting.

Nudity or nakedness are usually explored in anthropology through the lens of the "other" or the "primitive." Indeed, "a lack of clothing among colonized individuals has connoted primitiveness and savagery since at least the seventeenth century" (Levine 2008, 189). It is widely known that levels of dress and adornment vary widely from culture to culture, and that some cultures regard the clothing of other cultures as various states of nakedness. Nor, as Levine points out, is it possible to forget the ways in which being "properly" clothed has long been equated with being "civilized" by colonizing powers. Ruth Barcan notes that exposure, sin, sex, death, shame, anxiety, and savagery are all also symbolized or held to be associated with nudity (2004, 106–38). Yet the "absence of civilization" (Levine 2008, 196) and also the connections with poverty (or at least the rejection of capitalism) may be deliberately sought, as in the case of my informants and other groups that deliberately use nakedness.

It is notable that Philip Carr-Gomm's book, *A Brief History of Nakedness,* has very few photos of bodies that are not white, thin, young, and normatively heterosexual (2010). The only "queered" body performance is a photo of white performer Danny La Rue appearing as Lady Godiva; the only disabled body is a thin white woman in a wheelchair (94, 175). Meanwhile the enormous majority of bodies are white and thin, and a great number of them perform standard heterosexuality, pairing off male and female bodies. These bodies were overwhelmingly *not* like the bodies I was familiar with from women's land, which included old, fat, scarred, hairy, tattooed, disabled, and queer bodies. I argue, therefore, that the nudity of bodies on women's land is the nudity of abjected bodies, bodies that the hegemonic mainstream does not "want" or "permit" to be naked.

Levine notes tellingly that "indigenous people, with some notable exceptions, were widely regarded as ugly" in her discussion of photographs of nude "natives." Their differences were used to establish hierarchies between worthy and unworthy bodies, primitive bodies and civilized bodies, bodies that were suited to be ruled and bodies that should rule them (2008, 208). Similarly, bodies that fall outside the lines of "the tightly managed body—whether demonstrated through sleek, minimalist lines or firmly developed muscles [which] has been overdetermined as a contemporary idea of specifically female attractiveness" (Bordo 1993, 211) are also regarded as ugly by American mainstream culture. Bodies on women's land are not colonized—and largely also not bodies of color—but they are resistant to feminine body habitus. Thus instead of exposing these bodies to the "gaze" of the colonizer via the camera, these bodies are expected to hide themselves, neither fish nor fowl, neither colonizer nor properly colonized. They are failed "body projects," bodies which are abjected because they have rejected/failed civilization.

Positive associations with nudity among my informants include connections to "nature," rejection of modernity and artificiality, and the concept of freedom. Barcan lists and supports an even longer list of positive associations, including simplicity/lack of artifice, honesty or openness, innocence/humility (also childhood), freedom, nature, and authenticity (2004, 83–106). Another source of positive associations is the historical use of nudity in witchcraft/paganism (Carr-Gomm 2010, 25–51); indeed, the Wiccan use of the term "skyclad" to denote ritual nudity, which probably derives from Gardner's use (Carr-Gomm 2010, 43) has also been adopted by Dianic, feminist, and lesbian witchcraft traditions. However, for land-women, the naked body is also an assertion of authority and the lack of the male gaze. Barcan notes that "much of the history of female nakedness in the West is, however, a story of *restriction*—the curbing of its powers and the limiting of its meanings to erotic or domestic ones" (2004, 193). Land-women undermine both of these meanings with outdoor nudity that is nondomestic and not explicitly erotic (although lesbian eroticism is not denied).

Ruth Barcan writes, "Nudism is, then, a paradoxical example of 'deviant naturalism,' a form of sanctioned but circumscribed public nudity" (2004, 166). Except in situations like bathing or swimming, nudity is seldom practiced by everyone at once on women's land, but is instead accepted as part of a *range* of clothing choices. However, the concept of "deviant naturalism" is very apt, connecting back to the idea of "queering the natural," and the ways in which queer women challenge the "reprosexual" (Alaimo 2000) assumptions we make about the concept of nature, and reassert themselves as "natural." Barcan notes that "it is easy to romanticize nature, to forget that it is 'dirty,' 'messy,' or dangerous" (2004, 147). However, queer nature is always dirty, messy, and dangerous (Alaimo 2000); the connection of queerness with nature upsets the hegemonic definition of both.

This acceptance of the body is not wholesale, nor universal, as I will discuss in the next section. However, the *surface* of acceptance is near-universal. I have not experienced having another woman comment on my body, nor have I witnessed women commenting on each other's bodies while using an open-air shower.[6] Meg, who self-identifies as a fat landdyke, told me that at Michigan she went to the shower wearing only flip-flops, with "no openly negative reactions." Older women walked around without shirts at the Landdyke Gatherings. I could not imagine—and I did not witness—anyone making disparaging comments. Yet in the matrix culture such body discipline "is everywhere, and it is nowhere; the disciplinarian is everyone and yet no one in particular" (Bartky 1997, 36). In a culture where such negative comments are nearly unthinkable, women are encouraged not to participate in the panopticon of the male gaze. Such policing, in fact, may happen in reverse: women trained from birth to speak disparagingly of their bodies meet negative responses on women's land. One informant, Ivanova, told me that a self-deprecating body remark was met with "a firm but clear message that such talk was not only unnecessary here [at a Landdyke Gathering] but unwelcome and uncomfortable." She added ruefully that women communicate such messages "with varying levels of kindness or hostility" and stated that this led to conscious self-monitoring.

Bodily practices, even those as mundane as excretion and bathing, work to connect the body with a feminine/female landscape. The acceptance of women's bodies, including old bodies, bodies with mastectomies, tattooed bodies, scarred bodies, disabled bodies, and bodies of all shapes, works against the matrix definition of the feminine and its limitations on women and women's bodies. Practices such as public excretion that claims bodily products as part of a larger lifecycle connect women's bodies to a larger landscape, and help women see themselves as connected to cycles and communities and their bodies as "natural."

These body practices are in revolt against United States doxa. Yet they also refer to doxa in the concept that the body is some sort of natural, biological, precultural touchstone. The latter notion about the body is itself a cultural construction, as are *all* ideas of "the natural." These cultural uses of bodily experience make use of the concept of the supposed rawness or primacy of bodily experience to undermine other forms of gender doxa. Bodily experience convinces us, in women's space, that femaleness is not shameful, that femaleness can be the default, and does this through the unspoken assumption that our bodies and their experience are natural and thus legitimate.

Karma Eaters: The Body-Politics of Food and Fatness

Due to their interaction with the larger matrix culture, women's lands are *not* necessarily havens from the fatphobia of the United States. However, on women's land, the meanings of fatness, food, and the female body are inflected and changed by lesbian and feminist identity. In particular, the politics of food, environmentalism, and the overall rubric of "health" that connects both of these change what a fat body means in women-only space.

While doing fieldwork in this space, I have often been surprised and challenged as a fat person myself by this fatphobia and the ways in which it both mirrors and differs from the fatphobia of the American matrix culture. Although Bartky claimed that "women in radical lesbian communities have also rejected hegemonic images of femininity and are struggling to develop a new female aesthetic" (1997, 109), that rejection has not gone so deep as to abjure the aesthetics of the thin, muscular body. That thin, muscular body—firmly socially bounded and policed, as Douglas reminds us—may stand for a slightly different symbolism of discipline on women's land. However, the discipline itself and its ultimate meaning of being a properly "civilized" person (Farrell 2011) remains. Mary Douglas asserts that "the body is a model which can stand in for any bounded system. Its boundaries can represent any boundaries which are threatened or precarious" (Douglas 1984, 115). Thus the social structure of women's land, and how women's land relates to its setting in the larger matrix culture, is reflected in the politics of the body.

There is a persistent cultural myth in the United States (and elsewhere) that there is a one-to-one relationship between diet and the shape of the body (Campos 2004; Lupton 1996; Robinson, Bacon, and O'Reilly 1993). Among land-women, this belief is more specific: the idea that eating food that is "earth-friendly," including but not limited to food that is vegetarian or vegan, cruelty-free, raw diet, organic, or locally grown, will result in a thin body. Carol Adams, in *The Sexual Politics of Meat,* suggests that as meat has come to symbolize masculinity and patriarchy, vegetarianism (commonly practiced on women's land) symbolizes femininity and respect for nature and female power (2010). On women's land, this rejection of meat is viewed as not only political, but also having a visible impact on the body and the environment. An "earth-friendly" diet is thus exhorted as being not only healthy for the earth, but also healthy for the women eating it, where "health" encompasses bodily, mental, and spiritual aspects.

In the United States matrix culture, "health" has strong moral connotations and connections to the thin body (see Metzl 2010; Klein 2010 on moral connotations; Bordo 1993; LeBesco 2001; and LeBesco 2010 on connections of the thin/fat body). However, in the cultural networks of women's lands, this form of health is even more overtly moralized, since it impinges not only on the woman herself, but also on her politics, her spirituality, and on the environment around her. Thus the fat body may be negatively stigmatized *regardless* of whatever food practices actual fat women may have, both because of the symbolism borrowed from the matrix culture—lazy, lack of self-control, lower class, sinful, excessive, ugly (Bordo 1993; Farrell 2011)—*and* because of the symbolism adopted from the feminist environmental movement: parasitical, earth-hating, selfish, poisonous, subject to the patriarchy/kyriarchy,[7] and undeveloped/spiritually unaware (Dominy 1986). Thus the body and its shape comes to stand not only for its own internal moral state, but also for the relationship between that woman and the world around her. The thin body stands as a visible image of one's relationship not only with food/morality (as in the matrix culture) but with the larger ecological and spiritual system of the Earth.

In this way, the doxa of the meaning of women's bodies—particularly the "thin body" and the "fat body"—from the U.S. matrix culture persists into how such bodies are viewed in women's lands. Studies on the fatphobia of the United States and Europe are well known: for example, see Puhl, Luedicke, and Heuer on weight-based bullying of adolescents in the United States (2010); Puhl and Heuer's overview article on fatphobia and weight-based discrimination (2009); Andreyva, Puhl, and Brownell's article on how weight-based discrimination seems to be increasing over time (2008); and Greenhalgh's ethnography on the consequences of fat hatred (2015). Fatphobia (a term constructed on the same principles as homophobia) connotes the negative bias of the fatphobic towards bodies they deem excessive, stereotypes about fat people, and the ways in which body shape is blamed on a person's behavior (Robinson, Bacon, and O'Reilly 1993).

Amy Farrell, in her comprehensive volume *Fat Shame: Stigma and the Fat Body in American Culture,* narrates how fatness has been used to mark particular bodies (suffragette, African American, lower class/poor, or immigrant/ethnic) as uncivilized, primitive, and unworthy (2011). She notes that "theories of the 'uncivilized body' remain powerful today, although they show up in new and scientific terms" (81). Fatphobia thus relies on the idea that you can read the *moral* state of a person's mind/soul/social status through the body, to which they have a precultural, natural, *inevitable* one-to-one connection. Thus, both in the matrix culture and on women's land, what a fat woman *actually* eats or says she eats is not sufficient to exonerate her from the sin of having a fat body, which is tangible "proof" that she is not *really* performing "properly." This is held to be true whether or not a proper diet is held to be calorie-restricted to the point of penitence or whether the diet is "earth-friendly," as both of these are expected to produce thin, thus *visibly moral* bodies. The fat body is a testimonial against her health, her politics, her spirituality, and her honesty.

This double stigmatism often occurs under the banner of "health," as it does in the matrix culture. But "health" is reinterpreted and given different meanings through the emphasis on environmentalism and connection to the earth/the land. Yet these bodily ideals, particularly the assumption that a "good body" follows "naturally" from eating "right," are dangerously close to exactly the same extraordinarily stringent ideals that the mainstream has for women's bodies. These ideals, although they are interpreted differently, have been noted to impose pressures not only on middle-class white women, but on women and men of all races and classes (Thompson 1994; Bass 2000; Reddy and Crowther 2007; Campos 2004);[8] they are ideals that travel, ideals with legs.

My first personal encounter with such surprisingly narrow bodily ideals came at a Landdyke Gathering in New Mexico, where I was startled to find a slot on the schedule for an Overeaters Anonymous meeting. Discussions with other fat landdykes revealed that the presence of the item on the schedule was a clear message to us about how (certain) other women there felt that our bodies were ugly, wrong, and unwanted. One of the women I interviewed, Meg, identified as both a landdyke and a fat woman. In the interview she said that she had previously not noticed body consciousness at Landdyke Gatherings and had felt comfortable going nude. However, after seeing the posting on the notice board for Overeaters Anonymous, she was very careful not to go nude there. She added that she felt as though the problems with her body were "their problems, not really mine," but also indicated that she did not want to expose herself—either literally or metaphorically—to that hostility.

While overeating is not necessarily *empirically* linked to the fat body—it is, in fact, difficult to create a fat body via food intake alone, as bodies tend to have greatly different rates of metabolism and metabolic rate tends to vary with food intake (Campos 2004, 176–77)—it is intensely linked to the fat body in U.S. matrix culture. Deborah Lupton notes that "the link between body weight and the quantity and quality of food consumption is widely taken as a given, to the extent that any other explanation of heavy body weight is rarely countenanced" (1996, 16); this is unfortunately still true today, despite actual biological complexity. Fat characters in popular media are shown as gluttonous as well as morally corrupt, stupid, and cruel: see for example J. K. Rowling's popular series of children's books and Kathryn Nolfi's article on the fatphobic tendencies of young-adult novels (2011).

The moral status of the body is profoundly entwined with the folk belief that fat equals poor health, which is as active and important in the women's-land community as it is in the matrix culture. Meg told me that one of the reasons she could not live at a particular women's land was because one of the women there believed that she was in imminent danger of a heart attack. Meg said that the fact that she had low blood pressure and low cholesterol and was generally a healthy person meant nothing to this woman, who had told her, to her face, that she expected Meg to drop dead of a heart attack at any moment. Hidden in this statement was the unspoken comment that the heart attack would be Meg's fault because she was fat. Beliefs like this one display judgments about fat bodies and the way fat people are "supposed," in both senses of the term, to live. "It is expected that a 'healthy' diet will result in a slimmer body, thus providing a more permanent sign of self-discipline" (Lupton 1996, 16). Farrell notes that "in a culture permeated by fat stigma, a thinner body provides the illusion of health" (2011, 12). This equivalency of fat with un-health and thinness with health is everywhere.

Health is the main way in which land-women relate to the necessity of thinness. Beauty discourse is explicitly rejected, and class remains unspoken, just below the surface. Susan Bordo's classic analysis of the cultural meaning of slenderness implicates consumerism as the driving force behind the connection of the slender body with success, willpower, upper-class status, and beauty (1993); however, on women's land, the inhabitants have largely rejected that imperative to consume. It is "health" that drives that message home instead, and it does it just as effectively. Illness and death, as Lupton points out, are "failures of the self," which result from lack of proper regulation of the body (1996, 16). That regulation and success are visible as thinness, muscularity, and ability.

Indeed, if one peels back the skin of fatphobia on the morality of health, the "flesh" is formed of the aesthetic rejection of the fat body. Farrell notes, "What is clear from the historical documents, however, is that the connotations of fatness and of the fat person—lazy, gluttonous, greedy, immoral, uncontrolled, stupid, ugly, and lacking in will power—preceded and then were intertwined with explicit concern about health issues" (2011, 4). The bones or structure, however, is composed of ableism. Despite the fact that fat bodies are *not* necessarily disabled, the assumption that such bodies cannot or *should* not do certain things (ranging from competing in triathlons to having sex to being seen in public at all) is a potent theme in U.S. matrix culture. Susan Schweik expands the notion of what "disability" is in connection to "citizenship," showing how American "ugly laws," intended to limit the rights of disabled people to be in public, are connected to ideas about immigration. "We know what the normal body of the citizen is by knowing what it is not" (2011, 418)—not ugly, not fat, not brown/nonwhite, not disabled. Fat bodies, by being classed as a form of Other body, are excluded from certain social rights, and thus certain abilities—such as full citizenship and the status of being "civilized" (Farrell 2011)—regardless of the physical abilities of the body in question. Fat bodies are not socially *permitted* to be able. Schweik notes that the "ugly law undoubtedly was one way of punishing women whose appearance violated aesthetic norms of femininity" (Schweik 2009, 145).

It is a testament to the power of the metaphor of health when a mere generation after feminists fought to assert that a woman's worth was not in her bodily appearance, the necessity of the thin body crops up again—often among those *very same women*. For example, at one point at a Landdyke Gathering (the same one with the Overeaters Anonymous meeting), a woman called here Bea spoke feelingly on the topic of "waking up" from an earlier feminist consciousness of loving her body the way it was to the "medical dangers" of the fat body, and praised herself for putting her health above her feminist ideals. As a fat woman, I felt very uncomfortable about this, and replied that I thought that "health" stands for "morality" in today's culture.

In an act I believe was meant to turn the discussion and prevent conflict, Sirocco stepped in with a story of fostering a troubled child who used to steal and hide food because he had been starved by his parents and foster parents. She spoke about telling him that he would never have to do that in her house because he was always welcome to anything in the pantry and would never be punished for eating. By the end of her story she had several of us in tears and had successfully turned the conversation, a piece of diplomacy I was grateful for.

The very act of eating is gendered in the United States and other Western cultures. Bourdieu's famous study of food in France found powerful associations between meat and masculinity (1984), associations that Adams drew on in her work on vegetarianism and feminism (2010). Lupton notes "a symbiotic metaphorical relationship between femininity and vegetables: the eating of vegetables denotes femininity, while femininity denotes a preference for vegetables" (1996, 107), also noting that women were seen by her informants as more concerned about the environment and animal rights than men (106). Carole Counihan, in her ethnographic research among college students in the United States, found that while certain foods were seen as "masculine" and others as "feminine" (not unlike Adams 2010), she also discovered a more marked tendency among her informants to see the very act of eating itself as "masculine" (1999, 124). She writes "the sexes are enjoined to eat differently—men to eat heartily and abundantly, women to eat daintily and sparingly" and then notes that for her female informants, the act of eating in public at all is fraught with gendered danger. Male students, boyfriends, and fathers are all reported as commenting on, restricting, and forbidding the consumption of food by women (124–25). On women's land, the symbolic presence of a restricting gaze such as Overeaters Anonymous—not to mention a discussion of "health" through food restriction—calls to mind the ways in which the male gaze is not limited to male bodies. It is instead present in the ways in which female bodies are policed by each other.

At the Landdyke Gatherings, food is prepared and served communally, drawn from a common larder paid for by donations from the women present and utilizing volunteer labor. The basic menu is vegetarian or vegan, with vegan offerings present at every meal, as well as gluten-free offerings. Meat was cooked separately by women who wished to have it. The food was all freshly prepared and generally good. As Counihan reminds us, "sharing food ensures the survival of the group both socially and materially" (1999, 13): food sharing is both a basic human act and a complex and important cultural ritual. However, at this particular Gathering, with the Overeaters Anonymous group on the schedule, food became an unpleasantly tense topic at times.

One of the women who lived at the land hosting this Gathering, Aloe, ate a diet in which she allowed herself no sugars at all because she believed she was an addict. She eliminated sugar from her diet completely: not only all processed sugar, but also all natural sugar, such as that present in fruit. She served as the kitchen organizer one evening, and that evening the kitchen was tense with hostility and unprecedented errors in food preparation. For example, one side dish of mushroom gravy was burnt beyond saving and had to be recreated. During the hurried second preparation, people spoke curtly, assigning and deflecting blame for the mistake. In contrast, although there were some negative feelings about kitchen duty during other times, openly assigning blame was generally avoided. In fact, the usual method of scolding someone (for example, for not doing their fair share of the dishes) was to extravagantly praise someone *else* who had done their share in front of the shirker in question. Most of the work tension was thus indirectly expressed and did not result in the open hostility of this evening.

The difficulty of preparing the food on this occasion did not seem any greater than on previous nights, but it seemed to me and to my informants that Aloe's discomfort with food itself was communicated throughout the kitchen and made what was usually a pleasant communal task tense, hostile, and fraught with judgment. I did not know while helping in the kitchen that Aloe both instigated the inclusion of Overeaters Anonymous on the schedule and regarded herself as a sugar addict. One of my informants mentioned this when I tentatively brought up the subject of the kitchen problems afterwards, and she linked the hostility in the kitchen to Aloe's attitude towards food.

The belief that certain food substances are "addictive"—indeed, the belief that food itself, a substance that makes up one of the basic necessities of life, is addictive—has been borrowed from the matrix culture through alternative medicine. Such beliefs are visible through practices such as Overeaters Anonymous, which explicitly places food in the same category as alcohol and illegal drugs. While not all or even a majority of the women on the land hold these beliefs, enough do to make these ideas universally intelligible. Such images of food-as-drug are also common among the eating disordered, where images of binging as the addict getting high are frequently reported (Counihan 1999, 84). One fat landdyke deconstructed the entire idea of "food as addiction" on her blog, asking "Do food addicts miss work because they can't tear themselves away from the supermarket? Do the staties pull them over for operating under the influence of pudding? Do they crash their cars into bridge abutments after knocking back too many M&M's? Do they wake up on the sidewalk covered in powdered sugar without remembering how they got there?" (Feminist Reprise 2006). The idea of food as "drug" draws heavily on the morality of self-control.

The morality of self-control is heavily influenced by concepts of purity. Purity and impurity are relative. As Mary Douglas reminds us, "dirt is essentially disorder" (1994, 2). Food, then, exhibits great disorder, which must be ordered in order to control the food and thus control the body that the food enters. Food is liminal, as it bridges nature and culture, the human and the nonhuman, the outside and the inside (Atkinson 1983, 11; also Levi-Strauss 1966). Therefore, food is also highly important, as it will become part of ourselves; ordering food is a way of ordering the body and the self. It is significant that food can be seen as a troubling, dangerous, even *unclean* substance. It is then a short step to the belief that all food must be addictive, that all eating habits must be strictly controlled, and that the body is actively imperiled by nearly all the substances that enter into it. This dovetails with precise and frightening neatness with the beliefs of the diet industry and the morality of self-control.

Food as a substance is regarded as impure by many land-women, as are traditional pharmaceuticals, alcohol, other psychoactive substances (sometimes with exceptions), tobacco, air pollutants, water pollutants, most body care products including perfumes, and clothing and house cleansers produced with industrial chemicals.[9] Purity can be enhanced by using natural products, as in substituting organic for commercially-produced food or herbs for pharmaceuticals. There is a hierarchy of purity: herbs, especially organic ones, are seen as a very pure and health-giving substance, while perfumes—even if made from organic and natural essential oils—are impure.

This attitude towards food is similar to what Fischler called the "omnivore's paradox," the search for new foods restrained by the fear of poisoning (1988); however, this "poisoning anxiety" is clearly not some issue deep in the human psyche, but a clear and present danger kept fresh by constant new information about various possible "poisons" in food. This is true both for land-women and for the American matrix culture itself, which is saturated with media about the dangers in our food. On women's land, food is a contested substance—while it can be made more pure, there are still dangerous substances within the food itself. "Food is now commonly represented as a pathogen, a source of disease and ill-health" (Lupton 1996, 77). Food is *also* a source of morality, right action, and discourse about the body/self, and the common equation of nature and virtue is recalled in the hierarchy of purity that "natural" eating entails (89).

Meg told me about a time she was celebrating her birthday with a cake. Someone mentioned "how much sugar" the cake had in it and Aloe, who was a member of the community hosting the celebration, had to leave the table. Meg spoke eloquently about how painful the incident was for her and how much implied judgment there was regarding her food choices and her body. Meg later wrote a letter to the community about how her mother had denied her food since she was five and about how she had wanted the food at her birthday to be a celebration. However, the food contained symbolic danger: sugar. Food is not a neutral topic.

Food processing—adding preservatives, production in factories—now "breeds symbolic danger" (Lupton 1996, 89) through making food less natural. However, sugar and other similar substances are not additives and cannot always be "redeemed" out of the food using organic farming or less-processed forms of cooking: they are inherent in the food itself. Therefore, food cannot be a completely pure substance. "Health" foods create a bodily appeal that parallels the rural retreat of women's land in "their imputed ability to restore purity and wholesomeness, to retreat from the complexities of modern life to an idealized pastoral dream of the 'good life'" (89). Ashley et al. (2004) argue that there are two separate branches of vegetarianism—the "ethical," which focuses on the impact of meat farming on the environment, global economics, and ethics, and "lifestyle," which instead focuses on "eating healthy" (194). However, in the space of women's land, these things are *conflated*—the environment and the body are seen as having a reciprocal relationship. Thus "healthy food" and vegetarian eating, in their association with purity and femininity, nature and rejection of the "factory farm" (Atkinson 1983, 16), are a practice that links bodies to the very space of women's land. The practice of purity in eating, therefore, is not simply policing the boundaries and health of the self; it is policing the boundaries of the entire community.

In this context, it is easy to understand how food itself can be classified as a dangerous, impure, and addictive substance. Aloe's decision to classify herself as an addict and to control her diet so stringently is a logical outgrowth of sugar's classification as an evil, addictive substance. This is similar to Fischler's concept of "saccharophobia," which describes a fear of sugar as the source of disease because of its association with technology/food processing (1987, 87–88), but it is clear that sugar's evil is not confined to this association if it is also shunned in "natural" foods. It is not sugar's status as an industrial chemical that makes it impure. It is sugar's reputation as the creator of the unhealthy—fat—body.[10]

The link between healthy eating and the larger world is understood to reflect "naturally" and visibly in the body itself. The practice of healthy eating in and of itself is not enough. Thus the fat body is seen as *itself* a "disease" caused by laziness/indolence, lack of self-control, selfishness, and being spiritually undeveloped.[11] It is, according to these believers, the outward sign of the moral corruption of the soul. Health, in fact, is so overtly moralized in the matrix culture of the United States that sometimes sufferers from actual diseases such as cancer, heart disease, and AIDS are blamed for contracting their diseases (Beaulieu et al. 2014; Shepherd and Gerend 2014, for just a few examples; see also Sontag 1988). Thus the construction of morality around the fat body invokes powerful real-world effects. Within women's-land culture, the connection between relative food impurity, the symbol of the fat body, and the moral importance of health is well developed.

For example, my informant Marie seemed to assign blame to her lover for her diabetes. In the midst of several long stories about her lover, all of which were very affectionate, Marie said the following:

> And later on, you know, when she got cancer—she got cancer at 92—we weren't living together, of course, this was 2002. And what was also hard was she was eating a lot—she had diabetes in her family. She was 4'1"—you know, a tiny person, small person. She got up around 200 pounds. And when I first met her she was not, I think she'd just been on one of those weight-loss diets not too long before, that Colombian or whatever. One of those ones where you made the stuff and drank it. And I'm a nurse, and I'm a real health advocate, and it would be hard, real hard to see her eating. Drinking diet Coke and a lot of coffee all day, and, we'd go out for

something to eat and she'd have—those all-you-can-eat places and she'd have—and I'd say "Geez, [Name removed], watch out, I don't want you to have diabetes." And she got it.

And she'd say to me, "I'm not your patient! Let me alone!" You know. [Laughter] You know. So you know, we had our times.

Marie did not find it "hard" that her lover was doing a malnutritive weight-loss diet; instead she found it "hard" to "see her eating." Note also that she seems to blame her lover for getting diabetes because of her eating habits or her weight gain—this victim-blaming myth is well established.[12] Marie did not explicitly say what she thought the connection was between her lover's diabetes and her cancer at the age of ninety-two. In any case, ninety-two is a fairly advanced age at which to die, of cancer or any other cause, yet the way this story is told implies that even at ninety-two, women are expected to police their bodies for thinness, morality, and health.

The correlation to such reasoning is the idea that a moral body will naturally be free of disease and will also escape death. (This reasoning persists despite the evidence that no body, no matter how healthy or moral, escapes death.) The moral body among land-women is maintained through moral bodily action, which includes paying attention to food purity and impurity.

Processed foods often symbolize "what is wrong" with the matrix culture. It is interesting that "medical experts"—often white males, always people in positions of social power—have also often used processed foods, particularly sugary or fast foods, as symbols of "what is wrong with how people are eating today." Helene Dominy, in her study of lesbian separatists in New Zealand, reports that her informants "associate purity with nature" and "all agree that processed foods and professional medicine are examples of male control and power over women's bodies" (1986, 279). By rejecting processed foods, many women reject not only how they believe the matrix culture would have them eat, but also the entire industry of those foods.

The interpretation of *all* sugar as "addictive" is not only a rejection of the processed food industry, it is also an assertion of control over the body—perhaps even an act of taking control out of the hands of the matrix culture. Sugar is also coded feminine in the matrix culture, as anthropologists have noted (Mintz 1986; Lupton 1996). Rejection of sugar can thus also be seen as rejection of mainstream femininity. However, these practices of body discipline and food purity closely replicate the restrictions of matrix femininity. This rejection of "patriarchal control" leads to a policing of bodily boundaries that results in the slender, feminine, "docile body" (Bordo 1993), a body in which energy is being properly directed towards food and bodily control rather than other projects.

In the midst of women's lands devoted to the principle of removing women's lives from the reach of the kyriarchy, food practices and body shape ideals betray some of the ways that mainstream/matrix-culture ideas about gendered bodies persist. In particular, it is deeply ironic that such food practices essentially adopt the same standards for the female body—thin, muscular, and firm—that the matrix cultures of the United States insist on. The symbol of the thin body, although it is used to mean something different from self-restraint and heterosexual attractiveness, remains on women's land in spite of how the thin female body reflects a particularly gendered form of control. The surface of such bodily practice is interpreted differently, even in opposition to patriarchal control, but the deep doxa of the body—of limiting what a "properly gendered" female body should look like—remains.

However, discourse around bodies is varied. At other Gatherings, public nudity of a wide range of bodies, including older women, fat women, and scarred and disabled women, was encouraged. I have also witnessed self-denigration by a fat woman being flatly discouraged in a way diametrically opposed to many places in the U.S. mainstream, where female verbal self-denigration is a well-known and accepted conversational form. Ivanova said, "it was almost instructional correction: it was not acceptable for me to say something like that. It was rude. And the impression I was given was that to a certain extent it was self-aggrandizing—it was a means of getting attention and validation and reassurance. And that was what straight women did." Fat landdykes also practice a wide range of consciousness-raising, from writing about body issues to attempting to educate individual women and communities about the problems of fatphobia. However, not all such attempts are successful: Meg, in her interview with me, told me about her painful decision not to live at a particular women's land because of the fatphobia there and the attitudes some of the women had about her and her body.

Thus the attitudes of women in the community-at-large tend to reinforce ideas about the food purity hierarchy, and the ways a thin body signifies social, spiritual, moral, and bodily health. Thin bodies, like white bodies, are morally positive or neutral. Ironically, the thin body is also the properly feminine body of the matrix culture—the disciplined, controlled body that does not "take up space," and the body that is constructed to the mores of the heterosexual male gaze. An enormous aspect of proper femininity is body size, that, in the guise of bodily health, is extensively practiced by many land-women despite their rejection of mainstream/matrix ideas about gender and heterosexual roles.

The female body in its various guises—as an agent, acting in her environment; as a supposedly-malleable canvas for the impact of cultural forces, but that is instead interpreted as the mirror of the moral soul; and as a profoundly political canvas for the demonstration of boundaries, purity, and worth—reveals important ways in which land-women both resist and adopt ideas about gender from the matrix culture. While women's lands provide an important locus for the female body to act freely, unconfined by the presumed male gaze of the matrix culture, aspects of the patriarchal and heterosexual gender system still persist in terms of what body shape is interpreted as healthy and morally correct. This influences what bodies are viewed as proper, worthy, and good citizens of women's land.

In particular, the idea that the body is raw and precultural, an idea so rooted in the doxa of the United States that few, if any, of my informants thought to question it, provided the locus both for ways to resist forms of matrix-culture gender doxa and also to adopt it. In particular, the view of the body as "natural" provided a venue for the female body's "natural" experience in women's-land spaces to claim new ways of experiencing space and being in the world.

The idea that bodies "naturally" mirror behavior—a myth very prevalent in the matrix culture as well—leads to the rejection of fat bodies not simply as aesthetically unappealing but as morally wrong. If bodies are "naturally" transparent and display a one-to-one relationship between moral action and the body surface, then of course it is possible to read a woman's "true" nature in the shape of her body. The foodways of women's land may use the symbol of the thin body to mean something different than the matrix culture does, yet the standard of thinness for women's bodies persists. Such standards are still set by the matrix culture and still produce a female body who takes up less space, who spends much of her time and energy disciplining herself, and who adheres to a heterosexual standard of attractiveness in body shape, if not in other forms of femininity such as clothing and makeup. The doxa of the natural body, coupled with the discourse of health, produces a standard of thinness that carefully mirrors that of the mainstream United States.

The body is complex: a rich signifier of cultural meaning, the locus of societal discipline, and yet also agential, interacting with the world around her to claim space and create a differently gendered way of being. The body is the focus of deep cultural doxa—the cultural ideas we accept as natural—but also the focus of experience and action that allows cultural change itself.

· CHAPTER 7 ·

We Have Met the Enemy and She Is Us

Scapegoating Trans Bodies

> *We just want to identify the "real" freaks, so we can feel closer to normal. In reality, not a single one of us is so magically normative as to claim the right to separate out the freaks from everyone else. We are all freaks to someone. Maybe even—if we're honest—to ourselves.*
>
> —Kate Bornstein, *Gender Outlaw: On Men, Women, and the Rest of Us*

SOME OF US WERE EXTREMELY UNCOMFORTABLE with the turn the discussion had taken. Three women at the Landdykes Gathering were discussing a well-known trans woman who was living in a mixed-gender community.

The woman who was under fire was personally known (as I happened to know because it had come up in conversation earlier) to at least one woman there, my informant Artemis. She was sitting to one side, her face rigid and her expression at least as uncomfortable as I felt.

Then one of the women who was engaging in the trashing called the trans woman in question—whom the other women had been calling "he" throughout the discussion in a deliberately disrespectful act of misgendering—"it."

I wanted to say something, anything, about how nasty and vicious this all was. But I felt tied by my precarious status as a researcher, my age (I was the youngest present at the time), and my status as a guest. Anger and fear taste very similar.

I got up and left.

One of the best-known conflicts among women's-space enthusiasts is over the admittance of trans women. By "trans women" I mean people who have been diagnosed at birth as the male or masculine sex/gender, and who have then changed their gender to female through behavior, dress, and sometimes also through surgery and hormones. This conflict has produced some of the most bitter arguments I have seen on the many thorny topics that spark debate among women supporting women's space (the other two topics that leap immediately to mind are the use of BDSM in women's space[1] and whether male children are allowed). The online discussion board for the Michigan Womyn's Music Festival was perhaps the best-known forum for this debate, but it occurs in other spaces and among other women as well. This conflict also focuses heavily on the body and on body doxa that persists from U.S. matrix cultures: the body as a "natural," precultural object; the body as possessing some sort of experiential "truth"; and the body as performing or not performing gender correctly.

This chapter is the one that will be taken as a betrayal by at least some of my informants; but I cannot and will not betray my own knowledge and principles, which tell me that I cannot deny the humanity of trans folk. Gender is intimately tied into personhood in many cultures, including those practiced on women's land and in the matrix cultures of the United States. Indeed, as a scholar of gender, I would argue that gender is necessary to personhood—when your gender is denied, so is your humanity. Thus, the debate over trans women, as I argue below, is an epistemological war—a deep and sordid conflict of meaning-making with the humanity of certain people at its heart.

Among my informants, those who expressed openly transphobic views were about equally balanced with those who expressed disgust with such views, with the subject simply not occurring among most. Transphobia, while shocking, was not a common event in my fieldwork because I am a cis woman; I describe above one of only three occurrences I witnessed face-to-face. However, when I was writing this manuscript, the first thing editors and reviewers wanted to hear about was transphobia. Online, the very loud voices of some women's-space enthusiasts, especially centering around the Michigan Womyn's Music Festival, have foregrounded this debate. Also, debates in which some women express openly transphobic views on the Land-dyke mailing lists have occurred several times while I was following them. So, because of what happens online/in public, transphobia as an issue has heavily colored how women's land/women's space is seen.

One of the most disturbing aspects of the various arguments made against the inclusion of trans women is the way they bear an uncanny resemblance to arguments made against including lesbians in the second wave of the women's movement. Lesbians served as the scapegoats of the second wave, and separatists serve, even today, as the scapegoats of feminist lesbians, or lesbian feminists; the trans population serves as a collective scapegoat for the queer community at large. Julia Serano notes this similarity as well: "But what I find most dumbfounding about lesbian-feminist arguments that trans women might somehow threaten cissexual women's safety is how eerily similar they are to the arguments some heterosexual women have made in the past in their attempts to exclude lesbians from women's spaces and organizations" (2007, 242).

Those arguments stem from the same root: that people are not "doing" their gender correctly, and are therefore "wrong" in body, mind, or behavior. Proper gender expression in the North American matrix culture is heterosexual and compulsory (see Adrienne Rich's discussion of compulsory heterosexuality, 1986). Both transphobia and homophobia spring from gender discipline, or social attempts to police gender along hegemonic lines. Serano rightly points out that engaging in either transphobia or homophobia is also antifeminist (2007, 244). Yet at the same time they engage in transphobia, land-women also see themselves as resisting gender discipline by performing or welcoming lesbianism.

Thus, transphobia and homophobia are *both* types of gender policing: licensed hatred of people who step outside the heterosexual hegemony of dichotomous genders. Trans folk, even those who prefer male/female sexual expression, step farther outside these boundaries, and are statistically punished more severely. The Southern Poverty Law Center reports that hate crimes towards transgender people are on the rise, and their murder rate may in fact outpace all other hate killings (Moser 2007), while 2014–2017 saw a terrifying rise in the number of trans women killed. In 2015, twenty-four trans women were killed in the United States, twenty-one of whom were women of color. The Trans Murder Monitoring (TMM) project notes, "While the actual circumstances of the killings often remain unknown due to a lack of investigation and reports, many of the cases documented involve an extreme degree of aggression, including torture and mutilation" (Transgender Europe 2015).

The National Coalition of Anti-Violence Programs reports that 2017 saw a 29 percent increase in hate homicides against LGBTQ and HIV+ people, including the murders of sixteen trans women of color (Waters and Yacka-Bible 2017); the final number of trans women murdered in 2017 was twenty-six (and one trans man was also murdered). They also report a worrying rise in the murder of transgender (particularly transfeminine) minors (Transgender Europe 2014). Both transphobia and homophobia share a depressing range of repercussions, including the very low rates at which hate crimes are successfully prosecuted, the association with high stress levels and medical problems, and how both tend to lead to "invisible" crimes and discrimination (National Coalition of Anti-Violence Programs 2017).

Why, therefore, do some lesbian and lesbian-allied women exhibit such profound transphobia when dealing with women's space and trans women? Many of the issues regarding the inclusion of trans women in women-only space have to do with the definition of "women," and while that definition is both bodily and otherwise, it relies on the idea that there exists a precultural, natural, "raw" bodily experience that can be accessed. It also relies on the way our own privilege remains invisible to us, especially when we are in the process of exercising it. What we define, what becomes visible, and what we choose to speak of are all acts of power.

A Body Politic: Difference "All the Way Down"

The problem of "sisterhood"—that is, the assumption that women are a unified class with common experiences—occurs across all sorts of differences, including bodily ones. The ongoing debate over body and gender in both the U.S. matrix culture and in women's-land cultures encompasses both sides of the problem of women as an analytic category: the problem of eliding differences between women and women's experiences, and the problem of how to define women as a group.

Feminists of color first pointed out this problem in relation to assumptions that sisterhood somehow transcended racism. Although it is invidious to compare the issues of transgender oppression and racism, it is important to note the history of the "problematics of sisterhood" which applies as a concept to both racism and sexism, and to give credit to the theorists who first pointed out these issues. Audre Lorde notes that "beyond sisterhood, is still racism" (1983, 97), and doris davenport states, "Feminism either addresses itself to all wimmin, or it becomes even more so just another elitist, prurient white organization, defeating its own purposes" (1983, 89). The problems with considering women as a single category are well articulated by bell hooks:

The vision of Sisterhood evoked by women's liberationists was based on the idea of common oppression. Needless to say, it was primarily bourgeois white women, both liberal and radical in perspective, who professed belief in the notion of common oppression. The idea of "common oppression" was a false and corrupt platform disguising and mystifying the true nature of women's varied and complex social reality. Women are divided by sexist attitudes, racism, class privilege, and a host of other prejudices. (1997, 485–86)

In conclusion, hooks notes, "Women do not need to eradicate difference to feel solidarity. We do not need to share common oppression to fight equally to end oppression" (1997, 499). Such arguments against the need for a "common oppression," although written to address racial differences, also apply to cis women and trans women.[2]

Significantly, black feminists were among the earliest to voice suspicion of biological determinist arguments with regard to gender:

> We have a great deal of criticism and loathing for what men have been socialized to be in this society: what they support, how they act, and how they oppress. But we do not have the misguided notion that it is their maleness per se—i.e. their biological maleness—that makes them what they are. As Black women we find any type of biological determinism a particularly dangerous and reactionary basis upon which to build a politic. (Combahee River Collective 1986, 14)

This statement, first published in 1977, clearly and immediately rejects reliance on biological determinism to explain the origin of sexist and homophobic oppression. Black feminists had already seen the problems with biological determinism applied to race.

Nagoshi and Brzuzy say dryly that "a feminist theoretical approach to transgenderism that retains an essentialist view of gender would clearly be problematic" (2010, 435). Often, current gender theory, springing from Butler's classic work *Gender Trouble* (1999), holds that gender is entirely performative, as is sex itself: "No longer believable as an interior 'truth' of dispositions and identity, sex will be shown to be a performatively enacted signification . . . one that, released from its naturalized interiority and surface, can occasion the parodic proliferation and subversive play of gendered meanings" (44). In an article about performativity, Butler notes:

> Gender is performative insofar as it is the effect of a regulatory regime of gender differences in which genders are divided and heirarchized under constraint.... There is no subject who precedes or enacts this repetition of norms. To the extent that this repetition creates an effect of gender uniformity, a stable effect of masculinity or femininity, it produces and destabilizes the notion of the subject as well, for the subject only comes into intelligibility through the matrix of gender. (1993b, 21–22)

That is, not only is there no "raw" pregendered (or only-sexed) self, but the self only becomes "intelligible" *through* gender, which is a strict code of behavior. Gender is thus a necessary precursor to personhood.

Julia Serano proposes the term "experiential gender" to cover the ways in which gender is both embodied in a physical experience and also dependent on performance and acceptance of that performance (2007, 216–27). In discussing how her own trans-embodied experience of gender illuminates sexism, homophobia, and transphobia, she also touches on the ways in which gender is both localized to the bodily experience and presentation of a particular person (what Bourdieu would call the *habitus*[3]) and part of a larger regulating structure of symbols, behaviors, and beliefs. She challenges the idea that women are a *natural class:* that a category which we can call "women" somehow exists in the world even when we do not observe it, instead calling for the idea that "'woman' is a holistic concept" (227). Nagoshi and Brzuzy suggest that such an approach helps to unite notions of embodiment with gender as both individual performance and larger social structure, saying, "this transgender theory idea of fluid, embodied, and socially and self-constructed social identity can inform an understanding of intersectional oppressed identities" (2010, 437). Bobby Noble, writing about the similar problematics of defining the "women" in "women's studies," wryly notes that "trans bodies have always been present in feminism as a social movement, even as those bodies have been ghosted by a belief that such bodies have never been a part of feminism or women's studies" (2012, 48).

Yet, the idea that men and women exist as "natural categories," has haunted gender and feminist studies from its inception. Judith Butler notes that she originally wrote *Gender Trouble* in response to her "unease" with this:

> The binary between "men" and "women" seemed not only to be a constant presupposition within feminist work, but... the implicit and compulsory presumption of heterosexuality supported the normativity and irreversibility of that binary and posited relations of complementarity or asymmetry between its terms in ways that only shored up, without marking, the heterosexist assumptions of the paradigm. As I wrote against such moves, I meant to open up another possibility for feminist thought, one that would overcome its complicity in heterosexist presuppositions. (1999, 2)

Butler denaturalizes *assumed binary gender*, knocking away an important support of heterosexism. It is therefore important to analyze how cis lesbians (and some other feminist cis women) culturally wield notions of binary gender when addressing the issue of women's space and trans women. All too often these notions can wind up undercutting lesbian and feminist ideals, as binary notions of gender all too easily fall into heterosexist paradigms.

Ortner writes that "an emphasis on 'women' as an analytic category, when pushed too hard, tends to move in the direction of a very problematic naturalism" (1996, 137), also rejecting the concept of the natural class. Joan Wallach Scott suggests that while much of the usefulness of the term *gender* in the 1970s through the 1990s was its radical position, which has since slipped to a more codified and less questioning place, it can still be a useful overall category of analysis (2010). She writes:

> Gender is, I would argue, the study of the vexed relationship (around sexuality) between the normative and the psychic, the attempt at once to collectivize fantasy and to use it for some political or social end, whether that end is nation-building or family structure. In the process, it is gender that produces meanings for sex and sexual difference, not sex that determines the meanings of gender. If that is the case, then (as some feminists have long insisted) there

is not only no distinction between sex and gender, but gender is the key to sex. (Scott 2010, 13)

In this formulation, the term "gender" does remain useful as designating a field of inquiry; at the same time, however, we must question the more concrete categories of "men" and "women." Mary Hawkesworth also identifies a number of pitfalls in the deployment of gender as an analytic category (2006). She notes a shift whereby gender attains ontological status, and "these accounts suggest a universal and invariant role for gender. Race, class, ethnicity, and nationality disappear from these accounts as the cunning of culture produces species survival, compulsory heterosexuality, heightened sexual pleasure, or categories of the mind" (174). This shift from gender description to gender as explanation is problematic for scholarship, as it produces merely simplified "explanans" (175) reductive to biology without biology's data, and problematic for activism, as these "explanans" are non-inclusive and non-collective. "Universal claims about the invariability of gender and the unwarranted assumptions about the cunning of culture securing gender's psychic and social functions are self-defeating, for they signify the persistence of the natural attitude in feminist discourses" (175) Hawkesworth warns that "natural attitude" signals the hidden hand of biology and the body as a precultural object appears again. Although "natural attitude" thinking pushes us towards women as a natural class of objects, women are a cultural invention, like world peace, poetry, and the nature/culture divide.

The "anti" participants in the debate about trans women generally argue from three points: experiential, political, and essential. Experiential arguments state that trans women are not really women because they did not have the experience of growing up as women. Political arguments demand the exclusion of trans women on the basis that they represent a diminution of women's power/space/energy in a zero-sum game. Essential arguments consist of asserting that trans women are not women for reasons other than early or current experience, instead relying on either bodily, sometimes genetic, descriptions or on an undefined, assumed *essential* quality that "true women" are assumed to socially or spiritually share. All of these arguments are predicated on the doxa of the natural, precultural body; that is, the idea that a body exists *prior to* the application of gender is essential to the function of these arguments. This doxa of the natural body also undergirds the assumption that men and women occur as "natural classes."

The experiential argument holds that trans women are unable to experience "female oppression" or even simply female experience because of their a priori "male" bodies that shape their experience as male in childhood. This argument depends on the notion that a body exists prior to the cultural experience of it *and* that that cultural experience is filtered through the biological "meaning" of that body (rather than our experiences of "biological reality" being shaped by culture). Serano notes aptly that "claims that [cis women] somehow understand 'womanhood' better than trans women do by virtue of having been born and socialized female is just as naive and arrogant as my claiming to understand 'womanhood' better because, unlike most women, I have had a male experience to compare it to. Any claim that one has superior knowledge about womanhood is fraught with gender entitlement and erases the infinite different ways for people to experience their own femaleness" (2007, 227).

The political/zero-sum argument also relies on the doxa of the precultural body, as the idea that trans women "remove" resources from "real" women depends on a division between these two categories made on the basis of the body. Whether this argument is made on a simple biological basis—that biology is destiny—or predicated on the idea that biology comes before destiny, both are based on the premise that the body is without culture and exists (or at some time existed) in a precultural state. That is, any argument that boils down to biological essentialism assumes that bodies *operate the same way* regardless of their cultural context. Serano also notes that such biological essentialism is ironically phallocentric: "This 'penis' argument not only objectifies trans women by reducing us to our genitals, but propagates the male myth that men's power and domination somehow arise from the phallus. The truth is, our penises are made of flesh and blood, nothing more. And the very idea that the femaleness of my mind, personality, lived experiences, and the rest of my body can somehow be trumped by the mere presence of a penis can only be described as phallocentric" (2007, 239).

The idea that trans women lack the "essence" of femaleness, whether postulated as a directly biological ability to breed or as a spiritual feminine essence, is also predicated on the idea of a precultural body: either a biological "reality" based in a fertile reproductive tract (a bodily trait many cis women lack) that trumps cultural ideas about femininity, or a precultural, spiritual essence that resides in the biological body defined as female.[4] Again, Serano points out that such arguments are ironically antifeminist: "many argue that trans women should be barred from women's spaces because we supposedly still have 'male energy.' But by suggesting that trans women possess some mystical 'male energy' as a result of having been born and raised male, these women are essentially making the case that men have abilities and aptitudes that women are not capable of" (2007, 239). When arguments center around "the experience of menstruation," as they sometimes do, they do not call on the experience of many women who have never menstruated, who have ceased to menstruate, or who menstruate in nonstandard ways (such as women who have polycystic ovary syndrome).[5]

A focus on reproductive ability ignores the fact that many lesbians and other fertile women simply don't reproduce. What meaning should fertility invoke when many women not only have no intention of reproducing, but have been working for many years to define themselves as something other than reproductive bodies? Fertility arguments invoke the complication of women who have had hysterectomies or are past menopause, and also implicates the wide range of non-fertile women as "not really women." But reproductive ability is still seen by some as the centerpiece of femaleness: Alix Dobkin is quoted as saying that "a woman can make a man, a woman can make a woman, but a man can't make a woman, not even with a doctor's knife" (McDonald 1997, 6). This definition places reproductive power as the definitive point of being a woman. Helene Dominy reports that some lesbian separatists in Christchurch, New Zealand, "use a biological model based on the nature of female sexuality and on female powers of reproduction. They believe female sexuality fosters creativity and vitality.... Separatists do not think of gender as socially determined, but they do believe social structures reinforce gender differentiation. Thus they see biologically defined gender as a pervasive social fact" (1986, 276). Again, reproductive power defines femaleness; just as it does for conservative threads of the matrix culture.

Those who seek to ground essential gender difference in the body often turn to genetics. Yet this proves a feeble reed; for although biology is used in the matrix culture as the premier method to establish truths about humanity, biology is messy. The existence of people with genetics outside the XX and XY spectrum, as well as XY individuals who present entirely as anatomically female from birth and XX individuals who present entirely as anatomically male from birth, and individuals of both genetic structures with ambiguous genitalia, seem to mandate against a neat biological argument (Karkazis 2008). In fact, our society imposes narrow bodily ideals on a wide biological reality, as Anne Fausto-Sterling points out when she writes that one in a hundred people in our matrix society are outside medical norms, are considered intersex, and tend to be surgically corrected (1997, 245). Yet these binary bodily ideals are so entrenched that biological facts are not permitted to stand in the way of socially formed ideas about what men and women "are."

We do not experience the body except through the lens of our own particular culture. As Clifford Geertz points out, "Whatever else modern anthropology asserts—and it seems to have asserted almost everything at one time or another—it is firm in the conviction that men unmodified by the customs of particular places do not in fact exist, have never existed, and most important, could not in the very nature of the case exist" (1973, 35). This goes for women as well. We cannot understand our bodies except through culture; therefore, there *is* no pregendered body and there *is* no "raw" precultural body or body experience. While biological bodies undoubtedly exist—we are not brains in jars—how we interpret, understand, and experience those bodies is culturally shaped. We are our bodies, but culture affects *how* we are our bodies; they are completely entwined. And one of the primary cultural shapers is gender. Therefore, as Nicholson says:

> We cannot look to the body to ground cross-cultural claims about the male-female distinction.... We need to understand social variations in the male/female distinction as related to differences that go "all the way down," that is, as tied not just to the limited phenomena that many of us associate with gender (i.e., to cultural stereotypes of personality and behavior) but also to culturally various understandings of the body and to what it means to be a woman or to be a man. (1994, 83)

Our first and last understandings of our bodies are shaped by the language, gender, and culture we have learned to apply to them. However, the cultural *myth* that there is some "raw" bodily experience that we can access is prevalent in both the matrix culture and on women's land.

To return to the experiential, political, and essential arguments against the inclusion of trans women, all of these arguments also bear an eerie resemblance to arguments made against including lesbians in the second wave of the women's movement (Betty Friedan's "lavender menace" comment is perhaps the most famous of these). "Few dykes, even lesbian feminists, remember today that the first negative response to lesbian participation in the women's movement was the idea that we would contaminate consciousness-raising groups with male behavior—specifically, sexual predation. Straight feminists assumed lesbians had the equivalent of male identities" (Califia 2003, 3). This is similar to conservative arguments about trans women preying on cis women in bathrooms. Lesbians have been, and still are, accused of "taking resources away from the 'real' concerns of the women's movement" [Bunch 1972, 8] (zero-sum argument) and of lacking the *heterosexual* experience or essence that makes a "true" woman (experiential and essence arguments).

However, despite these similarities, women's space activists do not always perceive these connections. There are many possible reasons for this, foremost among which is the divide-and-conquer technique of straight hegemony and kyriarchy in general. Racism benefits white people most, but racism routinely occurs between and among people of color. Similarly—and in intersection with racism—transphobia primarily benefits the straight, cisgender, and male hegemony, but it also occurs among other groups whose gender and/or sexual identities are neither straight nor hegemonic. Lesbians and gay men (not to mention other queer types) are not performing their gender correctly according to the norms of the matrix society of the United States: proper gender expression is *heterosexual*. As Califia notes, lesbians are, to a certain extent, "unwomaned"[6] (2003, 4). To be properly gendered, you must participate in the compulsory heterosexuality of the Western matrix cultures so ably described by Adrienne Rich (1986); heterosexuality is compulsory *because* it is intertwined and part of the binary gender system, as Gayle Rubin aptly noted (1975).

Thus, both transphobia and homophobia are a form of gender discipline, bullying, or hatred directed at those who transgress gender boundaries. It is well known that trans folk are statistically punished more severely, and hate crimes towards transgender individuals, especially those who are nonwhite, are on the rise (Moser 2007). Like other queer folk, transgender people are often reluctant to contact the police or other "official" systems, having often endured violence or discrimination; for example, the well-known case of Tyra Hunter, who bled to death in Washington D.C. after being struck by a car because the EMT who had arrived to give aid laughed and told jokes about her to the other emergency service workers rather than give life-saving treatment. The case of CeCe McDonald, who was tried and convicted for second-degree manslaughter after defending herself in a transphobic attack on her in which she was stabbed and blinded by liquor tossed into her face[7] and the case of four lesbians in New York who were sentenced to prison merely for defending themselves against a homophobic attack[8] are extremely similar. Both cases are of black women (transphobic and homophobic violence is higher against women of color than against white women), attacked by a white man, and in both cases they were sentenced by a white jury or judge who refused to allow evidence that they were the victims of an attack (Signorile 2014). Both transphobia and homophobia stem from rigid gender policing, and both share a wide range of characteristics, including intersections with racism[9] and misogyny, a frightening tendency to violence, and an even more frightening tendency to make that violence as invisible and as normative as possible.

Given these similarities, why would a lesbian and lesbian-allied community engage in transphobia? The policing of boundaries of what it means to be a "woman" still relies on the idea of the precultural, "raw" bodily experience that contains or "is" some kind of binary-gendered, biological or spiritual truth. Furthermore, by rejecting those who transgress even farther against norms of proper gendered behavior, these communities have access to a useful scapegoat.[10]

Biology, in this case, is used as the "essential truth" behind the draperies of our social norms and our wishful thinking. Biology, it is implied, is what we "really are." Again we see the doxa of the "real," the "natural," and the precultural body. In the arguments of the anti-trans contingent, biology is a neat binary thing that follows the neat binary thinking of the matrix culture's strict dichotomy between men and women. Messy biological facts are elided, ignored, or discarded as "irrelevant." In this case, biology is made to serve societal ideas about the opposite, dichotomous nature of male and female, dressed up in scientific language. "People often squabble over what defines a person as a woman or a man—whether it should be based on their chromosomes, assigned sex, genitals, or other factors—but such reductionist views deny our indisputably holistic gendered realities" (Serano 2007, 224).

The phrase "women-born-women," which is used by many anti-trans women to refer to cis women, implies not so much a reliance on biological essentialism as on *contiguity of experience*. It suggests that only those who have had the experience of growing up as women are "true" women, neatly obviating the experience of trans women. This form of labeling goes with the assertion that trans women cannot "truly" be women because they lack the essential femaleness that can only be acquired through a *lifetime* of female experience.[11] It also de-legitimizes the experience of trans women who state that they have always been women, regardless of how other people have seen their bodies. Julia Serano unpacks how "contiguity of experience" is actually a form of biological essentialism after all:

> The fact that socialization is a specious argument became obvious to me during an exchange I had with a trans-woman exclusionist who insisted that my being raised male was the sole reason in her mind for me to be disqualified from entering women only spaces. So I asked her if she was open to allowing trans women who are anatomically male but who have been socialized female—something that's not all that uncommon for MTF children these days. She admitted to having concerns about their attending. Then, I asked how she would feel about a person who was born female yet raised male against her will, and who, after a lifetime of pretending to be male in order to survive, finally reclaimed her female identity upon reaching adulthood. After being confronted with this scenario, the woman conceded that she would be inclined to let this person enter women-only space, thus demonstrating that her argument about male socialization was really an argument about biology after all. In fact, after being pressed a bit further, she admitted that the scenario of a young girl who was forced against her will into boyhood made her realize how traumatic and dehumanizing male socialization could be for someone who was female-identified. This, of course, is exactly how many trans women experience their own childhoods. (2007, 241)

These arguments center around an assumed precultural, assumed nonproblematic natural-category female body. Yet besides the fact that there is no precultural body, no body with "sex before gender"—our understanding of the body is inevitably filtered through our cultural norms about the body—there is also another argument. This is the argument that bodies which have undergone hormonal or surgical alterations are "alien" or "wrong." Or, on the other hand, how an assumed male body that behaves in a female-gendered manner has "wrong/alien energy." What does it mean when some people argue that bodies are "wrong?"

Is There Any Way to Have a Wrong Body?
Wombs and Alien Energy

Arguments about biology, essence, or alienness often seemed to lie behind how some of my informants spoke about trans women. For example, some of their reactions to trans women included stereotyping them as "shrill," characterizing them as "female caricatures," and expressing fear in regard to their wrong bodies. This is extremely revealing, especially the word "shrill," usually applied to *women* stepping out of line. Trans women's "voices"—not only their literal voices, but their expressions and acts of speaking up—were thus characterized as unpleasant and grating in a dismissive fashion, in the same way that the matrix culture characterizes women's. I believe that "shrill" operates as a code word in both instances to signal improper female behavior; it is also dismissive and belittling. When land-women use it about trans women, it helps to call trans women's "femininity" into question, yet it uses precisely the same mainstream standards of behavior that land-women reject for themselves.

One of my informants told me that she thought trans women looked like "female caricatures." This kind of name-calling and fearing trans women for their bodies comes from an assumed *regulation of performance*. The act of "passing" depends on a gaze that has been trained in particular *cultural* ways and which looks for a very particular performance of femininity demanded by American matrix cultures. This is a performance that many cis women—particularly older cis women—fail at to some degree. In a community where androgyny and butchness are not only welcomed but favored, such policing is troubling. This comparison to a poor or exaggerated drawing suggests that variations from the mainstream standard are flawed and unacceptable. This implies that being a "real woman" depends on the image one projects, *and that image is the one drawn by the mainstream*. While those standards are largely rejected by land-women on their own behalf, they reappear as a way to police the femininity of others, and "ensure that trans women—whether they are feminine or masculine, whether they 'pass' or not—will invariably come off as 'fake' women no matter how they look or act" (Serano 2007, 49). Despite rejecting mainstream femininity for themselves, some of my informants apply it to trans women as an unattainable standard.[12] This problematic standard is characterized by Serano as "put[ting] trans women in a double bind: If they act feminine they are perceived as being a parody, but if they act masculine it is seen as a sign of their true male identity" (2007, 49).

Trans people are also feared by some of my informants for having "wrong" bodies. Trans women who have not yet undergone gender alignment surgery are shut out from some women's music festivals where there is obligate nudity, in the showers, for example. Women who attend these events state that the sight of male genitalia is anything from "wrong" to "disgusting" to "frightening." The United States segregates people according to gender for bathing and excretion and when that segregation is breached, the taboo causes violent reactions. Abuse survivor narratives are also commonly used as straw arguments, and to imply that trans women themselves, by the association of their genitalia with the genitalia of abusers, are sexual predators.[13]

One of my informants called trans men "crazy" for having breast reduction surgery, despite the fact that we both knew land-women who had had breast cancer that had resulted in a near-identical surgery. Some land-women view trans people as having simply *wrong* bodies, and moreover *perversely* wrong bodies, bodies that they have *made* wrong through surgery, hormones, and bodily practices. Califia notes that these wrong bodies are threatening because they remind us of our own gender transgressions: "The setting-aside or excommunication of the transsexual from the main body of society is a vital, and easy to miss, part of this conceptual process. I suspect this is a strategy for reducing the anxiety of a reader who might otherwise be forced to confront his or her own failures at living up to gender stereotypes" (2003, 2). This is also true for the removal of trans women from women's space: this reduces the ways in which trans folk remind us that there are times when cisgender people also do gender "wrong," and also when our own bodies may be seen as transgressive or perverse. The doxa of the correct female body runs deep. The implications of this doxa also point uncompromisingly to lesbian, disabled, old, fat, scarred, and androgynous women, but these bodies are not judged by the same standard, even when their flaws are essentially *the same ones* that are feared on trans bodies.

Because some land-women do not see trans women as being "female," trans women are seen as taking very limited resources away from women who truly need them. At times, they are also regarded as people who are "taking over," interlopers, or as "spies" for the patriarchy (Califia 2003, 93). This goes along with assertions that trans women somehow retain male privilege while living as women; for example, the idea that they retain "male energy." The extreme prejudice and physical danger that most trans women face would seem to argue against any male privilege being retained. Indeed, Serano notes that not only is she described solely in feminine terms by others since her transition, but that "all attempts to portray trans women as 'fake' females (whether media or feminist in origin) . . . require one to give different names, meanings, and values to the same behaviors depending on whether the person in question was born with a female or male body (or whether they are perceived to be a woman or a man). In other words, they require one to be sexist" (2007, 51).

Yet these accusations are still made, which indicates that male privilege is something that is seen by some women as intrinsic to "maleness," which is *essential* and cannot be changed. A statement by some separatists makes this clear:

> Man has learned to change sexual characteristics, and has been so successful that we can not even tell a natural woman from an altered man. Do not be fooled by their convincing performance. Fortunately modern paternal science falls far short. It will never be able to synthetically create women's spirit, women's energy, or women's wisdom. (McDonald 1977, 7)

Women's "spirit, energy, and wisdom" are things that women apparently are born with; therefore, these separatist women assert, there is some intrinsic female essence within the person of everyone born "with a female body." In their eyes, gender does not result from the body's shape or from social cues or performance. It is a spiritual essence somehow indelibly placed into the bodies of reproductively-enabled women. Thus the highly important "energy" term has become emotionally linked to visions of feminism/women-oriented events without trans people—that is, to *biological* ideas of what it means to be a woman. According to these dictates, a woman is only a woman if she can *function* as one in terms of heterosexual reproduction, a view identical to that of the heterosexual mainstream. Even more important than fertility, however, is the idea of "naturalness"—that having a body whose gender aligns with its apparent or approved sex produces the *essence* of being that gender.

The appearance of *essence* defines what exactly is "alien" or "wrong" about the bodies of trans folk, according to some of my informants. An essence—a single item that can serve as *both* the signifier and the signified—is elusive yet tempting. The essence is both a marker that will reliably signify a category and also the true nature of that category itself. In this case, "essence" (of maleness and femaleness) is inextricably bound to the physical body and binary sex diagnosis at birth, as well as gender performance. Most importantly, these things should *agree*, like an adjective and noun in a romance language. Bodies that change over time, bodies that are biologically "other," bodies that are "interfered with" or "self-made," and bodies that do not perform according to these binary standards do not have this "essence." Therefore, such bodies can be regarded, by those who hold to these essential beliefs, as not truly possessing gender and thus not being fully human.

Yet all bodies change over time, no body is biologically identical to another, and we have a history of thousands of years of "interfering with" human bodies. Many of us, including myself, would not be alive at this moment without some form of surgical interference. Current anthropological theory holds that human bodies and bodily experience do not exist "outside of" culture (Csordas 1994; Geertz 1973; Scheper-Hughes and Lock 1987), and thus the idea of there being some sort of "truthful, raw, sexed" body underneath the "mask" of culture/gender/surgery is deeply problematic. Nevertheless, like the concept of "nature," the concept of the "natural body" remains important. It is, however, telling that only bodies that fall along very particular axes of failing to perform as proper binary women/men are punished, by both the matrix culture and some landwomen, by being called "alien" or "wrong." As Serano passionately puts it, "Women who have struggled against patriarchal ideals of what makes a 'real' woman think nothing of turning around and using the word 'real' against trans women" (2007, 242).

Even when you are yourself violating gender norms, it can be important to have a scapegoat, someone who is worse than you are: as Joanna Russ points out, separatists are/have been the scapegoats of the feminist movement (1998, 85).[14] Similarly, trans people are the scapegoats of those who violate gender norms. Also, although the matrix culture defines lesbians, and to a lesser extent feminists, as violating gender norms, landwomen do not see themselves as doing so. Instead, they redefine gender norms to include themselves.

Those who argue against the inclusion of trans people seem to be using an unspoken but important idea of essential femaleness and maleness closely related to the concept of "energy." Female energy, or woman-energy, covers bodily essence, social actions, and spiritual beliefs. In its social actions guise, this concept can be used to exclude trans women on the grounds that they do not have the intrinsic experience of oppression, despite the fact that women's experiences of oppression vary widely. Instead, it is assumed that trans women have the experience of men, categorized as oppressors, who therefore cannot interact properly as women. In its guise as bodily essence, in the form of hormones, genetics, or mysterious brain functions, it serves to say that there is something "different" about women who are born as women. In the realm of spiritual beliefs, it relies on the binary, as though souls are born like bodies (except more carefully dichotomized, as bodies often fail to be "fully" male or female). This argument that bodies can be "wrong" or be filled with "wrong" or "alien" energy is, when unpacked, an argument that certain people *should not exist*—after all, we cannot exist without our bodies. A wrong body is not only an error in performance; it is a wrong identity and way of being-in-the-world. Thus although this argument may seem to be trivial in some ways, especially to those who do not use the "energy" term in their everyday vocabulary, it is not. An argument about "wrong energy" is, at its core, an argument that certain bodies and people should not exist. This is an epistemological (knowledge-making) argument about the humanity of other people.

The bodies of trans women are said, by this vocal minority, to be filled with "alien" energy, masculine energy, or simply "wrong" energy, because they lack an "essence" of femaleness. This essence may be said to come from a lifetime of experience as a woman, genetics/biology, or some undefined or defined spiritual source, but because it is lacking, trans women lack "female energy." And as we shall see, this energy cannot be gained. Gender in these terms is a zero-sum game.

Gender as a Zero-Sum Game: Trans Men

I have spoken at great length about trans women, yet the issue of trans men is also a thorny one in the community. Trans women are sometimes excluded from women's space while trans men are accepted or even fetishized (Serano 2007, 236–37). While this is sometimes seen as yet another form of biological essentialism—after all, trans men were (usually) identified female at birth—Serano suggests that this has little or nothing to do with the essentialist stance that underlies trans-misogyny (2007). She writes, "Rather, I believe that this preference for trans men over trans women simply reflects the society-wide inclination to view masculinity as being strong and natural, and femininity as being weak and artificial. In other words, it is a product of traditional sexism" (Serano 2007, 238).[15]

Yet some in the loosely-knit community of land-women view women transitioning into men as the loss of a limited resource. This is a powerful perception. One land-woman, Yawning Lion, posted on her blog about a letter she wrote to a former lover who had visited to tell her about deciding to transition to a man:

> I said her decision felt like a loss to me. I said I had loved her. I loved the woman she is. I loved her body, her mind, her heart. I loved her cowlicks and her awkward moments. I loved all the things she hated about her body. I had listened to her recount all of its betrayals, and she was still a woman. I loved the woman I loved, and I would miss her. I would miss knowing that she was out there. I grieved at the thought that a day would come when I would no longer recognize her, and not because of the passage of time but because of the work of hormones and surgeons. I grieved the loss of the woman I loved, even after we had parted. (2007)

She then noted, "She never wrote back."

The loss of even a single woman is constructed by Yawning Lion as a tragedy and a loss to the community. Of course this is a loss to the community only insofar as trans men are *excluded* from the community. Underneath the openly-expressed loss is another fear: the threat to one's own lesbian identity in a mainstream world convinced that all women, whatever they dare to express, must desire men.[16]

Yawning Lion obviates this problem by refusing to acknowledge her transitioned lover as male. Not only does she refer to him as "she" throughout her entry, she also notes that "I do not believe that her choice will soothe her pain or resolve the questions she wrestles with" (Yawning Lion, 2007), undermining her ex-lover's agency and rationality. Underlying the argument is doubt whether it is possible for someone born female to truly wish to become male. Her questioning of how freely anyone can make such a choice in a culture dedicated to devaluing femaleness is well taken. However, gender is not merely a matter of cultural values: there is also the matter of internal identity and desire (Weston 1993). Gayle Rubin suggests that contemporary rejection of FTM men among lesbians is connected to long-standing hostility towards butch-femme roles rooted in lesbian feminism,[17] as well as a fear of variation on the part of "gender vigilantes" (1992, 476).

Yawning Lion says, "I do not believe that becoming male answers the question of what it means to be a woman who doesn't fit what a woman is supposed to be in patriarchy" (2007). Some critics have asked whether transition merely reinforces traditional gender binaries instead of allowing people to have other gender expressions. This is the only criticism of transsexuality that does not seem to stem, itself, from those traditional, essential binaries. Yet this criticism paradoxically *limits* the gender expression of others by denying forms of gender diversity. Transsexuality does not erase the gender expression of non-traditionally gendered people who are not trans. As Serano notes, such "subversism"—the assumption that moving beyond the gender binary is good in and of *itself*—is merely a flip of preferred and outcast categories, reversing the hierarchy (2007, 346–47). Historically, transgender theorists are among some of the harshest critics of binary gender: Kate Bornstein likens it to drug addiction and racism (1994, 45, 105), Califia hopes that gender will become "voluntary" (2003, 10), and Serano questions "gender entitlement" (2007, 226).

Serano writes, "I would say that the assumption that distinct identities would automatically lead to exclusivity was entirely misplaced. . . . If we look beyond gender and sexual identity politics, we can find many examples of flexible and fluid identities" (2007, 353). She notes that the assumption that identities are fixed and "natural" is just that, an assumption. When Yawning Lion writes, "I do not believe changing one's sex does anything to change the system" (2007), she is confusing the issue.[18] Placing the onus for change on those who are *most* oppressed and endangered by the system is disingenuous and reminds me of how white women innocently ask why women of color don't feel comfortable in all-white communities. Still, the ways Yawning Lion are disturbed by this transition are deeply informative.

Beneath these arguments is the idea that transition is a loss to the community. This is predicated on two things: First, the assumption that trans men are unwelcome. Second, the notion that lesbians are a limited commodity. Certainly, the number of women who are able to openly live non-heteronormative lives is limited; but that limitation is not due to some arbitrary fixed number of lesbians. That limitation is due to the compulsory heterosexuality of North American matrix cultures, and the concomitant risk of living as an openly queer person. That risk is not reduced by choosing to transition, nor is it increased for the larger group. Gayle Rubin notes dryly that "some of these [FTM or genderqueer individuals] may not want to leave their lesbian communities, and they should not be forced to do so. They may cause confusion, repelling some lesbians and attracting others. But if community membership were based on universal desirability, no one would qualify. Our desires can be as selective, exclusive, and imperious as we like; our society should be as inclusive, humane, and tolerant as we can make it" (1992, 476).

Pushing the notion of loss further, I note that in this system "female essence" can be spoilt or lost by transitioning gender, and never gained. Women who express anti-trans sentiment state that trans men "lose" the things that make them women: note Yawning Lion's focus on "loss" predicated through hormones and surgeons. It is also important to note that Yawning Lion refused to address her FTM friend by his chosen pronouns, implying that he could not gain masculine status. Yet femaleness and femininity can be lost or ruined. However, as we saw in the previous section, "true" femaleness can never be gained: it is something that is only granted—by circumstances, a deity, or Nature.

This idea of what it is to be female parallels, with surprising aptness, traditional kyriarchy. In that system, "proper" feminine sexual behavior consists of "preserving" the virginity/virtue a woman is born with; one can "lose" it and thus become a "fallen" or improper woman, and former status can never be regained. Certain categories of people, traditionally women of color, women born into poverty, and abused or prematurely "adult" children were excluded automatically from having such feminine virtue (Blank 2007, 11). In the system of transphobia, the excluded are those whose bodies do not fit our arbitrary medical standards. If female energy, like virginity, can be lost but never gained, this is merely a replication of old patriarchal systems under a new guise. This is not a feminist conception of gender.

Michigan: One Woman One Vote

The Michigan Womyn's Music Festival was once the center of the debate over the admission of trans women to women-only space. From the politics of Camp Trans (an organization that seeks to end trans women's exclusion from women-only spaces, best known for their protest outside the gates of Michigan every year)[19] to the heated and often vitriolic online debates, Michigan Womyn's Music Festival has been a prominent symbol of trans exclusion from feminist events for decades.[20] With the closing of Michigan's gates in 2015, should we regard this as a victory for trans rights? Or, given the anti-trans woman rhetoric still common online, is the closing of Michigan merely tangential? Yet such rhetoric, even in a relatively small and private "Landdyke space" no longer goes unchallenged.[21]

While the closing of Michigan did provoke some discussion of trans issues on the Landdyke list, the discussion quickly veered to the fact that Lisa Vogel, as the sole holder of the deed to the land Michigan is held on, functioned as a gatekeeper and authority figure[22] despite the explicitly communal and consensus-based ethos of the festival. Whether or not Michigan closed in the face of pressure to be more inclusive was irrelevant, my informants pointed out, as the decision was made by one woman, and not by the community. Lisa Vogel announced on April 21 of 2015 in a Facebook post that the festival would be closing permanently, asking everyone "to remember that our 40 year Festival has outlived nearly all of her kin" (Vogel 2015) and not referring to any particular reason for closing, except that "We have known in our hearts for some years that the life cycle of the Festival was coming to a time of closure." Although she acknowledged that "the Festival has been the crucible for nearly every critical cultural and political issue the lesbian feminist community has grappled with for four decades," Vogel did not acknowledge any more specific issues, such as trans acceptance. As Vogel owned the land, once she decided it was closing, that was that.

Victoria Brownsworth, writing for *Curve*, lamented the loss of Michigan and collected "love letters" to and from Michigan from performers and festival-goers, and quotes comments on the MichFest Facebook page saying "MichFest has been my college, grad school and a safe home to learn and grow" and "I will never forget my time on The Land. It was nothing short of life changing" (2015). This sounds like what many of my informants say about women's land in general—the sense of safety, the "life changing" expansion of possibilities. Michigan served as a temporary women's-land experience for an enormous community. However, that experience was not open to all women. Despite the fact that only one trans woman had ever been expelled from the festival, in 1991, trans women were not welcome there. In April of 2013, Lisa Vogel sent an open letter via email to the community involved with the festival. Shortly afterward, the letter was also posted on the Landdykes email listserv as well as on Facebook. The letter was in response to a Change.org petition asking the artists and attendees of Michigan to welcome "all self-identified women," and continued the long-standing debate regarding the exclusion of trans women from the Michigan festival. Vogel wrote that she "rejected transphobia," but that the festival should remain for cis women, stating, "I believe that womyn-born-womyn (WBW) is a lived experience that constitutes its own distinct gender identity" (Vogel 2013).

Several women on the Landdykes email list replied with statements of support for the email, including one woman who remarked that she would not have been able to attend Michigan had the festival welcomed trans women, and another who stated that she liked having "womyn-born-womyn" (hereafter "WBW" for ease of reference) as a gender identity.[23] This is not to imply that the entire community supported the letter; at least one woman spoke up in support of trans women, but the expressions of support for Vogel were revealing.

The letter itself frames keeping a space separate for "WBW" as compatible with an anti-transphobic stance. Vogel writes, "Nobody should be asked to erase the need for autonomous spaces to demonstrate that they are sisters in struggle" (2013). Here the idea of "autonomous spaces" is linked with the image of "sisters in struggle" to create an argument that trans women and WBW should "work together." However, this relies on two problematic assumptions: the first is the assumption of equal access implied in "autonomous spaces," and the second is the assumption of shared oppression implied in "sisters in struggle." I have already unpacked the problematics of shared oppression earlier in this chapter, so I will concentrate here on "autonomous spaces."

"Space" is a very important concept. The ability to make a space "autonomous" means the ability to reserve that space to the use of a particular population—in this case, the Michigan festival to the use of WBW. The "autonomy" of the space is also dependent on the assumption that those who use it are disenfranchised or disadvantaged in some way. When applied to the exclusion of trans women at Michigan, this needs some very careful thinking around, as trans women are disenfranchised far more than cis women/WBW.[24] Bonnie Morris, in her book about Michigan, provides an excellent example of this kind of thinking: "Is it not possible for there to be *one* event, *one* annual festival, intended for women born female? One does not see any 'transracial' persons demanding entry to Michigan's Womyn of Color Sanctuary. But this analogy angers some activists" (Morris 1999, 173–74).

The reason the analogy is tone-deaf and offensive is that it appropriates the struggle of women of color.[25] This likens trans women to white women attempting to "crash" women of color space, attributing a social power to them not congruent with reality, in which trans women are far more likely to face discrimination and violence than cis women/WBW. Yet Vogel is essentially making the same argument, albeit without the offensive comparison: by stating that spaces are "autonomous," she assumes that trans women and WBW both start with the same amount of resources and societal backing. This is analogous, extending the comparison Morris made, to stating that "whites only" spaces are pretty much the same thing as "women of color" spaces. However, the idea of a space only for WBW is palatable to Vogel's readers because as members of groups historically discriminated against and disenfranchised (women and queer/lesbian women), they are unused to thinking of themselves as the dominant group, even though there is ample evidence that there are considerable social privileges given to the cisgender majority (Califia 2003; Serano 2007). Similar to the split in thinking about race into the binary discourse of "victim or perpetrator" (Scott 2000, 126), a split in gender thinking casts women as victims, not only replicating a strict gender binary but ignoring the complex ways in which kyriarchy works intersectionally.

Examining two particular paragraphs of Vogel's letter closely will reveal how some women can reconcile excluding trans women with not seeing themselves as transphobic. These paragraphs begin, "I passionately believe the healing in our community will occur when we unconditionally accept transwomyn as womyn while not dismissing or disavowing the lived experience and realities of the WBW gender identity" (Vogel 2013). On first reading, Vogel seems to "unconditionally accept" trans women as women. However, upon analysis, she is saying that the WBW gender identity has "lived experience and realities" that are not mirrored for trans women, thus setting up the gender identity of WBW as a "reality" trans women cannot hope to achieve. "Sadly, the extreme voices on this issue have driven much of the discussion, and the aggressive rhetoric leaves little room for building the alliances that are critical to everyone's survival, growth, and integrity" (Vogel 2013). This is a tone argument, policing the debate for being "extreme"; it leaves it unclear exactly who is being policed but the intended audience doubtless knows who they are.

She continues, "we must find ways to be allies in this discussion. I know that for some, WBW space seems flatly incompatible with honoring and supporting transwomyn within the larger womyn's communities." This is a clue as to whose tone was being policed above: activists noting that the WBW policy is exclusionary and supports privilege. "Regardless, we must listen to those who believe in the power of every woman's voice, and commit to stay in a process with open hearts, open minds, and abiding respect even when that conversation gets incredibly hard." The idea of the "power of every womon's voice" is another flattening of the playing field and refusal to see the ways in which certain women are disadvantaged or not heard, thus placing cis and trans women on an imaginary level.

Vogel's letter, upon analysis, seems to me to be saying that trans women are welcome in the community only as long as they are willing to accept a secondary, flawed gender identity, to give up resources to the more powerful WBW gender identity, and to speak *nicely* about all this. Some readers of the letter might see it instead as simply a way to reject the "transphobic" label while retaining the right to keep the important cultural institution of Michigan only for WBW—a clever gerrymander. However problematic this letter is, it does illustrate that there is a spectrum of understanding among land-women; this is not merely a case of vocal transphobia or the opposite.

However, the problems of "ducking transphobia" run deeper than this, and extend to a form of rhetoric that is similar to the ways in which MRAs (Men's Rights Activists), white supremacists, and homophobes structure debate. On the Landdyke mailing list, at least one transphobic discussion framed trans women's vocalization of their desire to be seen as women (that is, fully human) as "violent," and themselves as "victims," in the context of disappointment that Angela Davis was vocally supporting trans rights. By equating their emotional distress with another person's loss of humanity (or safety, or life, as these things are also on the line), the arguer creates the illusion of victimhood. This is a clever and effective tactic usually used by the far-right to disenfranchise minorities, and it is a profound and difficult-to-address act of epistemological violence. By recreating the very act of speaking up as "violent," such reframing silences trans women and dehumanizes them in one stroke without needing to even engage in debate; this is of course a weapon that cannot be used from below.

Welcoming Queerness

Not all of my informants expressed anti-trans sentiments. Indeed, there is a wide range of opinion on the subject, although the anti-trans faction I have analyzed above is certainly vocal. On the other hand, there are lands where trans women are welcomed; in fact, I interviewed two women who were in the process of founding one. Jan and Sara, whom I met at their art jewelry booth at the Michigan Womyn's Music Festival, had just purchased land—an old hippie commune—and were in the process of creating a women's land and artist's colony. I found them because they had put up flyers about their new community, which explicitly welcomed trans women. I talked to them about their welcoming of trans and queer women:

> ME: So, the community. I understand that it's an artists' community and the flyer was very clear on the fact that you had trans people—I thought it was very exciting that they were going to be welcomed there. So, are you trying to build a community that's—are you trying to attract a specific kind of people to your community is what I'm asking? Other than artists?
>
> JAN: The people—right. I would like to have people who are living outside the norm of gender of, of—and it's hard for me to talk about it without talking about the art piece, because it's people who are doing creative things.
>
> And it's—identifying it more as a queer community rather than a women's community attracts different people. I think the terminology. And that—I feel like it has its difference—to me it feels a bit different than lesbian land, which I've also—I mean, we've spent time on, and you know that was part of what we did

in Hawaii, and because I would like it to be less focused on—I guess more focused on kind of radical thinking and expressing that through artistic means.

And if people kind of identify with all of those things, it's not a specific type of person really that we're looking for, but having it open for anyone who identifies as queer.

And really, though—and this is part of what we're trying to figure out. Like, what does that mean? So if someone who is straight and identifies "but I'm queer," also—I mean, I've heard that, like how does that fall—like men are welcome passing through town. You know.

SARA: But not to live there.

JAN: Yeah. It's not a land where people are excluded from coming. We've had big parties with every type of person, you know. But the permanent spaces, it's like a queer space. So, that's pretty important.

Jan and Sara focus on creating an artistic space, but part of that is their vision of a space for queer women, which is inclusive of all women who identify as queer, in whatever way. This is very much linked to artistic identity and radical thinking in their discussion. Clearly, for them the process of identifying as "queer" and "woman" were *individual* processes, something that could be worked out with each person rather than by classifying people as part of categories. "Creativity," a term referring more to what people do than what they are, is the bond that will hold the community together, rather than ideas about gender or how gender is created/performed.

In another incident that illustrates differing views of what women's land is or should be, one of my informants, Sirocco, made an impassioned speech during one of the Landdyke Gatherings in defense of "queer spaces." Earlier that day, several women had spoken disparagingly about the term "queer," stating that it was used as a way for bisexuals or, worse, trans people to "sneak into" spaces that "should be" reserved for lesbians.[26] Then, during a session about a tangentially related topic, Sirocco spoke up, talking about her long history with women's land. She had a particular kind of legitimacy, as she was living on one of the oldest women's lands. She spoke with fervent emotion about her attachment to and how much she had learned from her "lesbian foremothers" and then spoke about the necessity for connecting to a wider, younger, and more diverse community with queer space. Her speech was listened to with respect by the other women present.

Afterwards, we talked about what had happened together, and she confessed to me that "she just felt that she had to speak out after what some of the other women were saying." She shook her head. "They were saying those things about bisexuals and trans people, and you know, I have friends."

I said, "I have friends, too."

Although a certain subset of land-women see trans women as being filled with alien energy—male or simply "confused" energy, and therefore not properly female—the arguments against their inclusion in the category of "women" are not only problematic, but also fall along the same continuum as homophobic attacks and *are made for the same reasons as those attacks.* Similarly, trans men are seen as having lost or ruined their femaleness or female energy, much the same way that women under kyriarchy can lose their respectability or virginity. These attacks stem from the definitions of gender that come from the matrix culture: the unexamined doxa of the precultural body and the idea that experience, culture, and gender are somehow layered on top of that body. They also come from the perception that the resources of land-women are limited and under attack. Yet trans people are not the true source of these attacks, any more than feminists are responsible for misogyny.

Divisions and scapegoating among marginalized groups is a deeply uncomfortable topic. It is particularly uncomfortable for me because as the writer of this text and the privileged voice at present, I feel as though I am implying, with Joanna Russ: "We haven't gone too far; *she* has. We aren't crazy; *she* is. *We* aren't angry or bad or out of control; *she* is. *We* don't hate men (the sin of sins); *she* does. Don't punish us; punish *her*" (1998, 85). In this case it's not hating men that is the sin of sins,[27] but hating ourselves. I do not wish to imply either that land-women—even land-women who are transphobic—are somehow therefore an acceptable scapegoat, or are in any way "more" accountable than our larger matrix culture, which still regards all deviations from the binary heterosexual as suspect and acceptable targets for hatred and violence. (One need only to look at the recent upsurge in "bathroom bills" for an example.) Indeed, the farther we go from that binary heterosexual, neatly bounded by the picket fence of respectable middle-class whiteness, the more suspect we become. And land-women are by their very nature far outside that fence.

The viciousness and hatred with which trans people are regarded by some land-women saddens and frightens me. Trans folk occupy the far end of the "unacceptable gender" spectrum that lesbians also inhabit. This is a loose-knit group who are judged to be unacceptable according to the rigid heteronormative binary gender model. While those within this group often do not see themselves as members of the same group at all, this does not change the fact that within the heteronormative matrix, all lesbians, all gay men, all bisexual people, all queer people, all asexuals, all genderqueer people, and all trans people of every stripe are committing varying degrees of the *same crime:* failing to be a proper man/proper woman. At the same time each of us, to varying degrees, reveals that gender is not rigid, not inborn, not necessarily dependent on any one aspect of gender performance, not necessarily linked to sexuality. Gender is more fluid, more complex, more interactive, more fundamental, and more informative than we had thought. These are dangerous insights, and we cannot help making them.

· CHAPTER 8 ·

The Hermit and the Family

Aging and Dis/Ability in Community

When I judge these people, I judge myself.
—Barbara Myerhoff, *Number Our Days*

"WHEN I GROW OLD," said Bluebird, a woman perhaps thirty years older than myself, "when I grow old, I am going to live on that mountain." The mountain she gestured to was directly before us, rising behind a small lake. We had just hiked to this spot, and were surrounded by land owned by Mountainview. Although Bluebird, like many of the other women of Mountainview, was past the usual "retirement age," she still worked, walked, and gardened with great energy.

We hiked around the lake and up the mountain, emerging finally into a clearing that gave us the most magnificent view yet. One side had been cleared of trees, and there was a wide vista that took in the rolling Appalachian mountains. It was full of huge recumbent boulders, and used by some of the women of the community as sacred space. As far as we could see was wilderness.

Everywhere I looked I could see only mountain and forest. As romantic as the idea of being an old crone on the mountain was, I wondered about its feasibility. What about groceries, running water, and health care? Is it possible for an old woman to be a hermit? Does women's land provide a family that can take care of aging and disabled women?

Many women's lands were founded during the 1970s and 1980s, and their founders and original population are aging. The bodies of older[1] women and the bodies of disabled women dynamically interact with the physical and social environments of women's-land cultures. They illuminate important aspects of those cultures, especially some of the images that illustrate and drive concepts of the "good life" on women's land. In particular, aging and disability alter how women's lands are constructed through the important concept of accessibility. They also illuminate the intersecting images of the hermit and the family, which help shape how life on the land is viewed.

My informants often remarked on how many of the women living on women's lands are older. While this was sometimes mentioned positively, most often it would come up in terms of anxiety about aging care, combined with a sense of cultural and personal loss as aging women died. In addition to the aging of the original founding cohort of land-women, "retirement" also has an impact as it is easier for women to retreat from the matrix culture when they are assured of a small steady income.[2]

This older portion of the community has a profound effect on the culture of land-women as a whole, spanning discussions on land-women's email lists, conferences for aging lesbians, and women from diverse communities in the United States and Canada. The issue of "aging in place" comes up frequently, as land-women pursue a desire to live in women's community as they age. For land-women, "aging in place" encompasses many complex needs. This term incorporates the need for lesbian community as opposed to a nursing home where they may need to be closeted. Aging in place also indicates the desire to continue to have contact with wilderness and "the land" as one ages, and a preference for remaining within a distinct community and culture. It also implies a wish for independence and self-determination rather than entry into an impersonal and restrictive system. All of these things are heavily symbolized by "place." One of my informants, Sirocco, put it this way: "Throughout my lifetime, no matter what has gone on in my life, there's always been a little index card filed away that says, 'I always have a place to go. I always have a place to belong.'"

Many of the concerns that aging women express about having access to women's land are echoed by women with various disabilities. Indeed, some disabled land-women speak of abled people as "temporarily abled," or "currently abled," highlighting the likelihood that we will all need assistance someday. During the Landdyke Gatherings I attended, there was a great emphasis on making the Gatherings as accessible as possible to disabled women. Because of the concerns of disabled women and aging women, music festivals, women's land, and other women's communities have been leaders in making their spaces accessible. From making their spaces scent-free to installing wheelchair ramps and providing sign-language interpreters, such concerns have been foregrounded for years (Dykewomon 2014).

Populations of disabled women have concerns that are parallel in some ways to the concerns of aging women: access for women who cannot walk long distances, wider doorways for wheelchairs, or more dependable electricity. However, the two populations differ in their relative ages, and in their relationship to women's land. Aging populations of land-women are largely strategizing to find ways to *remain* on land. Disabled women are often strategizing for *entrance* to women's land, to raise awareness of themselves as a population with particular needs, and to show that it is desirable and necessary to accommodate their needs. Populations of disabled women also face the problem of the "difference" of the disabled body. While the aging body is seen as *contiguous* with the "normal" body—after all, we will all age, if we're lucky—the disabled body is often perceived as the opposite of the "normal" body (Campbell 2009, 5).

Both the population of aging women and the population of disabled women highlight a primary tension that underlies women's-land culture. Because of their needs, they throw light on how women's land depends on the seemingly-paradoxical images of the hermit and the family. Women's lands, particularly rural lands, simultaneously support and valorize both solitude and community. Women's communities often work to make wild land available to women, and the image of living in a small cabin on wild land—the hermit image—is deeply important in the language land-women use to talk about their needs, dreams, and desires. On the other end of the spectrum is community—women with whom one shares basic cultural expectations that differ from the matrix culture. Particularly when women speak about ideal land-cultures, those communities approach the idea of "chosen family," (such as that explored in Kath Weston 1991) replete with the responsibilities and emotional entanglements that term implies. When aging and disabled women seek that solitude and community, their different needs throw the tension between these different "poles" of women's-land culture into relief.

In this chapter, I will examine one women's community, Mountainview, in depth because of their focus on aging options. Discussions of aging on women's land and access for disabled women were certainly not limited to the women of Mountainview. Disabled and aging women bring the tension between these different needs to the fore, as their needs throw into relief the different tendencies, priorities, and customary practices of individual communities. Their needs may highlight just how important the image of the hermit is, and how the community may have prioritized individualization over community effort in some areas. At the same time, these needs strengthen the image of and reliance on the family-community.

Options for Aging Lesbians: Institutional Problems, Community Solutions

Some studies have found that aging lesbians prefer lesbian community (Goldberg, Sickler, and Dibble 2005; Stein, Beckerman, and Sherman 2010); others have noted a preference not for lesbian community per se but for women's community (Phillips and Marks 2008). For my informants, this community is the one they have been building all their lives. In creating their own options for aging the women of Mountainview express the same doubts that the queer population in general expresses with regard to institutionalized systems. This fear and anxiety is well documented. A British study found that 77.5 percent of GLBT women and 62.8 percent of GLBT men saw nursing homes as "undesirable" (Heaphy, Yip, and Thompson 2004, 892). One of their informants said, "This is something that I've thought about [and I've] met a lot of people [who said that if you had] to go into a residential home as a gay person, your life would be hell." Johnson, Jackson, Arnette, and Koffman's 2005 U.S. study of 127 GLBT adults found that 60 percent reported discrimination in access to health and social services, 73 percent believed homophobic discrimination occurs in retirement facilities, and 34 percent thought they would have to return to the closet if they were placed in a retirement home (2005, 90). Stein, Beckerman, and Sherman, in a 2010 focus group study performed in New York City and New Jersey, found similar fears:

> When asked about their psychosocial challenges and concerns as a gay or lesbian senior, the following themes were articulated by most participants: (a) fear of being rejected or neglected by healthcare providers, particularly personal care aides; (b) fear of not being accepted and respected by other residents; (c) fear of having to go back into the closet if placed in a mainstream long-term care

facility; and (d) a preference for gay-friendly residential options if needed for long-term and end-of-life care. (427)

However, a "gay-friendly" residential option is not yet widely available, especially to the non-affluent aging population. My informants were keenly aware of this, and expressed both disdain for and fear of institutionalized care.

These fears are well founded: discrimination, homophobia, and outright abuse have been reported by many studies on LGBT elders (see Butler 2013). Hughes, Harold, and Boyer's survey of Michigan aging-services providers found that while providers indicated willingness to serve LGBT elders, there was little outreach to the community and a persistent perception of LGBT invisibility (2011). Cahill and South give several examples of actual homophobic abuse in nursing homes in the United States (2002). Studies in New York State found a high level of homophobia among nursing home staff, reporting language such as "the staff would be horrified" and "thought it was gross"; one facility outright banned admission of LGBT clients (Fairchild, Carrino, and Ramirez 1996, 166). My informants thus have plenty of reasons for their dislike of institutionalized options. The women of Mountainview openly indicated distaste and fear of nursing homes, as Robin did when she said, "How do we help each other stay in our homes, rather than having to go live in some crummy assisted-living place?"

Assisted living and medicalized care may necessitate going "back into the closet" as Stein, Beckerman, and Sherman found (2010). As Jane Wilkins learned from her interviewees, such strategies are often very painful. "Sheila's previous negative health-care experiences rendered her intensely private, terrified that she would not be treated if staff knew she and Maggie were partners. 'And when she became ill and she was in and out of hospital, I had to pretend to be her sister, not her partner. So, that was hard but there wasn't anything I could do about it'" (Maggie's interview in Wilkens 2015, 94). Kuyper and Fokkema show that loneliness among Dutch LGB older adults exacerbates minority stress, while social embeddedness helps relieve it (2010); thus closeting, while an important survival strategy, can actually increase other stressors by increasing loneliness and isolation.

Homophobia is not the only frightening thing about assisted living. Impersonality, loneliness, sexism, and being cut off from community are also feared. Instead, many land-women rely on friendship and community networks to replace institutionalized care systems. The importance of such networks is demonstrated by a group of women who gathered to "support each other through menopause and aging" (Ariel 2008, 285).[3] A similar emphasis on such friendship networks appears in the work of Masini and Barrett, whose study on lesbian, gay, and bisexual adults over age fifty found that "social support from friends did prove predictive of psychological outcomes while support from family did not. Support from friends predicted higher mental quality of life, and lower depression, anxiety, and internalized homophobia. . . . This finding speaks to the importance of networks that extend beyond the traditional familial boundaries" (2008, 104).

Heaphy, Yip, and Thompson discovered that "non-heterosexual community networks" were of great importance, quoting informants who described "the sort of feminist band, if you like, who have a history of organising and networking and getting together" [Daphne] and "I think it does go back to feminist groups for me. [For] lesbian feminists, you were supposed to rely on each other . . . and it worked well" [Anita] (2004, 895). Surveys of women who identify as lesbians in the United States "confirm that friendship networks remain a primary source of support and socialization for elder lesbians" (Goldberg, Sickler, and Dibble 2005, 207).

Wilkens finds that in the U.K., organized and dedicated groups catering to the needs of older LGBT people help provide alleviation for loneliness as well as a sense of community (2015, 99–100). Marcena Gabrielson confirms not only the importance of "friends as family" among lesbians in the United States, but also notes that this support network may need to augment or replace a not-always supportive natal family (2013). This reflects the expectations of my informants, who have said to me that within women's community, women should be able to rely on each other.

It is clear from a variety of research across disciplines that institutional care is feared by queer women for good reason: homophobic abuse, the need to closet one's self, and the stress of doing so all make the general impersonality and loneliness of institutionalized care much worse. At the same time, strong friendship networks and connections offset the problems of unsupportive natal family and also provide strong support for higher quality of life. Land-women strategizing to provide alternate options for aging rely on their already-existing communities to provide both these friendship networks and an alternative to the physical plant of the institution itself.

Growing Old Together: Old Women, They Plan for Roots on the Mountain

It is important to land-women to stay within the communities that they have created. However, aging creates life changes that require accommodations, planning, and resources. As this population ages, those changes are discussed and planned for in a variety of ways.

Mountainview has a sub-community planned for "aging in place," a term borrowed from the U.S. matrix culture. Usually this term indicates strategies to prevent older people from being placed in nursing homes. Among land-women, however, the term refers to ways to prevent women from having to leave women's lands as they age.[4] I am focusing largely on Mountainview and their planned community, but this focus is in the context of a larger population of self-identified "landdykes" and other interested women who keep in touch via email lists, and who live in (or have lived in, or are connected with) various women's communities throughout the United States. This population, especially the population settled in women's communities, tends to be older. Yet many of them first face aging not through needing care themselves, but through caring for aging parents. This is a common topic of conversation on email lists, since several of these women are caring for their parent(s) themselves.[5] Thus the planning demonstrated by the women of Mountainview is done within a larger cultural conversation in which the people providing eldercare are largely land-women themselves.

The community planned by the women of Mountainview is already named (I shall call the proposed community "Old Babeapalooza").[6] During my stay, many women discussed Old Babeapalooza with me, including details of planning, monetary considerations, location (on some land that the current community owned) and particularly, how the design of the community would accommodate aging. Mountainview itself is located in mountainous terrain in the Appalachian area, and the physical plant consists of separate houses—some self-built, some partly self-built and partly contracted, and some prefab trailer homes. The roads are winding and graveled and the houses are distant enough that it is difficult to see one from another, a planned feature to give the residents privacy.

Old Babeapalooza is planned as a separate but connected community. The land area the residents plan to use is contiguous with Mountainview, and several members of the current community say they will move there when they get "old enough."[7] Although none of the physical plant of Old Babeapalooza was in place during my interviews, the members discussed its design with me. One of the main differences in Old Babeapalooza is the shift to communal housing. This shift is intended to address both physical and mental needs of women as they age: by living together, women expect to be able to combine and lighten household chores, keep each other more mentally focused through social interaction, and check up on each other's medical needs.

One point of discussion among the Mountainview community was whether younger women were needed to care for the aging members, and if so, whether that care would be hired or whether the care would be carried out by younger members of Mountainview. These discussions introduced the concept of delayed reciprocity in terms of "giving to the community" and expecting a younger member of the community to "give back" in the form of unpaid elder care as a type of community service. In this framework, eldercare was expected to be "paid for" by previous services to the larger community in an open-ended, "paid-forward" exchange. At the same time, it was clear that *all* members of the community (without reference to previous contributions, in a form of generalized reciprocity) deserved comfort and care as a basic human right. Both of these care economies existed side by side. On the one hand, old women who would want to seek entrance to Old Babeapalooza, whether or not they came from Mountainview, were generally assumed to come from the larger lesbian community and thus to have contributed to community-building in a larger sense, thus enacting delayed or "paid-forward" reciprocity. On the other hand, in cases of women bringing their aging mothers to women's land, communal care was enacted as a form of generalized reciprocity or "basic human right."

Sarah Lamb discusses a similar long-term delayed reciprocity in her book on aging in West Bengal, in which the delayed reciprocity is contained within a parent–child relationship: "Just as parents once provided their children with the substance of household life, the children years later reciprocate with the same kinds of goods" (Lamb 2000, 50). She contrasts this reciprocity with the relationship between aged parents and adult children in North American society, which she classifies as advocating a "one-way flow of benefits" from the parent to the child, so that dependent parents are seen as "childlike" (Clark 1972; Clark and Anderson 1967; and Vesperi 1987 in Lamb, 52–53). Joel S. Savishinsky, in his work on American retirement, described financial and health worries as occurring within a similar "family" network (2000, 234), yet within those networks aging men and women strategize to maintain themselves and their spouses financially and physically—dependence on children is not a favored outcome (239).

The women of Mountainview have an understanding of aging and aging care that is not exactly like either the Bengali model or the prevalent North American one; while the Mountainview model depends on delayed reciprocity, it is not limited to biological family. Jane Traies's study of older lesbians in the U.K. found that the "family" model among her informants extends along the lines of intimate friendships that are cross-generational, residential and nonresidential, and along lines of ex-lovers, possible lovers, and lifelong friends. Traies suggests that drawing lines between "formally organized" groups and more "underground" networks is arbitrary and not useful to this analysis (2015, 40); I have found a similar lack of distinction between formally organized "lesbian groups" and informal friendship networks. These networks are especially important in terms of providing social and care support.

In the delayed reciprocity model espoused by the women of Mountainview, the women providing necessary care may not be those who benefited directly from contributions made by the older women, yet this model still sees such care as paid for or justified by those contributions.[8] At the same time, the idea of *generalized* reciprocity includes women who may not have made a significant contribution to this particular community in the group of those who still deserve care. Yet constraints, particularly monetary limitations and disinclination to use institutionalized care, oblige many women in women's-land communities to depend on their immediate biological families or to provide eldercare themselves. The population of women on women's land is largely working class or lower middle class, and economic concerns thus affect care choices.[9] This results in a complex network of ideas, preferences, and actual practices. My informants demonstrated a keen knowledge of the various options available to them. Not only were they engaged in discussing Old Babeapalooza, but also brought up lesbian retirement communities in Florida, the options of living with children, and the problems of traditional nursing homes. These women do not see themselves as passive; they are agential and engaged in choosing how they wish to live the rest of their lives.

An excellent example of this comes from Sophia, who spoke to me about "the issue of what do we do about retaining our lesbian culture when we age, when we're old":

> The group continued meeting about how do we manage our old age? What can we do to keep our lesbian identity as old dykes. And I was a part of that group that met. We traveled all over the state and met different people who wanted to be involved, so we met in their homes, and so . . . I mean, we talked about purchasing some sort of a group [home], a motel, or you know, a something where women, old women could be together, and we talked about a lot of things . . . [with] a real emphasis on *of*, not *for*, but an active community of [women] defining themselves and taking care of themselves as much as possible, of long-living lesbians. (Sophia)

Thus women's communities are not simply *managed* in order to make them physically accessible to older women, but are seen as a way for older lesbians to actively maintain and create social identity and community. Sophia's emphasis on women building the community for themselves is consistent with a common emphasis on the abilities of older women.

Although plans for Old Babeapalooza are focused specifically around the needs of aging women, Mountainview has already made many accommodations to age. For example, Freddie, the member with whom I was staying, pointed out their phone tree—a quick and efficient way for members to check in with each other in the event of a problem—and also the fact that there was a social get-together at least once a week. She also noted that they were holding meetings about how to make sure that they supported one another as they got older, another example of active decision-making about age by the community. Robin, another member, pointed out in a more personal and graphic sense that other women in the Mountainview community were "watching out for you":

> They made me promise, because my knee collapses on me, they made me promise if I did decide to do something really stupid like getting on the roof and cleaning out the chimney from my woodstove, I would call somebody first and then promise to call them within an hour. And if I didn't call them within an hour, they would come and see if I had fallen off the roof! Or was stuck on the ladder halfway down with only one leg working. (Robin)

Her physical problems are met with a community solution: checking in to make sure that she is not injured.

One aspect of Old Babeapalooza that was not discussed was the *medical* needs of the residents. There may have been many reasons for this, including that it may not have been something they felt like discussing with me. However, land-women tend to be very active and involved in their own health care. Many of them (although not all) use a wide variety of alternative medicines, including herbalism and other health-care systems. Although biomedical systems, including necessary hospitalizations, were also used, my informants did not tend to treat health and health care as something that must be referred to another's expertise or decisions. Because of this, I think that the discussions about Old Babeapalooza did not include overt medical attention because my informants did not envision themselves as needing to alter their current medical arrangements, in which they made their own medical decisions. That is, they did not *medicalize* aging to the extent that matrix cultures in the United States tend to, but saw health and medicine only as *adjuncts* to aging, the way they were adjuncts to their daily lives prior to being "elders."

One discussion about Old Babeapalooza started while we were sitting around one land-woman's living room. Bluebird spoke about taking her mother to Mass that morning, and how the two of them had run into "a crazy lady" they had never met before. This "crazy lady" had talked to them, demanding to know "why they hadn't taken her" and had said things like "no one cares about me," and "I'm going to lie down in the road and get run over and no one can stop me."

A lively discussion ensued about Old Babeapalooza, and the issue of "what do we do about our crazy women?" Was the woman who harassed Bluebird off her medication, and what should they do if a member of Old Babeapalooza did the same? Should there be a separate crazy house? "But what if a woman is vegan AND crazy? Is she going to have to go and live in Crazy House with all the meat-eaters?" asked Bluebird. "I think crazy trumps everything," said Baba Yaga with authority. "Look at us, assuming that none of us are going to be that crazy woman!" said Gentian. "I've done my time being crazy," said Bluebird. Everyone laughed.

Woven into this discussion is commentary on medication and mental factors as one ages: commentary that focused on group and community responses to needed medications, "crazy" behavior, and shifts in mental ability with age, as well as remarks on and perhaps fear of cognitive and behavioral disability. Although clearly some of the discussion referred obliquely to Alzheimer's and dementia, the use of the all-encompassing term "crazy" also opened the possibility of other forms of mental illness, and the ways this might impact a community that was welcoming to all its members and all of its members' needs.[10] The *owning* of the term "crazy" by one of the women there ("I've done my time being crazy") places it on a continuum with the memory and life of one of the members: "crazy" is not wholly Other, even if it does, according to another member, "trump everything." The discussants may not, however, agree on how to deal with these issues.

Just as the image of the hermit is based to a certain extent on physical ableism, it is also based on mental or emotional ableism; at the same time, such issues affect the entire community, not isolated members. If a member does not take her medication, or acts "crazy," this is not a problem she faces alone. The people who are engaged in these discussions are the ones who will be impacted by the decisions. These explorations of what it means to give up privacy in exchange for care, to organize around dietary "houses," what senility or mental illness "means" to the individual or the community—none of these are made by top-down caretakers but by those who will be most affected by the results. These women do not plan to give up their power and autonomy to anyone.

Mountainview members are not alone in considering these matters in a community context. The organization OLOC (Old Lesbians Organizing for Change) addresses aging and disability concerns.[11] Some of the women at Mountainview and some of my other informants (including Sophia) were part of this community, which holds conferences, publishes a newsletter, networks, and brings women together. This organization provides networking, a larger voice, and resources to older lesbians.

The aging body and mind form the point around which these negotiations turn. While acknowledging that aging changes bodies and minds, these models of aging still focus not on what abilities are lost, but on what abilities remain. A delicate balance between individual abilities and agency, community care, and response is being negotiated.

Beautiful Crones: Images of Aging

The aging body is experienced, spoken of, and imagined in different ways in women's-land cultures than it is in U.S. matrix cultures. The different ways women use their bodies in women's land, the influence of Goddess-oriented feminist spirituality,[12] and conscious feminist efforts to embrace a more diverse view of the beauty of the female body all influence how aging is seen.

The intersection of women's-land cultures with Goddess-oriented spirituality has lent great importance to the image of the Crone. In many branches of such spirituality the figure of the Goddess is divided into three aspects: the Maiden, the Mother, and the Crone.[13] The Crone, usually appearing in U.S. matrix cultures as a figure of comedy or evil,[14] has been adopted by many land-women as a powerful, resonant image. Some land-women celebrate menopause with Cronings, large life-event parties that celebrate their new identity. The power and respect that are offered to the Crone aspect of the Goddess are also in some small measure arrogated to the women who enter that part of their lives. At the same time, since women's lands are embedded within the United States matrix culture, ageism is still a part of how women interact. Baba Copper (2015), who lived at Heraseed, a feminist utopian collective, noted many aspects of ageism specific to the lesbian community, ranging from the assumption of wealth (9) to sexual erasure (10).

Although not all women's lands are explicitly associated with Goddess spirituality, the power and respect offered to crones "travels" through women's culture. For example, crones are often depicted in flattering ways in the feminist art favored by land-women. Crones are important and beautiful figures in feminist tarot decks. See, in particular, The Crone, Spiderwoman, and Maat, and the Crone cards of the four suits in the Daughters of the Moon Tarot (Morgan 1986); the Poet's Tarot (Cougar 1986); and the Amazon Empowerment Tarot (Rivers and Wiles 2000). This art offers a very different image of aging from the one available in the matrix culture.

A conscious effort on the part of many women involved in women's community to view aging differently helps create a new view of the aging body. Many women have made an effort to see aging as a strengthening, positive process and to see older women as vital parts of the community, in opposition to a matrix culture that increasingly values youth and conflates it with success, ability, and attractiveness. Cynthia Rich writes in her feminist aging manifesto: "But I cannot hear these voices clearly if I am still afraid of the old witch, the Terrible Mother in myself, or if I am estranged from the real old women of this world. For it is not the wicked witch who keeps Rapunzel in her tower. It is the prince and our divided selves" (1983b, 7).

Struggling against the ageism of the matrix culture is not an easy task and requires a conscious rejection of many of the cultural images, tropes, and hegemonic formulas about gender, the body, age, and death.

Older women are also seen as an important resource of knowledge and history in the women's-land community. Although women's-lands do use paper publications—print media of various kinds and now electronic media as well—oral tradition receives an importance and a pride of place that is alien to the mainstream. Older women, particularly those with a long history on women's lands, can thus wield a considerable amount of social power. As in many other cultures, the past is often looked to as a source of legitimization, and women who embody and interpret the past control access to this type of legitimacy.

As the creators of oral herstory, women are important archives. Older women, whose access to foundational herstory (e.g. the origin herstories of many women's lands) represents an unusual resource, are particularly important. The herstory of women's lands is sometimes viewed as something fragile that may be lost; many of the written records of their foundation were periodicals that were rarely archived. In response, the OLOC is currently engaged in the Arden Eversmeyer Old Lesbian Herstory project. They note, "The herstories of the women who lived through a unique period in time need to be preserved. The women deserve to be recognized for their experiences and contributions. And, just as importantly, there are thousands of other Old Lesbians who need to know they are not alone" (http://www.oloc.org/projects/herstory.php).

Another example, which has recently passed out of the realm of oral tradition into a written one, is the Landdykes Slideshow, which is a set of photographs and the information accompanying them. This slideshow—originally in the format of traditional slides and only recently transferred to digital format—is passed from woman to woman in order that a presentation using them can be given at women's events. The original narration that accompanied the slides was created by Sealion, who gathered all the information about the various lands and women documented. The transcript and the slides (and now, various copies thereof) are treasured for their narrative history, and Sealion is viewed as an expert and authority on this history.

Thus age is often associated with social importance, and narrative as well as conscious, positive images are adopted deliberately in the face of ageism.

The Hermit and the Family

During a meeting on aging I attended at a Landdyke Gathering held at Turtle Mesa in New Mexico, a woman related the following story: Two lesbians built a rural house and lived together until the death of one of the partners. The remaining partner, Julia, was still living in the house but because of the remote location and wood-stove heating, she knew she could not stay. Julia's daughter wanted her to live with her in the city, but Julia did not want to: she loved the country, and did not want to leave the house she and her partner had built. However, Julia's increasing age, coupled with her solitude, meant that she could not continue living the life that she and her partner had built together. She said, "I love my daughter, but I have never wanted to live in a city."

Queer and lesbian-identified women living in the U.S. matrix culture have expressed similar sentiments, including fears about whether surviving partners will be allowed to keep joint homes and fears of whether their current homes would continue to be viable for them as they aged (Orel 2004, 66). Julia's story, told by a woman who knew her, sparked an intense reaction in the meeting. Women expressed sympathy and several said that they, too, would prefer to live in a house with the memory of a beloved partner.

Lying underneath that discussion, cold and palpable as floodwater, was one of the most primal issues of women's land: community. A woman alone—a hermit—does not have an immediate family/community to depend on. As women age and need more assistance, the family model becomes more necessary. The tension between the hermit and the family, two completely different yet mutually included models of life in women's land, emerges in these conflicts. As an excellent example of this, Sylvie, from Mountainview, told me that she liked living in community because "she could live alone in the woods but have people she could rely on at the same time."

On the one hand, rural locations offer solitude, safety, and wilderness; on the other hand, women's communities offer mutuality, like-minded people, and a different, participatory culture. These tensions can be seen in their physical arrangements—which largely tend towards separate houses, but which often retain community space and structures—and in their locations, which are mostly rural. Women enter women's land both for the sense of participation in community and in order *not* to participate, to be alone. Sometimes, this is the same woman and the same community.

The tragedy of the woman who had to move away from her rural home was that she had no "family" of a larger local women's community to turn to. The paradox is that a family-community is often needed in order to support the hermit lifestyle as one ages. The hermit *needs* a family.

The image of the hermit depends on *ableism*. Women's land culture is largely rustic and technology is often eschewed: one may be expected to chop wood and carry water. Levels of technology vary but a large number of potential physical barriers, such as dirt roads and difficult-to-traverse terrain, tend to persist. The expense of building physical accommodations is a barrier as well. Aging land-women find themselves with more physical needs in sometimes remote situations that can be physically demanding,[15] with fewer options and resources over time with which to face those challenges. Disabled land-women may find themselves shut out from certain lands and locations by lack of accessibility. At the same time, land-women, many of whom are working class or who have chosen to live a non-affluent lifestyle, are often economically limited in their choice of support for their older years.

The growing awareness among land-women of such physical and social difficulties is typical of how women's-land communities focus on aspects of culture they see as problematic and in need of change. With the high proportion of aging women among land-women, issues of aging are foregrounded, and thus the tensions between the independent hermit and the interdependent family are brought to the table. As seen in the example of the women of Mountainview planning their "retirement community" of Old Babeapalooza on the lands of Mountainview itself, the desire to remain hermetic, to whatever degree possible, is addressed through the family-community. That desire is also held by some disabled land-women.

The Disabled Body-Self and Her Concerns

Disabled queer women stand at an intersection or "confluence," as Susan Schweik points out:

> The street-corner metaphor, particularly apt for the situation of the unsightly beggar, sharply underscores the harm that can happen there. "One of the dangers of standing at an intersection," writes duCille, "is the likelihood of being run over." (Schweik 2009, 143)

Indeed, the image of being "run over" at the intersection is vivid. Schweik, in writing about the "ugly laws" of the United States that regulated the public appearance of the disabled in concert with ideas about race, citizenship, gender, and class, notes that disability is often presented as a monolithic category, especially in oppressive discourse (141). However, "gender, race, sexuality, religion, and national identity are inexorably intertwined with disability and class in the culture(s) of ugly law, producing a variety of ugly identities." Disability itself is highly varied both in experience and in how disability theorists present it.

While disability is highly varied, how it is presented in the larger, ableist matrix culture is often as a monolith—a failure to reach a "normal" standard (Campbell 2009). This "failure" is similar to "queer failure" (Halberstam 2011) in that both are seen as deviations from the assumed normal body. Both people with disabilities and queer people have been presented in U.S. matrix culture as asexual or problematically sexual (Whitney 2006; Drummond and Brotman 2014). Queer women with disabilities are at a higher risk for health disparities, according to Drummond and Brotman, because they are likely to receive substandard health care (534). The very term *disabled* is too flexible, applied to a wide number of conditions, and unclear, describing physical, emotional, and learning or mental disabilities. The term is applied to those who are born with particular conditions as well as to those who acquire them through accident, violence, or illness, or through the passage of time.

Both those who are disabled and those who are queer *deviate* from an assumed normal.[16] However, as with those who identify as queer, we cannot assume a uniform experience among women who identify as disabled. Kay Inckle compares the wide variety of bodily and experiential difference among those called disabled to the wide variety of experience found in those grouped in the category "woman," and states that her "use of 'disabled embodiment' is a double move, something akin to Spivak's (1988) strategy of 'strategic essentialism' that materialises only in order to disrupt the structures which necessitate it." Inckle suggests that we remain suspicious of these overarching categories, calling for their disruption; yet these categories have something to say to each other about "the politics of visibility and exclusion where disabled embodiment disrupts both normative frameworks and radical gender theories and yet remains largely absent from both" (2014, 389). Indeed, both queer and crip embodiments resist normative standards.

However, despite the ways in which both the queer and the crip are "deviant," these experiences are not parallel, and women who experience both have particular intersectional identities. Chelsea Whitney writes that for queer women with disabilities, "identity becomes a complex and multifaceted process," with identity development drawn from both disability and queer models (2006, 46–47). Identity discourse in the queer community makes use of ableist language such as "strength" or "voice," equating these abilities with pride and alienating queer women with disabilities (41). D'Aoust also notes the "problematic image of the Amazon," which can be alienating for disabled women (1994, 570), while Corbett Joan O'Toole states that "disabled women challenge the foundation of the lesbian community's value of self-reliance" (2000, 212). Similarly, hospital and therapeutic resources for the disabled often assume a heterosexual orientation, particularly with regard to sexuality and child-rearing (Vaughn et al. 2015, 38; O'Toole 2000, 217). Female-partnered women in physical rehab also report negative reactions, and/or decisions to closet themselves (Hunt, Milsom, and Matthews 2009, 174–75), while disabled queer women report physical and social exclusion from queer spaces (Dykewomon 2014, 28–29).

In the same way black women are excluded in feminist analyses of domestic violence (Crenshaw 1991), disabled queer women face intersectional invisibility and the case of disabled women of color illustrates even greater intersectional issues. In 2000, O'Toole wrote, "There is very little understanding of how disability, lesbianism, and race intersect" (208). Her paper explores some of the ways in which these identities affect each other, quoting several disabled queer women of color, including an anonymous informant who stated, "People ask me which I am: Woman, disabled, Asian. I tell them I am all three, it's like a triangle. It just depends on what is on top right now."

The concerns of disabled women are similar to, but not identical with, those of aging women on land. These include physical alterations to make living on land easier, an increasing acceptance of members of communities who cannot do the labor that is often an integral part of caring for the physical plant of a community, and inclusion of the disabled in the planning stages of various women's communities and land events. The main difference between the disabled and aging women lies in their relative positions: many aging women have been part of the women's-land community for many years and thus have access to insider status. Disabled women, who face difficulties due to the physical and social barriers of remote rural living, often must struggle to overcome outsider status and be accepted as land-women.

Like aging women, disabled women have particular reason to want access to women's land as an alternative to institutional care. Such models for queer disabled populations are regarded by my informants with the same suspicion (and in some cases, outright fear) as institutional eldercare is regarded by aging lesbians, for many of the same well-founded reasons. Homophobia in disabled care is well documented, ranging from refusal or reluctance to support same-sex relationships for intellectually disabled clients (Abbot and Howarth 2007; O'Toole 2000, 220; O'Toole and Brown 2003) and clients undergoing treatment for mental illness (Cook 2000, 202) to the myth that relationships between women are pathological and only occur because disabled women are in a female-only space (segregated ward) or are undesirable to men due to their physical presentation (O'Toole 2000, 219, 208).[17]

The struggle of disabled women to create opportunities for themselves in women's land mirrors the struggle of disabled people in the matrix culture of the United States. Here, as Geyla Frank sums up, a growing cohort of activists "argued that the degree of a person's ability or disability is determined by access to public facilities, social support, protection against discrimination, and cultural acceptance. Exclusionary conditions, not impairments, are the root cause of disability" (2000, 44). In this model, currently fundamental in disability studies, disability as a concept is moved away from the body and into the interactions of that body with society. However, where Frank notes that in the matrix cultures of the United States, "activists encouraged people with disabilities to think of themselves not as patients but as consumers" (45), land-women do not primarily see themselves as consumers. Instead, disabled land-women see themselves as creators of culture and society.

In her discussion of queer theory and disability theory, Carrie Sandahl writes:

> Their primary constituencies, sexual minorities and people with disabilities, share a history of injustice: both have been pathologized by medicine; demonized by religion; discriminated against in housing, employment, and education; stereotyped in representation; victimized by hate groups; and isolated socially, often in

their families of origin. Both constituencies are diverse in terms of race, class, gender, sexuality, religion, political affiliation, and other respects and therefore share many members (e.g., those who are disabled and gay), as well as allies." (2003, 26)

These overlaps may not lead naturally to alliances, but there is a parallel relationship between the structures that create and reinforce "normality." One of Whitney's informants elucidates this: "Whereas, because I'm queer and I have a disability it's like all of a sudden I'm like ya know what we have this whole bullshit idea of normal that really doesn't apply to anybody.... Like nobody really fits into that anyway and I especially don't and there is no way I'm going to even if discrimination against queer people ends" (2006, 46). This concept of "abolishing the normal" intersects with the ways in which women's land seeks to actively change culture and social norms, including norms about the body and ability.

At Landdyke Gatherings there is visible, outspoken discussion of accessibility issues ranging from "invisible" disabilities such as asthma, arthritis, and other painful syndromes to chemical sensitivities, wheelchair and walking issues, to blindness and deafness. It is notable that what we might broadly call women-oriented spaces—women's music festivals,[18] women's lands, women's co-ops, and communal activist concerns run on feminist principles—have been leaders in terms of making spaces, gatherings, and organizations accessible in various ways. O'Toole notes that "in the early 1970s lesbians were providing wheelchair seating and sign-language interpreters at some major community events" (2000, 212). Yet on women's land the issue of accessibility is endemic due to the rural nature of many of the spaces and how the ethos of early women's lands was reflected in the physical structure of the buildings. The emphasis on "simple living" made it initially difficult for women with certain disabilities. However, beyond the emphasis on simplicity, a desire to be *inaccessible* to the matrix culture or the kyriarchy is sometimes flatly incompatible with a desire to be *accessible* to all women.

Here is another tension, one that parallels but is not exactly similar to that between the hermit and the family. This tension is between the ethos of "simple living," which encompasses rustic living, economic and communitarian values of living as cheaply/simply as possible, and ecological values, and the ethos of accessibility and diversity. For example, at WomanShare,[19] the homes were heated by wood cut on the land by individual women. As Nelly describes it, "My first three winters in the country I got my firewood in by hand. I don't mean my hand itself sawed the wood, but rather my hand pushed the bow saw or joined with a sister in pushing the two-person saw. At first it seemed quite romantic." Later, Nelly purchased a chainsaw to lighten this task (Sue et al. 1976, 108–10). However, certain types of disability would make living in an environment where one had to cut one's own wood difficult or impossible. Yet other forms of heating are more expensive—even the money for the chainsaw itself was earned with difficulty, as Nelly notes: "I wanted a chain saw so badly that I was even willing to work as a dishwasher to earn money to buy it!"

Not every form of accessible heat, roads, water, or other necessities are as easily purchased as a chainsaw. The widespread concern over physical accessibility, which dovetails to some extent with the concerns of aging in place, is thus in tension with *financial* accessibility. While some accommodations are merely a matter of forethought—for example, making sure you mow your paths wide enough for wheelchairs, or organize kitchens consistently for people who rely on memory or touch, or ask people not to use scented products—others require more economic outlay.

A Place for Us: Land-Women Strategizing against Disablism

Like aging women, disabled women create communities based around their own needs. I was able to visit one such community, Oaktrust, located in New England and home to one resident, Acorn. I was part of a crew of local women who volunteered to help clear roads and paths on the land after a tornado blew through. My wife and I, along with four other lesbians, worked with handsaws and hedge-trimmers to clear large branches from paths and driveways. This incident demonstrates networking to provide community support; a single resident, disabled or not, could not have dealt with the damage the tornado had left. In this instance, word of mouth among diverse communities provided the support needed for a single woman living alone in the woods.

Acorn's land, Oaktrust, was administered as part of a nonprofit organization specifically for the benefit of disabled women. The organization's charter did not specify any particular type of disability, but the land was reserved for the use of women who identified as disabled.[20] Acorn herself identifies as disabled pursuant to extensive health problems from environmental sensitivities. She maintains a wide network of community friendships through telephone and email and is an activist on behalf of women with disabilities. At the time of my visit, she was living in a small trailer on Oaktrust land.

Acorn regularly attends Landdyke Gatherings by telephone, and it is at least partly through her networking and efforts that phone access is provided. For example, the "spiderphone" adapted to teleconferencing used at the Gatherings I attended was provided by her organization. Also, at least partly at her suggestion, meetings are held to discuss the concerns of accessibility in women's lands and what can be done to adapt existing women's-land structures to be more accessible.

Elana Dykewomon demonstrates that even if "alternative" and women-oriented spaces have been leaders in accessibility, accessibility is not universal. She writes: "Many organizations meet the demands of the disabled community by saying: when we have the money; when we can; the benefit was at a private house, we cannot dictate to them; disabled people are not coming" (2014, 29). Accessibility is important, she writes,

> Not because it's "PC" but because we need each other, we need every perspective; and we need to ensure that we respect each other's dignity, each other's bodies, as we wish our own to be respected. Try to imagine an activist universe in which every venue is wheelchair accessible, signed, scent free; where no one supports the diet industry, and if T-shirts are sold, they come in sizes up to 6x; conferences where scooters, hearing devices, and captioning are provided for attendees.

This vision of an "activist universe" links community with accessibility, as does Dian when she writes, "i believe that the value placed on rugged individualism in our culture has to go and that cooperation must be emphasized if we are to survive. Collectivity is based on cooperation" (Sue et al. 1976, 137). The need to move beyond "rugged individualism" is a strong theme throughout *Country Lesbians*. Vicky D'Aoust explicitly connects this theme to disability in her essay "Competency, Autonomy, and Choice" (1994) when she writes about the "false truth" of feminist autonomy, and notes that "dependence is neither 'healthy' nor 'unhealthy' but rather as common and as much a part of life as being a lesbian or having a child" (567). In these visions we recognize the Family side of the Hermit and the Family.

Thus, the issue of dependence versus collectivity/interdependence helps replicate the Hermit/Family dynamic on women's land and in similar spaces. D'Aoust criticizes a collective ethos that values the work members provide rather than the members themselves, and goes on to state,

> On a collective level, this dynamic imitates the valued aspects of capitalist societies such as 'productive work' and creation of 'surplus value.' On an individual level, it teases women with disabilities by saying that we are all working for independence and autonomy, which you can never have because you are chronically dependent. (569)

Such understandings of collectivity appear from time to time on women's land. For example, at Mountainview, one member who took me hiking praised the work that several other members had done to help maintain the trails that wound around the mountains. Then she added, "Of course, not everyone can help with this." Recall from "Karma Eaters" that the usual way of disciplining someone for not doing their share of the work is to praise someone else for doing their share. Although this was not a direct form of "discipline," as those who did not maintain the trail were not present, I understood it as a clear way of expressing disapprobation without naming names. Drawing my attention to this seemed significant, especially in light of the way able and *working* bodies are often seen as good and *virtuous* bodies.

At the same time, land-women who identify as disabled also—collectively and individually—work against ableist/capitalist understandings of community based on work contributions, point out disablism, and help create more positive images of disabled and non-normative bodies. Like Oaktrust, other women's lands work to make their spaces more accessible, including wheelchair ramps installed on at least one house at Mountainview, ramps and wide wheelchair-accessible paths on the land at Wild Uprising, and scent-free events such as the Landdyke Gathering.

Portrayals of disabled women in feminist art, such as in women's tarot sets, vary widely. In the Poet's Tarot (Cougar 1986), the Witch figure,[21] Card I, is a woman in a wheelchair, and there are several other women with canes in the art, which also features elderly women and very androgynous women/figures. In this case, the woman who has the visibly-different body is placed in a central location as an important figure, with an accompanying text that reads, "My intentions are / pure harmony, / that I may / conduct / the powers / and ride them. / The forces will / back this / overture."

Also in the Poet's Tarot, the Seer (Card X of the major arcana)[22] has a cane and dark glasses, which implies that she is blind, and the Crone (Card VII of the major arcana)[23] walks with a cane; the illustrations show women of different races, ages, and sizes. The Daughters of the Moon Tarot, another woman-only tarot set, features a wheelchair race as the Six of Pentacles (Morgan et al. 1986, 92). The Amazon Empowerment Tarot has no images of visibly disabled women, although it does have a wide range of ages and races (Rivers and Wiles 2000). These positive images in feminist art illustrate a push towards seeing disability not only as part of the larger community, but also as beautiful and worthy of portrayal.

The gaze is a complicated issue when dealing with ableism/disablism, since as many theorists have pointed out, those who are visibly disabled are disciplined both by "the stare" and by social invisibility (Inckle 2014), while those who are invisibly disabled have their disabilities doubted and accommodations questioned or denied. Similarly, lesbianism is at one and the same time visible and stared at (when performed in particular ways) and still invisible and socially overlooked in others (D'Aoust 1994). When the two identities coincide, the gaze becomes particularly fraught. Catherine Odette, in her 1999 essay "Butchdom and Disability," writes:

> When I am looked at by those who cannot perceive me when they see me, I feel the long and increasing distance between us. I see her not see me.... She cannot imagine the strength it takes to live with a disability. She cannot imagine that she underestimates the vastness of who I am. She cannot imagine the special world that has disability at its core. I can no longer imagine not perceiving disabled people as they pass by me. I can no longer not imagine the additional community that exists for me because I know the secret handshake of disability. (96)

This discussion of seeing/not-seeing, perception and misperception, presence and invisibility, uses the image of both disability as presence (the visible figure in the wheelchair) and absence (being ignored, assumed to *not be*). This works in parallel to Odette's earlier discussion of butchness as both visible performance but also invisible, smothered/silenced (1999,

95). Queer presence and disability move together to assert humanness in the face of those who would ignore, efface, or see these expressions as less than human. On women's lands, land-women who identify as disabled work to keep both themselves and issues of disability visible. Through discussion, positive images, and the creation of spaces specifically for disabled women, they move themselves into the visible circle.

Aging women and disabled women bring interconnections between cultural expectations and individual needs to the fore in women's intentional communities. As they showcase the tension between the ideals of the Family and the Hermit, they also highlight the tensions and interactions between the community and the individual. By this, I mean that the community and the place must adapt to the needs of the individuals: for example, the physical place may have to be altered, or the community implement a procedure for checking in among its residents. The tension between the Family and the Hermit and the ways in which the Family can *support* the Hermit are reflected in these arrangements. In this way, the needs of the individual members also become the needs of the community, and are reflected in the physical space of the land. The bodies of aging and disabled women not only interact with the various cultures of women's lands differently, but also cause the physical surroundings—the literal place—to differ. Bodies and places have a reciprocal impact on one another.

That reciprocal impact changes the physical shape of women's land. The symbolism of accessibility is deeply important to disabled women and to women's-land culture as a whole. Consider, for example, how "all women" are defined, including aged and disabled women who are often seen as nonentities or relegated to very minor roles in many of the matrix cultures of the United States. Accessible women's lands represent not only an important resource for the women who live there or who use their resources, but also are an important symbol in the wider network of women's culture. They are the "open door" symbol, the ability for "any woman" to take advantage of the resources of women's land. While the actual ability of individual women to access women's lands varies a great deal, and how welcomed they might feel once they get there will also vary, the ethos or principle of women's lands being for all women is an important thread. At the same time, such accessibility is constrained by financial issues and by the white imaginary.

The issue of aging and accessibility thus comes full circle: while pointing out the conflict in women's-land culture between the archetypes of the Hermit and the Family, these issues also provide incentive for women to find resolutions for those tensions—ways for the family to support the hermit and for the hermit to live within the family. The emphasis on aging in place also points out the important connections between women and physical, as well as community, location. The images of the Hermit and the Family are cultural goals and potent images in the creation of the good life.

· AFTERWORD ·

Women's Lands, Women's Lives

The Ladies' Sewing Circle and Terrorist Society
—seen on a button, circa 1990

It wasn't different because we were women. It was different because we were creating something different.
—Tamara, speaking about the Seneca Women's Peace Camp

WOMEN'S LANDS ARE THE SITE of intense production of cultural difference. That difference is largely *constructed* by the women who form these communities, and it centers around gender. Gendered cultural variation is variation that goes all the way down, as gender is one of the deep supports of culture. Thus the women who have produced these cultures have successfully and intentionally generated profound differences. However, these differences do not absolve these communities from systems of power in the larger U.S. matrix cultures that surround them. Those systems of power still affect these nested cultures, perhaps most pervasively in how these communities replicate white ways of knowing (Finney 2014, 3) that help to exclude women of color.

The literal absence of the male gaze is used to signal and signify a space where women are considered full human beings without the heavy limitations of sexism imposed by the matrix societies of the United States. Sirocco expresses this very well:

> Because for me it's not about male or female, it's about being true to myself. And for me to be true to myself, I can't be around men without feeling like I have to behave or act or present myself in a certain manner. And I don't want to. I don't want to. I don't want to deny a portion of myself because it's socially not acceptable,

· 243 ·

> or it's deemed as "that girl's kind of weird because she doesn't want to wear dresses or act a certain way, or wear makeup or use certain language, or bow down, or you know." And regardless of whether ... to function in the real society, women pretty much need to do that.... You have to comply. And complying to me, the word complying sometimes means sacrifice. Sacrificing who I am, what I'm about.

This space where women are freed from what Bartky calls "the disciplinary techniques through which the 'docile bodies' of women are constructed" (1997, 41) allows the development of the self without such time-consuming and constraining practices, as well as direct rebellion against the mores of the matrix culture. Those mores are not simply rejected but also undone: the creation of a space where the female body-self can act *without reference* to those constraints is a site of revolution.

Yet this revolution is partial; for example, the thin body ideal continues in many spaces as the unchallenged meter of "health." And, like Bartky's article that focuses mainly on *white* body practice, the default body and the default self in these spaces is white. This continues to other the experiences of queer women of color, even as much of the theory, philosophy, and practice of these spaces has been contributed by feminist theorists of color.

This theoretical space of freedom is created in a paradoxical, liminal way. Women's land and women's culture are created by an ethos of *difference*,[1] based on ideas about gender difference which are both borrowed from matrix cultures (doxa) and constructed by land-women. Yet within that cultural space, women can and do expand to fill all cultural roles. Women's space itself is created by focusing on gender difference that is largely part of an unconsidered binary, yet *within* women's space women are free to explore a larger arc of gender roles, without reference to the binary of the matrix culture.

Using the body as a touchstone for debates on who should be permitted into the category of women also invites essentialism into the discussion—and the essentials are defined by the gender binaries of matrix cultures of the United States. At the same time, actual practices break down gender essentialisms, for where all roles are taken by women, women comprise *the entire human race*. Women take on all the range of human activity, roles, and abilities. In expanding themselves to their full human potential, they also explore the full range of the female gender, which stretches much farther within women's community than it does in most matrix cultures. When this is contrasted with the body-based essentialism of transphobia, the tension between theory and practice becomes deeply ironic: while expanding practice to take on all roles for themselves, some of the women of these spaces defend the boundaries by reverting to "biology is destiny" essentialism.

Still, gender ideas borrowed from the matrix culture are often exploded by the act of living within a society of women exploring the full range of human possibility. Thus, there are also women in these spaces who welcome gender questioning, the inclusion of "queer," and the inclusion of trans folk.

Land-women are consciously and deliberately engaged in the production of cultural difference. They also do their own analysis and critique of that difference. Despite this self-awareness, the fact that women's lands are embedded within the larger matrix culture of the United States leads to cultural tension, and the larger cultural "weight" of the United States gives it a great advantage in preserving capitalism, sexism, and racism. These are most visible in conflicts over class, the way white land-women tend not to question the whiteness of their communities, transphobia, and in the manner in which the thin, muscular body has been adopted as the visible mark of health. Despite this, the production of difference is profound, and in many cases women actively and openly question strands of the matrix culture, discussing class and race, creating lands for women of color, and criticizing transphobia and fatphobia. Women's lands are not homogenous; indeed, no land has members who agree about all aspects of "women's culture."

Attempted change of the matrix culture by women's-land women reaches from the macro-level, such as participating in nationwide legislation initiatives or traveling to other countries for feminist conferences and political actions, to the local level, in activities such as animal rescue, the support of a local clinic, or creating a riding school to help children at risk. Some women also regard the very fact that women's land exists as a banner for possible change. Indeed, by challenging the *doxa* of society, land-women have managed to change a portion of it into *orthodoxy*. Orthodoxy can be challenged by the heterodoxy of their own way of living, and some aspects of the matrix culture (for example, the social interactions referred to by my informants as gendered "energy") can be openly discussed and analyzed. Land-women, by creating their own cultural spaces within the matrix society, have exerted power. They have changed the terms on which the matrix culture operates, moving it from unquestioned and unquestionable doxa to questionable orthodoxy, and they do this not only for themselves but for anyone who knows of them. It does not *matter* whether we take them seriously or not: the very fact that they have questioned the terms of the matrix culture provides a means for other people to do so.

What this diverse community shows us is that the production of cultural difference based on gender is possible. Yet gender is still present: whether borrowed from the matrix culture or refigured to express wider possibilities, gender is still one of the primary means of organizing culture, even in a single-gender environment. Kath Weston suggests that gender is something beyond performance—something that individuals adopt as an internal identity (1993). That internal identity, however, is fashioned out of the messages of our culture(s), and when it comes to changing that identity and those messages, we are faced with the paradox of having internalized them. At the same time, gender is continually negotiated, something that we can influence and change both within ourselves and in the cultures that surround us.

Although threads from the matrix culture still remain, women's lands represent a differently-gendered space. Within that space, a fundamental truth that is still obscured and denied by the matrix culture is made clear and prominent: women are human beings. Not inferior, not "people of gender," not second-class citizens, not their bodies, and not their reproductive potential. Simply human beings—the unmarked category.

One of my informants, Sealion, once told me about how she joined the women's-land movement in the early seventies, "Why would I need a college degree to change the world?" She did not, and the world is changed. Making women an unmarked category is a profound and important change.

We Are Everywhere You Want to Be: Women's Lands around the World

Very briefly, I would like to put the hundred-plus women's lands in the United States in a more global and historical context. While they are a very particular historical and cultural form of women's land, they are not unique; we find self-determined single-gender communities throughout history and all over the world. In fact, here in the United States, American women's lands were presaged by the Women's Commonwealth, founded in 1879 by Mrs. Martha W. McWhirter as part of her conversion/religious experience (Sokolow and Lamanna 1984, 371–72). Women who joined the commune called themselves the Sanctified Sisters or the Sanctificationists, and claimed their rights to deal with property and divorce their husbands due to their spiritual call to "perfection," asserting that a "sanctified wife owes no duty to any unsanctified husband" (378).

The Sanctified Sisters challenged many ideas prevalent in society at the time. In addition to asserting their rights to divorce their husbands and forging new ideas about women's sexuality (the majority of them were celibate), they held down jobs and communally owned property (Sokolow and Lamanna 1984; Chmielewski 1993). "The women also formed new emotional bonds with each other and replaced the nuclear families from which they had come with a successful communal family based on equitable relationships" (Chmielewski 1993, 52). The community, based on a completely communal model, lasted for over a hundred years, until the death of the last member, without major schisms. Chmielewski writes:

> The Women's Commonwealth was one of the few intentional communities designed, controlled, and populated by women. It was shaped by the women inhabitants according to their needs and their beliefs. The Sisters demanded independence and self-determination and soon learned that this aspiration threatened traditional patriarchal society. By banding together the women could survive economically and fight against the hostility of the outside world. Believing that the communal life provided the best social family and environment for individuals, the women found that this mode of living fulfilled many of their needs. (65)

This long-lasting, stable community is not nearly as well known as Oneida (which did not last so long), yet it seems to have worked just as well. Living without male support in that historical period was revolutionary, and their religious focus echoes the utopian religious communities common in North America at the time, as well as nunneries.[2] The women-only community was also at once the reason for and the solution to "the hostility of the outside world"; a paradox that many women's spaces and communities face. Their egalitarian and communal ethos prefigures many North American women's lands existing today.

But women's lands and communes are not limited to North America. My interviewees told me about their experiences living all over the world: for example, one interviewee told me about living in a rural women's commune in New Zealand. There, on land unserved by electricity or running water, the women had built themselves handsome one-room houses of solid mahogany, the wood coming from old automobile shipping crates. "They used to ship cars crated in mahogany?" I asked, disbelief coloring my tone. She grinned. "Yep," she said. "And we recycled it into something useful rather than letting it be thrown away."

Glorious Dyke, who had lived on several women's lands, told me about visiting a lesbian commune in Japan, where the women lived in buses and didn't stay in one place. They traveled as a communal group and she stayed with them for a while. Another interviewee, who had grown up in England, told me about Greenham Common, where a large women's community protested against the United States military presence there, as well as her journey to the United States in search of a more permanent women's land to live on.

In the Carpathian Mountains in the Ukraine, a women's group called the Asgarda are empowering girls by teaching them a martial art in which they wield curved blades resembling scythes, as well as encouraging feminist thought and self-reliance (Howard 2010). Although the Asgarda are not a residential community, they run a two-month long women-only summer camp in which they train and empower women and girls. Katerina Tarnouska founded the Asgarda in 2004, and says, "I wanted girls to gain confidence to be themselves, and not just quiet wives working, working and swallowing all the time their own dreams—the lot of our mothers and grandmothers under the Soviets" (quoted in Howard). Although this is not a year-round community, like the Peace Camp and music festivals it forms a core of community and cultural change for these women.

Umoja, the village that provides shelter for survivors of rape in Kenya, is famous. "The village was founded in 1990 by a group of 15 women who were survivors of rape by local British soldiers. Umoja's population has now expanded to include any women escaping child marriage, FGM (female genital mutilation), domestic violence, and rape—all of which are cultural norms among the Samburu" (Bindel 2015). Here, women wear traditional dress, make bead jewelry to sell, support each other, and raise children in a community of forty-seven women and two hundred children. The leader, Rebecca Lolosoli, came up with the idea of the village after being beaten by a group of men in "an attempt to teach her a lesson for daring to speak to women in her village about their rights." Like similar women's communities in the United States, this village provides a haven from violence; like U.S. women's lands, it is not taken seriously by the culture around it. Bindel notes that "there is still suspicion of the village in the neighbourhood," and one of the neighboring men remarks, "They think they are living without men, but that is not possible" (2015). All the same, and even though many of the women tell horrific tales of rape and abuse, the story Bindel tells overall is of a thriving and supportive community:

> Many of the women tell me they cannot imagine living with a man again after they have been living in Umoja. Towards the end of my visit I meet Mary, 34, who tells me she was sold to a man of 80 for a herd of cows when she was 16 years old. "I don't want to ever leave this supportive community of women," she says.
>
> Mary shows me a handful of dried beans that she will be cooking soon for dinner. "We don't have much, but in Umoja I have everything I need."

Unlike women's lands in the United States, Umoja is not associated with queerness/lesbianism; all the women there are assumed to participate in heterosexual/reprosexual sex. However, by removing themselves from the economic support of men and rejecting the violence meted out to them, they are mirroring many of the reasons women around the world create such spaces.

On the other hand, Naisargi Dave, in her exploration of lesbian communities in India, writes that "lesbian activism in India, like lesbian activisms the world over, grew both out of and against the norms of the women's movement that presaged it" (2010, 598). While this movement did not create (as far as Dave records) residential communities, networks were created, "beginning to formulate an imagined Indian lesbian community where nothing of the sort had existed before" (597). These groups started as "informal collectives of 'single women' in Delhi" in 1987 (610) and quickly blossomed into larger networks first based on letter-writing, then publications, then, with the acquisition of space, social clubs. Dave's opening of the piece, in which she looks on with "awe" at Thadani, India's "first out lesbian" (295) at a club, sounds, despite historical differences and very different cultural ways of being a same-sex-loving woman, familiar to U.S. readers:

> There, just across the club from her, were the directors of India's first lesbian help line and support group, Sangini, which was organized as a distinct alternative to the lesbian collective Thadani founded in 1991. To my right were members of PRISM, a queer advocacy collective that was born, in turn, out of ideological differences with Sangini. Amid these known and watchful activists were, in the middle of the dance floor, two young women dancing together in a manner utterly unburdened by care and history. (596)

I do not want to imply that queer life in India is "just like ours, only more Indian,"[3] but the similarities between queer politics as depicted by Dave and queer politics of the 1980s and 1990s in any large city in the United States are apparent, including the ideological differences and the reference to a lesbian collective. Although Dave does not record residential communities, the lesbian collective itself seems to have existed in a particularly Indian form.

These are only a few examples of how women's communities can be found all over the world, exhibiting enormous cultural, political, and social diversity. While the particular form of women's land as it is thought, built, and lived in North America is unique, similar ideas, ranging from lesbians living together on buses to women teaching martial arts at camp to the concept of the lesbian collective, are far-reaching. The different ways these are implemented have much to teach us about gender, politics, queer history, and the ways in which small communities both resist and incorporate larger cultural ideas.

These efforts create communal space for women; they teach, exert political change, and network; and they are all spaces where gender is negotiated, performed, and changed. Such communities, like women's land in the United States, suggest spaces where gender and culture are raised to conscious attention, where they are examined by local critics, and where they are subject to change without notice.

Acknowledgments

As with all books, this one would not exist without the material assistance of many people other than myself. I would first like to thank the many women who were generous enough to welcome me into their lands and homes so I could find out about women's lands firsthand; it was a very magnanimous act. This book would not exist without your knowledge and your generosity. All the land-women, would-be land-women, once land-women, and traveling dykes who generously donated their time and thoughts to being interviewed for this project (as well as hosting me, introducing me about, and giving me vital information): thank you for your introduction to women's lands.

Many of my interviewees asked that their interviews be filed with the Lesbian Herstory Archives, but the Brandeis University Office of Human Subjects in Research forbade me from doing so despite my efforts to gain permission. I would like to take this space to formally apologize to my interviewees for being unable to provide this basic service for them. Due to the constraints of my original IRB application, and the fact that the Brandeis University Office of Human Subjects in Research did not allow me to alter it, all original interview recordings have been destroyed for privacy reasons, even against the wishes of the interviewees. I deeply regret the loss of these conversations and the fact that I could not place them on record for those of my interviewees who wished them archived.

I would like to thank the Brandeis University Department of Anthropology and the Brandeis University Provost's Dissertation Expense Fund for their financial support of this work while it was my dissertation project. All post-dissertation work was unfunded.

The Committee on Studies of Women, Gender, and Sexuality at Harvard University was unflagging in its encouragement and support of this book project, and I thank them profusely for it. Also, many thanks to Bear Bergman and his "gendernauts," for doing research off-the-cuff, Hanne

Blank for her scholarly and editorial support, and Katherine Angel Cross of CUNY Graduate Center for a detailed and very helpful reading of chapter 6. I remain deeply in debt to both of my anonymous manuscript readers for their excellent insights and helpful comments: many, many thanks. I also thank Chrystos for allowing me to reprint one of her blazing poems.

Lastly, I thank Jude McLaughlin, who not only reassured me I was capable and visited women's lands with me but also read and commented on the manuscript extensively. (Like many academic spouses, she is 90 percent an academic herself but is never given proper credit.)

Notes

Introduction

1. Due to the terms of the Institutional Review Board (IRB) agreement under which I did my original and continuing research, all interviewee names and the names of the women's lands where I did my research are pseudonyms.
2. http://www.cambridgewomenscenter.org/aboutus.html.
3. There were also similar collectives of gay men. "By the mid-1970s, collectivist gay men inspired by lesbian feminists formed rural collectives on principles of radical sexual politics, separatism, and feminist paganism, and by applying lesbian feminism's universalizing gestures to gay men. For instance, the gay men's collective at Magdalen Farm adopted Maoist principles and brought gay men together through rural gatherings" (Morgensen 2011, 132). Morgensen also discusses the still-extant Radical Faerie movement extensively (see chapter 4), which advocates temporary rural retreat for spiritual and social connection.
4. Where material is not word-for-word, it has been edited for clarity only (removing "um" and similar vocatives) or has been edited for length, indicated by ellipsis. There are also a few instances, indicated in the text, where I attempt to recreate a remembered conversation from field notes and memory.
5. Many books cover the experience of living on women's land for extended periods. For example, see Hawk Madrone's *Weeding at Dawn* (2000); Sue et al., *Country Lesbians* (1976); Juana Maria Paz, *The La Luz Journal* (1980); and Pelican Lee's *Owl Farm Stories* (2002).
6. https://wemoon.ws/pages/contact-us.
7. Okely uses the term "Gypsy" throughout her work (1998, originally published in 1983). This term is now widely acknowledged as pejorative.

1. The Political Is Personal

1. In quotes because these cultures are so diverse and embedded in the larger network of the North American and global matrix.
2. See chapter 3 and Arcadia's story about the community that started as a mixed-gender commune but ended up as women's land.

3. See chapter 7 for a full discussion of transphobia, body concepts, and gender.
4. Schlesinger archive papers of the Seneca Women's Peace Camp.
5. Schlesinger archive papers of the Seneca Women's Peace Camp.
6. Correspondence in the Schlesinger archive papers of Seneca.
7. Schlesinger archive papers of the Seneca Women's Peace Camp.
8. They used a true consensus model—a single dissent could block a decision.
9. Schlesinger archive papers of the Seneca Women's Peace Camp.
10. They never did this, although it was debated several times.
11. Schlesinger archive papers of the Seneca Women's Peace Camp; interviewee notes.
12. The tendency to position women as symbols rather than as agential human beings is highly pervasive in academia. Marina Warner explored this in art and visual symbolism in her classic *Monuments and Maidens,* writing that "the female form tends to be perceived as generic and universal, with symbolic overtones; the male as individual, even when it is being used to express a generalized idea" (1985, 12). However, this tendency is far more deplorable in academic writing about real people and their actions, whether these are living people (anthropology, psychology, medicine) or dead (history).
13. And also, possibly, global changes through their engagement with antinuclear politics.
14. One cannot make the Marion Zimmer Bradley connection here without acknowledging the problems raised by the known sexual abuse perpetrated by her husband, Walter Breen, who was tried and convicted in 1954. She and her local science fiction community condoned this and kept it as an open secret for many years. Even more troubling is the fact that her daughter recently revealed that Bradley was herself sexually abusing her (Moen 6/10/2014). This unspeakable behavior was not known beyond the Bay Area science fiction community until recently, and was likely to be entirely unknown to her feminist/land-women fan base. I was unaware of it until 2014, when the issue was highly publicized in the online science fiction community.

Thus, there are ethical issues associated with her work, but these were unlikely to have occurred to the population of hopeful women communards in the 1980s. Omitting references to her work when I knew the importance of it was not an option; however, it is essential to acknowledge the problems now and the issues raised by the science fiction community about the ethics of enjoying work by abusers and protecting abusers in a community. For more information about the history of these issues in the science fiction community, please see Moen 6/10/2014; Moen 6/3/2014; Anonymous/Community "The Breendoggle Wiki"; and Luhrs 6/16/2014. Links to the 1954 trial depositions can be found through Moen 6/3/2014.

15. These include *Journey to Zelindar, Daughters of the Great Star, The Hadra,*

Clouds of War, The Redline of Yarmald, Her Sister's Keeper, and *The Smuggler, the Spy, and the Spider.*

16. The Separatist Lesbian is reverse camp not only because she seems to stand for such opposite values than the Old Queen, but also because I don't want to close the door on the possibilities of lesbian camp *qua* camp: playful, ironic, sly, allusive, tongue-in-cheek. For an interesting discussion of the possibilities of fem lesbian camp, see Hemmings, "Rescuing Lesbian Camp" (2007).

17. One cannot say "apolitical" without invoking Sontag's famous "Notes on Camp" (1965) and the discussion over the potential politicization of camp (and the relative paucity of her connections between camp and homosexuality). While I cannot recapitulate the whole of this fascinating debate in a footnote, I must note that my use of "antipolitical" does not imply "apolitical," but instead indicates a camp that hides politics, as it hides pain, behind itself. Camp is a strategy, it is relational, and "this dialectical tension—between past and present, morbidity and camp, morality and aesthetics, sympathy and revulsion, melancholy and hope—is a space of ethics. It is also a reason to hold onto camp in a time of terror" (Pellegrini 2007, 184).

18. Online Equal Marriage advertisement, February of 2007, produced by HSI productions.

19. Bondage, domination, sadism, and masochism. The acronym serves as an overview term for a wide variety of sexual practices, as does the term "leather" in other contexts. This is a sexual practice in which one person voluntarily submits to another, that may or may not include bondage play, pain, and verbal domination and/or humiliation. A debate has gone on for many years among separatist women (and the greater lesbian community) as to whether this form of sexuality is inherently patriarchal, and whether women's lands should provide "safe space" for survivors of sexual abuse who may be triggered by BDSM equipment or terms. Meanwhile, there is a fairly large lesbian and queer women BDSM community.

20. Similarly, it is notable that Halperin's discussion of camp as cultural gay male queerness focuses largely on (unspoken) white aspects of camp, although camp itself is heavily inflected by race and there are black, Latinx, and Native variations on what it means to camp or be camp (see, for example, E. Johnson's *Sweet Tea: Black Gay Men of the South* [2008] for excellent discussions of gender presentation and camp; see also Brian Joseph Gilley's *Becoming Two-Spirit: Gay Identity and Social Acceptance in Indian Country* [2006]). Also, bell hooks argues that white appropriation of black gay male camp obscures its real purpose in her essay "Is Paris Burning?" (1996).

21. These are a series of fantasy novels by John Norman that feature a world in which women are brainless slave sex objects. As in the parody version in *The Killer Wore Leather,* these books have inspired a roleplay following, about which I can only say the world is certainly full of many kinds of people.

22. That is, make them admit that she is the ultimate authority.

23. In a curious show of coyness, the text does not refer to her lesbianism directly at all, but leaves it to an accusation from a highly unpleasant male character who only gets her involved in the plot because he resents her perceived choice of sexuality (117).

24. "Do women belong in higher education?"

25. I am sure I need not point out the doubtless deliberate "vulva" reference here.

2. Are the Amazons White?

1. I will return to Finney's argument about our national cultural imagination with regard to the environment and race in chapter 5.

2. Note that all of these early statements use the heavily-inflected "energy" term. For more on the use of "energy" among current land-women, see chapter 3.

3. See chapter 4 for more about Arco Iris, including how it is faring today.

4. There is a chapter in *Nuclear Summer* that focuses entirely on how upset two straight white women were about the lesbians, vegetarians, and witches in the encampment. This is an excellent example of the discomfort of the privileged when faced with a space in which nonprivileged bodies and identities do not have to remain invisible or subservient.

5. We must not overlook, however, that at least some of the women participating in women's-land cultures have probably been shaped by middle-class suburban upbringings.

6. As we will see in chapter 5.

7. This is a good place to point out that Oregon, the primary focus of Gagehabib and Summerhawk's ethnography of women's land, was originally founded as a white separatist state, and had laws forbidding the settlement of people of African ancestry until the 1960s (Richard 1983; Brooks 2004; for a good overview see Novak 2015).

8. Presumably, "you couldn't do this alone, because there were so many babies in the preemie unit."

9. For more on the Clark doll tests, black dolls, and their social impact, I recommend Robin Bernstein's *Racial Innocence* (2011).

3. "Now My Neighbors and Friends Are the Same People"

1. Like my informants, Felski makes the basic erroneous assumption that feminist aesthetics *must* produce feminine-gendered products. As an anthropologist, I keep a somewhat more open mind.

2. One has only to look at the organic food movements, the natural parenting movement, and the ways in which femininity and masculinity are expressed (for example, online) by their members for a current example.

3. I am indifferent to arguments about whether texts, actions, and even bodies can be/are *actually/intrinsically*/what have you "feminine" or "masculine." What I am investigating is what my informants define as feminine, how they make those distinctions, how their ideas of what is feminine are influenced by mainstream/hegemonic ideas of femininity, and to what extent such doxa is undermined or resisted. I am investigating a feminist aesthetics solely on the basis that ideas of what is "masculine" or "feminine" are human productions *all the way down.*

4. Much has been written on the problem of women as an analytic category; for two foundational texts in this field, see Mohanty 1984 and Ortner 1996.

5. All but one of the children were adults at the time of my interviews.

6. Including most of the women who had been married to men, several of whom identified as "life-long" lesbians who had not realized this aspect of their identity earlier, or who had chosen to remain closeted.

7. Note G.D.'s spelling, which is a deliberate ploy to remove the construction "he" and "men" from all positive words, not simply from "women," while emphasizing or constructing that spelling in negative words. This wordplay genders language, assigning it positive and negative meaning.

8. The original name of the community, which I cannot give here for confidentiality reasons, referred to lesbian women growing old together.

9. See the feminist classic "The Tyranny of Structurelessness" by Jo Freeman (1970).

10. I do not want to give the impression that nonmonogamy was a "phase" or theme associated with the second wave that can no longer be found in modern queer or lesbian circles. Polyamory, polyfidelity, and other nonmonogamous forms of love and dating are thriving today, but are, alas, beyond the scope of this book.

11. Other members of Mountainview may have identified this way, but Robin was the only one who mentioned it in her interview.

12. A circle is a space used for pagan, Witch, or feminist spiritual religious gatherings and rites. They can be constructed temporarily or can be made permanent. A circle is usually roughly circular, as the name implies, with items to mark the four compass directions, which are of symbolic importance.

13. For more on this connection, see chapter 5.

14. Landdykes listserv email 4/13/07: "2007 Landdyke gathering announcement."

15. Heterosexual women are not only free from the constraints of (open) homophobia (but see Rich 1986), but also have access to privilege such as greater income derived from association with men (who, statistically speaking, are paid at a much higher rate than women), greater respectability due to their girlfriend/wife/mother role, and access to male people who can use their greater cultural capital on the women's behalf.

16. A few women spoke to me about the need for "queer-friendly" lands, in

which "queer" seemed to stand for both trans women and for women who were uncomfortable with a lesbian label.

17. An expanded version of "Gender and Language: Women's Energy as Social Theory," was published in *Journal of Homosexuality* as "The Gender of 'Energy': Language, Social Theory, and Social Change in Women's Lands in the United States," 2015. https://doi.org/10.1080/00918369.2015.1037129.

18. See also chapter 2, in which the "energy" term comes up in close relation to early separatist texts.

19. A useful and more modern feminist term for this is "emotional labor."

4. The Giving Tree

1. One woman I spoke to referred to herself as "polylandrous," a charming pun on "polyamorous" (having many lovers) and "land."

2. The Dykelands slide show is a collection of slides and accompanying text that were sent with a volunteer to various gatherings (such as the Landdyke Gathering, MichFest, other women's music festivals, and other women's gatherings) to educate women about extant women's lands. When I viewed it, the slides were still in physical form and the information was oral; the slides were in the process of being transferred to digital format and the information transcribed at the last Landdyke Gathering I visited. For more information, see chapter 8.

3. To a certain extent, this is somewhat opposed to the matrix cultures in the United States, where advanced education tends to raise class. Ownership of land and income raises class in all cultures that I am aware of.

5. The Mountain Is She

1. See, for example, the famous print of America as a nearly-naked virgin welcoming the advent of Columbus, called "The Discovery of America," by Dutch artist Jan van der Straet, 1575.

2. It is important to note that Mohanty was criticizing not ecofeminism but feminism as a whole in her important 1984 paper.

3. This makes me think of Meg's case, where she was deliberately excluded from a land community for being "too fat" (i.e. for not being aesthetically pleasing) under the rubric of health/environmental awareness. (See chapter 6 for a more complete discussion of this incident.)

6. Primally Female

1. For example, see Calefato 2004; Cordwell and Schwartz 1979; Hansen 2004; Kroeber 1919; and Mascia-Lees and Sharpe 1992.

2. Long hair can be masculine for some Native American cultures; cutting hair is a sign of mourning in some cultures; and the appearance of natural, dread-

locked, and braided African hair all intersect with these "short/long" meanings in very different ways. One excellent example of this comes from a story told to me by a friend, about some white lesbians who decided that a black stud (masculine-leaning lesbian) was "fem" because she wore dreadlocks, which read to them as "long hair," despite the fact that dreads can be masculine. This incident illustrates the power dynamics of these racialized assumptions.

3. QUILTBAG stands for "Queer/Questioning, Undecided, Intersex, Lesbian, Trans, Bisexual, Asexual, Gay/Genderqueer," and was coined by Sadie Lee (2006, 144).

4. Marideth Sisco states that the incidents were prompted by one of the camp's newsletters falling into the hands of the pastor of a nearby Baptist Church, which then resulted in: "Gunshots in the night. Dead pets. Nails in the driveway, and Brenda's car run off the rural road" (2015, 143). Camp Sister Spirit was founded by Brenda and Wanda Henson, and served as "a feminist adult education center" (Sisco 2015, 143). Despite these rocky and violent beginnings, as local people got to know the women of the camp, they got on well, to the point where the camp was a major point of recovery and help during Hurricane Katrina, and reportedly, "Folks at the general store now refer to that original outraged Baptist as 'That little Hitler'" (Sisco 2015, 145). Camp Sister Spirit is now closed.

5. See also Millar, "Towards a Performance Model of Sex" (2008).

6. As opposed to, for example, walking down a public street fully clothed in any city in the United States.

7. "Kyriarchy" was created by Elisabeth Schüssler Fiorenza as an alternative term to patriarchy, in order to illustrate the ways in which domination operates in multiple ways simultaneously, not simply on the axis of gender, but also along race, class, dis/ability, access to wealth, sexuality, and via other means. For further information, see her book, *But She Said: Feminist Practices of Biblical Interpretation* (1992).

8. I especially recommend Campo's chapter "Fear and Loathing in Los Angeles," which does an excellent job of connecting the media fear of the fat body with the fear of the racially other body.

9. Note that the body ingests substances not only through eating, but also through breathing, through the skin, even through proximity. The body is seen as permeable and thus imperiled.

10. Food substances commonly classified as "addictive" are usually appetizing and pleasant, which might lead one to speculate about the Puritan background of the alternative health movement. The matrix culture, as well, seems to have a persistent belief that things that are pleasant must be either sinful or bad for one—and the fat body represents both.

11. Similar to how obesity is called a "disease" in U.S. matrix culture, full stop (Campos 2004, Farrell 2011).

12. Data suggest that the relationship between food intake and development of diabetes is not so simple. In the Whitehall II study, 7,321 white London civil

service workers, average age of 50, were recruited and their glycemic indexes and glycemic loads were calculated from detailed dietary information over 13 years. The study found that neither GI nor GL had any correlation on the development of diabetes; indeed, there was a slight negative correlation between high GL and development of diabetes (Mosdøl et al. 2007).

7. We Have Met the Enemy and She Is Us

This chapter is dedicated to the woman who told me, before our interview, that she had feared I was an FBI agent "because I was always writing in that notebook." Now you know I am something much worse than an FBI agent. With apologies to Walt Kelly for the title.

1. BDSM: Bondage, domination, sadism, and masochism. See note in chapter 1.

2. "Cis woman" or "cis women" refer to a woman or women whose gender presentation matches the genital diagnosis given at birth, while "cissexual" refers to the category of cis men and cis women both. Enke (2012) credits Dana Leland Defosse with the first widely public use of the term in a web document in 1994 (60). "Cis" is a deliberately neutral and non-loaded term, and comes either from a clever use of chemistry terms for molecular chirality, or possibly from the German; in either case, "cis" is simply the opposite of "trans." Some anti-trans advocates object to using the term "cis women"; objections to using the term seem to stem primarily from the fact that the term is used by the trans community (there is some debate over whether the term *originates* from the trans community) or possibly from the loss of being an unmarked and therefore privileged category (Enke 2012). Cf "straight."

3. Bourdieu suggests that "the habitus, the product of history, produces individual and collective practices" (1995, 54).

4. Since anti-trans arguments automatically discount a feminine spiritual essence existing in a body they do not define as biologically female. Note also that who gets to define what is female is *an operation of power.*

5. As anthropologists have pointed out, menstruation varies widely across cultures and is interpreted in very different ways, thus it is difficult to say what is "standard" or "non-standard." Menstruation that occurs once a month (as menstruation is largely constructed in North American matrix cultures) is very different from menstruation that may occur no more than 12–20 times over a woman's entire lifetime. For an overview see Buckley and Gottlieb 1988; for a more specific exploration of understandings of time and menstruation (as well as contraception) see Bledsoe 2005.

6. Important feminist theorist and lesbian Monique Wittig asserts that lesbians are not, in fact, women. See Les Guérillères (1969) and Le corps lesbien (1973).

7. The judge for McDonald's trial allowed evidence that McDonald had

written one bad check, but disallowed expert testimony about how transgender women are disproportionately victims of hate crimes, the dead man's history of violence towards women, and the dead man's toxicology report (Signorile 2014).

8. These women are Venice Brown (19), Terrain Dandridge (20), Patreese Johnson (20) and Renata Hill (24), who were sentenced in 2007 for defending themselves, nonlethally, from a man who held them down, choked them, ripped out their hair, spat on them, and threatened to rape them because they were lesbians (Henry 2007). Henry goes on to note, "All of the seven women [present at the incident] knew and went to school with Sakia Gunn, a 19-year-old butch lesbian who was stabbed to death in Newark, N.J., in May 2003. Paralleling the present case, Gunn was out with three of her friends when a man made sexual advances to one of the women. When she replied that she was a lesbian and not interested, he attacked them. Gunn fought back and was stabbed to death" (2007).

9. In these cases, it is relevant that the victims were black women, who have historically been regarded as more sexual, more violent, and more "masculine"/less "feminine" than white women (see Roberts 1997; Ritchie 2006).

10. Trans Exclusionary Radical Feminists (TERFs) are a group of women who actively seek to restrict the rights of trans people because they believe that trans people harm the gay community simply by existing. They run sites such as Gender Identity Watch and Pretendbians, and verbally attack and out trans people (particularly trans women), seek to get them fired from their jobs, evicted, denied medical treatment, or attacked by local bigots. Cathy Brennan is the most notorious/active of the TERFs, although there are several other prominent women in the movement such as Victoria Brownworth; Janice Raymond and her work are often cited. Although some TERFs attend the Michigan Womyn's Music Festival, none of my interviewees or other land-women have identified as a TERF, nor have any TERFs, to my knowledge, ever lived on women's land. However, their extreme stances, coupled with their activity online, means they are very visible. The way they commit violence, through "outing" and depending on the homophobia-transphobia of others who then evict, fire, etc., depends on a thorough knowledge of how transphobia works and on the violence of others who would likely also be violent to TERFs (who often identify as lesbian). This reveals a profound understanding of the violence trans people are subject to, yet does not prevent TERFs from asserting that trans individuals somehow have access to large amounts of privilege or somehow deserve that violence. This "alliance of hatred" has often been commented on by the trans community (Clark 2014). I add that most TERFs identify as "radical feminists" (which identity does not have a complete overlap with TERF identity) or "gender-critical feminists" (which does tend to overlap) and violently reject the TERF label (I am indebted to Katherine Cross, private communication, for reminding me of this).

11. That lifetime of experience, upon discussion, often hinges upon experiences of oppression, which circles around to bell hooks's pointed statement that women *cannot* unite around experiences of oppression.

12. Keep in mind that "complete femininity" is an unattainable standard for *anyone* in the United States, no matter how wealthy, heterosexual, thin, white, and compliant to beauty standards she is.

13. While it is *possible* that a trans woman *could be* a sexual predator, it is also possible for *any* woman to be a sexual predator, and cis women are not automatically assumed to be such by a categorical assumption of their genitalia with the ability to rape. I am sure I do not need to remind my readers that it is possible to rape someone without the use of masculinized genitalia. Such assumptions also make those who are victims of female abusers invisible. Lastly, accusations of rape against trans women are vanishingly rare (Serano 2007, 242).

14. I am not sure there are enough separatists left to count as scapegoats; surely the vitriol aimed at trans folk indicate that they are farther "down the ladder."

15. There has long been an academic focus on trans women rather than trans men, often explained as being because a voluntary transition from masculine to feminine must be *explained* (as loss of status and privilege) while a transition from feminine to masculine seems desirable and natural. Judith Butler points out that these analyses are "crude," and "don't ask whether it is easier to be *trans* than to be in a perceived bio-gender, that is, a gender that seems to 'follow' from natal sex" (2004, 94). Both Serano (2007) and Califia (2003, 178) point out that there is a considerable *media* focus on MTF and no corresponding focus on FTM, precisely because "striving for masculinity seems like a perfectly reasonable goal" (Serano 2007, 46). Weston notes that in anthropology, the very notion of "crossing" from one gender to another replicates a notion of binary gender that is not culturally universal (1993, 346). She also, tellingly, asks, "what is at stake when so much attention accrues to social science as a source of 'facts,' and so little to data's uses, derivation, and production?" (1998, 12). Katherine Cross points out that there are also greater numbers of trans men within academia, and that the greater visibility of trans women both within and outside academic study puts them "at the forefront of cis consciousness" (personal communication, 8/14/17). I would like to thank Marta S. Rivera Monclova for locating the Butler quotation for me, as well as the rest of Bear Bergman's "gendernauts" for searching their minds and shelves attempting to find a source quotation for the perversely enduring notion in academic circles that it makes sense for women to want to become more masculine, but not the other way around.

16. Current partners of lesbian-identified female-to-male trans men are isolated by rejection by people like Yawning Lion, as Califia notes: "The lesbian community has historically served as a haven for genetic females with gender conflicts, who have until recently labeled themselves as extreme butches rather than FTMs. As transsexual men became more visible, a growing number of 'butches' are rejecting a lesbian and female identity in favor of sex change. This creates a virtually undocumented state of crisis for their partners, who are usually lesbian-identified. The ideology of romance encourages the female partner to remain with the former butch, now FTM, but often this leaves the couple in isolation, rejected

by their lesbian extended family and unable to replace them with a heterosexual network" (2003, 216).

17. Although a full overview of this subject is not possible here, the volume *The Persistent Desire: A Femme-Butch Reader*, edited by Joan Nestle, contains excellent material on this history.

18. It could also be argued that disconnecting the doxa of the sexed body "naturally" producing gender *does* challenge and change the system.

19. Camp Trans was organized in response to the 1991 ejection of Nancy Jean Burkholder from Michigan, after she responded truthfully to another festival-goer's question about her transgender status (Califia 197, 227; Serano 2007, 234).

20. This is the only women-only space or event that Serano mentions by name in her chapter on exclusion from lesbian and women-only spaces, for example (2007, 232–45).

21. In one case, the challenger was another member of the list, who spoke against the "hateful" language. I do not have permission to quote the debate here, however.

22. Michigan Womyn's Music Festival is similar to Ankh-Morpork of the fictional Discworld, which "had dallied with many forms of government and had ended up with that form of democracy known as One Man, One Vote. The Patrician was the Man; he had the Vote" (Pratchett 2013, 167, footnote).

23. Although I use the phrase here in its shortened form as my informants use it, it is important to note that this is a way of not using the term cisgender. It is also a deeply problematic construction: "it does similar work to a phrase like 'normal born normal' in lieu of saying heterosexual, and this of course reveals how equally nonsensical the phrase is" (Cross, personal communication, 8/14/2017).

24. As one reader has pointed out, Michigan has often been described as a cultural necessity for *all* lesbians. (I do not agree.)

25. While ignoring the fact that trans women may be women of color, as well.

26. While this was the most prominent example of biphobia in my field notebook, the linking of biphobia to transphobia here is probably not incidental as both depend on highly fixed and essentialist understandings of sexuality and the body.

27. Although Russ is right, hating men is still seen by the matrix culture of the United States as The. Worst. Possible! Thing! Hating women of any kind is par for the course and can be forgiven if the hater is well-educated, a good writer, makes high-grossing films, is a scientist, etc.

8. The Hermit and the Family

1. Several readers have taken issue with my use of the term "older," which follows how my informants use it. However, like Sarah Lamb, I did "not decide in advance whom I would consider 'old'" (2000, 43) and like Lamb, I discovered that other scholars dislike not having a "bright line" of age defined (Lamb's advisor

seemed distressed over her not defining an age cutoff). Most lay readers grasp the "older" category without trouble, as this is a concept common in United States matrix cultures. However, the academic insistence on specific ages is troubling, as anthropology has shown that who is considered "old" varies considerably according to culture, specific context, and who is doing the judging. For more on this, please see Cohen 1994; Copper 2015; and Lamb 2000.

2. One of my informants had an income from a 401(k) retirement fund, but most of the "retired" women I interviewed or spoke to got their income from Social Security and from wage labor.

3. This group eventually created a life commitment together although, unlike my informants, they do not reside together (Ariel 2008).

4. For example, needing to move into a house in the suburbs would not be considered "aging in place" among my informants, while it might be considered a viable type of "aging in place" by the matrix culture.

5. One woman I know of has brought her aging mother to live with her on women's land.

6. For which name I am indebted to Hanne Blank. This name attempts to capture the playfulness of naming conventions among land-women.

7. This was a distinction they universally declined to give in actual years; "old enough" seems to be delineated by a certain need for help or care rather than a strict chronological measure.

8. In this case the care becomes part of the younger woman's "community donation" which she can expect to have repaid later.

9. Sandra Butler notes that there have been (and still are) institutionalized disadvantages to being LGBT while aging in the United States, particularly in regard to Social Security and Medicaid practices that do not recognize same-sex spouses (2004, 36–37). While government and law have shifted since 2004, there are still institutionalized disadvantages.

10. My interpretation here of the commentary is influenced by other interview data that included Bluebird's story of how a similar group had bonded together to deal communally and compassionately with an experience of mental illness.

11. https://oloc.org/.

12. There are a large number of different feminist religious approaches; I am referring here specifically to neo-pagan, Witch/Wicca, and Goddess-oriented versions of feminist spirituality and religion, although this is not the only form of feminist religion that can be found on women's land.

13. See, for example, Starhawk's *The Spiral Dance* (1989).

14. A full discussion of this is beyond the scope of this book, but the figures of the "wicked witch" and the "silly old bat" will be familiar to my readers. Cynthia Rich, in reviewing Sarah Matthews's *The Social World of Old Women* (Sage Publications 1979), reports also on ageism, the invisibility and poverty of old women, and on social incidents such as old women being asked why they aren't dead and being called "ugly, ugly, ugly" in public (Rich 1983a).

15. Solitude is also seen as emotionally and mentally healing by many of my informants, thus the paradox that situations that are physically demanding (alone in a cabin in the wilderness) are seen as emotionally or mentally healing or beneficial; living alone can also be dangerous or demanding emotionally.

16. Carrie Sandahl notes parallels between the term *queer* and the similarly reclaimed term *crip* (2003, 27).

17. It is important also to note that trans individuals who are disabled also experience similar prejudice and denial of care, with respect to blocking access to their chosen partners, denying them access to gender-affirming health care, and general mistreatment by health, clinic, and institutional staff (Gavriel Ansara 2010).

18. At Michigan Womyn's Music Festival, for example, there was a disability resource area known as DART, and there were organized efforts to include performers who identified as disabled.

19. Similarly, all the homes I saw at Turtle Mesa were wood-heated, and some of the homes at Mountainview were as well.

20. I am using the past tense here because Oaktrust has been dissolved and the property has been sold.

21. For those familiar with tarot, this is equivalent to the High Priestess, an important card of the major arcana.

22. Replacing the Hermit of the major arcana.

23. Replacing the Hierophant or Pope of the major arcana.

Afterword

1. Not all land-women subscribe to the ethos of difference—think of Tamara's quote that opens this chapter. It's not gender that makes difference, it is *intent*.

2. While religious communities such as nunneries are truly fascinating, due to their oversight by a larger authority and their very long and involved history, I have chosen to omit them from this brief overview.

3. It is not, and I recommend Dave's article for a fuller historical and cultural overview of the politics and cultural specificities of things like the use of the term "lesbian."

Bibliography

Abbot, David, and Joyce Howarth. 2007. "Still Off-Limits? Staff Views on Supporting Gay, Lesbian, and Bisexual People with Intellectual Disabilities to Develop Sexual and Intimate Relationships." *Journal of Applied Research in Intellectual Disabilities* 20: 116–26.

Abu-Lughod, Lila. 1993. *Writing Women's Worlds: Bedouin Stories*. Berkeley: University of California Press.

Adams, Carol. 2010 (1990). *The Sexual Politics of Meat: A Feminist-Vegetarian Critical Theory*. New York: Continuum.

Águila. 2015. "Arco Iris, Rainbow Land: The Vision of Maria Christina Morales." *Sinister Wisdom* 98: 43–52.

Alaimo, Stacy. 2000. *Undomesticated Ground: Recasting Nature as Feminist Space*. Ithaca, N.Y.: Cornell University Press.

American Anthropological Association. 2003 (1997). "Statement on 'Race.'" In *Applying Cultural Anthropology: An Introductory Reader*, edited by Aaron Podolefsky and Peter J. Brown. Boston: McGraw-Hill.

Andreyeva, Tatiana, Rebecca M. Puhl, and Kelly D. Brownell. 2008. "Changes in Perceived Weight Discrimination Among Americans, 1995–1996 through 2004–2006." *Obesity* 16: 1129–34. https://doi.org/10.1038/oby.2008.35.

Anonymous/Community. n.d. "Breendoggle Wiki." http://breendoggle.wikia.com/wiki/Breendoggle_Wiki.

Ansara, Gavriel. 2010. "Beyond Cisgenderism: Counselling People with Non-Assigned Gender Identities." In *Counselling Ideologies: Queer Challenges to Heteronormativity*, edited by L. Moon. Surrey, U.K.: Ashgate.

Antoniou, Laura. 2013. *The Killer Wore Leather*. Berkeley, Calif.: Cleis Press.

Anzaldúa, Gloria. 2007. *Borderlands/La Frontera: The New Mestiza*. 3rd ed. San Francisco: Aunt Lute Books.

Ariel, Jane. 2008. "Women Living Together in Community." *Journal of Lesbian Studies* 12 (2–3): 283–92.

Ashley, Bob, Joanne Hollows, Steve Jones, and Ben Taylor. 2004. *Food and Cultural Studies*. New York: Routledge.

Atkinson, Paul. 1983. "Eating Virtue." In *The Sociology of Food and Eating*, edited by Anne Murcott. Aldershot, U.K.: Gower.

Barcan, Ruth. 2004. *Nudity: A Cultural Anatomy*. New York: Berg.

Barnes, Shaba. 2005. "My Life in a Lesbian Community: The Joys and the Pain." *Journal of Lesbian Studies* 9 (1–2): 45–54.

Bart, Pauline, and Patricia O'Brien. 1985. *Stopping Rape: Successful Survival Strategies*. New York: Pergamon.

Bartky, Sandra Lee. 1997. "Foucault, Femininity, and the Modernization of Patriarchal Power." In *Feminist Social Thought: A Reader*, edited by Diana Tietjens Meyers. New York: Routledge Press.

Bass, Margaret K. 2000. "On Being a Fat Black Girl in a Fat-Hating Culture." In *Recovering the Black Female Body: Self-Representations by African-American Women*, edited by Michael Bennett and Vanessa D. Dickerson. New Brunswick, N.J.: Rutgers University Press.

Bauhardt, Christine. 2013. "Rethinking Gender and Nature from a Material(ist) Perspective: Feminist Economics, Queer Ecologies and Resource Politics." *European Journal of Women's Studies* 20 (4): 361–75.

Beaulieu, Marianne, Alix Adrien, Louise Potvin, and Clément Dassa. 2014. "Stigmatizing Attitudes Towards People Living with HIV/AIDS: Validation of a Measurement Scale." *BMC Public Health* 14: 1246.

Bechdel, Alison. 1986. *Dykes to Watch Out For*. New York: Firebrand Books.

Bechdel, Alison. 1990. *New, Improved! Dykes to Watch Out For*. New York: Firebrand Books.

Bechdel, Alison. 1993. *Spawn of Dykes to Watch Out For*. New York: Firebrand Books.

Bechdel, Alison. 2008. *The Essential Dykes to Watch Out For*. New York: Houghton Mifflin Harcourt.

Bell, Colin, and Howard Newby. 1972. "Theories of Community." In *Community Studies: An Introduction to the Sociology of the Local Community*, edited by Colin Bell and Howard Newby. New York: Praeger Publishers.

Benería, Lourdes. 1999. "Globalization, Gender, and the Davos Man." *Feminist Economics* 5 (3): 61–83. https://doi.org/10.1080/135457099337815.

Bengal, Rebecca. 6/25/2017. "Country Women." *Vogue* (online). http://www.vogue.com/projects/13532936/pride-2017-lesbians-on-the-land-essay/.

Bennett, Sara, and Joan Gibbs. "Racism and Classism in the Lesbian Community: Towards the Building of a Radical, Autonomous Lesbian Movement." In *Top Ranking: A Collection of Articles on Racism and Classism in the Lesbian Community*, edited by Joan Gibbs and Sara Bennett. New York: Come!Unity Press.

Bergland, Renée L. 2000. *The National Uncanny: Indian Ghosts and American Subjects*. Hanover, N.H.: University Press of New England.

Bernstein, Robin. 2011. *Racial Innocence: Performing American Childhood from Slavery to Civil Rights*. New York: New York University Press.

Bindel, Julie. 8/16/2015. "The Village Where Men Are Banned." *The Guardian* (online). http://www.theguardian.com/global-development/2015/aug/16/village-where-men-are-banned-womens-rights-kenya.

Blank, Hanne. 2007. *Virgin: The Untouched History.* New York: Bloomsbury.

Blank, Hanne. 2012. *Straight: The Surprisingly Short History of Heterosexuality.* Boston: Beacon Press.

Bledsoe, Caroline. 2005. "Reproductive Relativity: Time, Space and Western Contraception in Rural Gambia." *Ahfad Journal* 22 (1): 3–20.

Bordo, Susan. 1993. *Unbearable Weight: Feminism, Western Culture, and the Body.* Berkeley: University of California Press.

Bornstein, Kate. 1994. *Gender Outlaw: On Men, Women, and the Rest of Us.* New York: Routledge.

Bourdieu, Pierre. 1979. *Algeria 1960: The Disenchantment of the World; The Sense of Honour; The Kabyle House or the World Reversed: Essays.* New York: Cambridge University Press.

Bourdieu, Pierre. 1984. *Distinction: A Social Critique of the Judgment of Taste.* Translated by Richard Nice. Cambridge: Cambridge University Press.

Bourdieu, Pierre. 1991. *Language and Symbolic Power.* Translated by G. Raymond and M. Adamson. Cambridge, Mass.: Harvard University Press.

Bourdieu, Pierre. 1995 (1972). *Outline of a Theory of Practice.* Translated by Richard Nice. Cambridge: Cambridge University Press.

Bradley, Marion Zimmer (ed.) and the Friends of Darkover. 1985. *Free Amazons of Darkover: An Anthology.* New York: DAW Books.

Brooks, Cheri. 2004. "Race, Politics, and Denial: Why Oregon Forgot to Ratify the Fourteenth Amendment." *Oregon Law Review* 83 (2): 731–62.

Brotman, Shari, Bill Ryan, and Robert Cormier. 2003. "The Health and Social Service Needs of Gay and Lesbian Elders and Their Families in Canada." *Gerontologist* 43 (2): 192–202.

Brown, Teena Delfina (Dolphin). 1985. "D.W. Outpost." In *Lesbian Land,* edited by Joyce Cheney. Minneapolis, Minn.: Word Weavers Press.

Brownsworth, Victoria A. 4/23/2015. "Michigan Womyn's Music Festival to End After 40 Years." *Curve* (online). http://www.curvemag.com/News/Michigan-Womyns-Music-Festival-to-End-after-40-Years-447/.

Buckley, Thomas, and Alma Gottlieb, eds. 1988. *Blood Magic: The Anthropology of Menstruation.* Berkeley: University of California Press.

Bunch, Charlotte, for the Furies Collective. 1972. "Lesbians in Revolt." *The Furies* 1 (January): 8–9.

Bunch, Charlotte. 1994 (1979). "Learning from Lesbian Separatism." In *Lavender Culture,* edited by Karla Jay and Allen Young. New York: New York University Press.

Butler, Judith. 1993a. *Bodies That Matter: On the Discursive Limits of Sex.* New York: Routledge.

Butler, Judith. 1993b. "Critically Queer." *GLQ: A Journal of Lesbian and Gay Studies* 1: 17–32.

Butler, Judith. 1997. "Against Proper Objects." In *Feminism Meets Queer Theory*, edited by Elizabeth Weed and Naomi Schor. Indianapolis: Indiana University Press.

Butler, Judith. 1999 (1990). *Gender Trouble: Feminism and the Subversion of Identity*. New York: Routledge.

Butler, Judith. 2004. *Undoing Gender*. New York: Routledge.

Butler, Sandra S. 2004. "Gay, Lesbian, Bisexual, and Transgender (GLBT) Elders." *Journal of Human Behavior in the Social Environment* 9 (4): 25–44.

Cahill, Sean, and Ken South. 2002. "Policy Issues Affecting Lesbian, Gay, Bisexual, and Transgender People in Retirement." *Generations* 26 (2): 49–54.

Calefato, Patrizia. 2004. *The Clothed Body*. New York: Berg.

Califia, Patrick. 2003 (1997). *Sex Changes: The Politics of Transgenderism*. San Francisco: Cleis Press.

Cameron, Deborah. 2005. "Language, Gender, and Sexuality: Current Issues and New Directions." *Applied Linguistics* 26 (4): 482–502.

Campbell, Anne. 1993. *Men, Women, and Aggression*. New York: Basic Books.

Campbell, Fiona Kumari. 2009. *Contours of Ableism: The Production of Disability and Ableness*. Houndmills, U.K.: Palgrave-MacMillan.

Campos, Paul. 2004. *The Obesity Myth: Why America's Obsession with Weight Is Hazardous to Your Health*. New York: Gotham Books.

Carr-Gomm, Philip. 2010. *A Brief History of Nakedness*. London: Reaktion Books.

Chang, Grace. 2000. *Disposable Domestics: Immigrant Women Workers in the Global Economy*. Cambridge, Mass.: South End Press.

Cheney, Joyce, ed. 1985. *Lesbian Land*. Minneapolis, Minn.: Word Weavers Press.

Chmielewski, Wendy E. 1993. "Heaven on Earth: The Women's Commonwealth, 1867–1983." In *Women in Spiritual and Communitarian Societies in the United States*, edited by Wendy E. Chmielewski, Louis J. Kern, and Marlyn Klee-Hartzell. Syracuse N.Y.: Syracuse University Press.

Chrystos. 1991. *Dream On*. Vancouver: Press Gang Publishers.

Chun, Allen. 2002. "Flushing in the Future: The Supermodern Japanese Toilet in a Changing Domestic Culture." *Postcolonial Studies* 5 (2): 153–70.

Clark, Lucian. 2014. "Southern Poverty Law Center: TERFs Are a Hate Group." *Genderterror* (blog). 2/12/2014. http://genderterror.com/2014/02/12/splc-terfs/.

Clarke, Victoria, and Katherine Spence. 2013. "'I Am Who I Am?' Navigating Norms and the Importance of Authenticity in Lesbian and Bisexual Women's Accounts of Their Appearance Practices." *Psychology & Sexuality* 4 (1): 25–33.

Clarke, Victoria, and Kevin Turner. 2007. "Clothes Maketh the Queer? Dress, Appearance and the Construction of Lesbian, Gay and Bisexual Identities." *Feminism & Psychology* 17 (2): 267–76.

Cliffe, Nicole. 2013. "The Comment Section for Every Article Ever Written about Intimate Grooming." *The Toast* (blog). 7/2/2013. http://the-toast.net/2013/07/02/all-you-can-say-about-pubes-online/.

Cohen, Lawrence. 1994. "Old Age: Cultural and Critical Perspectives." *Annual Review of Anthropology* 23: 137–58.
Cohen, Lawrence. 1998. *No Aging in India: Alzheimer's, the Bad Family, and Other Modern Things*. Berkeley: University of California Press.
Combahee River Collective. 1986 (1977). "A Black Feminist Statement." *The Combahee River Collective Statement: Black Feminist Organizing in the Seventies and Eighties*. Freedom Organizing Series #1. New York: Kitchen Table: Women of Color Press.
Conley, Terri D., and Laura R. Ramsey. 2011. "Killing Us Softly? Investigating Portrayals of Women and Men in Contemporary Magazine Advertisements." *Psychology of Women Quarterly* 35 (3): 469–78.
Cook, Judith A. 2000. "Sexuality and People with Psychiatric Disabilities." *Sexuality and Disability* 18 (3): 195–206.
Copper, Baba. 2015. "Ageism in the Lesbian Community." *Journal of Lesbian Studies* 19 (1): 7–12.
Cordwell, Justine, and Ronald Schwartz. 1979. *The Fabrics of Culture: The Anthropology of Clothing and Adornment*. New York: Mouton.
Cougar, Jesse. 1986. *The Poet's Tarot*. Little River, Calif.: Tough Dove Books.
Counihan, Carole. 1999. *The Anthropology of Food and the Body: Gender, Meaning, and Power*. New York: Routledge.
Crenshaw, Kimberlé. 1991. "Mapping the Margins: Intersectionality, Identity Politics, and Violence against Women of Color." *Stanford Law Review* 43 (6): 1241–99.
Critical Resistance and INCITE! Women of Color Against Violence. 2006. "Gender Violence and the Prison Industrial Complex." In *Color of Violence: The INCITE! Anthology*, edited by INCITE! Women of Color Against Violence. Cambridge, Mass.: South End Press.
Cross, Amanda. 1981. *Death in a Tenured Position*. Ballantine Books: New York.
Csordas, Thomas J. 1994. "Introduction: The Body as Representation and as Being-in-the-World." In *Embodiment and Experience: The Existential Ground of Culture and Self*, edited by Thomas J. Csordas. Cambridge: Cambridge University Press.
Daly, Mary. 1990. *Gyn/Ecology: The Metaethics of Radical Feminism*. Boston: Beacon Press.
D'Aoust, Vicky. 1994. "Competency, Autonomy, and Choice: On Being a Lesbian and Having Disabilities." *Canadian Journal of Women and the Law* 7 (2): 564–78.
Dave, Naisargi N. 2010. "To Render Real the Imagined: An Ethnographic History of Lesbian Community in India." *Signs: Journal of Women in Culture and Society* 35 (3): 595–619.
davenport, doris. 1983. "The Pathology of Racism: A Conversation with Third World Wimmin." In *This Bridge Called My Back: Writings by Radical Women*

of Color, edited by Cherríe Moraga and Gloria Anzaldúa. New York: Kitchen Table Press.

Daynes, Sarah, and Orville Lee. 2008. *Desire for Race.* Cambridge: Cambridge University Press.

Desjarlais, Robert R. 1992. *Body and Emotion: The Aesthetics of Illness and Healing in the Nepal Himalayas.* Philadelphia: University of Pennsylvania Press.

Dimpfl, Mike, and Sharon Moran. 2014. "Waste Matters: Compost, Domestic Practice, and the Transformation of Alternative Toilet Cultures around Skaneateles Lake, New York." *Environment and Planning D: Society and Space* 32: 721–38.

Dominy, Helene. 1986. "Lesbian-Feminist Gender Conceptions: Separatism in Christchurch, New Zealand." *Signs* 11 (2): 274–89.

Doris, Margaret. 1983. "The Summer of Peace? With the Women of the Romulus Encampment." *Boston Phoenix,* July 19, 1983.

Douglas, Mary. 1984 (1966). *Purity and Danger: An Analysis of Concepts of Pollution and Taboo.* Boston: Ark Paperbacks.

Drummond, J. D., and Shari Brotman. 2014. "Intersecting and Embodied Identities: A Queer Woman's Experience of Disability and Sexuality." *Sex & Disability* 32: 533–49.

Duncan, Nancy. 1996. "Renegotiating Gender and Sexuality in Public and Private Spaces." In *BodySpace: Destabilizing Geographies of Gender and Sexuality,* edited by Nancy Duncan. New York: Routledge.

Dutton, Michael, Sanjay Seth, and Leela Gandhi. 2002. "Plumbing the Depths: Toilets, Transparency and Modernity." *Postcolonial Studies* 5 (2): 137–42.

Dykewomon, Elana. 2014. "Living 'Anyway': Stories of Access." *Journal of Lesbian Studies* 18: 21–30.

Edwalds, Loraine. 1995. Introduction to *The Woman-Centered Economy: Ideals, Reality, and the Space In Between,* edited by Loraine Edwalds and Midge Stocker. Chicago: Third Side Press.

Elgeziri, Moushira. 2010. "Wading through Treacle: Female Commercial School Graduates (CSGs) in Egypt's Informal Economy." *Feminist Formations* 22 (3): 10–50.

Enke, Anne. 2012. "The Education of Little Cis: Cisgender and the Discipline of Opposing Bodies." In *Transfeminist Perspectives in and Beyond Transgender Studies,* edited by Anne Enke. Philadelphia: Temple University Press.

Fairchild, Susan K., Gerard E. Carrino, and Mildred Ramirez. 1996. "Social Workers' Perceptions of Staff Attitudes Toward Resident Sexuality in a Random Sample of New York State Nursing Homes: A Pilot Study." *Journal of Gerontological Social Work* 26 (1/2), 153–69.

Falcon, Sylvanna. 2006. "'National Security' and the Violation of Women: Militarized Border Rape at the US–Mexico Border." In *Color of Violence: The INCITE! Anthology,* edited by Incite! Women of Color Against Violence. Cambridge, Mass.: South End Press.

Farrell, Amy. 2011. *Fat Shame: Stigma and the Fat Body in American Culture.* New York: New York University Press.

Fausto-Sterling, Anne. 1997. "How to Build A Man." In *The Gender/Sexuality Reader: Culture, History, Political Economy*, edited by Roger D. Lancaster and Micaela di Leonardo. New York, Routledge.

Felski, Rita. 1989. *Beyond Feminist Aesthetics: Feminist Literature and Social Change.* Cambridge, Mass.: Harvard University Press.

Feminist Reprise Forum. 2006. "The Trouble with Food Addiction." *Feminist Reprise.* http://www.dimensionsmagazine.com/forums/showthread.php?t=17117.

Filipovic, Jill. 2008. "Offensive Feminism: The Conservative Gender Norms That Perpetuate Rape Culture, and How Feminists Can Fight Back." In *Yes Means Yes! Visions of Female Sexual Power and a World Without Rape*, edited by Jaclyn Friedman and Jessica Valenti. Berkeley, Calif.: Seal Press.

Finney, Carolyn. 2014. *Black Faces, White Spaces: Reimagining the Relationship of African Americans to the Great Outdoors.* Chapel Hill: University of North Carolina Press.

Fischler, Claude. 1987. "Attitudes Towards Sugar and Sweetness in Historical and Social Perspective." In *Sweetness*, edited by John Dobbing. Berlin: Springer-Verlag.

Fischler, Claude. 1988. "Food, Self, and Identity." *Social Science Information* 27 (2): 279–82.

Fishman, P. M. 1978. "Interaction: The Work Women Do." *Social Problems* 25 (4): 397–406.

Fonesca, Isabel. 1995. *Bury Me Standing: The Gypsies and Their Journey.* New York: Vintage.

Foucault, Michel. 1990 (1976). *The History of Sexuality.* Volume I, *An Introduction.* Translated by Robert Hurley. New York: Vintage Books.

Foucault, Michel. 1995. *Discipline and Punish: The Birth of the Prison.* Translated by Alan Sheridan. New York: Vintage Books.

Frank, Gelya. 2000. *Venus on Wheels: Two Decades of Dialogue on Disability, Biography, and Being Female.* Berkeley: University of California Press.

Freeman, Jo. 1970. "The Tyranny of Structurelessness." *Women's Studies Quarterly* 41 (3 and 4): n.p. (online version) http://www.jofreeman.com/joreen/tyranny.htm.

Gaard, Greta. 2011. "Ecofeminism Revisited: Rejecting Essentialism and Re-Placing Species in a Material Feminist Environmentalism." *Feminist Formations* 23 (2): 26–53.

Gabrielson, Marcena L. 2013. "'We Have to Create Family:' Aging Support Issues and Needs Among Older Lesbians." *Journal of Gay and Lesbian Social Services* 23 (3): 327–28.

Gagehabib, La Verne, and Barbara Summerhawk. 2000. *Circles of Power: Shifting Dynamics in a Lesbian-Centered Community.* Norwich, Vt.: New Victoria Publishers.

Gal, Susan. 2002. "A Semiotics of the Public/Private Distinction." *Differences: A Journal of Feminist Cultural Studies* 13 (1): 77–95.
Garber, Marjorie. 1992. *Vested Interests: Cross-Dressing and Cultural Anxiety.* New York: Routledge.
Geertz, Clifford. 1973 (1966). "The Impact of the Concept of Culture on the Concept of Man." In *The Interpretation of Cultures,* edited by Clifford Geertz. New York: Basic Books.
Geertz, Clifford. 1973 (1966). "Thick Description: Towards an Interpretive Theory of Culture." In *The Interpretation of Cultures,* edited by Clifford Geertz. New York: Basic Books.
Gibbs, Joan, and Sara Bennett, eds. 1980. *Top Ranking: A Collection of Articles on Racism and Classism in the Lesbian Community.* New York: Come!Unity Press.
Gibson-Graham, J. K. 2006. *The End of Capitalism (As We Knew It).* Minneapolis: University of Minnesota Press.
Gilley, Brian Joseph. 2006. *Becoming Two-Spirit: Gay Identity and Social Acceptance in Indian Country.* Lincoln: University of Nebraska Press.
Goldberg, Sheryl, Joanna Sickler, and Suzanne L. Dibble. 2005. "Lesbians Over Sixty: The Consistency of Findings from Twenty Years of Survey Data." *Journal of Lesbian Studies* 9 (1–2): 195–213.
Gorgons, The. 1991 (1978). "Response by the Gorgons." In *For Lesbians Only: A Separatist Anthology,* edited by Sarah Lucia-Hoagland and Julia Penelope. London: Onlywomen Press.
Gray, John. 2003 (1999). "Open Spaces and Dwelling Places: Being at Home on Hill Farms in the Scottish Borders." In *The Anthropology of Space and Place: Locating Culture,* edited by Setha M. Low and Denise Lawrence-Zúñiga. Oxford: Blackwell Publishing.
Greenhalgh, Susan. 2015. *Fat-Talk Nation: The Human Costs of America's War on Fat.* Ithaca, N.Y.: Cornell University Press.
Gregory, Roberta. 1999. *Bitchy Butch: World's Angriest Dyke.* Seattle, Wash.: Fantagraphics Books.
Gupta, Akhil, and James Ferguson. 2001 (1992). "Beyond 'Culture': Space, Identity, and the Politics of Difference." In *Culture Power Place: Explorations in Critical Anthropology,* edited by Akhil Gupta and James Ferguson. Durham, N.C.: Duke University Press.
Halberstam, Jack. 2011. *The Queer Art of Failure.* Durham, N.C.: Duke University Press.
Halberstam, Judith. 1998. *Female Masculinity.* Durham, N.C.: Duke University Press.
Halberstam, Judith. 2005. *In a Queer Time and Place: Transgender Bodies, Subcultural Lives.* New York: NYU Press.
Halperin, David M. 2012. *How to Be Gay.* Cambridge, Mass.: Belknap Press of Harvard University Press.

Hammidi, Tania N., and Susan B. Kaiser. 1999. "Doing Beauty." *Journal of Lesbian Studies* 3 (4): 55–63.
Hammonds, Evelynn. 1997. "Black (W)holes and the Geometry of Black Female Sexuality." In *Feminism Meets Queer Theory*, edited by Elizabeth Weed and Naomi Schor. Indianapolis: Indiana University Press.
Hansen, Karen Tranberg. 2004. "The World in Dress: Anthropological Perspectives on Clothing, Fashion, and Culture." *Annual Review of Anthropology* 33: 369–92.
Haraway, Donna. 2003. *The Companion Species Manifesto: Dogs, People, and Significant Otherness*. Chicago, Ill. : Prickly Paradigm.
Harvey, David. 2000. *Spaces of Hope*. Berkeley: University of California Press.
Hawkesworth, Mary. 2006. "Gender as an Analytic Category." In *Feminist Inquiry: From Political Conviction to Methodological Innovation*, edited by Mary Hawkesworth. New Brunswick, N.J.: Rutgers University Press.
Heaphy, Brian, Andrew K. Yip, and Debbie Thompson. 2004. "Ageing in a Non-Heterosexual Context." *Ageing & Society* 24: 881–902.
Helliwell, Christine. 2000. " 'It's Only a Penis': Rape, Feminism, and Difference." *Signs: Journal of Women in Society* 25 (3): 789–831.
Hemmings, Clare. 2007. "Rescuing Lesbian Camp." *Journal of Lesbian Studies* 11 (1/2): 159–66.
Henry, Imani. 2007. "Lesbians Sentenced for Self-Defense: All-White Jury Convicts Black Women." Workers World (website), July 21, 2007. https://www.workers.org/2007/us/nj4-0628/.
Hewitson, Gillian J. 1999. *Feminist Economics: Interrogating the Masculinity of Rational Economic Man*. Northampton, Mass.: Edward Elgar Publishing.
Hillman, Betty Luther. 2013. " 'The Clothes I Wear Help Me to Know My Own Power': The Politics of Gender Presentation in the Era of Women's Liberation." *Frontiers* 34 (2): 155–85.
Hollister, John. 1999. "A Highway Rest Area as a Socially Reproducible Site." In *Public Sex/Gay Space*, edited by William Leap. New York: Columbia University Press.
hooks, bell. 1996. *Reel to Real: Race, Sex, and Class at the Movies*. New York: Routledge.
hooks, bell. 1997. "Sisterhood: Political Solidarity Between Women." In *Feminist Social Thought: A Reader*, edited by Diana Tietjens Meyers. New York: Routledge.
Howard, Sally. 9/8/2010. "Fight Club." *The Telegraph* (online). http://www.telegraph.co.uk/culture/7987322/Fight-club.html.
Hughes, Anne K., Rena D. Harold, and Janet M. Boyer. 2011. "Awareness of LGBT Aging Issues among Aging Services Network Providers." *Journal of Gerontological Social Work* 54 (7): 659–77.
Hunt, Brandon, Amy Milsom, and Connie R. Matthews. 2009. "Partner-Related

Rehabilitation Experiences of Lesbians with Physical Disabilities." *Rehabilitation Counseling Bulletin* 52 (3): 167–78.

Inckle, Kay. 2014. "A Lame Argument: Profoundly Disabled Embodiment as Critical Gender Politics." *Disability & Society* 29 (3): 388–401.

Internet Movie Database (IMDb). 2015. "Mad Max: Fury Road." http://www.imdb.com/title/tt1392190/.

Jervis, Lisa. 2008. "An Old Enemy in a New Outfit: How Date Rape Became Gray Rape and Why It Matters." In *Yes Means Yes! Visions of Female Sexual Power and a World Without Rape*, edited by Jaclyn Friedman and Jessica Valenti. Berkeley, Calif.: Seal Press.

Jo, Bev. 1991 (1981). "Female Only." In *For Lesbians Only: A Separatist Anthology*, edited by Sarah Lucia-Hoagland and Julia Penelope. London: Onlywomen Press.

Johnson, E. Patrick. 2008. *Sweet Tea: Black Gay Men of the South*. Chapel Hill: University of North Carolina Press.

Johnson, Michael J., Nick C. Jackson, J. Kenneth Arnette, and Steven D. Koffman. 2005. "Gay and Lesbian Perceptions of Discrimination in Retirement Care Facilities." *Journal of Homosexuality* 49 (2): 83–101.

Johnston, Jill. 1973. *Lesbian Nation: The Feminist Solution*. New York: Simon & Schuster.

Jones, Lynne. 1983. "On Common Ground: The Women's Peace Camp at Greenham Common." In *Keeping the Peace*, edited by Lynne Jones. London: The Women's Press.

Karkazis, Katrina. 2008. *Fixing Sex: Intersex, Medical Authority, and Lived Experience*. Durham, N.C.: Duke University Press.

Kenny, Lorraine Delia. 2000. "Doing My Homework: The Autoethnography of a White Teenage Girl." In *Racing Research, Researching Race: Methodological Dilemmas in Critical Race Studies*, edited by France Winddance Twine and Johnathan W. Warren. New York: New York University Press.

Kilbourne, Jean. 2010. *Killing Us Softly 4: Advertising's Image of Women* (documentary film). Northampton, Mass.: Media Education Foundation.

King, Ynestra. 1983. "All Is Connectedness: Scenes from the Women's Pentagon Action, USA." In *Keeping the Peace*, edited by Lynne Jones. London: The Women's Press.

Klein, Richard. 2010. "What Is Health and How Do You Get It?" In *Against Health: How Health Became the New Morality*, edited by Jonathan M. Metzl and Anna Kirkland. New York: New York University Press.

Kolodny, Annette. 1975. "Surveying the Virgin Land: The Documents of Exploration and Colonization: 1500–1740." In *The Lay of the Land: Metaphor as Experience and History in American Life and Letters*, edited by Annette Kolodny. Chapel Hill: University of North Carolina Press.

Krasniewicz, Louise. 1992. *Nuclear Summer: The Clash of Communities at the Seneca Women's Peace Encampment*. Ithaca, N.Y.: Cornell University Press.

Kroeber, Alfred L. 1919. "On the Principle of Order in Civilization as Exemplified in Changes in Fashion." *American Anthropologist* 21: 262–63.
Kümbetoğlu, Belkıs, İnci User, and Aylin Akpınar. 2010. "Unregistered Women Workers in the Globalized Economy: A Qualitative Study in Turkey." *Feminist Formations* 22 (3): 96–123.
Kuyper, Lisette, and Tineke Fokkema. 2010. "Loneliness Among Older Lesbian, Gay, and Bisexual Adults: The Role of Minority Stress." *Archives of Sexual Behavior* 39: 1171–80.
Lamb, Sarah. 1999. "Aging, Gender, and Widowhood: Perspectives from Rural West Bengal." *Contributions to Indian Sociology* 33 (3): 541–70.
Lamb, Sarah. 2000. *White Saris and Sweet Mangoes: Aging, Gender, and Body in North India*. Berkeley: University of California Press.
Lane, Riki. 2009. "Trans as Bodily Becoming: Rethinking the Biological as Diversity, Not Dichotomy." *Hypatia* 24 (3): 136–57.
LeBesco, Kathleen. 2001. "Queering Fat Bodies/Politics." In *Bodies Out of Bounds: Fatness and Transgression*, edited by Jana Evans Braziel and Kathleen LeBesco. Berkeley: University of California Press.
LeBesco, Kathleen. 2010. "Fat Panic and the New Morality." In *Against Health: How Health Became the New Morality*, edited by Jonathan M. Metzl and Anna Kirkland. New York: New York University Press.
Lee, Anna. 1991 (1981). "A Black Separatist." In *For Lesbians Only: A Separatist Anthology*, edited by Sarah Lucia-Hoagland and Julia Penelope. London: Onlywomen Press.
Lee, Pelican. 1985. "Nozama Tribe." In *Lesbian Land*, edited by Joyce Cheney. Minneapolis, Minn.: Word Weavers Press.
Lee, Pelican. 2002. *Owl Farm Stories*. Ribera, N.M.: West Wind.
Lee, Richard. 1979. *The !Kung San: Men, Women, and Work in a Foraging Society*. Cambridge: Cambridge University Press.
Lee, Richard. 2003. *The Dobe Ju/'hoansi*, 3rd edition. *Case Studies in Cultural Anthropology*, series edited by George Spinder. London: Thompson Learning.
Lee, Sadie. 2006. "Final Call: Kate Bornstein." *Diva Magazine* 125 (October): 114.
Levine, Phillipa. 2008. "States of Undress: Nakedness and the Colonial Imagination." *Victorian Studies* 50 (2): 189–219.
Levi-Strauss, Claude. 1966. "The Culinary Triangle." *Partisan Review* 33 (4): 586–95.
Levitt, Heidi M., and Sharon G. Horne. 2002. "Explorations of Lesbian-Queer Genders." *Journal of Lesbian Studies* 6 (2): 25–39. https://doi.org/10.1300/J155v06n02_05.
Lewin, Ellen. 1991. "Writing Lesbian and Gay Culture: What the Natives Have to Say for Themselves." *American Ethnologist* 18 (4): 786–92.
Lewin, Ellen, and William L. Leap. 1996. Introduction to *Out in the Field: Reflections of Lesbian and Gay Anthropologists*, edited by Ellen Lewin and William L. Leap. Chicago: University of Illinois Press.

Lipsitz, George. 1998. *The Possessive Investment in Whiteness: How White People Profit from Identity Politics.* Philadelphia: Temple University Press.

Lorde, Audre. 1983. "An Open Letter to Mary Daly." In *This Bridge Called My Back: Writings by Radical Women of Color,* edited by Cherríe Moraga and Gloria Anzaldúa. New York: Kitchen Table Press.

Lorde, Audre. 2001 (1984). "The Master's Tools Will Never Dismantle the Master's House." In *Feminist Frontiers,* edited by Laurel Richardson, Verta Taylor, and Nancy Whittier. Boston: McGraw-Hill.

Low, Setha. 2011. "Claiming Space for an Engaged Anthropology: Spatial Inequality and Social Exclusion." *American Anthropologist* 113 (3): 389–407.

Low, Setha M., and Denise Lawrence-Zúñiga. 2003. "Locating Culture." In *The Anthropology of Space and Place: Locating Culture,* edited by Setha M. Low and Denise Lawrence-Zúñiga. Oxford: Blackwell Publishing.

Luhrs, Natalie. 2004. "Silence Is Complicity." *Pretty Terrible* (blog). 6/16/2014. http://www.pretty-terrible.com/2014/06/16/silence-is-complicity/.

Lupton, Deborah. 1996. *Food, the Body, and the Self.* Thousand Oaks, Calif: Sage Publications.

Lynch, Lee. 1988. *The Amazon Trail.* Tallahassee, Fla.: Naiad Press.

Madrone, Hawk. 2000. *Weeding at Dawn: A Lesbian Country Life.* New York: Alice Street Editions/Harrington Park Press.

Malkki, Liisa H. 2001. "National Geographic: The Rooting of Peoples and the Territorialization of National Identity among Scholars and Refugees." In *Culture, Power, Place: Explorations in Critical Anthropology,* edited by Akhil Gupta and James Ferguson. Durham, N.C.: Duke University Press.

Maltry, Melanie, and Kristin Tucker. 2002. "Female Fem(me)ininities." *Journal of Lesbian Studies* 6 (2): 89–102.

Maltz, Daniel N., and Ruth A. Borker. 1982. "A Cultural Approach to Male–Female Miscommunication." In *Language and Social Identity,* edited by John J. Grumperz. Cambridge: Cambridge University Press.

Mascia-Lees, Frances E., and Patricia Sharpe, eds. 1992. *Tattoo, Torture, Mutilation, and Adornment: The Denaturalization of the Body in Culture and Text.* New York: State University of New York Press.

Masini, Blaise E., and Hope A. Barrett. 2008. "Social Support as a Predictor of Psychological and Physical Well-Being and Lifestyle in Lesbian, Gay, and Bisexual Adults Aged 50 and Over." *Journal of Gay & Lesbian Social Services* 20 (1/2): 91–110.

Massey, Doreen. 2005. *For Space.* Thousand Oaks, Calif.: Sage Publications.

Mauss, Marcel. 1990. *The Gift: The Form and Reason for Exchange in Archaic Societies.* Translated by W. D. Halls. New York: W. W. Norton.

Mays, Vickie M. 1980. "Making Visible the Invisible: Some Notes on Racism and Women-Identified Relationships of Afro-American Women." In *Top Ranking: A Collection of Articles on Racism and Classism in the Lesbian Community,* edited

by Joan Gibbs and Sara Bennett. New York: Survival of Sharing/Come!Unity Press.
McCandless, Cathy. 1980. "Some Thoughts About Racism, Classism, and Separatism." In *Top Ranking: A Collection of Articles on Racism and Classism in the Lesbian Community*, edited by Joan Gibbs and Sara Bennett. New York: Survival of Sharing/Come!Unity Press.
McDonald, Sharon. 1977. "Transsexuals: The Woman Within or Women Without?" *Lesbian Tide* 6 (6): 6–7.
McWeeny, Jennifer. 2014. "Topographies of Flesh: Women, Nonhuman Animals, and the Embodiment of Connection and Difference." *Hypatia* 29 (2): 269–86.
Metzl, Jonathan M. 2010. "Introduction: Why Against Health?" In *Against Health: How Health Became the New Morality*, edited by Jonathan M. Metzl and Anna Kirkland. New York: New York University Press.
Millar, Thomas Macaulay. 2008. "Towards a Performance Model of Sex." In *Yes Means Yes! Visions of Female Sexual Power and a World Without Rape*, edited by Jaclyn Friedman and Jessica Valenti. Berkeley, Calif.: Seal Press.
Miller, D. A. 1990. "Anal Rope." *Representations* 32: 114–33.
Miller, George. 2015. *Mad Max: Fury Road* (feature film). Warner Brothers/Village Roadshow.
Miller, Peggy, and Nancy Biele. 1993. "Twenty Years Later: The Unfinished Revolution." In *Transforming a Rape Culture*, edited by Emilie Buchwald, Pamela Fletcher, and Martha Roth. Minneapolis, Minn.: Milkweed Editions.
Miner, Horace. 1956. "Body Ritual Among the Nacirema." *American Anthropologist* 58: 503–7.
Mintz, Sidney. 1986. *Sweetness and Power: The Place of Sugar in Modern History*. New York: Penguin Books.
Moen, Deirdre. 2014. "Marion Zimmer Bradley Gave Us New Perspectives, All Right." *Sounds Like Weird* (blog). 6/3/2014. http://deirdre.net/marion-zimmer-bradley-gave-us-new-perspectives-all-right/.
Moen, Deirdre. 2014. "Marion Zimmer Bradley: It's Worse Than I Knew." *Sounds Like Weird* (blog). 6/10/2014. http://deirdre.net/marion-zimmer-bradley-its-worse-than-i-knew/.
Moghadam, Valentine M. 2011. "Women, Gender, and Economic Crisis Revisited." *Perspectives on Global Development and Technology* 10: 30–40.
Mohanty, Chandra Talpade. 1984. "Under Western Eyes: Feminist Scholarship and Colonial Discourses." *boundary 2* 12/13 (3/1): 333–58.
Mohanty, Chandra Talpade. 2002. "'Under Western Eyes' Revisited: Feminist Solidarity Through Anticapitalist Struggles." *Signs* 28 (2): 499–535.
Mohr, Richard. 1996. "Parks, Privacy, and the Police." *The Guide* 16 (1): 16–19.
Moore, Niamh. 2008. "The Rise and Rise of Ecofeminism as a Development Fable: A Response to Melissa Leach's 'Earth Mothers and Other Ecofeminist

Fables: How a Strategic Notion Rose and Fell.'" *Development and Change* 39 (3): 461–75.
Morales, Margaret del Carmen, Leila Harris, and Gunilla Öberg. 2014. "Citizenshit: The Right to Flush and the Urban Sanitation Imaginary." *Environment and Planning* A 46: 2816–33.
Morena, Naomi Littlebear. 1991 (1981). "Coming Out Queer and Brown." In *For Lesbians Only: A Separatist Anthology*, edited by Sarah Lucia-Hoagland and Julia Penelope. London: Onlywomen Press.
Morgan, Ffiona et al. 1986. *Daughters of the Moon Tarot* [deck and book]. Willits, Calif.: Daughters of the Moon.
Morgensen, Scott Lauria. 2011. *Spaces Between Us: Queer Settler Colonialism and Indigenous Decolonization*. Minneapolis: University of Minnesota Press.
Morris, Bonnie J. 1999. *Eden Built by Eves: The Culture of Women's Music Festivals*. New York: Alyson Books.
Mosdøl, Annhild, Daniel R. Witte, Gary Frost, Michael G. Marmot, and Eric J. Brunner. 2007. "Dietary Glycemic Index and Glycemic Load Are Associated with High-density-lipoprotein Cholesterol at Baseline but Not with Increased Risk of Diabetes in the Whitehall II Study," in *American Journal of Clinical Nutrition* 86 (4): 988–94.
Moser, Robert. 2007. "Disposable People." Intelligence Report of the Southern Poverty Law Center. http://www.splcenter.org/intel/intelreport/article.jsp?pid=276.
Mujeres de Arco Iris. 1985. "Arco Iris." In *Lesbian Land*, edited by Joyce Cheney. Minneapolis, Minn.: Word Weavers.
Mulvey, Laura. 1999. "Visual Pleasure and Narrative Cinema." In *Film Theory and Criticism: Introductory Readings*, edited by Leo Braudy and Marshall Cohen. New York: Oxford University Press.
Mushroom, Merrill. 2015. "'A Great Big Women of Color Tent': Blanche Jackson and Maat Dompim." *Sinister Wisdom* 98: 150–56.
Myerhoff, Barbara. 1978. *Number Our Days*. New York: Simon & Schuster.
Nagoshi, Julie L., and Stephan/ie Brzuzy. 2010. "Transgender Theory: Embodying Research and Practice." *Affilia: Journal of Women and Social Work* 25 (4): 431–43.
Nestle, Joan, ed. 1992. *The Persistent Desire: A Femme-Butch Reader*. Boston: Alyson Publications.
National Coalition of Anti-Violence Programs. 2017. "Lesbian, Gay, Bisexual, Transgender, Queer, and HIV-affected Hate Violence in 2016." NCVAP. https://avp.org/ncavp/.
Newton, Esther. 2000. *Margaret Mead Made Me Gay: Personal Essays, Public Ideas*. Durham, N.C.: Duke University Press.
New York City Hollaback! 2015. "About." *Hollaback New York*. http://nyc.ihollaback.org/about/.

Nicholson, Linda. 1994. "Interpreting Gender." *Signs: Journal of Women and Culture in Society* 20 (1): 79–105.
Noble, Bobby. 2012. "Trans. Panic. Some Thoughts Toward a Theory of Feminist Fundamentalism." In *Transfeminist Perspectives in and Beyond Transgender Studies*, edited by Anne Enke. Philadelphia: Temple University Press.
Nolfi, Kathryn. 2011. "YA Fatphobia." *The Horn Book Magazine* (January/February): 55–59.
Novak, Matt. 2015. "Oregon Was Founded as a Racist Utopia." *Gizmodo* (blog). 1/21/2015. http://gizmodo.com/oregon-was-founded-as-a-racist-utopia-1539567040.
Odette, Catherine. 1999. "Butchdom and Disability." *Sexuality and Disability* 17 (1): 93–96.
Okely, Judith. 1998. *The Traveller-Gypsies*. Cambridge: Cambridge University Press.
Orel, N. A. 2004. "Gay, Lesbian, and Bisexual Elders." *Journal of Gerontological Social Work* 43 (2–3): 57–77.
Ortner, Sherry. 1972. "Is Female to Male as Nature Is to Culture?" *Feminist Studies* 1 (2): 5–31.
Ortner, Sherry. 1996. *Making Gender: The Politics and Erotics of Culture*. Boston: Beacon Press.
O'Toole, Corbett Joan. 2000. "The View from Below: Developing a Knowledge Base about an Unknown Population." *Sexuality and Disability* 18 (3): 207–24.
O'Toole, Corbett Joan, and Brown, Allison. 2003. "No Reflection in the Mirror: Challenges for Disabled Lesbians Accessing Mental Health Services." *Journal of Lesbian Studies* 7 (1): 35–49.
Paz, Juana Maria. 1980. *The La Luz Journal*. Fayetteville, Ariz.: Paz Press.
Pellegrini, Ann. 2007. "After Sontag: Future Notes on Camp." In *A Companion to Lesbian, Gay, Bisexual, Transgender, and Queer Studies*, edited by George E. Haggerty and Molly McGarry. Malden, Mass.: Blackwell Publishing.
Penney, Joel. 2013. "Eminently Visible: The Role of T-Shirts in Gay and Lesbian Public Advocacy and Community Building." *Popular Communication: The International Journal of Media and Culture* 11 (4): 289–302. https://doi.org/10.1080/15405702.2013.838251.
Pham, Minh-Ha T. 2010. "The Right to Fashion in the Age of Terrorism." *Signs: Journal of Women in Culture and Society* 36 (2): 385–410.
Phillips, Joy, and Genée Marks. 2008. "Ageing Lesbians: Marginalising Discourses and Social Exclusion in the Aged Care Industry." *Journal of Gay & Lesbian Social Services* 20 (1–2), 187–202.
Pickering, Lucy. 2010. "Toilets, Bodies, Selves: Enacting Composting as Counterculture in Hawai'i." *Body & Society* 16 (4): 33–55. https://doi.org/10.1177/1357034X10383882.
Piercy, Marge. 1982. *Circles on the Water: Selected Poems of Marge Piercy*. New York: Knopf.

Polhemus, Ted, and Lynn Procter. 1978. *Fashion and Anti-Fashion: An Anthropology of Clothing and Adornment.* London: Cox & Wyman.
Potts, Billie Luisi. 1991 (1982). "Owning Jewish Separatism and Lesbian Separatism." In *For Lesbians Only: A Separatist Anthology,* edited by Sarah Lucia-Hoagland and Julia Penelope. London: Onlywomen Press.
Pratchett, Terry. 2013 (1987). *Mort.* New York: HarperCollins.
Puhl, Rebecca M., and Chelsea A. Heuer. 2009. "The Stigma of Obesity: A Review and Update." *Obesity* 17: 941–64.
Puhl, Rebecca M., Joerg Luedicke, and Chelsea Heuer. 2011. "Weight-Based Victimization toward Overweight Adolescents: Observations and Reactions of Peers." *Journal of School Health* 81: 696–703.
Radicalesbians. 1991 (1970). "The Woman-Identified Woman." In *For Lesbians Only: A Separatist Anthology,* edited by Sarah Lucia-Hoagland and Julia Penelope. London: Onlywomen Press.
Reddy, S. D., and J. H. Crowther. 2007. "Teasing, Acculturation, and Cultural Conflict: Psychosocial Correlates of Body Image and Eating Attitudes Among South Asian Women." *Cultural Diversity & Ethnic Minority Psychology* 13: 45–53.
Revolutionary Lesbians. 1991 (1971). "How to Stop Choking to Death, Or: Separatism." In *For Lesbians Only: A Separatist Anthology,* edited by Sarah Lucia-Hoagland and Julia Penelope. London: Onlywomen Press.
Rich, Adrienne. 1986 (1980). *Blood, Bread, and Poetry: Selected Prose 1979–1985.* New York: W. W. Norton.
Rich, Cynthia. 1983a. "Aging, Ageism, and Feminist Avoidance." In *Look Me in the Eye: Old Women, Aging, and Ageism,* edited by Barbara Macdonald and Cynthia Rich. San Francisco: Spinsters Ink.
Rich, Cynthia. 1983b. "The Women in the Tower." In *Look Me In the Eye: Old Women, Aging, and Ageism,* edited by Barbara Macdonald and Cynthia Rich. San Francisco: Spinsters Ink.
Richard, Keith. 1983. "Unwelcome Settlers: Black and Mulatto Oregon Pioneers." *Oregon Historical Quarterly* 84 (1): 29–55.
Rifkin, Mark. 2011. *When Did Indians Become Straight? Kinship, the History of Sexuality, and Native Sovereignty.* New York: Oxford University Press.
Ring, Trudy. 2015. "This Year's Michigan Womyn's Music Festival Will Be the Last." *The Advocate.* 4/21/2015. https://www.advocate.com/michfest/2015/04/21/years-michigan-womyns-music-festival-will-be-last.
Riordan, Michael. 1996. *Out Our Way: Gay and Lesbian Life in the Country.* Toronto: Between the Lines.
Ritchie, Andrea J. 2006. "Law Enforcement Violence Against Women of Color." In *Color of Violence: The INCITE! Anthology,* edited by INCITE! Women of Color Against Violence. Cambridge, Mass.: South End Press.
Ritzdorf, Marsha. 1997. "Family Values, Municipal Zoning, and African American

Family Life." In *Urban Planning and the African American Community*, edited by June Manning Thomas and Marsha Ritzdorf. Thousand Oaks, Calif.: Sage.

Rivers, Chris Harrison, and Pat Wiles. 2000. *The Amazon Empowerment Tarot: An Amazon Journey to Self-Actualization*. Guffey, Colo.: Amazon Moon Productions.

Roberts, Adrienne. 2015. "Gender, Financial Deepening and the Production of Embodied Finance: Towards a Critical Feminist Analysis." *Global Society* 29 (1): 107–27.

Roberts, Dorothy. 1997. *Killing the Black Body: Race, Reproduction, and the Meaning of Liberty*. New York: Pantheon Books.

Robinson, Beatrice, Jane G. Bacon, and Julia O'Reilly. 1993. "Fat Phobia: Measuring, Understanding, and Changing Anti-Fat Attitudes." *International Journal of Eating Disorders* 14 (4): 467–80.

Rosaldo, Michelle Zimbalist. 1974. "Woman, Culture, and Society: A Theoretical Overview." In *Woman, Culture, and Society*, edited by Michelle Zimbalist Rosaldo and Louise Lamphere. Stanford, Calif.: Stanford University Press.

Rosing, Ina. 2003. "The Gender of Space." *Philosophy & Geography* 6 (2): 189–211.

Rubin, Gayle. 1975. "The Traffic in Women: Notes on the 'Political Economy' of Sex." In *Toward an Anthropology of Women*, edited by Rayna Reiter. New York: Monthly Review Press.

Rubin, Gayle. 1992. "Of Catamites and Kings: Reflections on Butch, Gender, and Boundaries." In *The Persistent Desire: A Femme-Butch Reader*, edited by Joan Nestle. Boston: Alyson Publications.

Rubin, Gayle, and Judith Butler. 1997. "Sexual Traffic: Interview." In *Feminism Meets Queer Theory*, edited by Elizabeth Weed and Naomi Schor. Indianapolis: Indiana University Press.

Rudolph, Karen. 1995. "Feminist Fundraising Phobia." In *The Woman-Centered Economy: Ideals, Reality, and the Space In Between*, edited by Loraine Edwalds and Midge Stocker. Chicago: Third Side Press.

Russ, Joanna. 1985. *Magic Mommas, Trembling Sisters, Puritans, and Perverts: Feminist Essays*. New York: Crossing Press.

Russ, Joanna. 1998. *What Are We Fighting For? Sex, Race, Class, and the Future of Feminism*. New York: St. Martin's Press.

Sandahl, Carrie. 2003. "Queering the Crip or Cripping the Queer? Intersections of Queer and Crip Identities in Solo Autobiographical Performance." *GLQ* 9 (1–2): 25–55.

Sanday, Peggy Reeves. 2007. *Fraternity Gang Rape: Sex, Brotherhood, and Privilege on Campus*, 2nd edition. New York: New York University Press.

Sandilands, Catriona. 1994. "Lavender's Green? Some Thoughts on Queer(y)ing Environmental Politics." *UnderCurrents: Journal of Critical Environmental Studies* 6: 20–24.

Sandilands, Catriona. 2002. "Lesbian Separatist Communities and the Experience of Nature: Toward a Queer Ecology." *Organization & Environment* 15 (2): 131–63.
Saunders, Lisa, and William Darity Jr. 2003. "Feminist Theory and Rational Economic Inequality." In *Feminist Economics Today: Beyond Economic Man*, edited by Marianne J. Ferber and Julie A. Nelson. Chicago: University of Chicago Press.
Savishinsky, Joel S. 2000. *Breaking the Watch: The Meanings of Retirement in America*. Ithaca, N.Y.: Cornell University Press.
Scheper-Hughes, Nancy, and Margaret M. Lock. 1987. "The Mindful Body: A Prolegomenon to Future Work in Medical Anthropology." *Medical Anthropology Quarterly* 1 (1): 6–41.
Schüssler Fiorenza, Elisabeth. 1992. *But She Said: Feminist Practices of Biblical Interpretation*. Boston: Beacon Press.
Schweik, Susan. 2009. *Ugly Laws: Disability in Public*. New York: New York University Press.
Schweik, Susan. 2011. "Disability and the Normal Body of the (Native) Citizen." *Social Research* 78 (2): 417–42.
Scott, Ellen Kaye. 2000. "From Race Cognizance to Racism Cognizance: Dilemmas in Antiracist Activism in California." In *Racing Research, Researching Race: Methodological Dilemmas in Critical Race Studies*, edited by France Winddance Twine and Johnathan W. Warren. New York: New York University Press.
Scott, Joan Wallach. 2010. "Gender: Still a Useful Category of Analysis?" *Diogenes* 225: 7–14.
Serano, Julia. 2007. *Whipping Girl: A Transsexual Woman on Sexism and the Scapegoating of Femininity*. Berkeley, Calif.: Seal Press.
Sheir, Rebecca. 2015. "Inside the HQ of D.C.'s Short-Lived but Influential Lesbian Separatist Collective." American University Radio. 11/6/2015. http://wamu.org/programs/metro_connection/15/11/06/inside_the_hq_of_dcs_short_lived_but_influential_lesbian_separatist_collective.
Shepherd, Melissa A., and Mary A. Gerend. 2014. "The Blame Game: Cervical Cancer, Knowledge of Its Link to Human Papillomavirus and Stigma." *Psychology & Health* 29 (1): 94–109.
Shostak, Marjorie. 1981. *Nisa: The Life and Words of a !Kung Woman*. New York: Vintage Books (Random House).
Shugar, Dana R. 1995. *Sep-a-ra-tism and Women's Community*. Lincoln: University of Nebraska Press.
Signorile, Michelangelo. "CeCe McDonald, Transgender Activist, Recalls Hate Attack, Manslaughter Case." *Huffpost Queer Voices* (online). 2/22/2014. http://www.huffingtonpost.com/2014/02/22/cece-mcdonald-manslaughter-case_n_4831677.html.

Silverstein, Shel. 2002 (1964). *The Giving Tree*. New York: HarperCollins.
Sinott, Megan. 2013. "Dormitories and Other Queer Spaces: An Anthropology of Space, Gender, and the Visibility of Female Homoeroticism in Thailand." *Feminist Studies* 39 (2): 333–56.
Sisco, Marideth. 2015. "'A Saga of Lesbian Perseverance and Steadfast Resolve': The Hensons and Camp Sister Spirit." *Sinister Wisdom* 98: 142–45.
Sklar, Deidre. 2001. *Dancing with the Virgin: Body and Faith in the Fiesta of Tortugas, New Mexico*. Berkeley: University of California Press.
Smith, Andrea. 2005. *Conquest: Sexual Violence and American Indian Genocide*. Cambridge, Mass.: South End Press.
Smith, Andrea. 2010. "Queer Theory and Native Studies: The Heteronormativity of Settler Colonialism." *GLQ: A Journal of Lesbian and Gay Studies* 16 (1–2): 42–68.
Smith, Barbara. 1986. Foreword. *The Combahee River Collective Statement: Black Feminist Organizing in the Seventies and Eighties* (Freedom Organizing Series #1). New York: Kitchen Table / Women of Color Press.
Smith, Henry Nash. 1970 (1950). *Virgin Land: The American West as Symbol and Myth*. Cambridge, Mass.: Harvard University Press.
Sokolow, Jayme A., and Mary Ann Lamanna. 1984. "Women and Utopia: The Woman's Commonwealth of Belton, Texas." *The Southwestern Historical Quarterly* 87 (4): 371–92.
Sontag, Susan. 1964. "Notes on Camp." *Partisan Review* 31 (4): 515–30.
Sontag, Susan. 1988. *AIDS and Its Metaphors*. New York: Farrar, Straus and Giroux.
Spivak, Gayatri. 1988. "Can the Subaltern Speak?" In *Marxism and the Interpretation of Cultures*, edited by Cary Nelson and Lawrence Grossberg. Urbana: University of Illinois Press.
Starhawk. 1989 (1979). *The Spiral Dance: A Rebirth of the Ancient Religion of the Great Goddess*. San Francisco: Harper and Row.
Starling, Phaedra. 2009. "Schrodinger's Rapist: Or a Guy's Guide to Approaching Strange Women Without Being Maced." *Shapely Prose* (blog). 10/8/2009. http://kateharding.net/2009/10/08/guest-blogger-starling-schrodinger%E2%80%99s-rapist-or-a-guy%E2%80%99s-guide-to-approaching-strange-women-without-being-maced/.
Stein, Gary L., Nancy L. Beckerman, and Patricia A. Sherman. 2010. "Lesbian and Gay Elders and Long-term Care: Identifying the Unique Psychosocial Perspectives and Challenges." *Journal of Gerontological Social Work* 53 (5): 421–35.
Sterk, Claire E. 2000. *Tricking and Tripping: Prostitution in the Era of AIDS*. Putnam Valley, N.Y.: Social Change Press.
Stewart, Pamela J., and Andrew Strathern. 2003. Introduction to *Landscape, Memory and History: Anthropological Perspectives*, edited by Pamela J. Stewart and Andrew Strathern. Sterling, Va.: Pluto Press.

Strathern, Marilyn. 1980. "No Nature, No Culture: The Hagen Case." In *Nature, Culture, and Gender,* edited by Carol P. MacCormack and Marilyn Strathern. Cambridge: Cambridge University Press.

Sue, Nelly, Dian, Carol, and Billie. 1976. *Country Lesbians: The Story of the Woman-Share Collective.* Grants Pass, Oreg.: WomanShare Books.

Swerdlow, Amy. 1993. *Women Strike for Peace: Traditional Motherhood and Radical Politics in the 1960s.* Chicago: University of Chicago Press.

Thompson, Becky W. 1994. *A Hunger So Wide and So Deep: American Women Speak Out on Eating Problems.* Minneapolis: University of Minnesota Press.

Traies, Jane. 2015. "Old Lesbians in the UK: Community and Friendship." *Journal of Lesbian Studies* 19 (1): 35–49.

Transgender Europe's Trans Murder Monitoring Project (TMM). 2014. "TGEU Press Release, TDoR 2014." https://transrespect.org/en/research/trans-murder-monitoring/.

Transgender Europe's Trans Murder Monitoring Project (TMM). 2015. "Transgender Europe: IDAHOT TMM Press Release." 5/8/2015. https://transrespect.org/en/research/trans-murder-monitoring/.

Turner, Edith. 2012. *Communitas: The Anthropology of Collective Joy.* New York: Palgrave-McMillan.

Turner, Terence. 1993 (1980). "The Social Skin." In *Reading the Social Body,* edited by Catherine Burroughs and Jeffrey Ehrenreich. Iowa City: University of Iowa Press.

Turner, Victor. 1974. *Dramas, Fields, and Metaphors: Symbolic Action in Human Society.* Ithaca, N.Y.: Cornell University Press.

Twine, France Winddance. 1996. "Brown-Skinned White Girls: Class, Culture, and the Construction of White Identity in Suburban Communities." *Gender, Place, and Culture* 3 (2): 205–21.

Twine, France Winddance, and Charles Gallagher. 2008. "Introduction; The Future of Whiteness: A Map of the 'Third Wave.'" *Ethnic and Racial Studies* 31 (1): 4–24.

Twine, France Winddance, and Bradley Gardener. 2013. "Introduction," in *Geographies of Privilege,* edited by France Winddance Twine and Bradley Gardener. New York: Routledge.

Valentine, Gill. 1997. "Making Space: Lesbian Separatist Communities in the United States." In *Contested Countryside Cultures: Otherness, Marginalisation, and Rurality,* edited by Paul Cloke and Jo Little. Routledge: London.

Vaughn, Genevieve. 1995. "The Philosophy Behind Stonehaven." In *The Woman-Centered Economy: Ideals, Reality, and the Space In Between,* edited by Loraine Edwalds and Midge Stocker. Chicago: Third Side Press.

Vaughn, Mya, Kurt Silver, Sophia Murphy, Renee Ashbaugh, and Amanda Hoffman. 2015. "Women with Disabilities Discuss Sexuality in San Francisco Focus Groups." *Sexuality and Disability* 33: 19–46.

Vogel, Lisa. 2013. "Letter to the Community." Open letter/email posted to the Landdykes email list. 4/12/2013.
Vogel, Lisa. 2015. "Dear Sisters, Amazon, Festival family." Open letter/Facebook post. 4/12/2015. https://www.facebook.com/michfest/posts/10153186431364831.
Ward, Sally. 2003. "On Shifting Ground: Changing Formulations of Place in Anthropology." *Australian Journal of Anthropology* 14 (1): 80–96.
Waring, Marilyn. 1988. *If Women Counted: A New Feminist Economics*. San Francisco: Harper & Row.
Warner, Marina. 1985. *Monuments and Maidens: The Allegory of the Female Form*. New York: Athenaeum.
Warner, Michael. 1999. *The Trouble with Normal: Sex, Politics, and the Ethics of Queer Life*. New York: Free Press.
Waters, Emily, and Sue Yacka-Bible. 2017. "A Crisis of Hate: A Mid Year Report on Lesbian, Gay, Bisexual, Transgender, and Queer Hate Violence Homicides." National Coalition of Anti-Violence Programs. www.ncavp.org.
Weiner, Annette B. 1992. *Inalienable Possessions: The Paradox of Keeping-While-Giving*. Berkeley: University of California Press.
We'Moon Company (Mother Tongue Ink). 2017. https://wemoon.ws/pages/contact-us.
Weston, Kath. 1991. *Families We Choose: Lesbians, Gays, Kinship*. New York: Columbia University Press.
Weston, Kath. 1993. "Do Clothes Make the Woman? Gender, Performance Theory, and Lesbian Eroticism." *Genders* 17 (Fall): 2–21.
Weston, Kath. 1998. *Long Slow Burn: Sexuality and Social Science*. New York: Routledge.
Weston, Kath. 2002. *Gender in Real Time: Power and Transience in a Visual Age*. New York: Routledge.
Whitney, Chelsea. 2006. "Intersections in Identity: Identity Development among Queer Women with Disabilities." *Sexuality and Disability* 24 (1): 39–52.
Wilkens, Jane. 2015. "Loneliness and Belongingness in Older Lesbians: The Role of Social Groups as 'Community.'" *Journal of Lesbian Studies* 19 (1): 90–101.
Williams, Karen. 1995. "Lesbian Riches." In *The Woman-Centered Economy: Ideals, Reality, and the Space In Between*, edited by Loraine Edwalds and Midge Stocker. Chicago: Third Side Press.
Wittig, Monique. 1969. *Les Guérillères*. Paris: Les Éditions de Minuit.
Wittig, Monique. 1973. *Le corps lesbien*. Paris: Les Éditions de Minuit.
Woodward, Sophie. 2005. "Looking Good: Feeling Right: Aesthetics of the Self." In *Clothing as Material Culture*, edited by Suzanne Kuchler and Daniel Miller. New York: Berg.
Woody, Imani. 2014. "Aging Out: A Qualitative Exploration of Ageism and Heterosexism Among Aging African American Lesbians and Gay Men." *Journal of Homosexuality* 61 (1): 145–65.

Yawning Lion. 2007. "Puzzles." *Fe-muh-nist*. http://feh-muh-nist.blogspot.com/.
Young, Iris. 1990. *Justice and the Politics of Difference*. Princeton, N.J.: Princeton University Press.
Zimmerman, Bonnie. 1990. *The Safe Sea of Women: Lesbian Fiction 1969–1989*. Boston: Beacon Press.

Index

ableism, 177, 232, 233
Abu-Lughod, Lila, 14
accessibility, 218, 232, 236–37, 238, 241–42
Adams, Carol, 173–74, 178
addiction narratives, 179–80, 182, 183, 259n10
ageism, 229–30, 264n14
agency: and energy concept, 101; and racism, 53, 54–55, 65; vs. symbolization, 254n12
aging, 217–18, 220–32; and accessibility, 218, 241–42; and arrival routes, 83–84, 257n8; and care for aging mothers, 223, 224, 264n5; definitions of, 263n1, 264n7; and dis/ability, 234–35; and gift economies, 113, 224, 225, 264n8; and hermit image, 218, 219, 228, 231–32, 241, 265n15; images of, 228–30; and informants, 4–5; and institutional options, 220–22, 225, 264n9; and medical needs, 227; and mental illness, 227–28, 264n10; planning for, 223–28, 264n4; terminology, 263n1, 265n16
aging in place, 218, 264n4
Águila, 125, 126–27
Alaimo, Stacy, 145, 146
alien energy. *See* wrongness

Amazon Empowerment Tarot, 229, 240
Amazon Trail, 3, 20
Amazon Trail, The (Lynch), 6
American Anthropological Association, 57
androgyny, 157
Antoniou, Laura, 39, 41–42, 255n21
Anzaldúa, Gloria E., 94
Aodagain, Ni, 147
architecture, 73
Arco Iris, 51, 54–55, 124–27, 133
Arden Eversmeyer Old Lesbian Herstory project, 230
ARF, 119
Asgarda, 248
Ashley, Bob, 181
Association of Lesbians in Community, 3
autonomy, 82, 210–11

balanced reciprocity, 111, 113
Barcan, Ruth, 170, 171
Barnes, Shaba, 60
Barrett, Hope A., 222
Bartky, Sandra, 158, 161, 173, 244
BDSM, 32, 41, 188, 255n19
Bechdel, Alison, 17, 33–39
Bell, Colin, 94
Benería, Lourdes, 108

· 289 ·

Bengal, Rebecca, 4
Beyond Feminist Aesthetics (Felski), 75
Bindel, Julie, 248, 249
biphobia, 214, 263n26
Bitchy Butch (Gregory), 39, 40
Black Faces, White Spaces (Finney), 141
"Black Separatist, A" (Lee), 49
body, 153–86; acceptance of, 172, 184, 259n6; and biological determinism, 199; and boundaries, 94, 173, 199; and dis/ability, 219; docile, 158, 161, 244; and essentialism, 196–97, 244; and genetics, 196–97; individual presentation, 155–60, 258n2; and wrongness, 201–5. *See also* fatphobia; food; natural body; social body
Bordo, Susan, 171, 176
Bornstein, Kate, 207
boundaries, 93–97; and body, 94, 173, 199; and fatphobia, 97, 258n3; and food, 181; and gender, 95, 97–98, 103; and gendered landscape, 130, 142; and lesbian identity, 81, 94–95; and matrix cultures, 93–94, 96; and transphobia, 198–99
Bourdieu, Pierre, 10, 62, 143, 178, 192, 260n3
Bradley, Marion Zimmer, 27, 28–29, 254n14
Breen, Walter, 254n14
Brennan, Cathy, 261n10
Brief History of Nakedness, A (Carr-Gomm), 170
Brownsworth, Victoria, 162, 209–10, 261n10
Brzuzy, Stephan/ie, 191, 192
Bunch, Charlotte, 82–83
"Butchdom and Disability" (Odette), 240
butch/fem roles, 157–58, 207. *See also* butch identity

butch identity, 95, 156–57, 169, 207, 240, 262n16
Butler, Judith, 9, 191–92, 193, 262n15
Butler, Sandra, 264n9

Califia, Pat, 198, 202, 207, 262nn15–16
Cambridge Women's Center, 3
Cameron, Deborah, 98
camp, 30, 255nn16–17, 255n20. *See also* reverse camp
Campos, Paul, 259n8
Camp Sister Spirit, 164, 259n4
Camp Trans, 209, 263n19
Canyon Sam, 61
capitalism, 106; and ecological consciousness, 138; feminist economics on, 107–8; and gift economies, 114, 117, 118; and land ownership, 120; and money, 119; suspicion of, 109
Carr-Gomm, Philip, 170
Charnas, Suzy McKee, 27
Cheney, Joyce, 6, 54, 119
children, 77, 146, 257n5
Chmielewski, Wendy E., 247
chosen family, 146, 147, 219, 222
Circles of Power (Gagehabib and Summerhawk), 6, 56, 59, 60–61, 63–65, 79, 92, 118, 121, 123, 131, 147, 256n7
cis women, 191, 195, 199–200, 260n2, 263n23
City of Sorcery (Bradley), 27
Clark doll tests, 70
Clarke, Victoria, 158
class: and gift economies, 112, 118; and land ownership, 121, 125, 258n3; and matrix cultures, 119, 258n3; and money, 119; and racism, 56; and separatism, 121–22; and sharing, 88
clothing, 155–58, 159–60

colonialism, 130, 131–33, 170–71, 258n1
colorblindness, 57–58, 60, 72. *See also* whiteness
Combahee River Collective Statement, 48, 51, 191
"Coming Out Queer and Brown" (Morena), 49–50
commensality, 74, 89–91
"common lesbian experience." *See* universalization
communitarian living, 19–20, 35
Communitas (Turner), 58
communitas, 58, 76, 93, 94, 96. *See also* community
community, 86–97; and aging, 231–32, 241; and boundaries, 93–97; and commensality, 74, 89–91; and dis/ability, 238–39, 241; and feminist aesthetics, 76, 91–93, 257n10; importance of, 86–87; and networking, 88–89; and nostalgia, 58, 93, 94; and sharing, 87–88
"Competency, Autonomy, and Choice" (D'Aoust), 238
compulsory heterosexuality, 194, 198, 208
consensus decision-making, 19, 22, 23, 89–90, 254n8, 254n10
Cooper, James Fenimore, 131
Copper, Baba, 229
Counihan, Carole, 178–79
Country Lesbians (Sue, Nelly, Dian, Carol, and Billie), 6, 79, 91–92, 110, 122–23, 238
"Country Women" (Bengal), 4
Cowan, Liza, 157
crafts, 21
Crenshaw, Kimberlé, 50, 72
Crone image, 229, 264n14
Cross, Amanda, 42–43, 256nn23–24
Cross, Katherine, 262n15

Daly, Mary, 75, 138
D'Aoust, Vicky, 234, 238, 239
Daughters of a Coral Dawn (Forrest), 27
Daughters of the Moon Tarot, 229, 240
Dave, Naisargi, 249–50
davenport, doris, 190
Davis, Angela, 212–13
Daynes, Sarah, 57
Death in a Tenured Position (Cross), 42–43, 256nn23–24
Defosse, Dana Leland, 260n2
delayed reciprocity, 224–25
diet. *See* food
difference, ethos of, 73–74, 244, 245
dignity, 114–15
Dimpfl, Mike, 166–67
Directory of Wimmin's Lands and Lesbian Communities (Shewolf), 52
dis/ability, 218–19, 232–41; and accessibility, 218, 232, 236–37, 238, 241–42; and aging, 234–35; and body, 219; and fatphobia, 177; images of, 239–40, 265nn21–23; institutional options, 235; and intersectionality, 232–34; and invisibility, 240–41; and matrix cultures, 233, 235–36; and Michigan Womyn's Music Festival, 265n18; and simple living, 236–37, 265n19; strategizing, 237–41, 265n20; terminology, 265n16; and trans people, 265n17
Dobkin, Alix, 196
docile body, 158, 161, 244
Dominy, Helen, 183, 196
Doris, Margaret, 24–25
Douglas, Mary, 173, 180
doxa: and body, 167, 184, 202–3; defined, 10–11; and ecological consciousness, 138; and energy concept, 101, 102; fatphobia as, 174;

and feminist aesthetics, 257n3; gender as, 103; and gift economies, 117; and land ownership, 127; matrix cultures as, 245–46; and money, 123; natural body as, 102, 188, 194–95, 199; transphobia as, 10; whiteness as, 10, 62–63
Duncan, Nancy, 144
Dykelands Slideshow, 230, 258n2
dyke presentation, 157
Dykes to Watch Out For (Bechdel), 17, 33–39
Dykewomon, Elana, 238

eating. *See* food
ecofeminism. *See* ecological consciousness
ecological consciousness, 92–93, 130, 137–41, 145, 175, 258n2
economics, 105–28; anthropological approach to, 106–7; feminist approach to, 107–9; fundraising, 110; and money, 78, 118–24, 218, 237, 264n2; and resistance, 127–28. *See also* gift economies
Eden Built by Eves (Morris), 21, 27
Edwalds, Loraine, 108
888 Memorial Drive, 3
emotional labor, 100, 258n19
energy concept: in fictional portrayals, 34, 35; and gender, 95, 97–103; and transphobia, 98, 196, 203, 205, 215
England, 22, 25, 248
erasure, 30–31
essentialism: and consensus decision-making, 91; and ecological consciousness, 137–38, 139–40; and energy concept, 102; and trans men, 206, 208; and transphobia, 194, 195–97, 199–201, 203–4, 205, 245, 260n4; and women's culture, 95, 244–45
exclusion. *See* boundaries
experiential argument for transphobia, 194, 195, 199–200
experiential gender, 192

Farm, The, 19–20
Farrell, Amy, 175, 176, 177
fatphobia, 173–78; and boundaries, 97, 258n3; challenges to, 184; and food, 173–74, 175–76, 178, 259n10; and health, 174, 175, 176–77, 182–83, 244; and matrix cultures, 173, 174, 175, 176, 177, 184–85, 259nn10–11; and natural body, 185–86; and racism, 259n8
Fat Shame (Farrell), 175
Fausto-Sterling, Anne, 197
Felski, Rita, 75, 256n1
Female Man, The (Russ), 27
femininity: and body, 158, 159, 161, 185, 244; and boundaries, 95, 97; and feminist aesthetics, 75, 257n3; and gendered landscape, 140, 144; and gift economies, 116–17, 128; and trans men, 208–9, 215; and wrongness, 201–2, 262n12. *See also* gender
feminist aesthetics: and community, 76, 91–93, 257n10; and language, 77; and women's culture, 74–76, 256nn1–2
feminist art, 229, 239–40, 265nn21–23
feminist consciousness, 74, 76. *See also* commensality; community; feminist aesthetics
Ferguson, James, 13
fictional portrayals, 26–44; Antoniou, 39, 41–42, 255n21; and construction of lesbian culture, 27–28, 29–30;

current production of, 29, 254n15; *Dykes to Watch Out For,* 17, 33–39; and herstory, 39, 40; nonqueer media, 42–44; Seneca Women's Encampment, 33–35; and separatism, 31–33, 43–44; and utopianism, 26–27, 28–29, 33, 39, 41–42, 254n15, 255n22; and whiteness, 32–33, 39

Finney, Carolyn, 46, 62, 76, 141, 142
Fiorenza, Elisabeth Schüssler, 259n7
Fischler, Claude, 180, 182
Fishman, P. M., 100
Fonesca, Isabel, 166
food, 178–84; addiction narratives, 179–80, 182, 183, 259n10; and fatphobia, 173–74, 175–76, 178, 259n10; and gender, 178, 183–84; and health, 181, 259n12; purity narratives, 180–82, 183–84, 259n9; and sharing, 178–79
foraging societies, 111
Forrest, Katherine V., 27
Foucault, Michel, 127–28, 161
Frank, Geyla, 235
Free Amazons of Darkover (Bradley), 28–29
Freeman, Jo, 115, 123
Friedan, Betty, 198
Furies, The (Furies Collective), 3, 6
Furies Collective, 3, 6, 48, 82

Gaard, Greta, 138–39
Gabrielson, Marcena, 222
Gage, Carolyn, 163
Gagehabib, La Verne. See *Circles of Power*
Gal, Susan, 144–45
Garber, Marjorie, 130, 169
Gardener, Bradley, 141
gay male culture, 30–31, 144

gay men's land, 15, 253n3
Gearhart, Sally Miller, 27
Geertz, Clifford, 197
gender: as analytic category, 193–94; and boundaries, 95, 97–98, 103; as doxa, 103; and economics, 108; and energy concept, 95, 97–103; and fatphobia, 177, 178, 185; and feminist aesthetics, 75, 76, 93, 256n1, 257n3; and food, 178, 183–84; and identity, 79–80, 257n7; and individual presentation, 156–57, 159, 160; and male gaze, 161–62, 169; and matrix cultures, 102, 246; as performative, 191–92, 260n3; and scapegoating, 205, 215–16, 262n14; and trans men, 207; unmaking of, 95, 103; and wrongness, 201–2, 262n12. *See also* gendered landscape
gendered landscape, 129–42; and colonialism, 130, 131–33, 258n1; and ecological consciousness, 130, 137–41, 258n2; and femininity, 140, 144; and healing, 133–34; and intimacy, 130; and land as individual, 136; and language, 129, 136–37, 140; and networking, 135–36; and nostalgia, 151; and utopianism, 134–35; and whiteness, 130, 141–42; and women's culture, 135
Gender Identity Watch, 261n10
Gender Trouble (Butler), 191–92, 193
generalized reciprocity, 105–6, 110–13, 114, 115, 224, 225, 264n8. *See also* gift economies
genetics, 196–97
Gibbs, Joan, 50
gift economies, 105–6, 109–18; action vs. discussion, 112–13; and aging, 113, 224, 225, 264n8;

anthropological definitions, 110–11; and balanced reciprocity, 111, 113; and capitalism, 114, 117, 118; and connection, 113, 114; and dignity, 114–15; and matrix cultures, 109–10, 115; and networking, 110, 111–12, 113, 258n1; and power, 115–18, 128; and woman-built housing, 110
Giving Tree, The (Silverstein), 117, 118
Goddess spirituality, 5, 92, 131, 133, 171, 229, 264n12
Goffman, Erving, 31, 32
Gorgons, 82
Gray, John, 146
Greenham Common Peace Camp, 22, 25, 248
Gregory, Roberta, 39, 40
Griffin, Susan, 75
guesting, 111
Gupta, Akhil, 13
Gwynn, Bethroot, 79
Gyn/Ecology (Daly), 138

habitus, 102, 192, 260n3
hair, 159, 160, 258n2
Halberstam, Jack, 94. *See also* Halberstam, Judith
Halberstam, Judith, 146. *See also* Halberstam, Jack
Halperin, David M., 17, 19, 30–31, 255n20
Hammidi, Tania N., 159
Hammonds, Evelyn, 59
Haraway, Donna, 137
Harris, Leila, 167
Harvey, David, 134–35
Hawkesworth, Mary, 194
healing, 44, 133–34, 265n15
health: and dis/ability, 233; and fatphobia, 174, 175, 176–77, 182–83, 244; and food, 181, 259n12

Heaphy, Brian, 222
Helliwell, Christine, 165
hermit image, 218, 219, 228, 231–32, 241, 265n15
herstory, 38, 39, 230
heterodoxy, 10–11
heterosexism, 96, 193, 198, 257n15
heterosexual matrix, 9
Hewitson, Gillian, 107
Hillman, Betty Luther, 157, 158, 159
hippie communes, 19–20
Hollister, John, 144, 145
home, 148–50
homophobia: and aging, 220–22, 264n9; and boundaries, 96; and compulsory heterosexuality, 194, 198, 208; and dis/ability, 234, 235; and second-wave exclusion of lesbians, 82, 189, 198; and transphobia, 189, 198–99, 215, 261n8; and violence, 199, 261n8
hooks, bell, 190–91, 255n20, 261n11
"Houston, Houston, Do You Read?" (Tiptree), 27
How to Be Gay (Halperin), 30–31
"How to Stop Choking to Death, Or: Separatism" (Revolutionary Lesbians), 48
Hunter, Tyra, 199
hypermasculinity, 108

identity, 77–83; and alternate spellings of "women," 80–81, 257n7; and body, 156–57; and gender, 79–80, 257n7; and individual presentation, 159–60; and parent status, 77, 257n5; QUILTBAG, 160, 259n3; and separatism, 81–83; and terminology, 78–79. *See also* lesbian identity
Inckle, Kay, 233

India, 249–50, 265n3
individual body, 155–60, 258n2
intersectionality, 46, 49–50, 72, 192, 232–34
intersex people, 197
invisibility: and dis/ability, 240–41; and privilege, 141–42; of women of color, 59–61, 63, 64–65
"Is Female to Male as Nature Is to Culture?" (Ortner), 137

Jackson, Blanche, 52
Japan, 248
Jewish identity, 78
Jo, Bev, 82
Johnston, Jill, 27
Journal of Lesbian Studies, 6–7

Kaiser, Susan B., 159
Kenny, Lorraine Delia, 57, 58
Kenya, 248–49
"Kids Story" (Lee), 14–15
Killer Wore Leather, The (Antoniou), 39, 41–42, 255n21
Krasniewicz, Louise, 22, 23, 24, 25, 256n4
kyriarchy, 184, 198, 208–9, 215, 259n7. See also matrix cultures

Lacan, Jacques, 130, 169
La Luz Journal, The (Paz), 6
Lamb, Sarah, 166, 224, 263n1
land: and ecological consciousness, 145; and placemaking, 146–47; and public/private division, 143–45, 146; and rooting, 147; and urination/excretion, 169; and whiteness, 46, 62. See also gendered landscape; land ownership
Landdyke Gatherings: and arrival routes, 78; and body acceptance, 184; and consensus decision-making, 90; and dis/ability, 218, 236, 238; and fatphobia, 175–76, 177–78; and fictional portrayals, 29; and food, 178–79; and landdyke identity, 79; and lesbian identity, 94–95; and methodology, 4; and nudity, 172; and transphobia, 187; and women of color, 57
land ownership: and class, 121, 125, 258n3; and gift economies, 106; and home, 148–50; and money, 122–23; and racism, 50–51; types of, 120; and women of color land, 124–27
land trusts, 120, 123, 126
language: and feminist aesthetics, 77; and gendered landscape, 129, 136–37, 140; and identity, 80–81, 257n7
La Rue, Danny, 170
Leap, William, 13
Lee, Anna, 49, 50
Lee, Orville, 57
Lee, Pelican, 6, 14–15, 91, 119, 146
Lee, Richard, 111
Lee, Sadie, 259n3
Left Hand of Darkness, The (Le Guin), 27
Le Guin, Ursula K., 27
Lesbian Connection, 5
lesbian culture: and architecture, 73; and BDSM, 255n19; and camp, 255n16; construction of, 18–19, 27–28, 29–30, 38–39; and *Dykes to Watch Out For*, 17, 33–39; global/historical context, 249–50, 265n3; and universalization, 56, 57–58, 59, 72. See also fictional portrayals; separatism; women's culture
lesbian identity: and aging, 218, 226; and boundaries, 81, 94–95; coming

out, 85; and definition of women's land, 79; and economics, 108–9; and freedom from patriarchy, 79–80; and individual presentation, 157–58, 159; and informants, 77–78, 79–80, 257n6; and the "natural," 145–46; as outside norms, 198, 260n6; and separatism, 81–83; and trans men, 206; and transphobia, 189, 261n10

Lesbian Land (Cheney), 6, 54
Lesbian Land Directory (Shewolf), 6
Lesbian Nation, 27–28
Lesbian Nation (Johnston), 27
lesbian separatism. *See* separatism
"Lesbian Separatist Communities and the Experience of Nature" (Sandilands), 6
"Lesbians in Revolt" (Furies), 48
Levine, Phillipa, 170
Lewin, Ellen, 13, 14
Lipsitz, George, 141
Lock, Margaret, 155
Lolosoli, Rebecca, 249
Lorde, Audre, 49, 55, 190
Low, Setha, 142
Lupton, Deborah, 176, 177, 178, 181
Luz de la Lucha, La, 51, 52–53, 54
Lynch, Lee, 6

Maat Dompim, 51–52
Mad Max: Fury Road, 17, 43–44, 256n25
Madrone, Hawk, 136–37
Magdalen Farm, 253n3
Magic Momma/Trembling Sister dyad, 116–18
mainstream. *See* matrix cultures
Maize: The Country Lesbian Magazine, 5, 6, 78–79, 81
"Making Space" (Valentine), 6

male absence, 161–66, 243–44; assumption of, 162–63; and energy concept, 98–99; and male gaze, 161–62, 166, 169, 172, 243–44; and rape culture, 164–66; and safety, 163–64; and urination/excretion, 169
male access, 7, 88–89, 188
male gaze, 161–62, 166, 169, 172, 243–44
Malkki, Liisa H., 147, 148
Maltry, Melanie, 159
"Mapping the Margins" (Crenshaw), 50
masculinity. *See* gender
Masini, Blaise E., 222
Massey, Doreen, 144
matrix cultures: and aging, 229–30, 264n1, 264n4, 264n14; and body acceptance, 172; and boundaries, 93–94, 96; and capitalism, 106; and class, 119, 258n3; and compulsory heterosexuality, 194, 198, 208; defined, 9; and dis/ability, 233, 235–36; as doxa, 245–46; and ethos of difference, 244, 245; and fatphobia, 173, 174, 175, 176, 177, 185, 259nn10–11; and fictional portrayals, 42; and food, 183, 184; and gender, 102, 246; and gendered landscape, 130, 131, 146; and gift economies, 109–10, 115; and land, 62; and land ownership, 121; and male dominance, 100–101; and menstruation, 260n5; and methodology, 13, 14; and money, 123; and nested cultures, 9–10, 26, 243; and racism, 64, 243; and rape, 165; and transphobia, 22; and urination/excretion, 169. *See also* doxa; political engagement
Matthews, Sarah, 264n14
Mauss, Marcel, 114

Mays, Vickie, 51
McCandless, Cathy, 50, 121–22
McDonald, CeCe, 199, 260n7
McWeeny, Jennifer, 140–41
McWhirter, Martha W., 247
menstruation, 196, 260n5
mental illness, 24, 227–28, 264n10
methodology, 4–6, 12–15
Michigan Womyn's Music Festival, 18; and dis/ability, 265n18; and gift economies, 116; and male gaze, 162; and methodology, 4; and safety, 163; and transphobia, 10, 21, 188, 209–13, 261n10, 263n19
middle-class culture, 60, 63, 90, 142, 256n5
Miner, Horace, 166
Mists of Avalon, The (Bradley), 27
modernity, 167
Moghadam, Valentine, 108
Mohanty, Chandra Talpade, 138, 258n2
Mohr, Richard, 144, 145, 146
money, 78, 118–24, 218, 237, 264n2
Moore, Niamh, 139, 151
Morales, Margaret del Carmen, 167
Moran, Sharon, 166–67
Morena, Naomi Littlebear, 49–50
Morgensen, Scott Lauria, 132–33, 253n1
Morris, Bonnie, 21, 27, 211
Motherlines (Charnas), 27
Mother Tongue Ink, 6

Nagoshi, Julie L., 191, 192
Native cultures, 133, 258n2
"natural," the: and food, 183; and individual presentation, 159, 160; and lesbian identity, 145–46; and queerness, 171–72. *See also* natural body
natural body: and arguments for transphobia, 195–96, 260nn4–5; and boundaries, 199; challenges to, 263n18; as doxa, 102, 188, 194–95, 199; and energy concept, 101; and essentialism, 195–96, 200–201; and fatphobia, 185–86; nonexistence of, 197; and social body, 172–73; and wrongness, 204
naturecultures, 137
neoliberalism, 107–8
nested cultures, 9–10, 26, 243
networking: and aging, 222, 225, 228, 264n3; and arrival routes, 83, 84, 88–89; extent of, 5; and fund-raising, 110; and gendered landscape, 135–36; and gift economies, 110, 111–12, 113, 258n1; organizations for, 3; and scholarship on women's lands, 8; and Seneca Women's Encampment, 6; and women's music festivals, 21; and word of mouth, 64–65. *See also* Landdyke Gatherings
Newby, Howard, 94
Newton, Esther, 7, 32
New Zealand, 248
Nicholson, Linda, 197
Noble, Bobby, 192
Nolfi, Kathryn, 176
nonmonogamy, 91–92, 257n10
Norman, John, 41, 255n21
nostalgia, 94, 95, 103, 151
Nozama Tribe, 119
Nuclear Summer (Krasniewicz), 22, 256n4
nudity, 170–72, 175–76, 202

Öberg, Gunilla, 167
Odette, Catherine, 240
Okely, Judith, 10, 12, 167, 253n7
OLOC (Old Lesbians Organizing for Change), 228, 230
oral herstory, 230

orthodoxy, 10, 11, 245–46
Ortner, Sherry, 137, 193
O'Toole, Corbett Joan, 234, 236
OWL Farm, 3, 14–15, 20, 123, 146
Owl Farm Stories (Lee), 6, 14–15, 146

Pascual, Amanda Jasnowski, 4
Paz, Juana Maria, 6, 51, 52–53, 165
Penney, Joel, 159
performativity, 191–92, 260n3
Pham, Minh-Ha, 159
Pickering, Lucy, 167, 168–69
Piercy, Marge, 27
placemaking, 146–47
Poet's Tarot, 229, 239–40, 265nn21–23
political argument for transphobia, 194, 195
political engagement: and camp, 31, 255n17; and clothing, 159–60; and gendered landscape, 139; as intrinsic to women's lands, 21, 24–26, 139, 245–46, 254n13. *See also* Seneca Women's Encampment
Pratchett, Terry, 263n22
precultural body. *See* natural body
prejudice model, 66
Pretendbians, 261n10
privilege: heterosexual, 96, 257n15; invisibility of, 141–42; and Seneca Women's Encampment, 256n4; and transphobia, 203, 211, 212, 260n2; white, 45–46, 47, 53, 54, 71
public/private division, 143–45, 146
purity narratives, 180–82, 183–84, 259n9

queerness: and gendered landscape, 132, 133, 134, 143, 146; and individual presentation, 156–57, 158; and the "natural," 171–72; and nudity, 171; welcoming, 213–15, 245, 257n16; and whiteness, 59–60
QUILTBAG, 160, 259n3

race. *See* whiteness
racism, 45–72; and agency, 53, 54–55, 65; and boundaries, 96; and concept of race, 57; and fatphobia, 259n8; and gift economies, 112, 117, 118; and intersectionality, 46, 49–50, 72; and invisibility of women of color, 59–61, 63, 64–65; and matrix cultures, 64, 243; prejudice model, 66; and separatism, 47–51; and transphobia, 211, 263n25; and universalization, 190–91; and victim/perpetrator discourse, 53–54, 65–66; and whiteness as absence of race, 55–61, 71, 72, 76, 142, 244; and whiteness as doxa, 10, 62–63; and white privilege, 45–46, 47, 53, 54, 71; as "wrong-feeling," 66–71, 256n8. *See also* women of color
Radicalesbians, 48
Radical Faerie movement, 132–33, 253n3
rape culture, 164–66
Raymond, Janice, 261n10
religion, 92, 257n12
resistance, 127–28
reverse camp: and fictional portrayals, 42, 43, 44; and separatism, 17–18, 19, 31, 32, 38, 44, 255n16
Revolutionary Lesbians, 48
Rich, Adrienne, 198
Rich, Cynthia, 229, 264n14
Rifkin, Mark, 132
Riordan, Michael, 134
Ritzdorf, Marsha, 95–96
Rivers, Diana, 29, 254n15

rooting, 147
Rosaldo, Michelle, 143, 144
Rosing, Ina, 135
Rowling, J. K., 176
Rubin, Gayle, 8, 198, 208
Rudolph, Karen, 109
Russ, Joanna, 27, 31, 82, 116–17, 118, 128, 205, 215

Safe Sea of Women, The (Zimmerman), 6, 27–28
safety, 163–64, 165
Sahlins, Marshall, 111
Sanctified Sisters, 247
Sandahl, Carrie, 235–36, 265n16
Sandilands, Catriona, 6, 133, 138, 139, 145, 146
Sassafras collective, 124–27
Savishinsky, Joel S., 224–25
Scheper-Hughes, Nancy, 155
Schweik, Susan, 177, 232
Scott, Ellen, 53, 54, 65, 66
Scott, Joan Wallach, 193–94
second-wave feminism: exclusion of lesbians, 82, 189, 198; and history of utopianism, 18, 20; and Seneca Women's Encampment, 22; and separatism, 3
Seneca Women's Encampment for the Future of Peace and Justice, 18–19, 22–26; archive of, 5–6; and consensus decision-making, 22, 23, 254n8, 254n10; fictional portrayals of, 33–35; and networking, 6; political engagement as intrinsic to, 24–26, 254n13; and privilege, 256n4; and racism, 55–56, 61
separatism: articulation of, 48; and class, 121–22; and ecological consciousness, 138; as embarrassing, 3, 7, 31, 32, 82; and energy concept, 97–98; and fictional portrayals, 31–33, 43–44; and gendered landscape, 133; and lesbian identity, 81–83; and racism, 47–51; and rape culture, 165; and reverse camp, 17–18, 19, 31, 32, 38, 44, 255n16; scapegoating of, 31, 205, 262n14; stereotypes of, 35–38; and stigmaphobe/stigmaphile concept, 31–32; and transphobia, 7; and whiteness, 32–33; and women of color, 32–33, 48–49, 51. *See also* male absence
Sep-a-ra-tism and Women's Community (Shugar), 6, 27
Serano, Julia, 189, 192, 195, 196, 200, 204, 206, 207, 262n15, 263n20
sexuality: BDSM, 32, 41, 188, 255n19; and boundaries, 94–95; and dis/ability, 233; and identity, 80; and methodology, 13–14; nonmonogamy, 91–92, 257n10; and separatism, 32; and whiteness, 59–60. *See also* lesbian identity
Sexual Politics of Meat, The (Adams), 173–74
sharing, 87–88, 178–79
Shattered Chain, The (Bradley), 27
shaving, 158
Shewolf, 6, 52
Shugar, Dana, 6, 27
silencing, 7–8
Silverstein, Shel, 117, 118
simple living, 236–37, 265n19
Sinott, Megan, 143
Sisco, Marideth, 259n4
Smith, Andrea, 132, 133
Smith, Barbara, 48
Smith, Henry Nash, 131

social body, 160–73; and male absence, 161–66; and natural body, 172–73; and nudity, 170–72; and urination/excretion, 153–54, 166–70
socialization, 194, 195
solitude. *See* hermit image
Sontag, Susan, 255n17
Southern Oregon Women's Community, 64, 65, 86, 92, 131, 139
Spence, Katherine, 158
Spiral Dance, The (Starhawk), 138
spirituality, 92, 124–25, 257n12
Spivak, Gayatri, 233
Starhawk, 138
"Statement on 'Race'" (American Anthropological Association), 57
Stewart, Pamela, 136
stigmaphobe/stigmaphile, 31–32
Stonehaven, 109
Strathern, Andrew, 136
subculture, 94
Summerhawk, Barbara. See *Circles of Power*
Sundance-Woman, Maya, 60
symbolization, 25, 254n12

Tarnouska, Katerina, 248
tarot, 229, 239–40, 265nn21–23
TERFs (Trans Exclusionary Radical Feminists), 261n10
Thadani, 249
Thendara House (Bradley), 27
Thompson, Debbie, 222
Thornton, Sarah, 94
Three Rivers, Amoja, 52
Tiptree, James, Jr. (Alice Bradley Sheldon), 27
Tönnies, Ferdinand, 57
Traies, Jane, 225
Trans Exclusionary Radical Feminists (TERFs), 261n10

trans men, 102, 206–9, 215, 262nn15–16, 263n18
trans people: and boundaries, 257n16; and dis/ability, 265n17; and energy concept, 102; violence against, 189–90, 198–99, 211, 260n7, 261nn9–10; welcoming, 22, 213–15, 245. *See also* transphobia
transphobia, 187–216; arguments for, 194–98, 199–200, 202, 211–12, 260nn4–5; and autonomy, 210–11; and biological determinism, 191, 199; and biphobia, 214, 263n26; and boundaries, 198–99; challenges to, 209, 210, 263n21; as doxa, 10; and energy concept, 98, 196, 203, 205, 215; and essentialism, 194, 195–97, 199–201, 203–4, 205, 245, 260n4; and gender as analytic category, 193–94; and gender as performative, 191–92, 260n3; and genetics, 196–97; and homophobia, 189, 198–99, 215, 261n8; and physical transition, 203, 204; and privilege, 203, 211, 212, 260n2; and racism, 211, 263n25; as rare in fieldwork, 7, 21–22, 188; and scapegoating, 205, 215–16, 262n14; and sexual predation, 202, 262n13; and trans men, 206–9, 215, 262–63nn15–16; and universalization, 190–91, 261n11; and victim/perpetrator discourse, 211, 212–13; and violence, 189–90, 198–99, 211, 260n7, 261nn9–10; and women's music festivals, 10, 21, 188, 202, 209–13, 261n10, 263n19; and wrongness, 201–5, 215
Trouble with Normal, The (Warner), 31–32
T-shirts, 159–60
Tucker, Kristin, 159

Turner, Edith, 58
Turner, Terence, 156
Turner, Victor, 58
Twine, Frances Winddance, 59, 60, 61, 141
"Tyranny of Structurelessness, The" (Freeman), 115, 123

Ukraine, 248
Umoja, 248–49
universalization: and lesbian culture, 56, 57–58, 59, 72; and Michigan Womyn's Music Festival, 263n24; women of color on, 48–49, 190–91, 261n11
urban women's lands, 3
utopianism: and fictional portrayals, 26–27, 28–29, 33, 39, 41–42, 254n15, 255n22; and gay male culture, 31; and gendered landscape, 134–35; history of, 19–20; and scapegoating, 31; and separatism, 17–18; and women's music festivals, 18, 20–21

Valentine, Gill, 6
Vaughn, Genevieve, 109
vegetarianism, 173–74, 178, 181
victim/perpetrator discourse, 53–54, 65–66, 211, 212–13
violence: against women, 95, 248–49; against women of color, 52–53, 165, 199, 261n9; and homophobia, 199, 261n8; and transphobia, 189–90, 198–99, 260n7, 261nn9–10; on women's lands, 52–53, 165–66
Virgin Land (Smith), 131
Vogel, Lisa, 116, 209, 211–12

Wanderground, The (Gearhart), 27
Ward, Sally, 93–94, 150

Waring, Marilyn, 107, 108
Warner, Marina, 254n12
Warner, Michael, 31–32
Waterloo Bridge incident, 23
WBW (womyn-born-womyn), 199–200, 210, 263n23
Webber, Charles W., 131
Weil, Simone, 147
Weiner, Annette, 114
We'Moon Company, 6
Weston, Kath, 13, 76, 219, 246, 262n15
"When It Changed" (Russ), 27
whiteness: as absence of race, 55–61, 71, 72, 76, 142, 244; awareness of, 55, 71; and boundaries, 96, 97; and camp, 255n20; as doxa, 10, 62–63; and feminist consciousness, 76; and fictional portrayals, 32–33, 39; and gendered landscape, 130, 141–42; and individual presentation, 159, 258n2; and informants, 4, 7, 56–57, 78; and land, 46, 62, 141; and privilege, 45–46, 47, 53, 54, 71; and racism as "wrong-feeling," 68; and scholarship on women's lands, 7; and separatism, 32–33; and sexuality, 59–60. *See also* racism
White Privilege Conference, 71
Whitman, Walt, 131
Whitney, Chelsea, 234, 236
wilderness, 62, 130, 131–32, 134, 135, 141
Wilkens, Jane, 221, 222
Williams, Karen, 108–9
"Will the Real Lesbian Community Please Stand Up" (Newton), 7
witches. *See* Goddess spirituality
Wittig, Monique, 260n6
woman-built housing, 73, 110
Woman-Centered Economy, The (Edwalds), 108

"Woman-Identified Woman, The" (Radicalesbians), 48
Woman on the Edge of Time (Piercy), 27
WomanShare, 64, 79, 123, 236–37. See also *Country Lesbians*
women as natural class, 192–93. *See also* natural body
"Women Men Don't See, The" (Tiptree), 27
women of color: fictional portrayals of, 33, 35; and gift economies, 118; and identity, 78; and individual presentation, 156–57, 258n2; as informants, 78; and intersectionality, 46, 49–50; invisibility of, 59–61, 63, 64–65; land communities for, 51–54, 63–64, 97, 124–27; and separatism, 32–33, 48–49, 51; separatist participation, 32–33, 49; on universalization, 48–49, 190–91, 261n11; violence against, 52–53, 165, 199, 261n9. *See also* racism
Women's Commonwealth, 247
women's culture: and commensality, 74, 89–91; and consensus decision-making, 89–90; delineation of, 8, 76; and dis/ability, 236; and essentialism, 95, 244–45; and ethos of difference, 73–74, 244, 245; and feminist aesthetics, 74–76, 256nn1–2; and gender, 93; and gendered landscape, 135; and universalization, 59. *See also* community; lesbian culture
women's lands: arrival routes, 83–86; contemporary, 3–4; definitions, 3, 12; global/historical context, 246–50, 265n2; herstory of, 230, 258n2; history of, 19–22; imaginings of, 17–18; networks of, 3, 5, 6, 8; scholarship on, 6–8
women's music festivals, 20–22, 87, 202, 236. *See also* Michigan Womyn's Music Festival
women's peace movement, 22
Women's Pentagon Action, 22
womyn-born-womyn (WBW), 199–200, 210–12, 263n23
Woodward, Sophie, 160
wrongness, 201–5, 215

Yip, Andrew K., 222
Young, Iris, 58, 95, 96

Zimmerman, Bonnie, 6, 27–28, 29, 57–58, 59, 63, 82, 97, 98, 132

Keridwen N. Luis is lecturer in anthropology and in the Women's, Gender, and Sexuality Studies Program at Brandeis University, and lecturer in Women's, Gender, and Sexuality Studies and sociology at Harvard University.